DRY MANHATTAN

DRY MANHATTAN

Prohibition in New York City

MICHAEL A. LERNER

HARVARD UNIVERSITY PRESS

Cambridge, Massachusetts

London, England

2007

FLIP

Cataloging-in-Publication Data available from the Library of Congress
ISBN-13: 978-0-674-02432-8
ISBN-10: 0-674-02432-X

For "Two-Sip" Susie

Contents

Introduction

Nothing so needs reforming as other people's habits.
—MARK TWAIN

In the fall of 1929, the mayor of Berlin, Gustav Boess, paid an official visit to the city of New York. In the course of his week-long stay, the mayor toured the subway and Chinatown, dined with German-American civic groups, visited parks and hospitals, examined a municipal incinerator, and marveled at New York's skyscrapers, which he described as "the most amazing array of buildings I ever saw." Struck by the tempo of life in the city, he awkwardly noted, "It goes here faster." Before he left, Boess made an equally salient observation when he reportedly asked Mayor James J. Walker, "When does the Prohibition law go into effect?" The problem with Boess's question was that Prohibition had been federal law for nearly a decade. The fact that this failed to register with the city's European visitor signaled how poorly Prohibition was faring, and not just in New York City.[1]

Boess's casual observation indicated that the boldest attempt at moral and social reform in the history of the United States had fallen far short of its ambitious goals. When the Prohibition experiment commenced in 1920, the results were supposed to have been very different. The United States government, at the behest of a powerful dry lobby, had barred the manufacture, sale, and transportation of alcohol through the force of a constitutional amendment, leaving most Americans to conclude that the liquor trade in the United States had come to a permanent end. The guiding principle behind this undertaking, which arrived at the end of the Progressive era, was

1

that the prohibition of alcohol and the elimination of the saloon would morally uplift the people of the United States, ultimately creating a healthier citizenry, safer cities and workplaces, and a more efficient society.

In 1928 President Herbert Hoover hailed Prohibition as "a great social and economic experiment, noble in motive and far reaching in purpose." Though the nickname "the noble experiment" stuck, President Hoover's appraisal was far too generous. The Eighteenth Amendment had committed the United States to a seemingly impossible mission. Never before had the federal government attempted to regulate the private lives of adults to the degree that Prohibition did, and never before had the Constitution been used to limit, rather than protect, the personal liberties of individuals. For the better part of a generation, the United States doggedly pursued this experiment, spending millions of dollars annually on its administration and enforcement, and arresting tens of thousands of Americans each year for violating the dry laws.[2]

The experiment failed. The efforts to enforce Prohibition, concentrated especially in large cities like New York, overwhelmed the nation's law enforcement agencies and engendered widespread opposition to the Eighteenth Amendment. Whether in the form of buying bootleg liquor, drinking in nightclubs, or supporting political efforts to undermine the reach of the dry law, Americans in many parts of the United States vigorously resisted Prohibition, their rebellion against the Eighteenth Amendment growing more pronounced as the years went by. By the time President Hoover offered his remarks about the "noble experiment," numerous polls indicated widespread dissatisfaction with Prohibition in the United States by margins of almost three to one. The experiment finally ended in 1933, when the Eighteenth Amendment was repealed at the onset of the New Deal.[3]

Though it failed as social policy, Prohibition has fascinated Americans for generations, especially in the realm of popular culture. The flappers, jazz, speakeasies, and gangsters of the era have been depicted exuberantly in films like Billy Wilder's *Some Like It Hot* (1959), Howard Hawks's *Scarface* (1932), and Woody Allen's *Bullets over Broadway* (1994), and in novels ranging from F. Scott Fitzgerald's *The Great Gatsby* to Toni Morrison's *Jazz*. The period has been romantically (and often inaccurately) recalled as one of the most glamorous and thrilling in modern American history. Fitzgerald famously characterized it as an era defined by "what was fashionable and what was fun."[4]

While American popular culture has kept the excitement of the Prohibition era alive, it has rarely succeeded in conveying the importance of Prohibition to the history of the twentieth-century United States. Given the frivolous nature of our popular depictions of the "Roaring Twenties," it is easy to dismiss the dry laws as part of a comical attempt to stop Americans from drinking. But there was much more at stake in Prohibition than booze. In addition to being the most ambitious attempt to legislate morality and personal behavior in the history of the modern United States, Prohibition embodied a fourteen-year-long cultural conflict over the nature of American identity, the reach of moral reform movements, and the political future of the nation. Prohibition indeed was the defining issue of the 1920s, one that measured the moral and political values of the nation while shaping the everyday lives of millions of Americans. Prohibition thus provides a key to understanding the cultural divides that separated Americans in the 1920s, as the United States was transformed by rapid economic growth and demographic changes.

The history of the Prohibition experiment in New York City deserves particular consideration. Nowhere in the United States were the clashes over Prohibition more visible or the questions about its wisdom more pressing than in New York. As the nation's cultural capital, financial center, media headquarters, and largest city, it was the foremost battleground in the war against demon rum. Though other cities, namely New Orleans, Chicago, and Detroit, could claim to have been "wetter," New York was notorious in the 1920s for its defiance of the dry laws and its more than 30,000 speakeasies and nightclubs. Resistance to the Eighteenth Amendment proved especially strong in the city's many ethnic working-class neighborhoods, whose residents experienced Prohibition, not as the "noble experiment" Hoover described, but as a crusade rooted in the bigotry of the dry movement and its distrust of ethnic and racial minorities. As the decade progressed, opposition to the Eighteenth Amendment mounted among the members of the city's middle and upper classes as well, as they embraced the cosmopolitan culture and nightlife that flourished under the restrictions of

Prohibition. Looking to associate themselves with the "smart" sensibility of New York's nightclub scene, they resisted Prohibition as openly as their ethnic counterparts. Taken as a whole, the resistance to Prohibition in New York City, which extended from the bottom of the city's social ladder to the more "respectable" types at the upper levels of society, confirmed New York's place as the center of opposition to the dry laws, and the most serious challenge to the viability of the dry movement's agenda.

That New York would play a central role in the opposition to Prohibition came as no surprise to the "drys" who had campaigned for and won the ratification of the Eighteenth Amendment. Since the 1880s, American temperance groups had been infatuated with the problem of alcohol in New York City, and they closely monitored everything from its consumption to the distribution of saloons in the city. They clearly recognized New York as the ultimate test of their ideology, and anticipated that making Prohibition work in New York would require a Herculean effort. The Anti-Saloon League, the lobbying group most responsible for engineering the ratification of the Eighteenth Amendment, was so preoccupied with New York's compliance with the dry mandate that it sent one of its most able officials to the city to lead the crusade to reform Gotham. Viewing New York and its wet ways as a contaminating influence on the United States, the league vowed to dry up Broadway at any cost. If the dry experiment failed in New York, drys feared, it could not be sustained in the rest of the nation. If Prohibition succeeded in New York, however, the league and its allies hoped to make the city the trophy example of temperance reform. Given what was at stake in New York, dry leaders condemned the resistance to the noble experiment in the city in no uncertain terms. Bishop James Cannon, Jr., of the Anti-Saloon League damned the city as "Satan's Seat," while "wets" in return mockingly called Gotham "the city on a still."[5]

The cultural rebellion against Prohibition in New York, and the dry movement's attempts to uphold the Eighteenth Amendment in the city, continued for nearly a decade and a half. As the debate over Prohibition raged in the city, it influenced almost every aspect of daily life, from employment opportunities to law enforcement, and from real estate trends to race relations. It fostered new forms of urban culture, redefined leisure and amusement in the city, and promoted corruption and crime. It changed the relationship between the middle class and reform, and challenged traditional gender roles that assumed women were the moral guardians of society. Eventually, and perhaps most importantly, the rebellion against Prohibition in New York reshaped politics.

Historians of the twentieth-century United States have long complained that the politics of the 1920s was devoid of meaning, even "dreary."[6] Yet New Yorkers came to realize during the 1920s that while drinking all night long in speakeasies was fun, it would do little to repeal an unwanted and ill-advised constitutional amendment. Out of necessity, New Yorkers slowly turned to the political arena—first on the local level, then on the national level—to counter what the dry crusade had wrought. In doing so, New York ultimately produced many of the nation's most outspoken wet political leaders, including James J. Walker, the city's "nightclub mayor"; Representative Fiorello LaGuardia, who demonstrated how to brew beer in his congressional office; Governor Al Smith, whose bid for the presidency offered the first real hope for an end to Prohibition; and Pauline Sabin, the New York socialite who became the leader of the largest repeal organization in the country. As these leading political opponents of the dry crusade emerged, the rest of the United States watched events unfolding in New York with great interest, and slowly began to be persuaded by the arguments against Prohibition coming out of the wet metropolis. The repeal issue, as promoted by New Yorkers, finally played an unheralded role in galvanizing national support for Governor Franklin D. Roosevelt, a reluctant wet whose election to the presidency in 1932 both doomed Prohibition and ushered in the New Deal. In this sense, the political response of New Yorkers to the "noble experiment" not only paved the way to repeal but also played a major role in shaping the political leadership of the nation into the 1930s and beyond.

While the problems associated with alcohol at the heart of the dry agenda were genuine, the solution imposed upon the nation had proved an anachronistic approach to reform. By the 1920s, New Yorkers' rejection of the dry agenda, their turn from cultural rebellion to political opposition, and their eventual embrace of the New Deal marked the emergence of a very different approach to addressing social problems. Rather than endure the demands of moral crusaders, they championed a style of political reform better suited to modern America.

Readers familiar with New York City today will no doubt recognize a great deal in the accounts of how New Yorkers resisted Prohibition—the energy and chaos of the modern metropolis, the remarkable landscape of the city, the bewildering diversity of its inhabitants, and its unmistakable attitude. What they may also find familiar is New Yorkers' refusal to abide by a moral vision imposed on them by reformers with no understanding of, nor concern for, the complexities of urban life. In their resistance to Prohibition, New Yorkers demonstrated that the city, its people, and its culture had come of age in the twentieth-century United States and would have to be accommodated as an integral part of American life.

Almost seventy-five years after repeal, we can understand that what was at stake in the "noble experiment" was not something as simple as the right to have a drink, but a much more significant set of issues. The battle between the dry movement and wet New Yorkers was a debate about competing visions of American society. It revealed deep divisions within the United States over individual rights, personal liberty, and the limits of reform. Through their role in the rebellion against Prohibition, New Yorkers made the most enduring claim of this cultural conflict. By the end of the 1920s, they had made it abundantly clear that the biggest challenge facing the United States in the twentieth century would be to demonstrate that Americans from different backgrounds and holding different beliefs could co-exist in an increasingly pluralistic, cosmopolitan nation without being subjected to the moral demands of a movement as unforgiving and unrealistic as the dry crusade.

1

The Dry Crusade

On New Year's Day, 1914, H. L. Mencken reported to his readers in the *Baltimore Sun* that William H. Anderson, the state superintendent of the Maryland chapter of the Anti-Saloon League, had arrived safely in New York, "carrying a toothbrush, a copy of Baxter's *Saints' Rest* and a change of medicated flannels." Anderson's arrival in New York was greeted as welcome news in Baltimore, and not just by Mencken. For seven years, Anderson had been the nemesis of Baltimore's bartenders, saloon owners, and liquor dealers, waging a ceaseless campaign against the alcohol trade as the city's leading temperance lobbyist. On New Year's Day, however, Anderson now set his sights on a more challenging target—New York City.[1]

During his tenure in Maryland, William Anderson had come to embody a new American reform movement, a "dry crusade" characterized by a desire to impose temperance on the United States, and especially on American cities, through lobbying, legislative efforts, and the enforcement of ever-stricter liquor laws. In contrast with the earlier temperance movements of the nineteenth century, which had emphasized moral suasion and the reform of the individual, this new movement sought to end the liquor trade in the United States completely. Spearheaded by the Anti-Saloon League, it aimed to pass an amendment to the U.S. Constitution abolishing forever the alcohol traffic in the United States.[2]

William Anderson had been extraordinarily successful in advancing the dry crusade in Maryland. Mencken, a longtime observer of Anderson's ex-

ploits, dubbed the dry lobbyist "the vampire and hobgoblin of every bartender's nightmare." (His allies in the Prohibition movement took a more
generous view of his talents, calling him "the most skillful politician in the
state.") While opinions of Anderson varied across Maryland depending on
one's wet or dry leanings, no one questioned his effectiveness. In seven
years, Anderson and the Anti-Saloon League had closed more than a thousand saloons in Baltimore, nearly half the city's total. Even the unabashedly
wet Mencken confessed an admiration for the dry lobbyist's talents. Seeing
no way to stop Anderson's crusade against drink, Mencken joked in 1912,
"My advice to the saloon keepers is that they imitate the Anti-Saloon
League and send to distant climes for some super-Anderson."[3]

William Anderson's departure from Baltimore was an indication that the
national leadership of the Anti-Saloon League had big plans for one of its
most effective officers. As the nation's leading temperance lobby, the Anti-
Saloon League had spent twenty years orchestrating state campaigns against
the liquor trade like the one Anderson had just waged in Maryland. Now
the league turned to its national goals. In 1913, it had won a major victory
in Congress with the passage of the Webb-Kenyon Act, a federal law banning the interstate shipment of liquor into dry states. Having dealt this major blow to the liquor industry, the league now opened a more ambitious
drive to enact a national Prohibition amendment, and it directed William
Anderson to lead that campaign in New York.[4]

Anderson's success or failure in New York would prove critical to the national campaign for Prohibition. The Anti-Saloon League needed no less
than thirty-six states to ratify the Prohibition amendment in order to make
it law. While New York was only one state, it loomed larger than most in
the battle for a dry United States. To the leaders of the Prohibition movement, New York embodied the immigrant city, a place full of foreign habits.
It was defined by its cosmopolitan culture, which drys considered antitheti-
cal to American identity. They warily eyed New York City as a source of
profound wet influence on the rest of the United States, on account of both
its penchant for drink and its ability to reach the rest of the nation through
newspapers and the media. In the national battle for Prohibition, the Anti-
Saloon League expected New York to put up the toughest fight of all. If
William Anderson could somehow reproduce what he had accomplished in

Maryland by bringing wet New York into the dry column, he would boost the Anti-Saloon League's efforts to reform the entire nation.

When William Anderson set foot in New York City on that cold New Year's Day, the city was still sleeping off the festivities of the previous evening. From working-class saloons in Brooklyn to Tenderloin cafés, and from theater district cabarets to lavish balls held at the city's grand hotels, New Yorkers had rung in 1914 with dining, singing, the tango, and enough drink, according to the *New York World,* to make "quite a few residents of the town kinda headachy." With its richly varied drinking culture, New York was the wettest city William Anderson had ever encountered, and he would have his work cut out for him.[5]

Once in New York, Anderson quickly made his way to the Hotel McAlpin on Thirty-fourth Street. Having settled into his suite, he went to work immediately, and by six o'clock that evening, reporters from the city's leading papers had gathered in Anderson's room for a press conference. There, Anderson introduced himself and outlined the moral and legislative agenda of the Anti-Saloon League. Outspoken, opinionated, and energetic, Anderson began by declaring, "From now on, the attention of the National Anti-Saloon League will be directed toward New York as the liquor center of America." Calling conditions in New York "deplorable," he promised to dry up the state from the Battery to Buffalo. "I'm willing to work, night and day," he added, vowing to transform New York into a national model of temperance.[6]

The reporters assembled in Anderson's hotel room greeted the dry warrior's claims with polite skepticism and plenty of questions. Was he aware that Tammany Hall, the powerful Democratic machine that controlled city politics, would bitterly oppose his efforts? Where did Anderson intend to find allies to support his campaign in New York? How long would the Prohibition campaign take?

Anderson was aware of the challenges ahead of him. He admitted it would be impossible to implement an immediate ban on alcohol in the state, and expected New York City to be particularly difficult to reform. He conceded, "I haven't the slightest idea that we can close up the saloons and cafés on Broadway and completely alter the character of what is known as the 'Great White Way.'" Nevertheless, Anderson promised to eliminate

New York's liquor trade in short time by raising money, recruiting supporters, and making the Anti-Saloon League a force to be reckoned with in state politics. As Anderson shared the specifics of his strategy with his audience, he vowed to lobby for the passage of a statewide "local option" law, which would allow voters to ban saloons on a town-by-town, district-by-district basis. Beginning in the smaller towns and cities of upstate New York, Anderson promised to use local option to stage a long, dry march, bringing the crusade closer to New York City with each victory. "We are going to carry this fight into all the counties of the state, educate the people, and stir up support for this proposed law," he insisted. "We shall win the state by degrees."[7]

As combative as he was methodical, Anderson pledged to punish anyone who stood in the way of the dry crusade. He insisted that neither liquor lobbyists, nor brewing magnates, nor wets of either party would hinder his efforts. Once his campaign was under way, Anderson promised, he would bring New York in line with the league's ultimate goal, a constitutional amendment outlawing the liquor trade. "It is going to be a real fight," he remarked, "and we won't admit to defeat."[8]

The day after his arrival, Anderson saw his bold predictions splashed across the city's papers. "Hey, Demon Rum, Watch Out! He's Here to Get You," announced the headline of the *New York World*. New Yorkers had endured their share of dry fanatics and temperance prophets before, but in Anderson they were encountering a new kind of dry leader. With his conservative business attire and law degree from the University of Michigan, the forty-year-old Anderson defied the stereotypical image of the American temperance crusader, once defined by the infamous Carry Nation, who had raged against the liquor trade in the 1890s with a Bible in one hand and an axe in the other. Anderson, by contrast, was a professional lobbyist who worked fourteen-hour days on the Anti-Saloon League's legislation and public relations campaign. With his instinct for politics, his tenacity as a lawyer, and his sharp tongue, he would accomplish far more than Carry Nation's hatchet ever had.[9]

While Anderson's bravado grabbed the attention of the reporters who met with him on New Year's Day, 1914, few of them, and likely fewer of their readers, believed the Anti-Saloon League's crusade would ever accomplish anything more than drying up a few towns in Herkimer County or imposing higher license fees on New York City saloons. The idea of a national Prohibition amendment seemed even more laughable. But Anderson was not fazed. When a young reporter told him he didn't expect to see the United States enact Prohibition in either of their lifetimes, Anderson shot back, "I hope nothing happens to you . . . but I, who am much older, expect to see it. It will come within ten or twenty years."[10]

In January 1919, only five years after William Anderson arrived in New York City, the United States stood on the verge of national Prohibition. After waging one of the most successful reform campaigns in American history, the Anti-Saloon League had ushered through both houses of Congress a constitutional amendment that declared "the manufacture, sale, or transportation of intoxicating liquors within, the importation thereof into, or the exportation thereof from the United States and all territory subject to the jurisdiction thereof for beverage purposes is hereby prohibited." On December 17, 1917, the House of Representatives had voted in favor of the proposed Article XVIII by a bipartisan vote of 282 to 128, just more than the two-thirds required for passage. The next day, the Senate followed suit with a 47 to 8 vote in favor of the dry amendment. It then sent the legislation to the states for ratification.[11]

Once it passed Congress, ratification of the Prohibition amendment seemed almost automatic. Through its lobbying efforts, the Anti-Saloon League had been lining up support for the amendment in dry-leaning states for several years. Now, state legislatures rapidly moved to endorse it. In 1918, fifteen states approved the amendment. As 1919 began, the pace quickened. On January 7, Ohio and Oklahoma ratified; the next day, Idaho and Maine; the following day, West Virginia. After a weekend lull, fifteen more states approved the dry amendment in the span of four days, including states that had only recently shifted into the dry camp. On the afternoon of January 16, 1919, Nebraska became the thirty-sixth state to ratify the Eighteenth Amendment, giving it the three-fourths majority necessary for enactment. According to the provisions of the resolution, the ban on alcohol would go into effect in one year, with Congress and the states "given concurrent power to enforce this article by appropriate legislation." Despite the claims of skeptics that it could never happen, the Eighteenth Amendment to the Constitution had become law.[12]

And what of New York, that bastion of wet sentiment and the so-called liquor center of America? In the spring of 1918, as the Prohibition amendment made its way through the states, the *New York Times* promised that "the federal Prohibition amendment will not be ratified by this legislature." It joked that New York, at least to drys, would always remain "Satan's last stronghold." Yet less than two weeks after Nebraska's decisive vote, and to the astonishment of many observers, New York also narrowly cast its vote in support of Prohibition.[13]

The amendment's passage in New York was a surprising development indicative of the dry lobby's formidable power. The Anti-Saloon League had engineered this victory in the face of overwhelming opposition from New York's Democrats, who spoke out against the proposed amendment in no uncertain terms. On January 28, 1919, as the amendment came up for debate in the State Senate, Senator James J. Walker, one of New York City's most vocal opponents of Prohibition, blasted the dry lobby for wanting "to take a glass of beer away from the workingman while allowing the rich to have their cellars filled with wine." But Walker's passion was no match for William Anderson's political maneuvering. Taking advantage of a quirk in the New York State Constitution that gave disproportionate power to upstate Republicans, Anderson and the Anti-Saloon League had corralled enough Republican votes to ensure that the dry measure would pass. Furious at having been outmaneuvered, Walker predicted that national Prohibition would never be fairly enforced, and shouted in disgust, "This measure you Republicans are fathering was born in hypocrisy, and there it will die."[14]

The following day, the senators staged a "spectacular fight" over ratification as wets and drys traded barbs for ten hours. As the debate wound down, Democrats used every parliamentary move imaginable to forestall a final vote, but failed. The Senate approved the Prohibition amendment along party lines by the narrow margin of twenty-seven to twenty-four. (The State Assembly had given its blessing to the dry law six days earlier by another party-line vote of eighty-one to sixty-six.) It had been a bitter fight, as William Anderson had predicted, but the Anti-Saloon League had prevailed. Contrary to all popular wisdom, New York had been pushed into the dry column, if only by the slimmest margin.[15]

From a legal standpoint, New York's ratification of the Eighteenth Amendment meant nothing. Having already been ratified by three-quarters of the United States, Prohibition would become law no matter how New York voted. But New York's ratification of the Eighteenth Amendment carried enormous symbolic importance for the Anti-Saloon League. For decades, drys had lamented New York's resistance to reform and feared that New York's enormous influence on American culture would undermine the dry crusade. Now the dry crusade had triumphed in the state most hostile to its cause, proving, William Anderson argued, that Prohibition had won the blessing of the entire nation, even those states that had once scoffed at the idea of a dry amendment to the Constitution. Calling it a "jubilee," the Anti-Saloon League celebrated the ratification of the Prohibition amendment in New York as the sweetest victory the dry movement had won, next to the ratification of the Eighteenth Amendment itself.[16]

The Anti-Saloon League's victory in 1919, which resulted in the passage of a constitutional amendment, was less an expression of popular will than the product of political opportunism and a generation's worth of aggressive lobbying. Though genuine concerns over alcohol abuse gave the dry cause a moral imperative, fear of America's growing cities, suspicion of the immigrants who lived in them, and outright prejudice were decisive factors in the campaign for ratification. Fortuitously for drys, the campaign concluded just as the United States entered World War I, a factor that had a profound effect on silencing opponents of the dry amendment. Prohibition's passage therefore should be attributed, not to a democratic yearning for social and moral reform, but to what William Anderson described as "outguessing and outgeneraling the foe . . . hard hitting and merciless fighting." In short, it was a victory based more on the Anti-Saloon League's skillful lobbying than on a national call for moral reform.[17]

It was no mistake that New York figured so prominently in the dry crusade. The prevalence of both alcohol and waves of immigrants in the city led the Anti-Saloon League to emphasize the need to reform New York and its inhabitants. Alcohol had been part and parcel of everyday life in New York City since the seventeenth century, when colonial Dutch settlers brought a fabled fondness for gin to New Amsterdam. (They opened the city's first distillery on Staten Island in 1640, beginning a long pattern whereby New York's drinking habits reflected the latest wave of arrivals.) By the late nineteenth century, a proliferation of working-class saloons, wine-soaked bohemian cafés, tawdry pleasure palaces, and ritzy hotel bars filled New York's neighborhoods, reflecting a drinking culture that was as varied and rapidly changing as the city itself. When William Anderson arrived in 1914, more than 13,000 drinking establishments dotted the city; in some districts there was a saloon for every six inhabitants. Ranging from respectable cafés to illegal "blind tigers," they gave life to the fact that New York City had been granted more licenses to sell liquor than had many states.[18]

From the perspective of the Anti-Saloon League, reform of New York's drinking habits was long overdue. By 1913, according to the league, New Yorkers were spending $365 million a year on alcohol, a figure that translated neatly to the tune of a million dollars a day. That was more than double what the nation spent annually on the salaries of its public school teachers. In one week, the league claimed, New Yorkers consumed 30 million quarts of draft beer, a million quarts of bottled beer and ale, a half-million quarts of whiskey, 75,000 quarts of gin, 76,000 quarts of brandy, 500 quarts of absinthe, 40,500 quarts of champagne, 60,000 quarts of wine, and nearly 500,000 quarts of other miscellaneous beers and liquors. Statewide, the league estimated that New Yorkers drank six quarts of alcoholic beverages a week for every man, woman, and child, indicating that per capita consumption of alcohol in New York was roughly three and a half times the national average.[19]

Though the Anti-Saloon League had been fighting the liquor traffic in the state since 1899, by 1913 it had advanced the dry cause only in upstate New York, where the number of dry towns had increased from 276 to 400. The league's directors remained stymied by the enormous problem New York City and its inhabitants posed to its efforts, and feared they would never be able to promote the vision of a dry America unless they could claim some measure of success in the wet metropolis. For this reason, the Anti-Saloon League sent William Anderson to New York in 1914, expecting him to inject a new urgency into the debate over alcohol in the state.

Anderson was eager for the challenge. Arguing that "New York is far from hopeless on this question," he insisted that he would soon have New York as wrapped up in the debate over liquor as the rest of the country. He exclaimed, "The Empire State and even New York City are about due for some agitation on this subject."[20]

Having been sheltered in their wet ways for so long, New Yorkers proved entirely unprepared for William Anderson's challenge to their way of life. Shortly after Anderson's arrival in the city, journalist Edward Marshall wrote in the *New York Times* that "the drinking New Yorker, smug in his conceit of living in the metropolis . . . has slight conception of the true strength of the anti-liquor movement which has been sweeping through the nation as of late years." While the Anti-Saloon League had surged ahead as a force in national politics during the 1910s, many New Yorkers remained oblivious to the mounting dry crusade. Dry politics might have a place in Ohio or Indiana, they reasoned, but certainly not in New York. With Anderson's arrival, however, Marshall argued that New Yorkers were about to become acquainted with the "amazing strength" of the Anti-Saloon League, which had "become one of the great forces in American life."[21]

True to Marshall's assessment, the league had enjoyed a spectacular rise since its founding in Berea, Ohio, in 1893. Launching a national campaign against the liquor trade and the influence of the saloon on public life, the league expanded into state after state, setting up local chapters and raising substantial sums of money for its lobbying efforts. (It benefited considerably from the contributions of John D. Rockefeller, Sr., a loyal supporter of the league.) It established a strong base of support in the Midwest and South, and expertly used that base to build the organization into a formidable political, social, and moral force with the strength to advance its agenda nationally.[22]

As it grew in power, the Anti-Saloon League eclipsed the Woman's Christian Temperance Union (WCTU), which had been the leading force in the American temperance movement since the 1880s. In contrast with the WCTU's emphasis on voluntarism and its desire to promote a broad social reform program, the Anti-Saloon League's great innovation was to pioneer the modern craft of political lobbying in the service of a single moral cause. Modeling itself after modern business organizations, the league was well suited to the political climate of the early twentieth century. At a time when Progressive reformers promoted the ideal of "government by experts," the league embodied this ideal by employing a professional staff of college-educated lawyers, statisticians, publicists, and researchers to carry out its work.[23]

The league's tactics were focused and effective. In lieu of fielding its own political candidates as the Prohibition Party had in earlier decades, the league instead used its influence to sway elections in favor of dry candidates, regardless of party, and then used their loyal support to advance the dry agenda. The league employed a subsidiary, the American Issue Publishing Company, to publish its own newspaper and to print the millions of pieces of dry literature it distributed across the United States. Embracing modern advertising techniques, the league used billboards and streetcar posters to disseminate its dry message. ("It brings lasting results," commented the league's general superintendent, Purley Baker.) Combining their political influence and public relations work, league lobbyists drafted pieces of dry legislation and pressured legislators to turn them into local, state, and federal laws. The league responded to political opposition to its program by mobilizing a dry voting bloc, which it used to oust any legislators who failed to support the Prohibition agenda. Through these efforts, the league established itself as a leading force in American politics, mastering what Peter Odegard, a political scientist of the era, described as the new art of "pressure politics."[24]

When William Anderson brought the Anti-Saloon League's pressure politics to bear upon New York, he was delighted to find New Yorkers woefully ignorant of the league's strength. In an interview with the *New York Times,* Anderson told Edward Marshall that "New York is one of the backward states. It is curiously insular. It seems to have no conception of what is going on in the Middle West and what is sure to happen here." Taunting Marshall's readers, Anderson added, "I wonder if New Yorkers would resent the statement that in some things their ignorance is great enough to be appalling." He concluded, "New York will presently wake up."[25]

And wake up it did. During Anderson's first two years in New York, he developed the Anti-Saloon League into a powerful force in state politics.

He met regularly with church groups, campaigned for Sunday closing laws, and built alliances with other dry groups and moral reformers. Drawing upon a base of subscribers who paid monthly pledges to the Anti-Saloon League ranging from twenty-five cents to two dollars, Anderson paid off the debt the state organization had incurred under his predecessor. Through constant speeches, press conferences, and publicity stunts, Anderson kept his name in the newspapers and built what he described as "the greatest permanent Anti-Saloon League organization ever built in any state."[26]

Anderson's crusading style could best be seen in his fearless charge into the rough-and-tumble world of New York politics. As a demonstration of his resolve, Anderson quickly made a point of challenging some of the most visible political figures in state politics, including the speaker of the State Assembly, the state chairman of the Republican Party, and the mayor of New York. These brash moves yielded great publicity for the league and quickly established Anderson's reputation as a figure to be reckoned with in state politics.[27]

In 1914 Anderson's battles with Thaddeus Sweet, a moderate dry who served as the speaker of the New York State Assembly, showcased the dry warrior's talents at their most cutthroat. Convinced Sweet would never cooperate fully with the league, Anderson decided the dry agenda would best be served by driving Sweet out of office. To accomplish this, Anderson sent a private investigator to Sweet's district in Oswego County to circulate rumors that the speaker had taken bribes from liquor interests in exchange for his pledge to vote against temperance legislation. Anderson then attempted to frame Sweet with a bogus letter of support from a fictitious liquor dealer. Using this evidence to insinuate that Sweet had betrayed the dry cause, Anderson urged voters in Sweet's county to replace the speaker with a "bone-dry" candidate more to Anderson's liking. When Anderson's antics were exposed before election day, Sweet succeeded in saving his job only by publicly confronting the dry warrior about his ruse. Sweet was reelected, but he and every other legislator in New York had been given a demonstration of William Anderson's style of politics. Anderson's tactics, Sweet noted, were enough to "make your blood run cold and your hair stand up."[28]

Anderson engineered an equally noteworthy run-in in 1914 with William Barnes, the chairman of the Republican State Committee. In an open letter to the press, Anderson blasted Barnes for opposing local option legis-lation favored by the league, and denigrated him as the "Boss of the Liquor End of the Republican Party." Taking offense at Anderson's use of the word "boss," arguing that it was an "odious and opprobrious epithet" connoting corruption and influence peddling, Barnes sued Anderson for libel, asking for $5,000 in damages, plus court costs. Being unfamiliar with Anderson's tactics, Barnes could be forgiven for thinking the threat of a lawsuit would put the dry crusader in his place. Those who had seen Anderson at work knew better. Commenting on Barnes's suit against Anderson, the *Baltimore News* wrote, "It is rather evident that . . . 'Bill' Barnes has not had the time to get on to the curves of 'Bill' Anderson." The *News* continued, "He is in for a terrible awakening . . . To be sued for libel on such an issue as Mr. Barnes had made is probably pretty close to Mr. Anderson's heart's desire."[29]

As the *Baltimore News* predicted, Anderson turned the tables on Barnes. First, he offered to retract his statements against Barnes, but only if Barnes agreed to a public debate on the liquor issue. When Barnes refused, Ander-son mocked the Republican leader, telling the press, "We don't know how long it will take to make Mr. Barnes politically worthless to the liquor traffic in this state, except that it will come sooner than bonehead politi-cians or indifferent good people imagine." Having embarrassed Barnes, An-derson put all of New York's Republicans on notice, showing them what they could expect if they failed to support the program of the Anti-Saloon League. (Democrats had less to fear. Convinced that he had no chance of winning them over, Anderson mostly spared Democrats his shenanigans and focused his energies on bringing Republicans in line with the league's objectives.)[30]

As Anderson honed the use of pressure politics in Albany, he also made his presence felt in New York City politics. In 1915 he attacked Mayor John Purroy Mitchel and Police Commissioner Arthur Woods for failing to en-force the state law requiring saloons to close on Sunday. Mitchel initially seemed an unlikely target for Anderson. The thirty-five-year-old "boy mayor" had been elected on a reform ticket in 1913, briefly knocking Tammany Democrats out of power in the city. While Mitchel's reform stance might have marked the mayor as a potential ally under other circum-stances, Anderson picked a fight nonetheless. Claiming league investigators had found 721 saloons in the city in violation of Sunday closing laws, Anderson asked Governor Charles Whitman to remove both Mitchel and Woods from office for neglecting their official duties, and insisted that the New York Police Department (NYPD) be investigated on the basis of the league's findings. Whitman declined Anderson's request, remarking, "I do not think I shall remove either—at least, not tonight," but the matter handed Mitchel and the NYPD a front-page embarrassment and provoked several religious leaders to come out against Mitchel. Most of all, the episode gave New Yorkers a closer view of Anderson's crusading style.[31]

Even by New York standards, Anderson's escapades raised eyebrows. After witnessing what he had done to Sweet, Barnes, and Mitchel, wet opponents and dry sympathizers alike learned to think twice before risking an encounter with the dry warrior. Republicans especially were forced to reconcile themselves with the dry cause, even if they disagreed with it, on account of Anderson's growing power in state politics. (Governor Whitman, for one, curried Anderson's favor by expressing support for the Anti-Saloon League's agenda, though critics pointed out that Whitman himself did not abstain from drink.) Anderson's efforts, which resulted in the ouster of several wet legislators, saw the number of state lawmakers pledged to Prohibition increase by 60 percent in 1915. These were remarkable gains in a legislature that the Anti-Saloon League had described in its 1914 annual report as "owned, body and soul, by Tammany Hall." At the same time, Anderson's active campaigning increased the dry contingent among New York's congressional delegation from three to thirteen in the span of a few years. William Anderson's activism forced New Yorkers to accept the liquor question as a central issue in state politics. Taking notice of Anderson's success in moving Prohibition to the top of the state's political agenda, the *New York World* wrote, "Six months ago prohibition was about as much of an issue as Mormonism, pragmatism or the fourth dimension." Crediting Anderson, it added, "in a few short months since his arrival, he has changed the whole political line up in New York State."[32]

Having established himself on the political scene, Anderson turned his attention to the enactment of dry legislation. Even with the growing power of the Anti-Saloon League, he entertained no illusions that ending the liquor trade in New York would come without a prolonged fight. But by

1917, the local option law that Anderson had spoken of at his first press conference had become a real possibility. The Anti-Saloon League's proposal for local option was essentially an attempt to introduce Prohibition to the state on the local level. Earlier local option laws, which simply allowed localities to ban the sale of alcohol, had already resulted in 412 townships in the state going dry, but almost all of them concentrated in the rural areas of western New York. By 1913 only 7 percent of the state population lived in these dry areas. To expand the reach of local option legislation, the Anti-Saloon League proposed a new law that would divide the state into even smaller districts for the purposes of liquor regulations. Basically, the league proposed a form of dry gerrymandering that would allow counties, towns, and local districts in the state to vote themselves dry by unshackling them from the political dominance of wet cities. The league's plan would divide the state's population centers into three categories. Small cities with populations under 50,000 would vote as a single entity; counties would vote separately from cities of more than 10,000; and larger cities would hold separate votes on local option in each election district. From the league's perspective, revising the local option statutes in this manner would enormously increase the chances for dry voters to prevail in local elections, paving the way for substantial dry gains.[33]

By the Anti-Saloon League's design, local option opened the astonishing possibility of dry pockets being created in New York City. William Anderson explained it this way: "Now suppose you live in a residential district uptown. You and your neighbors decide you do not want saloons in that district. The members of the adjoining district . . . agree with you, and so do their neighbors beyond them." "Why," he asked, "shouldn't they have a right to vote upon that local matter, and if they don't want saloons near their homes, abolish them?" To Anderson, it was a very simple proposition. "If the people for a time want their district dry, let them vote and say it shall be dry," he explained. By Anderson's reasoning, half of New York City would go dry if given the opportunity.[34]

To combat the notion that the league's lobbyists were forcing local option on New Yorkers, William Anderson repeatedly emphasized one aspect of the league's local option proposal—that it was democratic. According to Anderson, the Anti-Saloon League was simply asking the state legislature to "give the people their rights." Bowing to Anderson's influence, Governor Whitman supported the local option measure, telling legislative leaders, "I am going to stand for giving them that right, entirely aside from what my personal views on the liquor trade might be." Arguing that local option laws merely gave the citizenry a fair way to decide the liquor question for themselves, the governor insisted that "this local option bill has got to go through. Any man who gets in the way of it is going to get hurt." If wets in the state legislature opposed the proposal, Anderson insisted, the burden would be on them to explain their apparent mistrust of the will of the people. Though the press reported that the "measure [was] bitterly fought in the legislature," Anderson saw his local option bill enacted statewide in May 1917. The provisions of the law allowed New York City to hold a separate referendum on the measure, but its passage marked a major victory for Anderson, who was presented with a ceremonial pen by Governor Whitman at the signing of the law as a reward for his work on its behalf.[35]

In the face of Anderson's relentless politicking, it was no wonder that opponents of the league failed to stop the dry advance. Few New Yorkers had the nerve to take on a political force like Anderson, and those who did often regretted their decision. But Anderson's routine was not all intimidation. It was also part disguise. His success was linked to his ability to latch onto two related causes dear to many New Yorkers—Progressivism and a desire to reign in the notoriously corrupt Tammany Hall machine.

William Anderson had arrived in New York at a unique moment in the history of American reform. Alongside Anderson's campaign for Prohibition, women campaigned for suffrage, labor advocates marched for an end to child labor, and city planners called for new zoning laws. Reform-minded New Yorkers demanded the improvement of sanitation and health care, better housing, more parks and playgrounds, better public education, and a host of other urban improvements. In the context of the Progressive era, the dry movement appealed to urban reformers who shared the league's desire to bring order and sobriety to American cities.

To make reformers allies in the campaign against the liquor trade, Anderson couched his agenda in Progressive terminology. He described the league's local option proposal as a "distinctly progressive" piece of legislation. He promised that the Anti-Saloon League's efforts would involve "a campaign of education" and address "questions of health and industrial efficiency." To reach the New Yorkers most in need of reform, Anderson called for "the circulation of literature, especially on the scientific aspect of the question, in many languages, and the ultimate employment of workers of different nationalities." In short, Anderson presented the league's work as part of a modern, scientific campaign that had much in common with the work that Progressive-minded New Yorkers had been attempting since the turn of the century through settlement houses and reform associations.[36]

To Anderson's advantage, Progressives had long shared the Anti-Saloon League's concerns over alcohol abuse and the negative influence of the liquor trade on society. In the years before the Prohibition campaign reached its peak, journals like *McClure's, Collier's Weekly,* and the *Atlantic Monthly* published articles with titles like "Beer and the City Liquor Problem" and "The Story of an Alcohol Slave" to expose problems stemming from the alcohol trade. They voiced concern over the urban saloon in particular, which Progressives and drys alike regarded as a unique threat to American life. As one muckraking reporter of the era declared, "There is but one large temperance problem now waiting to be solved in America—the problem of the city saloon."[37]

Scoffing at nostalgic depictions of the saloon as the "workingman's club," Progressives argued that the two hundred thousand saloons that dotted the United States posed "a distinct menace" to the country. "They disregarded the law," one reformer exclaimed. "They sold to minors. They sold to inebriates. They sold on Sunday. They harbored crooks, blacklegs, prostitutes, gamblers, and every sort of disreputable people. They entered politics and controlled our municipal life." To many Progressives, the campaign of the Anti-Saloon League against drinking establishments was long overdue, and they eagerly joined forces with it.[38]

As targets of reform, the American brewing and distilling industries came under equal fire. Just as Progressives had excoriated the meat, food, and drug industries in the early twentieth century for their corrupt practices, they railed against the nation's brewing and distilling industries as dangerous monopolies. Progressives pointed out that in 1914 more than half of the beer production in the United States was concentrated in the hands of only one hundred breweries, while the distilling industry was dominated by the huge Distilling Company of America, a holding company whose subsidiaries controlled more than 90 percent of the nation's liquor production. To maintain their market dominance and to protect yearly revenues exceeding three billion dollars, brewers and distillers funded an extensive lobbying network composed of the United States Brewers Association, the National Wholesale Liquor Dealers Association, and the National Liquor League. Envisioning these lobbies as having a powerful grip on state and federal legislators, drys and Progressives depicted them as "a parasitic class which has fattened on human weakness." Though the brewers' and distillers' lobbies were in fact far weaker and more disorganized than their critics imagined, Progressives insisted that the alcohol industry was a corrupt and reckless force that had to be countered by some form of government intervention.[39]

Reformers were just as eager to sever the legendary connections between saloons and Tammany Hall that characterized New York City politics in the late nineteenth and early twentieth centuries. When it came to links between corrupt political machines and the alcohol trade, New York City was seen as one of the nation's worst offenders. In 1890, eleven of the city's twenty-four aldermen listed their professions as saloon owners. Prominent Tammany Hall figures like Timothy "Dry Dollar" Sullivan, "Big Tom" Foley, and Charles Francis Murphy, the Tammany boss who controlled most of New York City politics during the 1910s and 1920s, had all launched their political careers through saloon ownership or other dealings in the liquor trade. In Greenwich Village in the years before Prohibition, one-third of the neighborhood's fifty-seven saloon owners had actively pursued careers in politics, and even those who had not sought office wielded enormous influence as community leaders because of their links to Tammany Hall. Given these connections, it was accurate to claim, as one critic did, that "the bulwark of Tammany Hall has always been the bar room."[40]

By the time Tammany Hall entered its sixth decade of control over New York City government in the 1910s, it had finely honed the technique of using the saloon as a political instrument. Tammany Hall's rise to power had been achieved through the organized use of graft and voter fraud, and saloons had continued to play a central role in its plans. Neighborhood saloons provided Tammany Hall operatives with convenient sources of cash to pay for political favors, while also serving as headquarters for ward bosses to dole out patronage and jobs. Saloons also supplied the votes of "repeaters," vagrants and petty criminals recruited to cast multiple ballots for Tammany candidates on election day. In exchange for their services, Tammany-linked drinking establishments rewarded these hired voters with free food, cigars, and whiskey, allowing bosses like Sullivan, Foley, and Murphy to build political empires. Through these methods, Tammany commandeered more than $150 million worth of city contracts and public works projects each year, while fending off sporadic challenges from reformers.[41]

Given the plentiful evidence of the corrupt influence of the saloon on city politics, not only in New York but also in other cities across the United States, the Anti-Saloon League struck a chord of resentment when it declared, "If we wish to purify politics, the saloon must be destroyed." Still, building any sort of alliance between drys and Progressives in New York was a delicate affair. New York's Progressives were a varied lot, and often far less inclined to embrace moral reform causes like temperance than they were to support economic or social causes. With their disparate concerns, causes, and approaches to reform, it would have been impossible to appeal to all of New York's Progressives as one entity. But William Anderson didn't need the support of all New York Progressives; he only needed the support of enough of them to give the Anti-Saloon League's campaign for Prohibition an additional boost. By borrowing Progressive language and appealing to Progressive concerns, he succeeded in doing just that.[42]

Part of Anderson's appeal to Progressive New Yorkers was that the Anti-Saloon League was now poised to accomplish through its local option campaign what other reformers had long failed to do in New York. While Chicago, Denver, Seattle, Portland, and Berkeley, for example, had all seen alliances between Progressives and the Anti-Saloon League limit or even eliminate the alcohol trade in those cities, reformers in New York had been repeatedly frustrated, if not humiliated, by their failures.[43]

It had not been for lack of trying. Reform associations like the Committee of Fifty for the Investigation of the Liquor Problem and the Committee of Fourteen had brought together industrialists, university professors, settlement house directors, public health advocates, religious leaders, and other experts to combat the alcohol trade, prostitution, and other vices in the city. In particular, the Committee of Fourteen, organized by the City Club and the Anti-Saloon League in 1905, was a model anti-vice organization. Its investigators collected extensive data on drinking establishments in New York, while its leaders pushed for curfews, called for the stricter licensing of cabarets, condemned breweries for sponsoring "disorderly houses," and repeatedly urged mayors to take action against the proliferation of vice and prostitution in the city.[44]

Despite the efforts of these groups, the only notable Progressive-era legislation to address the liquor trade in New York was the infamous Raines Law, passed in 1896, which raised licensing fees for saloons and prohibited the sale of alcohol on Sundays, except in restaurants and in hotels with ten or more beds. Though initially seen as a legislative victory for reformers, the Raines Law ultimately failed to reform the city saloon. Because the law exempted restaurants from Sunday closing regulations, savvy saloon owners learned to circumvent the law by serving "meals" with drinks. The "meals" were often only pretzels, but sympathetic city magistrates ruled that pretzels were enough of a meal to excuse many saloons from the Sunday closing laws. The statute also encouraged the proliferation of seedy "Raines Law hotels," created by saloon owners who partitioned the back rooms and upper floors of their bars into "bedrooms" to meet the new licensing requirements. Not only did this innovation allow Sunday drinking in the city to continue unabated; it also prompted saloon owners to rent out their back "bedrooms" to prostitutes to meet the higher cost of the new licensing fees. With time, the Raines Law resulted in the establishment of more than 1,000 "Raines Law hotels" in the city, giving prostitution a new thriving commercial base.[45]

To make matters worse, the Sunday closing provisions of the Raines Law proved unenforceable. A 1908 report indicated that more than 5,000 of the 5,820 saloons in the Bronx and Manhattan were serving alcohol on Sundays in defiance of the law. In 1910 a new effort to enforce Sunday closing was undermined by Mayor William J. Gaynor, an independent with no sympathy for the dry cause, who openly told saloonkeepers that they could violate the Sunday closing laws as long as they kept their shutters drawn. In addition, he forbade uniformed and plainclothes police officers from entering saloons in search of evidence of Sunday closing violations.[46]

The Raines Law was blatantly ignored in New York because the city's political climate favored its evasion more than its enforcement. Tammany Hall bosses had nothing to gain from enforcing the Raines Law, and independent mayors like Gaynor saw that the Sunday closing laws were unpopular, especially with working-class saloon patrons who wanted their weekend beer. Beginning in 1914, William Anderson's challenge was to change the political climate that doomed initiatives like the Raines Law, and to do so quickly. Calling for an end to "the flagrant lawlessness in New York on Sunday," Anderson pushed to eliminate the loophole that allowed hotels to sell alcohol on Sundays. Why, he asked, should the wealthy be allowed to drink on Sundays in expensive hotels when the working classes could not? Extending Sunday closing regulations to hotel bars, Anderson reasoned, would make the enforcement of the law fair and simple. To strengthen his case, Anderson sent Anti-Saloon League investigators to several prominent New York hotels in 1915 and 1916 to test their compliance with the existing regulations. The reports came back indicating that the Waldorf-Astoria, the Knickerbocker, the Belmont, and the McAlpin were all violating the Raines Law by selling liquor after hours and on Sunday without meals. Anderson's findings bolstered the Anti-Saloon League's position that more uniformly restrictive regulations were needed.[47]

Anderson's push for local option, his appeal to Progressive New Yorkers, and his vigilance over alcohol sales in the city terrified the liquor and beer lobbies. "The liquor men are quite literally in a panic," Anderson told journalist Edward Marshall. Faced with a greater threat in Anderson than they had ever seen before, the beer and liquor lobbies fervently searched for ways to combat the growing dry crusade. Some beer brewers naively advocated an end to the hard liquor trade, hoping that beer and wine would remain legal if distillers succumbed to the league's campaign. Others fatalistically contended that it was time to give up the fight altogether. A 1914 editorial in the *National Liquor Dealers' Journal* revealed a sense of doubt and self-blame pervading the industry as a result of pressure from the Anti-Saloon League. Admitting openly that brewers and distillers had "formed alliances with the slums that repel all conscientious citizens" and aided "the most corrupt political powers," the editorial opined that the alcohol trade was facing nothing less than "doom." It concluded that "for this the liquor business is to blame."[48]

Sensing their weakness, Anderson continued to goad the liquor interests at conferences, in debates, and in statements to the press, accusing them of trying to resist the inevitability of Prohibition. In the state legislature, Anderson harassed them further by introducing a bill in 1916 that would have required any drink containing more than 1/2 of 1 percent alcohol to carry a warning label that read, "This preparation contains alcohol, which is a habit-forming, irritant, narcotic poison." Though the bill failed by a narrow margin, Hugh Fox, the secretary of the United States Brewers Association, called it the most clever piece of publicity ever used against the liquor industry. Anderson later admitted that he never expected the bill to pass. His strategy had simply been to "keep the New York liquor men so busy at home with local fights that they will have no time nor money to contribute energy and funds to the national fight."[49]

With this constant barrage of attacks on liquor lobbyists, hotel and saloon owners, and wet politicians, Anderson kept his critics off balance. As the dry campaign advanced, few opponents remained who dared to take on the dry warrior. At best, all wets could hope for was to see if Anderson's outspoken nature would finally get the best of him. Wet hopes of such a turn in Anderson's fortune rose briefly in 1917, when the dry warrior, in trademark fashion, sent word to 300 newspapers across New York that a secret Canadian "slush fund" had been set up by liquor interests to bribe New York lawmakers to vote against the legislation sponsored by the league. Wets in the state legislature raised a storm over Anderson's allegations, demanding he come forward with proof of the slush fund to support his claim, threatening to subpoena the dry leader if necessary. Unflappable, Anderson stood his ground. He said he would welcome a subpoena, but refused to divulge any more evidence until compelled to do so.

The matter came to a head in March 1917, when Anderson appeared in Albany for a hearing on several pending liquor bills sponsored by the Anti-Saloon League. In front of a crowd of several hundred howling spectators, Senator Ogden L. Mills lambasted Anderson for maligning the character of state legislators with unsubstantiated rumors of corruption. In a heated exchange with Anderson, punctuated by raised voices and finger pointing, Mills demanded that Anderson produce his evidence or recant his accusations. Siding with Mills, Assemblyman Martin McCue called for legislators to boycott the hearings on the league's proposed laws, insisting, "We should not listen to people who have cast reflections on us and insulted us." He continued, "I for one will refuse to sit with this committee while Anderson talks." The chairman of the committee then barred Anderson from testifying unless he submitted proof to support his earlier claims about the existence of the slush fund used to bribe legislators. Unable to offer any proof, Anderson was dealt a rare setback. Forced to retreat to the front row of the chamber, he watched the proceedings in silence as wets in the gallery cheered.[50]

Anderson's accusations infuriated his opponents, who now desperately wanted to give Anderson a taste of his own medicine. When a dry supporter cautioned wets that attacking Anderson would make a martyr of him, one wet assemblyman retorted, "You couldn't make a martyr of that creature any more than you could make a warthog appreciate a Mozart symphony." It was an early sign that Anderson's penchant for making enemies would come back to haunt him.[51]

Anderson's lack of restraint also had the effect of revealing prejudices that ran deep in the Prohibition movement. By the late 1910s, Anderson began to display an anti-Catholic streak that would become even more pronounced as the dry era unfolded. In 1918 he unleashed a blistering attack on a former Maryland foe, Cardinal Gibbons of Baltimore, accusing him of serving as a tool of "the largest and wealthiest distillers of Maryland," and calling Gibbons "an enemy of the American republic." The *New York Times*, startled by Anderson's bluntly anti-Catholic tone, called his comments a display of "fanatical intolerance and intemperance of the tongue" and reminded him that "not only Cardinal Gibbons, but the obscurest and humblest man in America has a right to express his opinion of Prohibition." Anderson's comments hinted at something observers of the dry movement had known for some time—that key members of it were as motivated by a distrust of Catholics, Jews, and the ethnic groups that populated cities like New York as they were by concerns over the saloon.[52]

As this trait of his emerged, the press began to take a more critical view of the style and tone of Anderson's pressure politics. Having watched the dry movement in New York grow from a curiosity into a political juggernaut, the *New York World* and the *New York Times* voiced concern about its unwavering dogmatism, and Anderson's zealotry in particular. Describing the Anti-Saloon League as "a pretentious lobby, pious and paid," the *World* warned that dry efforts to impose moral reform on the public threatened to render the Constitution meaningless. The *Times* expressed similar concern that William Anderson's extremism had become more pronounced as his dry campaign had progressed. Waxing for the day when Anderson "used to have some sense of humor," it complained that Anderson and "the professional prohibitionists" had ended any chance for the nation to reach a reasonable compromise on the liquor question with their insistence that any plan that called for less than a total prohibition of alcohol was a "scheme of the liquor interests."[53]

Four years into his campaign, Anderson was at a critical juncture. He had made a name for himself in New York politics, and made the dry agenda a central topic of debate in the state. Confounding his critics, he had nearly silenced the opposition to the dry cause in New York. Now, just as a backlash was emerging against him in response to his increasingly intolerant manner, Anderson was unexpectedly aided by the emergence of a national crisis that would factor significantly in the final enactment of Prohibition. The U.S. entry into World War I in April 1917 added a new dimension to the dry crusade. It was an element the dry crusade did not invent and could not control, but it was one the drys took advantage of masterfully.

The Anti-Saloon League couldn't possibly have planned for such an auspicious intrusion of world events into its campaign for Prohibition, but the league nevertheless seized the opportunity to make the dry crusade indistinguishable from what historian Frederick Lewis Allen called "the spartan fervor of wartime." As the conflict in Europe raged, the Anti-Saloon League quickly shifted strategies to present the alcohol problem in a new light as an issue of national security. With wartime slogans like "Booze or Coal?" and "Save 11,000,000 Loaves a Day," the league called for an immediate halt to distilling and brewing to conserve fuel and grain for the war effort. Building on its earlier arguments for stricter dry laws, the league also promoted the benefits of temperance for American soldiers, arguing that sober soldiers were safer, healthier, and less likely to divulge wartime secrets. Tapping into the rapid rise of anti-German sentiment in the United States, the league also questioned the loyalty and political activities of German-American brewers, demonizing them as a threat to domestic productivity.[54]

With the war in Europe now dominating the national agenda, the league's ability to link the dry cause to the war effort translated into quick legislative advances, each bringing the country closer to national Prohibition. Helped by a new influx of drys into the House of Representatives and United States Senate after the 1916 elections, the Anti-Saloon League found Congress more compliant than ever.

In August 1917, the Anti-Saloon League helped pass the Lever Food and Fuel Control Act, a wartime measure that gave President Woodrow Wilson broad powers to regulate the nation's food supply. It also banned the use of grain for distilling and allowed the president to regulate wine and beer production for the duration of the war. Drys also lobbied for and won statutes prohibiting the sale of alcohol on or near military bases, as well as regulations making it a crime to sell or serve alcohol to uniformed soldiers under any circumstances. The passage of these laws provided the dry lobby with important precedents for imposing national restrictions on the alcohol trade. The progress the drys made in this brief period was so great, and their momentum seemed to be growing so rapidly, that dry leader Bishop James Cannon, Jr., proclaimed, "Our people are now beginning to believe that nothing is impossible."[55]

The fusion of wartime patriotism with "anti-saloonism" further fueled calls for national sacrifice. William Jennings Bryan, the famed orator, presidential candidate, and former secretary of state, carried this message of sacrifice to the American public for the dry movement, asking in one 1918 address, "We have heard of meatless days and wheatless days. Why doesn't someone suggest a few beerless days?" Bryan's call for national sacrifice was echoed locally in New York when the Anti-Saloon League pressed Mayor John Purroy Mitchel to impose a 1:00 A.M. closing time for the city's cafés, saloons, and cabarets at the beginning of the war. Mitchel complied, winning praise from the *New York Times,* which noted, "One o'clock in the morning is a late enough bedtime for a people who are awaiting the summons to war."[56]

With wartime patriotism advancing the Prohibition cause, the conflict in Europe boosted the drys' chances for success in another important regard. The Anti-Saloon League had always regarded New York's large population of first- and second-generation immigrants as a significant obstacle to Prohibition, as they were expected to protest strenuously against any pending dry legislation. The conflict in Europe, however, unleashed a new wave of anti-ethnic sentiment in the United States cloaked as patriotism, which undermined the ability of ethnic Americans to challenge the dry movement in any meaningful fashion. In the context of the war, German Americans came under scrutiny as possible sympathizers of the kaiser, Irish Americans were criticized for opposing the U.S. alliance with Great Britain, and Southern Europeans and Eastern European Jews drew suspicion for their perceived radicalism. As a result, many ethnic New Yorkers grew reluctant to speak out against the dry agenda as long as the war raged in Europe. With the Anti-Saloon League loudly proclaiming, "The challenge to loyal patriots of America today is to demand the absolute prohibition of the liquor traffic," many ethnic New Yorkers simply swallowed their opposition to the dry campaign for fear of appearing disloyal.[57]

German Americans suffered the greatest affronts in the hostile climate of wartime. With hysteria against the German "Hun" sweeping the nation, the Anti-Saloon League took pains to emphasize the domination of the American brewing industry by German families. In 1917, one Anti-Saloon League publication crowed, "German brewers in this country . . . have rendered thousands of men inefficient and are thus crippling the Republic in its war on Prussian militarism." Another league pamphlet spoke out against "the un-American, pro-German, crime-producing, food-wasting, youth-corrupting, home-wrecking, treasonable liquor traffic." It asked, "How can any loyal citizen, be he wet or dry, help or vote for a trade that is aiding a pro-German Alliance?" Raising the specter of sabotage and alien infiltration, another Prohibitionist publication declared, "We have German enemies in this country too." Reciting the names of the country's prominent brewing companies, it noted that "the worst of all . . . are Pabst, Schlitz, Blatz, and Miller."[58]

This demonization of German Americans by the dry camp was exacerbated by the embarrassing revelation, made public by the *New York World* in 1916, that several American breweries had been funding the activities of the

German-American Alliance, a civic organization with more than two million members of German descent. While the alliance had been established
for the general purpose of fostering and promoting German culture in the
United States, a great deal of its resources had been spent opposing Prohibition. When the *World* revealed that the alliance had not only made payments to American newspapers to run articles critical of the Prohibition
movement, but also engaged in political lobbying on behalf of the German
kaiser, the Anti-Saloon League demanded action. Heeding the league's call,
Congress launched an investigation of the alliance's political activities and
outlawed the group in July 1918.[59]

The ban on the German-American Alliance silenced one of the Anti-
Saloon League's few remaining effective opponents. Having defeated the
alliance, the league stayed with its anti-German message, proclaiming in a
pamphlet, "Everything in this country that is pro-German is anti-American.
Everything that is pro-German must go." These wartime accusations had a
visible effect on New York City as its German institutions sought to distance themselves from the commotion. The German Hospital and Dis-
pensary, for example, changed its name to the Lenox Hill Hospital. The
Germania Life Insurance Company renamed itself the Guardian Life Insurance Company. At the same time, the Metropolitan Opera refused to per-
form German operas; German-language newspapers in the city declined in
circulation, and German churches began conducting services in English, all
in response to the anti-German frenzy of the war years.[60]

The Anti-Saloon League's contribution to this atmosphere of intolerance
understandably turned most of the city's German Americans vehemently
and permanently against the Prohibition movement. However, while German Americans had been boisterously vocal about their opposition to dry
laws as far back as the 1840s, the political climate of World War I severely
limited their opportunities to speak out. New York's German-American
newspapers offered surprisingly restrained commentary on Prohibition at
the height of the dry crusade, and German Americans in the city found it
nearly impossible to take a public stand against Prohibition, though they
opposed it almost universally.[61]

New York's Irish community also suffered from the dry movement's use
of the war effort to advance the Prohibition campaign. With Ireland in the

midst of its own bloody war for independence from Great Britain, many Irish New Yorkers opposed America's wartime alliance with England. One of the city's Irish newspapers, the *Gaelic American,* went so far as to express its support for Germany before the United States entered the war. At the same time, Irish New Yorkers opposed Prohibition overwhelmingly. As both Catholics and participants in a strong tradition of barroom culture, the Irish were doubly wary of the militancy of dry Protestants like William Anderson. Yet like German Americans, Irish New Yorkers risked being branded disloyal if they vocally opposed either the war or Prohibition. Faced with this dilemma, they restrained their obvious dislike for both. When called upon to serve in the military, New York's Irish donned American uniforms to fight, forcing themselves to distinguish American war interests from those of the British. At the same time, they offered no more than moderate criticism of the dry movement while the war was being waged. Though angered by stereotypes of Irish drinking and the anti-Irish and anti-Catholic sentiments stirred by many drys, Irish New Yorkers were more concerned about appearing "un-American" in the intolerant climate of the war. To the benefit of the dry campaign, papers like the *Gaelic American* carried almost no mention of Prohibition as it neared ratification; nor did Irish community groups in the city mount any significant opposition to the Eighteenth Amendment.[62]

This treatment of German and Irish New Yorkers was enough to silence the rest of the city's ethnic communities for the duration of the war years. With "foreign" habits already coming under close scrutiny in Progressive-era America, few ethnic minorities desired to draw any more attention to themselves by challenging Prohibition. While the foreign-language press in the city grumbled from time to time about the dry movement and the prejudices the Anti-Saloon League exploited to promote Prohibition, none dared speak too loudly.

Using the war to silence opponents of Prohibition clearly benefited the Anti-Saloon League in the short run, but the strategy also had long-term costs. Quietly suffering the attacks of Prohibitionists, many of New York's ethnic communities developed an undying enmity for the nation's drys, especially William Anderson. Prohibition's future success would ultimately depend on the cooperation of these minorities, but the intolerance that characterized the wartime push for Prohibition instead planted the seeds of a fierce resistance that would emerge later.

For the time being, William Anderson and the Anti-Saloon League were delighted to see World War I pushing the nation closer to Prohibition. On the national level, important legislative victories and wartime measures passed in 1917 greatly improved the outlook for the ratification of the national Prohibition amendment in the near future. When Congress finally approved the Eighteenth Amendment and sent it to the states for ratification in December 1917, Anderson and his fellow drys could step back and let momentum take its course. Where conventional wisdom had once dictated that the dry campaign would never win, the Anti-Saloon League seemed to be coasting to a victory that was not just about banning alcohol but about defining the culture of the United States.

In the final days of the dry campaign, it was not clear, even in New York, that the citizenry understood all that was at stake in the Anti-Saloon League's campaign. Boosted by the war effort, the movement for Prohibition suddenly had an irresistible appeal that masked the bigotry embedded in it. As the editors of the *New York Times* saw it, the rapid advancement of the dry amendment through the state legislatures in 1918 was a sign that Americans were rushing to "get on the bandwagon." The paper could only conclude that "Prohibition seems to be the fashion, just as drinking used to be."[63]

Indeed, as the dry fashion took hold in 1918, the Prohibition cause continued to attract new, and often surprising, supporters, even in New York City. In some cases, the dry campaign simply benefited from the help of ethnic groups with a predisposition to the temperance cause. Elements of New York's Norwegian community, for example, actively campaigned for Prohibition through Det Huite Baand (The White Ribbon), a women's group allied with the Woman's Christian Temperance Union. In Brooklyn and Staten Island, Norwegian church groups, the Atlantic Total Abstinence Society, and the lodges of the Norwegian Good Templars all circulated petitions in support of the Eighteenth Amendment. When it passed in 1919, two hundred members of the Norwegian community held a victory banquet at the Bethesda Mission in Brooklyn. While their support was probably rooted more in the strong temperance tradition of Norway than in any affinity for the Anti-Saloon League, it helped William Anderson dispel the notion that Prohibition was opposed universally by immigrant communities.[64]

The Prohibition movement also found pockets of support within the African American community. From their office in New York, A. Philip Randolph and Chandler Owen of the International Brotherhood of Sleeping Car Porters promoted the dry cause in their journal *The Messenger*. Though Randolph and Owen believed Prohibition would benefit workers of all races, they were especially optimistic about the gains Prohibition would yield for African Americans. From their perspective, Prohibition promised to lower crime and insurance rates, lift wages, and cleanse the political process, all to the benefit of working-class blacks. Noting that "the corruption of the Negro vote has been through the use of liquor plentifully served," they hoped that ending the liquor trade would give new power to black voters. In pledging their support for the dry laws, they concluded that "Prohibition is a promise, a splendid promise to the masses of working people."[65]

Other African American leaders expressed support for Prohibition for constitutional reasons. Many of New York's leading black intellectuals and politicians reasoned that enforcement of the Eighteenth Amendment, beyond curbing alcohol abuse, would strengthen the authority of the Fourteenth and Fifteenth Amendments, the landmark acts that extended civil rights and voting rights to African Americans after the Civil War. As both amendments were routinely ignored in the American South at the time, America's leading black intellectual of the day, W. E. B. Du Bois, suggested strict enforcement of a Prohibition amendment would result in the stricter enforcement of constitutional rights of African Americans. Other black leaders in New York took up the cause as well, arguing that Prohibition offered an excellent opportunity for blacks to represent themselves as respectable, law-abiding citizens, which would improve their overall standing in American society.[66]

With the "splendid promise" of Prohibition now looking likely to be realized, New Yorkers found more and more reasons to support the Eighteenth Amendment, ranging from altruistic to self-serving. Many of them had little to do with the agenda of the Anti-Saloon League. In the theater industry, producers optimistically hoped that, without liquor, people would turn to Broadway for their entertainment. The editors of *Variety* reminded readers that in previous years dry states had seen box office increases of 50 to 100 percent after alcohol had been outlawed. Though most producers and theater managers were, as *Variety* put it, "not adverse to the taste of the cocktail," they nonetheless "rooted for Prohibition, knowing that at least a healthy portion of the money which had been flowing into the coffers of the liquor interests would be diverted into the box offices." Seeing the potential for new business, theater mogul Lee Shubert endorsed the dry experiment heartily. He told his colleagues, "Personally, I am against liquor and a believer in Prohibition, and I think its going into effect in this country will help the theatrical business." George M. Cohan and others in the theater business agreed, expressing open-mindedness if not outright support for the dry experiment.[67]

Similarly, soda fountain manufacturers, tea merchants, candy manufacturers, car dealers, ice cream and soft drink vendors, members of the motion picture industry, and New Yorkers in other leisure trades joined the Prohibition bandwagon, expecting a surge in business to accompany the dry laws. "With national prohibition, the soda habit will largely increase," one soda manufacturer told the *New York Times*. Expecting a windfall if local saloons were converted into soda fountains, he was delighted at the prospect of having his business multiply on account of the dry laws. "At the first smell of Prohibition," the *Times* added, "tea merchants went crazy with delight, danced madly around their desks, and prepared for years of fabulous profits." S. H. Meinhold, the local manager of the Loew's theater chain, was also excited. "We certainly welcome Prohibition," he told a reporter. "It should make a lot of difference to our business." Expressing only scant support for Prohibition as a moral or social reform, these New Yorkers instead viewed it simply as an economic opportunity. Regardless, their support was all that mattered. It gave the dry campaign more momentum as it came to a climax.[68]

Even New York's newspapers, which had mocked William Anderson when he arrived in New York in 1914, offered a surprising degree of support for the dry cause in early 1919. With the Eighteenth Amendment already having made its way through numerous state legislatures and nearing ratification, the editors of the *New York Evening Post* approvingly wrote, "Not since slavery have we had a question which so plainly showed the readiness of the American people to respond to a moral appeal." Aware that support for the dry experiment was not universal, the *New York Evening Post* asked those who opposed Prohibition to put aside their reservations and show "cheerful submission to the majority." An editorial in the *New York Sun* declared that Prohibition gave proof of "the growing belief on the part of millions of temperate citizens . . . that the time has come when they ought to surrender something of what they have been accustomed to regard as the rightful liberty of personal choice for the sake of others." Even the *New York Times,* which often criticized William Anderson, chimed in. Its editors wrote, "May the amendment surprise its foes, surpass the hopes of its enthusiasts, and the nation be as easy to rehabilitate and improve as Article XVIII was to sweep through the legislatures."[69]

By this time it seemed that the only remaining opposition to Prohibition was disorganized, scattered, and overdue. Ironically, the last gasp of opposition to the dry campaign came from World War I veterans who objected to the way the dry lobby had used the war and the protection of soldiers as a rationale for Prohibition. They argued that Prohibition would undermine the very ideals they had been sent to die for in Europe. In a letter to the *New York Times,* one Brooklyn veteran voiced his discontent. "I volunteered my services as a soldier for Uncle Sam to help make the world safe for democracy," he wrote. "Am I now to sit idly by and permit freedom to be denied me?" In the *New York Sun,* another nascent anti-Prohibition group argued, "Our army was brave enough, moral enough and dependable enough to stop the German hordes on the way to Paris, but the National Prohibitionists say they cannot be trusted to drink a glass of beer or wine!" The group urged veterans, who reportedly opposed the Eighteenth Amendment by a nine-to-one margin, to demonstrate their opposition to Prohibition publicly.[70]

As the national magazine *The Outlook* pointed out, however, "the opponents of national prohibition have waked up too late." By the time one newly formed wet group, the Association Opposed to National Prohibition, was organized, time had already run out. The group ran a large ad in the *New York Sun* in January 1919 warning the public, "Interest your legislator today! Tomorrow may be too late!" Two days later, the Eighteenth Amendment became law.[71]

When New York ratified the dry amendment two weeks later, William Anderson proved to his skeptics that even New York could be brought into the dry fold. The ratification of the Prohibition amendment, and New York's surprising approval of it, capped off one of the most stunning campaigns in the history of American reform. Through its public relations efforts and political pressure, the Anti-Saloon League had made the eradication of the liquor trade a central issue in American public life, and convinced a broad cross-section of the American population of the need to rid the United States of liquor dealers and saloons. Through the relentless campaigning of dry warriors like William Anderson, who seemed to relish the battle as much as he believed in the cause, the drys had taken up the war against demon rum as a struggle for the soul of the country, and had won, even in as unlikely a battleground as New York.

Reaction to the dry victory in New York was mixed, but initially many New Yorkers were surprisingly receptive to the idea of Prohibition. The dry campaign had succeeded because it had offered something to nearly everyone, and with the passage of the Eighteenth Amendment, it seemed that plenty of New Yorkers had become enamored with the cause.

In that brief moment of optimism, however, it was easy to lose sight of how Anderson and the dry crusade had prevailed. The success of the dry movement, in New York especially, was neither a triumph of the democratic process nor a sign that an American consensus had been reached on the liquor question. The arrival of Prohibition was instead the result of the well-funded, well-organized, and tireless efforts of moral reformers and lobbyists who attacked their foes, silenced their critics, and built alliances of opportunity that had allowed drys to re-write the Constitution in their own vision. Theirs was an astonishing victory, but one that in all likelihood would have fallen short had it not been for the timely arrival of World War I and the masterly exploitation of that conflict by the Anti-Saloon

League. William Anderson and his compatriots had successfully imposed their agenda on the American people, but in doing so, they failed to see the costs of their strategy. Having pushed their reforms into the Constitution through pressure politics rather than democratic debate, they had set the stage for a spectacular wave of resistance to Prohibition, and for the dramatic failure of their own agenda.

2
A New Era?

As national Prohibition took effect on January 17, 1920, a jubilant William Anderson sent a message to the *New York Herald*. Still savoring the Anti-Saloon League's victory in the campaign for the ratification of the Eighteenth Amendment, the dry boss proclaimed, "It is here at last! Now for a new era of clean thinking and clean living! The Anti-Saloon League wishes every man, woman and child a Happy Dry Year, and a share of the fruits of prosperity which are bound to come with National Prohibition."[1]

Anderson's optimism was unfounded. Had he and his colleagues acknowledged the nature of their victory, or recognized how the patriotic hysteria of wartime had been used to silence their opponents, they might have greeted the final arrival of Prohibition with a dose of humility, or perhaps a cautious understanding of how much work remained to be done to implement the dry agenda. Instead, the drys congratulated themselves, confident that the Eighteenth Amendment's place in the Constitution spelled the permanent and irreversible demise of the alcohol trade in the United States. If any American believed that the Anti-Saloon League's experiment would fail, the dry response, bluntly summarized in a 1920 editorial in the magazine *Current Opinion,* was "Don't fool yourself."[2]

The unlikely success of the Anti-Saloon League's crusade, and its victory in New York in particular, blinded drys to the problems ahead of them. Since 1890, when the National Temperance Conference had held its annual convention in New York City, the dry movement had depicted the city as hopelessly wet. Now drys quixotically expected to make New York the trophy city of national Prohibition. As Reverend Dr. Rollin O. Everhart of the Anti-Saloon League told local papers in 1919 immediately after the ratification of the Eighteenth Amendment, "Successful administration [of Prohibition] here will be an answer for all time to those who say, 'it can't be done.'"[3]

In fact, once Prohibition finally arrived, many drys spoke of New York as the starting point of an even more ambitious campaign—the implementation of worldwide Prohibition. As Anderson explained to the *New York Times,* the Anti-Saloon League expected to use the example of New York to convert thousands of foreign visitors and tourists to the dry cause each year. All it would take was a firsthand look at how well Prohibition worked in New York City for these guests to return to their native countries and spread the dry gospel, sparking an international crusade against the liquor trade. As Anderson put it, "The failure or success of Prohibition as far as the world is concerned is its failure or success in New York." Emphasizing the visibility and prominence of the city in international circles, he argued that "the people of Europe are not concerned with Kansas or California, Oregon or Alabama. To them New York City is America."[4]

Dry leaders gave little thought to the possibility that Prohibition might fail. Some conceded that the initial enforcement of the law might prove difficult, but, backed by the force of a constitutional amendment, they believed, the dry mandate would unquestionably prevail in New York as well as the rest of the nation. As Anderson and his colleagues issued these rosy predictions, they failed to foresee the eventual, and in many ways inevitable, emergence of opposition to the dry experiment in the city. Angered both by the Anti-Saloon League's tactics and by the glimpses they had caught of William Anderson's bigotry during the campaign for ratification, many New Yorkers now finally found the resolve to stand up to the dry lobby. Their opposition came too late to prevent the ratification of the Eighteenth Amendment, but it would seriously challenge Prohibition enforcement efforts and keep the debate over the alcohol question alive for years to come.

According to the terms of the Eighteenth Amendment, national Prohibition would begin at midnight on January 17, 1920, one year after the amendment's ratification. Thanks to the aggressive maneuvering of the dry crusade, however, Prohibition actually came to the city incrementally through a series of wartime restrictions on alcohol consumption designed to put the dry agenda in place and get Americans accustomed to life without alcohol before the Eighteenth Amendment went into effect. In 1917, Mayor John Purroy Mitchel's declaration of a 1 A.M. curfew in the name of wartime sacrifice made the city noticeably drier. By the winter of 1918, additional wartime regulations forbidding the use of grain for the manufacture of alcohol resulted in widespread beer shortages in the city and in the entire Northeast. In February 1919 those restrictions became so severe that local breweries were forced to pool their grain supplies to stay in business. By April 1919 the city's beer supply had dwindled away almost entirely.[5]

The biggest advance for the dry crusade came in the form of the Wartime Prohibition Act, a temporary federal measure passed in September 1918 that barred the manufacture of beer and wine in the United States after May 1919, and prohibited the sale of beverages containing more than 2.75 percent alcohol anywhere in the nation after July 1, 1919. These restrictions, which essentially allowed only the sale of weak "war beer" and diluted wine until national Prohibition went into effect, were enacted under the guise of conserving national resources and fostering national sacrifice until the demobilization of American troops was complete. But many critics argued that wartime Prohibition, even as a temporary measure, was completely unnecessary, as it was enacted ten days *after* the signing of the armistice on November 11, 1918. Calling it "a dishonest, hypocritical, and superficial law," the *New York Times* argued that there was no reason for it, adding that even "the drys themselves confessed [the reasons for wartime Prohibition] were humbug." Though opponents of the measure denounced wartime Prohibition as a political favor to the Anti-Saloon League from Congress, aimed at pushing the nation into the dry era six months ahead of schedule, the dry lobby prevailed. Despite the opposition of President Wilson, who doubted the need for the measure, drys forced wartime Prohibition into law by attaching it to an emergency agricultural appropriations bill, signed by a reluctant Wilson in November 1918.[6]

Wartime Prohibition gave New York City its first glimpse of life under a legal ban on alcohol. William Anderson and the Anti-Saloon League optimistically looked at this moment as an opportunity to prepare New York for its dry future, but if wartime Prohibition offered a preview of what was to follow once the Eighteenth Amendment went into effect, it should have served as a warning to drys of trouble ahead. What wartime Prohibition demonstrated was that no amount of legislation could by itself succeed in changing the social mores of a city. Though New Yorkers had been open to some elements of the dry argument, their response to wartime Prohibition indicated that they were not ready to submit *en masse* to the demands of the Anti-Saloon League.

Less than six months after the "dry fashion" had narrowly swept the Eighteenth Amendment through the state legislature, New Yorkers greeted the impending arrival of wartime Prohibition with what the *New York Evening Post* could only describe as a "liquor stampede." With liquor prices soaring and advertisements in the newspapers warning, "Protect Yourself against the Dry Days" and "Buy Liquors and Wines in Bulk NOW," New Yorkers spent the months leading up to wartime Prohibition buying every last bottle of liquor and wine to be found in the metropolis. Liquor stores did brisk business holding liquidation sales, while other merchants plied soda waters and mixers as means of extending personal caches of alcohol well into the upcoming "long, dry spell."[7]

The frenzy culminated on June 30, 1919, with what the newspapers colorfully described as "New Year's Eve in June." Amid threats from the Justice Department that wartime Prohibition would be strictly enforced, New Yorkers crowded into bars, restaurants, and saloons for a final evening of legal merriment, drinking well past the deadline of midnight and into the morning. As dawn broke on the supposedly dry city, Leonard Steinberg of Brooklyn, the eighteen-year-old son of a hotel manager, earned the dubious distinction of being the first New Yorker to be arrested for violating wartime Prohibition after he sold a pint flask of whiskey to a New York City detective. The same night, the *Evening Post* reported, the Special Services division of the Police Department arrested four more Brooklynites for selling hard cider in the German-American Stubes of Bushwick. With the city hardly living up to the spirit of the new law, the *Evening Post* joked that New York could not stay dry for even one day.[8]

With no clear mechanism yet in place to enforce wartime Prohibition, the number of arrests for liquor violations remained relatively low. Within weeks, however, widespread resistance to the new alcohol regulations had emerged. Despite threats of an impending crackdown, many saloon owners simply ignored wartime Prohibition. According to a report published in the *New York Times,* a great number of the city's bars continued to engage in the "more or less open sale of harder liquors, including whiskey," figuring they had little to lose before the Eighteenth Amendment took effect and put them out of business for good. Only New York's hotels readily complied with the wartime dry regulations, unwilling to risk their entire businesses for the sake of liquor sales.[9]

With wartime Prohibition off to a rocky start, numerous questions remained over what exactly the new law prohibited. The Wartime Prohibition Act as passed by Congress barred the sale of "intoxicating beverages," but Congress had failed to legally define the term "intoxicating." Although "war beer" containing 2.75 percent alcohol was widely understood to be legal under the new regulations, the Anti-Saloon League insisted on a stricter threshold, arguing that the law banned any beverage containing more than 1/2 of 1 percent alcohol. When the Justice Department agreed to this stricter standard, New York's saloon keepers protested vehemently, declaring their intention to continue selling war beer to force a courtroom challenge to the law. In the meantime, demand for war beer remained strong in the city, especially with a heat wave gripping New York in July 1919. As temperatures in the city soared over one hundred degrees, New Yorkers broke records for beer consumption at Coney Island as bar keepers "worked almost to exhaustion." With questions over the legality of war beer lingering, the Justice Department dropped the issue in the hopes of avoiding a public outcry.[10]

Not until after the passage of the Volstead Act in October 1919 did it become clear to Americans exactly what Prohibition outlawed. Named after the bill's sponsor, Representative Andrew J. Volstead of Minnesota, the act defined the federal government's role in enforcing both wartime Prohibition and the Eighteenth Amendment. Working in close consultation with the general counsel of the Anti-Saloon League, Wayne Wheeler, Volstead sought to put a quick end to the violations of wartime Prohibition occurring in New York and elsewhere. The Volstead Act outlined "air tight" provisions for the enforcement of national Prohibition and defined the federal standard of "intoxicating" in accordance with the Anti-Saloon League's preferred standard of 1/2 of 1 percent alcohol. It charged the U.S. Treasury Department with the task of Prohibition enforcement, and it outlined penalties for the violation of the law, beginning with six months in prison and a $1,000 fine as the maximum penalty for first offenses, and increasing penalties for subsequent violations.[11]

The crafting of the Volstead Act after both the ratification of the Eighteenth Amendment and the imposition of wartime Prohibition indicated that the dry lobby had spent more time planning the enactment of Prohibition than considering its enforcement. Reflecting this lack of foresight, the Volstead Act was riddled with inconsistencies. At the same time, its strict enforcement provisions caught many Americans off-guard. Only under the Volstead Act did it become clear to the American people that Prohibition would ban beer and light wines as well as hard liquor. This angered numerous American labor organizations, some of which had supported the dry movement under a naive belief that beer and light wine would remain legal under the Eighteenth Amendment. Feeling duped, the American Federation of Labor and other labor organizations issued calls of "No Beer, No Work," and threatened general strikes in 1919 if the stricter provisions of the Volstead Act were enforced.[12]

At the same time, the Volstead Act left open several glaring loopholes. It allowed doctors to prescribe whiskey for medicinal purposes. It allowed the distillation of alcohol for industrial use, and it allowed each American household an annual allocation of ten gallons of sacramental wine for religious purposes. The biggest loophole was that while the Eighteenth Amendment outlawed the manufacture, transportation, and sale of alcohol, neither the amendment nor the Volstead Act prohibited the *possession* of alcohol. Passing such an extreme measure would have been politically impossible for Congress, especially given the Anti-Saloon League's long-standing argument that it opposed the brewing and distilling trades, not their customers. The practical implications of this particular loophole, however, proved particularly disastrous for those charged with enforcing Prohibition. It invited Americans with the means to do so to stockpile as much liquor as they could afford, and would leave thousands of criminal cases hanging in the balance over questions about whether defendants were selling, transporting, or merely possessing liquor.[13]

The Volstead Act had numerous other flaws as well, none of which was immediately visible. It grossly overestimated the level of cooperation state and local officials would lend to federal Prohibition enforcement efforts. It initially committed a modest sum of only $4.75 million to fund federal Prohibition enforcement, under the assumption that the mandate of the Eighteenth Amendment would suffice to dry up the country. The most ill-advised provision, made at the insistence of the Anti-Saloon League, dictated that political appointees, not civil servants, would administer and enforce Prohibition, even at the street level. While the league intended that this provision would give the dry lobby greater influence over the selection of national Prohibition administrators, in practice it meant that Prohibition enforcement agents and their superiors were coming to their jobs, not as experienced law enforcement officers, but as beneficiaries of political patronage. In time, this arrangement would open up widespread opportunities for corruption within the Prohibition enforcement system. While none of these problems was self-evident in 1919, all would ultimately play an enormous role in the difficulties the dry lobby faced in holding the Prohibition experiment together.[14]

When Congress first passed the Volstead Act in October 1919, President Woodrow Wilson vetoed it, viewing it as too extreme and objecting in particular to the provisions in it that applied to wartime Prohibition. Brewers were delighted with Wilson's decision. One commented, "I hope that the action of the President will put some manhood and backbone into our lawmakers." It did not. Bending to the will of the dry lobby, Congress overrode Wilson's veto within days, clearing the way for national Prohibition to go into effect.[15]

When the Supreme Court upheld the constitutionality of the Eighteenth Amendment in June 1920 by rejecting several legal challenges to the Eighteenth Amendment, dry leaders believed the legal debate over Prohibition had ended. Prohibition had been safely nested in the U.S. Constitution and appeared destined to remain the law of the United States indefinitely. From a purely legal perspective, Prohibition was an accomplished fact. But what the dry lobby failed to see was that the legal debate was not all that mattered. The hoarding of liquor in the city, the continued sale of liquor in defiance of federal regulations, and resistance to the enforcement of the dry laws indicated that the surge of support for Prohibition that had materialized in the final months before ratification was fading just as quickly as it had appeared. With each passing month in 1919 and into 1920, criticisms of Prohibition emerged that had not been heard in the patriotic climate of World War I. Instead of offering unwavering support for the dry agenda, New Yorkers now expressed concern that Prohibition would result in a dangerous expansion of police powers, and that strict enforcement of the law would come at the expense of their civil liberties and right to privacy. In a letter written to the *New York Herald* just as national Prohibition went into effect, a reader complained that "there never has been a greater wrong perpetuated on the American people." Though there was still little in the way of organized opposition to Prohibition, many New Yorkers who had expressed support for Prohibition were clearly having a change of heart. Through anecdote and observation, signs indicated that popular resistance to the dry experiment was mounting in the city as New Yorkers ignored the dry mandate and continued to drink openly throughout wartime Prohibition and into 1920.[16]

During the first weeks of July 1919, this state of affairs caught the attention of a columnist for the *New York Clipper,* who noted what he called "an interesting sidelight on the effect of Prohibition." At the popular rooftop show of the New Amsterdam Theater, he observed "patrons at two separate tables . . . drinking whiskey, which they had brought with them in small bottles." He went on to describe "their tables laden with bottles of ginger ale, the people . . . pouring the whiskey which they had brought with them into long narrow glasses and then adding ginger ale, which made them ginger ale highballs as of yore." He added, "Should this practice become common at . . . roof shows, the managements will accept the 'inevitable' and even tacitly encourage it, for it means the survival of the roof-show business."[17]

Every day, countless similar stories made their way into the city's papers. Gossip columns reported that elite private clubs in midtown Manhattan were drawing complaints from neighbors for hosting the loud, drunken revelries of well-to-do New Yorkers. The Fifty-Fifty Club on Fifty-fourth Street was jokingly described as an "unbonded warehouse" by the *New York Clipper* because it was so "heavily stocked with firewater." At the other end of the spectrum, Kelly's on Hester Street was reported to be crowded with clientele from all over the city, with one observer noting that "liquor is sold here freely to everybody." Soon *Variety* would note, "There isn't a restaurant, cabaret or dance place of any description where a drink isn't obtainable if you are known, and there are a great many places where one does not have to be known."[18]

If anything, the arrival of Prohibition seemed to inspire New Yorkers not to change their ways to comply with the demands of the dry lobby, but rather to devise new, more creative ways to evade the law. Many restaurants and clubs simply skirted the ban on the sale of liquor by charging higher cover prices and giving away "free" drinks to customers. At the same time, the city's newspapers published advertisements for homebrew kits, which promised to produce "a wonderful drink . . . rich in foam with the real taste and guaranteed to give results." One such advertisement ended with the disclaimer, "Don't use yeast, it is against the law." The *Evening Telegram* published a recipe for homebrewed beer, and for the benefit of New Yorkers looking to purchase bootleg liquor, both *Variety* and the *New York Clipper* printed weekly price quotes for cases of scotch, gin, and other spirits, noting when enforcement pressures had driven prices up, and when a glut of supplies meant bargains were to be had on the black market. (The Bureau of Prohibition, angered that these publications were treating liquor prices as if they were stock quotes, threatened to fine the papers $500 for each violation if they persisted.) For those inclined to make their own booze, hardware stores displayed inexpensive copper stills for sale in their windows. Though none of this was technically illegal, it made clear that New Yorkers were violating the spirit of the law, if not the letter of it.[19]

On New Year's Day, 1920, six months into wartime Prohibition and two weeks before the Eighteenth Amendment would go into effect, alcohol consumption in the city reached such levels that the *New York Herald* reported, "A common subject of discussion in this city yesterday was whether or not the New Year's Eve celebration of 1919–20 had been the wettest on record." The *Herald* added, "It is to be expected that the Anti-Saloon

League and the WCTU will find in the cheerfulness of Manhattan another proof of the wicked determination of this metropolis not to change all its habits at the orders of those who have none except meddlesome ones."[20]

Though opposition to Prohibition in the city was rising, in 1920 there were still plenty of New Yorkers who approached Prohibition with a "wait and see" attitude. Many urged compliance with the dry laws, out of either resignation or a sense of civic responsibility. The *New York Evening Post,* for example, expressed skepticism about the wisdom of the dry laws, but conceded that the window of opportunity to oppose the Eighteenth Amendment had closed. Its editors argued that New Yorkers, regardless of their feelings toward Prohibition, "owe it to themselves as well as to the country to manifest . . . respect for the opinion of their fellow-countrymen." Another cautious observer was quoted in the press as saying, "As long as Prohibition remains part of the fundamental law, obviously there is no other course for the government and law abiding citizens than to see that it is enforced." Given that Prohibition was a long-term inevitability, these conciliatory voices reasoned, supporting the dry experiment would ultimately make its effects less painful. In this spirit, the Columbia Amusement Company barred all satirical references to the dry law from its stage productions for the duration of the 1920 theatrical season. The theater house of Keith, Proctor, and Moss similarly argued that the new law must be respected, and banned Prohibition jokes not just in New York but in all of its nationally affiliated theaters. The Music Publishers Association likewise urged its members not to market songs that slighted Prohibition, arguing that to do so would undermine public respect for the law.[21]

To give the dry experiment the opportunity to prove itself, business owners and reform groups in the city talked about cooperating to create "substitutes for the saloon" that would both promote temperance and turn a profit. The Salvation Army, eager to contribute to the success of the dry experiment, took the lead by opening a model "temperance saloon" in the Hotel Argonne on West Forty-seventh Street, which offered coffee, buttermilk, and ginger ale as alternatives to beer and whiskey. While the Salvation Army's main goal was to advance temperance, it also saw this "liquorless saloon" as a source of potential income to fund its charitable work. The publicity director of the Salvation Army, Elmore G. Leffingwell, told the *New York Times*, "People need not think that the Salvation Army is going to spend foolishly . . . We mean to have our 'saloons' [function as] paying investments." After opening this first saloon, the Salvation Army expressed interest in establishing up to twenty-five more "beerless bars" if the demand proved sustainable.[22]

Prohibition also fostered examples of less charitable entrepreneurial efforts, as businesses looked to attract the dollars that New Yorkers had previously spent on drink. The Adams Gum Company, for example, appealed to New Yorkers to try chewing gum as a replacement for their cocktails. Waving "Good-bye, Old Pal!" to the mixed drink, Adams's advertisements in the New York dailies promised that Chiclets, with their "exhilarating flavor that tingles the taste," would let drinkers forget all about alcohol. Brewers, desperate for business, marketed alcohol-free "near beers" with such universally unappealing brand names as Bevo, Famo, Kippo, Yip, and Bone Dry. Welch's Grape Juice and Coca-Cola made more successful business pitches, urging consumers to consider their products as readily available alternatives to beer, wine, and liquor.[23]

While the dry lobby hoped that a city populated with buttermilk-drinking, gum-chewing, law-abiding New Yorkers would suggest that the debate over alcohol in the city had come to a close, in reality it was just beginning. The city was becoming even more divided over the noble experiment, and New Yorkers who opposed Prohibition were more willing to speak out against it now that the war was over. On one hand, drys promised that Prohibition would bring a new era of sobriety, health, and prosperity to a city transformed by "beerless saloons" and other similar innovations. On the other hand, wets forecast disorder, crime, and economic ruin for the city under Prohibition. To make their respective cases, each side began to measure and debate every conceivable effect of the Prohibition experiment as it unfolded in the city, and dissected everything from arrest records to hotel occupancy rates. Was Prohibition changing drinking habits in the city? What were the dry laws doing to New York's poor? Would Prohibition improve public health in the city? On these and a host of other questions, wets and drys disagreed vehemently.

Initially, wets and drys in New York focused on the economic impact of

Prohibition. The two sides agreed that Prohibition would have a pronounced effect on the city's economy, but they presented those effects in
drastically different lights. Wets asked where New York State would recover
the $22.6 million in annual liquor tax revenue that it would lose under Pro-
hibition, funds that constituted more than a quarter of the state budget.
Wets also argued that the dry laws would wreak havoc on the vital entertainment, restaurant, and tourism trades, and especially on New York's hotel
industry. With the onset of wartime Prohibition, they pointed out, hotels
had suffered drastic reductions in revenue as a result of having to close their
bars. The glamorous Hotel Knickerbocker, a luxury Times Square establishment renowned for its bar (and reputedly the birthplace of the dry martini),
was only one of several notable hotels in New York to close in 1920, ostensibly because of the effects of Prohibition. Faced with the sudden loss of a
half million dollars of annual liquor revenue, the owners sold the hotel and
converted it into an office building. The Holland House on Fifth Avenue
and the Manhattan Hotel (whose bar reputedly gave birth to the Manhattan
cocktail) suffered similar fates, as neither could survive the loss of income
that accompanied the end of liquor sales. The Eastern Hotel on the Battery,
the oldest hotel in the city and the past home of such eminent New Yorkers
as Robert Fulton, Commodore Vanderbilt, and P. T. Barnum, also closed,
another casualty of Prohibition.[24]

The closing of these landmarks, wets argued, was not only robbing the
city of some of its great institutions but also costing the city jobs. According
to the Association Opposed to National Prohibition, a hastily formed group
of representatives from the hotel and real estate trades, hotel owners would
have no choice but to raise their lodging rates to make up for lost liquor
sales. Other hotels around the city, including the Astor, the Claridge, and the
Bretton Hall converted their barrooms into retail spaces in efforts to remain
solvent, hoping that the rent from commercial tenants would replace the income once derived from liquor sales. Slowly, this trend transformed the familiar landscape of the city as bars disappeared from hotel lobbies to be replaced by lunchrooms, bank branches, and shops.[25]

Drys responded that the hotels themselves were to blame for their financial woes. The World League against Alcoholism, an offshoot of the Anti-
Saloon League, insisted that many New York hotels were antiquated and in-

efficient, and that those that had closed "were driven out of business not by Prohibition but simply because they could not meet the demands of the day." Eschewing any sentimentalism over the passing of old New York landmarks, drys insisted that the closing of prominent hotels like the Knickerbocker had been more than offset by the opening of newer, modern hotels, and that the net number of hotel rooms in the city had actually increased by several thousand since the beginning of Prohibition. Drys also disputed whether the increase in room rates that hotel owners had complained of had anything to do with Prohibition. Wayne Wheeler of the Anti-Saloon League simply attributed rising hotel rates to postwar inflation, arguing that "the cost of all things has increased, and hotel expenses have been no exception." At the same time, Wheeler took the opportunity to blast the hotel industry for its long-standing reliance on liquor sales, arguing that hotels simply used alcohol to take advantage of their patrons. "If hotel keepers must first intoxicate their guests in order to rob them," Wheeler argued, "it will be a good thing for them to have to change that policy."[26]

Wets and drys engaged in similarly heated arguments over the economic effects of Prohibition on restaurants, nightclubs, and theaters in New York City. Because these businesses relied heavily on alcohol sales as sources of revenue, they suffered serious economic declines with the enactment of Prohibition, further fueling the wet argument that Prohibition was harming the city's economy. The city's main show-business publications, *Variety* and the *New York Clipper,* issued dire predictions that nightclubs and cabarets would die off altogether because business had declined so sharply with the arrival of Prohibition. Though some clubs tried to survive the dry experiment by selling non-alcoholic drinks, the *Brooklyn Eagle* noted that "no cabaret can be sustained on ginger ale and near beer."[27]

Undoubtedly, Prohibition hurt famous nightclubs and revue theaters like Reisenweber's, Churchill's, and the Hotel de France, where check totals dropped to one-quarter of what they had been before Prohibition. Without revenue from liquor sales, many clubs abandoned their floor shows, unable to pay their entertainers. Florenz Ziegfeld, the Broadway impresario who had staged his "Midnight Frolic" revues at the roof garden of the New Amsterdam Theater since 1915, saw his business drop so precipitously that he was forced to close the show altogether in 1922.[28]

Prohibition had an equally pronounced effect on the city's restaurant business. The liquor ban cut deeply into the revenue of New York's most elegant restaurants. Rector's, Shanley's, and Murray's, which had hosted New York's elite since the turn of the century, were among several legendary establishments to close at the onset of the dry era. Unable to serve wine and drinks legally, they found their nightly receipts cut in half by the liquor ban. As several hotels and cabarets had done, some restaurants tried to devise alternatives to liquor as sources of revenue. The renowned Mouquin's on Fulton Street tried to replace its traditional cocktails with liquor-free imitations, considered watering down its famous wine selection to legal strength, and even marketed its own line of non-alcoholic cocktails. The owners of Lüchow's, the famous German restaurant and beer parlor on Union Square, thought it so inconceivable to do business without serving beer that they contemplated giving free beer to patrons in an effort to skirt the law. But most restaurants simply could not come up with an alternative plan. Given the choice between going out of business and breaking the law, many restaurants closed their doors, taking with them numerous jobs and a good part of the cosmopolitan character of the metropolis.[29]

Luxury establishments were not the only ones to suffer on account of the dry laws. Reports in *Variety* stressed that smaller, inexpensive restaurants fared even worse than their pricier counterparts. While more expensive dining rooms could at least attempt to recover their lost liquor income through higher cover charges and menu prices, average restaurants could not. Their patrons were not willing to pay cover charges, and higher menu prices only drove their regular customers away. With the arrival of Prohibition, these restaurants saw their revenues dwindle, their workers saw smaller paychecks, and their waiters received fewer and smaller tips. In Brooklyn, a waiter at an Eastern Parkway restaurant complained bitterly to a customer that business, which had been lively before Prohibition, had dropped considerably since its enactment. In Manhattan, a Sixth Avenue café owner similarly complained that his business had been devastated by Prohibition. With the dry laws in effect, he said, his patrons had "deserted him."[30]

Of all the trades to feel the effects of Prohibition, New York's breweries, bars, and saloons were hit hardest. New York had been a leading brewing state in the United States before Prohibition, and though many of the city's twenty-three breweries survived Prohibition by converting to the production of soft drinks, milk products, ice, or alcohol-free beer, they invariably suffered a decline in revenue, which resulted in the loss of jobs. The Pabst Brewery in Long Island City closed altogether and was converted into a printing plant, while the Peter Doelger Brewery in Brooklyn offered $10,000 to anyone who could present the company with a profitable plan for its plant. Saloons and bars fared worse, as they faced only two realistic alternatives—closing or breaking the law. Many saloon keepers who had enjoyed respectable and prosperous careers could not stomach the idea of becoming federal prisoners, so they gave up the trade. John Dunstan, the proprietor of Jack's at Sixth Avenue and Forty-third Street, reportedly locked his door at dawn the morning Prohibition went into effect and threw the key to his bar in the gutter. As saloons like Jack's voluntarily closed, they were converted into grocery stores, cigar shops, or dry goods stores. A small percentage lingered on, ostensibly selling soft drinks and non-alcoholic beer. Whereas approximately 15,000 saloons had been licensed in the five boroughs before Prohibition, only a fraction remained in business after 1920. According to the World League against Alcoholism, the city saw a 52 percent reduction in saloons between 1918 and 1922, and an 80 percent reduction between 1916 and 1924.[31]

Confronted with these examples of the economic hardships brought upon the restaurant, hotel, and entertainment trades, the Anti-Saloon League countered that the economic benefits of Prohibition far outweighed the losses. In spite of wet claims that Prohibition had cost New Yorkers thousands of jobs, drys argued that Prohibition had opened up far more opportunities for work than it had eliminated. The league claimed that the opening of nearly 7,000 new restaurants in the city in the first four years of Prohibition more than compensated for the loss of saloon jobs, as each restaurant employed more workers on average than the saloons had. By the estimates of the World League against Alcohol, the city may have lost as many as 16,000 saloon jobs as a result of Prohibition, but it had gained anywhere from 32,000 to 35,000 new jobs in the restaurants, stores, and other new establishments that had taken root where saloons had closed. According to drys, Prohibition had clearly "opened a new cycle of prosperity" in New York City.[32]

The league also refuted claims made in some trade publications that Broadway's entertainment business was suffering on account of Prohibition. It insisted that the "unanimous verdict" on Broadway was that Prohibition had boosted the amusement receipts. Drys argued that "more persons than ever before" were coming to Times Square, and that Prohibition had improved the area by taking "a lot of the coarseness and vulgarity" out of the theater district. They concluded that Prohibition had done nothing to hurt the entertainment or theater trades; it had simply "infused a new moral tone into Broadway."[33]

To strengthen the argument that Prohibition was transforming New York for the better, drys argued that Prohibition had fostered a new real estate boom in New York City, especially in commercial districts, where the closing of saloons had stimulated the market for retail space. The city did indeed enjoy a remarkable real estate boom in the 1920s, spurred by further extension of subway and commuter rail lines that fostered new development in Queens and Long Island. Reports authored by the World League against Alcoholism claimed that real estate assessments of former saloons in Manhattan increased between 39 and 55 percent during the first two years of Prohibition, while rents for commercial spaces jumped anywhere from 75 to 300 percent. Even on the Bowery, where a proliferation of boozy dives and flophouses had once made it an unappealing area for commercial tenants, rents increased significantly. New tenants were now paying 75 to 100 percent more in rent as "legitimate businesses" took over the spaces once occupied by the lowest class of saloons.[34]

In turn, drys argued, this real estate boom sparked other forms of economic growth in the city. As barrooms were converted into restaurants, retail spaces, and other commercial businesses, the labor market for contractors and construction workers improved, as did the demand for building supplies. The emergence of new businesses in place of former saloons had sparked a wave of consumer spending on dry goods, clothes, and general merchandise. Because New Yorkers could (theoretically) spend none of their money on alcohol, drys argued, their dollars were being channeled into other purchases, boosting the market for everything from basic material items to luxury goods.[35]

Both the wet and the dry arguments greatly oversimplified the economic situation in the city, however. Neither the wet assertions of economic disaster nor the dry predictions of unbounded prosperity were entirely credible, and neither side acknowledged that larger economic trends linked to the end of World War I—high inflation, a wave of labor unrest, and a sharp postwar depression in 1920 and 1921—undoubtedly influenced the city's financial health more than Prohibition did. Yet drys and wets continued to insist that every fluctuation of the city's economy was tied to Prohibition.

Dry forces had much more at stake in this debate. As the engineers of the social experiment now regulating the city, they had been the ones to proclaim that New York would be radically transformed by Prohibition. But having made so many lofty promises about Prohibition for so long, they now seemed unable to live up to them. With vocal opposition to Prohibition emerging in New York, drys suddenly found their promises falling short.

Motion picture theater managers, Broadway producers, amusement park owners, and other members of entertainment and show business industries had all been promised bountiful profits as a result of the dry experiment. They had been told to expect larger audiences and increased revenues as New Yorkers turned to popular amusements as replacements for the saloon, but during the first two years of Prohibition, the anticipated economic windfall never materialized. While theater owners enjoyed a brief boom in the summer of 1919 as former patrons of cabarets and cafés flocked to Broadway shows, by 1921 theater attendance was down, suffering from a general decline in the tourism and nightlife trades. Nor did Coney Island concessionaires see any of the profits they had expected to reap from the closing of nightclubs and bars. Instead, their amusement businesses lost two million dollars. Most surprisingly, the motion picture business also suffered a decline, which trade publications could only attribute to Prohibition's overall dampening of nightlife and the leisure trade in the city. With the arrival of Prohibition, New Yorkers were not seeking out alternatives to the saloon. Instead, it seemed, they had stopped going out altogether.[36]

The only thing more damning to the dry position than the decline in the entertainment trades was the slowly emerging evidence of alcohol consumption in the city. At first the evidence heartened the dry movement. According to an early study compiled by the National Temperance Council, arrests for intoxication in New York fell sharply with the beginning of Prohibition, from 22,505 in 1910 to 5,562 in 1919. Corroborating this statistic was a similar decline in the number of arraignments for intoxication, which dropped from 22,748 in 1911 to 5,657 in 1919. In 1920, hospitals also showed drastic decreases in the number of patients admitted for alcoholism and related illnesses. According to Dr. Frederick Green of the United Hospital Fund, city hospitals saw alcohol-related admissions decline between 70 and 90 percent within the first two months of Prohibition. Green, delighted by this development, commented, "Thanks to Prohibition, seven thousand beds have been released for the care of maternity, mental, tuberculosis, and general cases." The chief medical superintendent at Bellevue Hospital, Dr. George O'Hanlon, expressed similar satisfaction. According to O'Hanlon, admissions to the alcoholism wards at Bellevue had dropped precipitously, from 9,293 in 1916 to a low of 2,091 in 1920. As a result, O'Hanlon announced, Bellevue had "practically closed the wards formerly used for the cure and treatment of patients suffering from alcoholism."[37]

This initial spate of good news bolstered claims that Prohibition was drying up the city, prompting leading reformers in New York to raise a chorus of praise for Prohibition. Bird S. Coler, the city's commissioner for charities, told reporters that he had seen vast improvements because of the noble experiment, especially on the Bowery and in the area around Chatham Square. Coler delighted in reporting that of the ten worst dives around Chatham Square, only two remained, and they were "wobbling" at best. Coler added that the charities and missions that served New York's indigent had also seen a change for the better. Although he knew he was breaking with his Democratic colleagues in the administration of Mayor John Hylan by doing so, Coler concluded that the dry experiment was a success.[38]

But soon the initial impression that Prohibition was transforming New York into a safer, healthier environment gave way to widespread signs that drinking was actually continuing unabated, only in different places. The turning point came in a May 1920 New York Times article that surveyed the drinking habits of New Yorkers under the Volstead Act. The reporter's conclusion was readily obvious from his title—"Making a Joke of Prohibition in New York City." After spending weeks observing New York under the dry experiment, the reporter noted that Prohibition violations were occurring daily all over the city. Liquor was being sold openly from taxicabs. Unreformed saloons were selling alcohol disguised in soda bottles with fictitious names like "Moonland Moss." Bartenders were hiding miniature flasks of whiskey in cigar boxes, or concealing it in bottles attached to their belts like holsters. Though many hotels had closed their bars, their lobbies had become very popular with patrons desiring suspicious brews of "coffee" or "tea," curiously served without cream or sugar. Wine was sold openly in some restaurants, while in others patrons were seen drinking liquor out of teacups. Waiters had quickly mastered the art of exchanging flasks under tablecloths, carefully avoiding any indication that they were selling alcohol. In select nightclubs, patrons were welcome to bring their own flasks of liquor, which waiters would collect for a bartender to mix out of sight in a back room. Even strangers to the city had no trouble finding alcohol. The *Times* reporter told the story of a man from the Midwest in search of a drink who was told by a waiter to go to a nearby saloon. "Walk right in and tell the man at the bar that Charley sent you," the waiter said. "He'll fix you up." True enough, the visitor had found a reliable source for a two-dollar pint of whiskey.[39]

The *Times* article was just the beginning of what would prove to be an avalanche of reports from the early 1920s on the creative determination of New Yorkers to buy, sell, and manufacture liquor, illegal or not. The *Amsterdam News* reported that a candy shop on Wythe Avenue in Brooklyn sold chocolate bunnies filled with whiskey. Farm trade journals reported 17,000 trainloads of grapes being shipped to New York, and estimated that only 20 percent were consumed as fruit. A Staten Island hearse was stopped carrying 60 cases of liquor. Saloon owners went to watch court proceedings in an effort to learn the identity of Prohibition agents, and to see which legal loopholes were effective in getting defendants off the hook. An olive oil dealer on Chrystie Street actually turned out to be selling rye in olive oil tins. Art studios in Greenwich Village were rented out and set up as speakeasies, and more new pharmacies opened in New York between 1920 and 1923 than in the ten previous years combined, undoubtedly because pharmacies, which could legally dispense prescription whiskey, offered a perfect front for bootleggers.[40]

This wealth of anecdotal evidence publicly highlighted in the press illustrated the speed with which New Yorkers were devising methods to evade the dry laws. If these anecdotes were not enough to call into question the statistics set forth by Prohibitionists just months earlier, within a short time wets had sufficient statistics of their own to question the worthiness of the dry experiment. Though the Anti-Saloon League proudly claimed arrests for intoxication had declined sharply between 1910 and 1919 as the dry movement swept the state, the trend began to reverse itself immediately after Prohibition took effect in 1920. According to the New York City Police Department, arrests for intoxication rose sharply in 1920, increased again in 1921, and rose even more sharply in 1922. Arraignments for intoxication in the city magistrates' courts showed a similar increase.[41]

These new numbers stunned the dry lobby. Reformers and public health officials who had applauded the apparent success of Prohibition in 1919 and 1920 were forced to recant their earlier support. Bird Coler, the commissioner of public welfare who had praised Prohibition in March 1920, complained in May of the same year that hospitalizations for alcohol abuse had begun to rise dramatically. By January 1921, the city's Department of Public Welfare reported that the number of men and women in the city's alcoholism wards had doubled since the beginning of Prohibition, and Bellevue Hospital, which had recorded a sharp drop in admissions to its alcoholism wards between 1916 and 1920, saw steady increases between 1920 and 1924.[42]

As quickly as the dry fashion had swept the nation, William Anderson's vision of a dry New York had collapsed. There would be no more celebrations and no further assertions that Prohibition was ushering in "a new era of clean thinking and clean living." Rather than uniting New Yorkers behind a single moral agenda, as Anderson and his fellow drys had hoped, the imposition of Prohibition on the city had polarized New York between irreconcilable dry and wet camps, one bent on enforcing Prohibition at any cost and the other set on rebelling against it.

This contentious debate would set the tone for Prohibition in New York City for the next decade, as every aspect of the dry agenda came under the skeptical questioning of wet New Yorkers. Furthermore, as New York's half-dozen daily newspapers reported widely on New Yorkers' penchant for violating the Volstead Act, devoting as much as a page a day to Prohibition news, the effect of the city's opposition to Prohibition carried even further. Magazines with national circulation like the *Atlantic Monthly*, the *Nation*, and *McClure's* all reported on the opposition to Prohibition in New York, as did newspapers in other cities. The cumulative effect of this coverage over the next decade was devastating to the drys. William Anderson blasted the *New York World* in particular for "inciting lawlessness" with its coverage of Prohibition violations. Another dry would later tell Congress that "the great metropolitan newspapers of the country are dropping poison in the breakfast cups of millions of people" with their reporting of wet violations of the law.[43]

The same drys who had succeeded in stifling debate over Prohibition before the ratification of the Eighteenth Amendment now had to begin the debate all over again, with the added irony that the amendment in question was already part of the Constitution. With the dry experiment already under way, the Anti-Saloon League and its allies still enjoyed the advantage of political power and organization, as well as the backing of the law. Nonetheless, a full-scale revolt against the Eighteenth Amendment had begun in New York, and the drys had to fight desperately to keep the Prohibition experiment from unraveling.

3

A Hopeless and Thankless Task

Just before midnight on December 25, 1920, Monk Eastman left his boarding house at 801 Driggs Avenue in Williamsburg and walked to the Court Café, a neighborhood speakeasy, to meet up with friends for drinks. After a few rounds, Eastman and company decided to move on to Manhattan. They hired a taxi to take them over the Williamsburg Bridge to the Bluebird Café on Union Square, where they spent the remainder of the night singing, drinking, and swapping stories.

By closing time, Eastman was thoroughly drunk, and he began quarreling with his friend Jeremiah "Jerry" Bohan over how much to tip their waiter. It was Christmas, and Eastman was feeling generous. Bohan was not. After the two men exchanged some rough words, Bohan prevailed. The group then stepped out of the café and onto the sidewalk at 4:00 A.M. Despite the late hour on Christmas night, the streets were busy with holiday patrons heading home from the all-night restaurants and motion picture palaces that ringed Union Square. As the group milled about outside the Bluebird, the argument between Bohan and Eastman flared up again. Yelling and cursing, Eastman grabbed his friend and shook him, saying, "Jerry, you've become a rat since you got that Prohibition job." Eastman then thrust his hand into his coat pocket.

Bohan and Eastman had fought like this before. Only a few months earlier, Eastman had pulled a gun on Bohan in a Williamsburg saloon, vowing to kill him if the opportunity arose again. Eastman later apologized for his temper, but this time Bohan was taking no chances. With close to twenty eyewitnesses looking on, Bohan drew a revolver and shot Eastman once at close range. As Eastman fell to the sidewalk, Bohan drew closer and fired four more times. He then tossed the gun away, hopped onto the running board of a passing taxi, and disappeared into the night. While the crowd of onlookers kept a distance, Eastman died on the sidewalk in front of a candy shop, just outside the subway entrance at Fourteenth Street and Fourth Avenue.[1]

In the following days, reports of Monk Eastman's murder filled the pages of the city's newspapers. Eastman had once been New York's most feared gangster, known as "the king of the strong-arm men." On the Lower East Side where he grew up, he was infamous for perpetrating countless robberies, assaults, and murders-for-hire. At the height of his notoriety, he had led his gang in pitched street battles against rival outfits like the Yakey Yakes, the Whyos, and the Red Onions.

Always looking for sensational stories to help sell their papers, city editors had a field day with the Eastman murder. When last in the news, Eastman had been the toast of the town for his efforts to reform himself. Released from Sing Sing in 1917 after serving a ten-year sentence for robbery, Eastman publicly declared his intention to set his life straight. At age forty-four, the former gangster volunteered for the 106th Infantry and went off to fight in the trenches in France. He came back a highly decorated veteran and received a pardon from Governor Al Smith as a reward for his battlefield valor. Eastman had proved to all New York that even the most violent street hoodlum could be reformed. Since then, Eastman had dropped out of the spotlight and settled into a quiet life, busying himself with odd jobs and moving between Williamsburg rooming houses.

Eastman's murder naturally raised doubts as to whether the gangster's reformation had been complete. The press circulated rumors that Eastman had been killed for having become a stool pigeon for the police. Others claimed he was running a small dope-dealing ring out of a saloon on South Fourth Street in Williamsburg. Some excitedly surmised that Eastman had recently begun a bootlegging operation, and that his murder stemmed from business dealings gone sour. Until Jerry Bohan was questioned, the real story was anyone's guess.

While the press busied itself chasing down the details of the Eastman case, the Bureau of Prohibition, the federal agency charged with enforcing the Volstead Act, viewed the gangster's passing with considerably less excitement. Reports had begun circulating that a Prohibition agent had committed the murder after spending the night drinking with one of New York's most notorious, albeit possibly reformed, gangsters. This development posed a public relations nightmare for the bureau, even if, as it turned out, the reports were not entirely accurate. Monk's alleged murderer, Jeremiah Bohan, was not actually a Prohibition agent but an administrative employee of the bureau. Nonetheless, reports implicating Bohan in Eastman's murder, and his subsequent disappearance, were only the beginning of the embarrassments the bureau would face from the Eastman case. Soon the press would reveal not only Bohan's long-standing association with Eastman, something that in itself should have disqualified Bohan from a position with the Bureau of Prohibition, but also the fact that Bohan was himself a former liquor dealer. Worse, Bohan had been tried for murder in 1911 and, though acquitted, he had been arrested four additional times since then for disorderly conduct. When questioned about the character of his employee-turned-fugitive, State Director Charles O'Connor of the Bureau of Prohibition commented only that Bohan had come to him "highly recommended by a politician in Brooklyn," and that he "was trusted and his work was highly satisfactory."[2]

Detectives were unable to sort out the situation until Jerry Bohan turned himself in on New Year's Day, 1921, at which time he confessed to shooting Eastman in self-defense. Recalling Eastman's earlier threat after their brawl in a Williamsburg saloon, Bohan had feared that his drunken friend was going to kill him when they fought on Christmas night. Convinced by the explanation that the murder of Monk Eastman was not premeditated and that Bohan was acting in self-defense, a Manhattan jury spared Bohan the death penalty but convicted him of the lesser charge of manslaughter. He was sentenced to three to ten years in prison but was later paroled after serving a year and a half of the sentence.[3]

The Bureau of Prohibition, however, faced lingering questions long after the court sentenced Bohan to prison. Why was a former liquor dealer, with ties to a gangster like Eastman, working for the bureau? Why was he out drinking when his job was to enforce the Prohibition laws? What did Bohan's case say about the employees the bureau was hiring? The Eastman episode brought harsh criticism upon the bureau, including a comment from U.S. Representative Lester B. Volk of Brooklyn, who denounced the incident as "a public scandal." According to Volk, the incident "was only one instance demonstrating the need for improvement in the personnel of the [Prohibition] enforcement core." With employees like Bohan, it was no wonder the Bureau of Prohibition was having such a hard time enforcing the Eighteenth Amendment.[4]

The Eastman episode, which captivated the entire city in December 1920, was not simply a case of a rogue law enforcement agent or a once-reformed gangster sliding back into old habits. It revealed much larger problems inherent in the dry effort to impose a new moral standard on the nation. The ambitious plan to uphold Prohibition in the United States would depend heavily on the integrity and effectiveness of its enforcers. In New York City, however, those efforts would be continuously undermined by staggering cases of corruption and abuse of power.

When Congress passed the Volstead Act in 1919, it assigned the task of enforcing the Eighteenth Amendment to the U.S. Department of the Treasury under the assumption that the Cabinet department already responsible for levying and collecting alcohol taxes was best suited for the job. Within the Treasury Department, the Prohibition Unit (later called the Bureau of Prohibition) was created as a division of the Internal Revenue Service, and put under the charge of a national commissioner, who in turn supervised forty-eight state directors. All aspects of Prohibition enforcement were given to the bureau: policing the nation's borders for illegal smuggling; making raids and arrests for alcohol sales; licensing the manufacture, storage, and distribution of industrial alcohol; regulating the supply of medicinal alcohol; and monitoring the dispensation of sacramental wine. It was an enormous assignment, and one that overwhelmed the bureau from the beginning.[5]

In its first fiscal year, the Bureau of Prohibition operated on a meager budget of $4.75 million, with a national force of only 1,500 enforcement agents and an equal number of administrative employees. While the bureau's group of agents constituted the largest nonmilitary federal law enforcement body in the country, even larger than the Federal Bureau of Investigation, it was inadequately staffed for policing something as prevalent as alcohol. The reasoning behind the minimal level of staffing was the assumption made by Congress that the bureau would be readily assisted by local law enforcement agencies, the Coast Guard, the U.S. Customs Service, and other agencies, as well as charitable groups and temperance organizations. Despite agreement in wet and dry circles that New York would be the most important test of the dry experiment, the bureau assigned only 129 of its Prohibition agents to New York State and paid them the modest sum of $150 a month.[6]

Congressional reluctance to commit more funds to Prohibition enforcement posed a continual problem for the bureau. While congressional drys were always eager to show their support for the Prohibition experiment with votes, even the staunchest of them were unwilling to raise taxes if Prohibition enforcement proved too expensive. The Anti-Saloon League similarly hesitated to push for more funds, unwilling to admit that Prohibition enforcement might wind up costing far more than the league had anticipated, and wary of stirring more opposition to Prohibition enforcement on the basis of its cost. Both Congress and the Anti-Saloon League believed that state enforcement efforts would make up for any shortcomings in federal Prohibition enforcement, though they failed to consider that state governments, already suffering large losses in liquor tax revenue, were even less likely than Congress to allocate funds for Prohibition enforcement.[7]

The lack of foresight that went into implementing a reform as far-reaching as Prohibition was striking, though clearly visible to many observers, even within the bureau. The effects of chronic underfunding were clear. One New York–based Prohibition agent told a reporter in 1921, "Give me the money and I'll dry up the place in a jiffy . . . But it will take money and plenty of it." He believed that enforcing Prohibition in New York was possible, but added that "it will take a great deal more money than the Government will ever consent to spend to make it dry." Clearly, the lobbying effort that went into the passage of Prohibition did not translate into the formulation of effective policy.[8]

Beyond the problems of underfunding and understaffing, the issue of political patronage interfered with the Bureau of Prohibition's ability to do its job properly. When the Volstead Act was drafted in 1919, it specified that positions within the Bureau of Prohibition were to be filled by political appointment rather than through the federal civil service system. The logic behind this arrangement, insisted upon by the Anti-Saloon League's general counsel Wayne Wheeler, was that it would give the league maximum leverage in the selection of the national Prohibition commissioner and other upper-level Prohibition administrators. Through the use of political appointments, dry reformers sought to guarantee that Prohibition administrators remained accountable to the league and its agenda. In 1919, true to plan, Wayne Wheeler and his colleagues virtually handpicked as the nation's first Prohibition commissioner John F. Kramer, an unknown Ohio lawyer and legislator whose principal qualification for the job was his loyalty to the dry cause.[9]

In Kramer, the Anti-Saloon League got the loyal partisan it sought for the position of commissioner. In terms of other appointments, however, what worked at the highest levels of the bureau failed at the lower levels. Avoiding civil service regulations gave the Anti-Saloon League its pick of state directors; yet without civil service requirements, the appointment of Prohibition agents was left wide open to the whims of local politicians who often had little interest in the dry cause.[10]

In New York City, positions with the bureau were handed out like candy to candidates with no experience in law enforcement. Through political connections, dishwashers, baseball players, boxing managers, shopkeepers, and returning veterans were all nominated to the bureau by local politicians. They were quickly sent into the field as dry agents with minimal training and little genuine regard for the dry agenda. The best of these men were attracted to the job by the promise of a regular government paycheck. The worst of them, as repeat episodes would show, were violent, unstable, or lured to the job solely by the potential riches to be made while policing the liquor trade. Given this scenario, the Bohan case proved to be only one, and not even the most remarkable, in a long series of embarrassments involving bureau agents and employees.

The scandals that plagued the Bureau of Prohibition were stunning, as a March 1920 case involving Prohibition Agent Stewart McMullin demonstrated. McMullin's notoriety stemmed from the shooting death of a Manhattan cab driver during a botched liquor deal. The circumstances of the shooting immediately raised questions about the professional conduct of Prohibition agents. Initial reports indicated that Agent McMullin had never identified himself as a Prohibition agent and, according to the medical examiner, had shot his victim point-blank in the back of the head. Though McMullin claimed the cab driver had wielded a knife, police investigators found no weapon at the scene. Suspecting that McMullin was actually trying to rob the cab driver of several cases of liquor, the Manhattan District Attorney's office charged Agent McMullin with homicide.

The scandal worsened while McMullin sat in jail awaiting trial. In an interview with a reporter from the *New York World*, McMullin confessed that he was not actually "Stewart McMullin" at all, but John Conway, an ex-convict who had served six years in Dannemora State Prison for armed robbery. Conway admitted to two additional felony convictions, as well as to a guilty plea to a charge of involuntary manslaughter at the age of fourteen. Despite his lengthy criminal record, "McMullin" had won an appointment with the Bureau of Prohibition while in prison as his reward for giving the Department of Justice information about a radical bomb plot. Like the Monk Eastman murder, the McMullin episode served as a troubling reminder that positions within the bureau were being given out to inappropriate candidates as a result of the dry lobby's insistence on avoiding civil service regulations.[11]

Other incidents highlighted the agents' lack of training and professional decorum. In April 1920, for example, Prohibition agents James Muck and Michael Grisi got into a fistfight with a waiter in Reisenweber's Café on Columbus Circle. When the waiter ordered the agents to leave the restaurant, Agent Muck drew his revolver, unleashing panic in the restaurant. When another waiter joined the scuffle, Agent Grisi also drew his revolver before the two fled the restaurant shouting obscenities. The agents then led several police cars on a high-speed chase through midtown Manhattan. When finally apprehended, the two agents were taken into custody and charged with disorderly conduct.[12]

In a similar case in December 1920, Agents Peter Reger and Joseph Ernsthal shot and wounded Richard O'Hara, the owner of a café at 165th

Street and Amsterdam Avenue. The agents had insisted on searching the café after O'Hara had served them whiskey. But when O'Hara demanded they present a search warrant, the agents shot him, slightly injuring him. The agents were later charged with felonious assault.[13]

In addition to the overzealous gunplay of its agents, the Bureau of Prohibition had to contend with cases of corruption, graft, and bribery that sometimes reached into the highest levels of the agency. In the same month as the O'Hara shooting, investigators auditing the bureau's New York office discovered 116 forged permits requesting the withdrawal of $2.75 million worth of stockpiled liquor from bonded government warehouses. Further investigation of the matter uncovered an illegal liquor ring operating in the office of the bureau's state director, Charles O'Connor. According to the *New York Times,* Regina Sassone, an employee who reported directly to O'Connor, acted as the inside connection for the ring, which also included three former bureau employees. With their access to the liquor permits, the four had set up a system to divert legally warehoused liquor to be sold on the black market. These episodes appalled but did not surprise New Yorkers. Before the Volstead Act was passed, the *New York Times* had warned that "those who are familiar with the workings of prohibition laws in certain states years ago know what pickings for dishonest fingers, what rich potentialities of blackmail, prohibition offers to the men immediately charged with its enforcement." Leaving Prohibition enforcement in the hands of political appointees, the *Times* predicted, was practically an open invitation to bribery and plunder.[14]

The invitation was well received. Staggering sums of money were being exchanged in New York's illegal alcohol trade in the early 1920s, and the underpaid and undertrained agents in the bureau's employ found it difficult to resist the bribes they were offered on a daily basis. Liquor dealers and saloon owners throughout the city made it a regular practice to offer dry agents payments ranging from $50 to $500 to leave them alone or tip them off in advance of raids, and many agents were happy to cooperate. (The problem was so extensive that the bureau had to cut off outgoing telephone service from its headquarters on the nights when raids were scheduled in order to stop tips from being phoned out by agents on the take.) In a business that could easily yield profits of $4,000 to $5,000 a week, such bribes were a small price to pay for protection.[15]

While small-scale liquor dealers offered small bribes, large-scale dealers offered enormous bribes. When Agent George Golding entered a bonded warehouse at 999 Freeman Street in the Bronx in 1920 to investigate why a truck parked in front of the warehouse was loaded full of liquor, he gained firsthand knowledge of how enormous the sums of money involved in the nascent illegal liquor trade could be. Venturing into the warehouse, Agent Golding asked the owners, Bernard and Nathan Bornstein, if they had the proper federal permits to transport liquor legally. According to later court proceedings, Bernard Bornstein informed Agent Golding "that he did not have any permit and that he did not need any permit; that he was being protected by people downtown." Nathan Bornstein added that "he was surprised that any officer should visit his place as he understood that all agents had instructions to leave him and his brother alone." When Golding persisted, demanding the Bornsteins produce permits or be arrested, the brothers offered him $200. When Golding refused the bribe, Nathan Bornstein insisted that "every man had his price," and finally offered the agent $20,000 to let the brothers continue their business unmolested.[16]

While Agent Golding refused the payoff in this case and arrested the Bornsteins, the bulk of historical evidence suggests that many of his fellow agents were far less principled. Policing a trade that routinely involved $25,000 shipments of liquor, and contending with racketeers who were amassing millions of dollars, bureau agents quickly succumbed to the corrupting influence of liquor money. As the illegal economy of Prohibition grew, Prohibition agents began to resemble, both in appearance and in conduct, the bootleggers and racketeers they were supposed to be policing. With consternation, bureau supervisors noted agents arriving for work in new cars and wearing diamond jewelry clearly beyond the reach of what they could afford on their government salaries. Agents who once reluctantly accepted bribes from nightclub owners, saloon proprietors, and bootleggers soon graduated to demanding payments from them. In one instance in 1921, a group of renegade Prohibition agents was so displeased with the payoff offered by the owners of a nightclub that they demanded additional payments from the club's patrons. They passed a hat and refused to allow customers to leave until more money was collected.

Other entrepreneurial endeavors followed. Taking advantage of the vast supplies of liquor they encountered daily, Prohibition agents learned that dealing in confiscated liquor was as lucrative and easy as soliciting bribes. A cache of liquor seized from one saloon could easily be sold to a competing saloon, and on a few occasions agents had the audacity to sell liquor bottles back to their original owners, complete with evidence markings. One agent reportedly became so familiar with the illegal alcohol trade through his side dealings that he left the Bureau of Prohibition altogether to open his own speakeasy in Greenwich Village.[17]

Money was not the only corrupting influence in the bureau. In the early years of Prohibition in New York, the abuse of power proved as big a problem as bribery or liquor dealing. Armed with revolvers and badges, many Prohibition agents stormed about New York City with an "anything goes" attitude, exhibiting behavior that rivaled that of criminal gangs. During raids, agents smashed up illegal bars and speakeasies, planted evidence, and often acted in complete disregard for public safety, firing their revolvers haphazardly, or engaging in high-speed chases on city streets. They also tended to show an impertinent disregard for the dry laws when it came to their own drinking. Prohibition agents had no qualms about patronizing speakeasies and illegal saloons in and about the city, and showed little concern if anyone knew it. In 1922 the owner of a roadhouse outside the city boasted that Prohibition agents were some of his best customers, adding that they drank in full view of other customers without making any attempt to conceal their identities.[18]

Once given a taste of the power that came with a badge and a gun, Prohibition agents found limitless ways to take advantage of it. In October 1921, a group of fifteen agents caused a near-riot at the Polo Grounds in upper Manhattan when they tried to force their way into Game Four of the World Series between the Yankees and the Giants by claiming they were on "official business." When ticket takers at the stadium would not let them in, the agents refused to leave until police forcibly removed them from the line, as angry fans looked on. The following day, federal Prohibition Commissioner Roy Haynes, chastened by the embarrassing conduct of his agents, issued new orders barring agents from using their badges to gain admission to places of amusement.[19]

These scandals and escapades cemented the bureau's reputation for hiring underqualified, untrained, and improperly supervised agents. While some of the bureau's renegade agents were fired for misconduct, and the worst offenders were prosecuted and sent to federal prison, the punishments were not enough. In the first year of the noble experiment, the Bureau of Prohibition lost the public's trust. It would never regain it.

By the end of 1921, the *New York Times* declared that corrupt agents had turned Prohibition into a farce. William Ross, the United States Attorney for Brooklyn, was so displeased with the work of the Prohibition agents he encountered that he complained to the press that "many of the [bureau's] men were absolutely crooked, and a still larger number absolutely inefficient." A federal grand jury for the Southern District of New York expressed a similar opinion in a 1921 report: "Almost without exception the agents are not men of the type of intelligence and character qualified to be charged with this difficult and important duty and Federal law." And in 1923, an editorial in *Variety* commented that recent press stories on corruption in the bureau barely scratched the surface of the problem. It argued that "the federal men . . . are doing more to make prohibition detested than anyone else, even the drys."[20]

With their stock plummeting, bureau supervisors were left with no other choice but to dismiss agents *en masse* and replace them with fresh appointees or recruits brought in from other states. By the end of 1920, New York Bureau Supervisor Daniel Chapin had dismissed 47 of his 200 agents. One year later, the *New York Times* reported that more than 100 agents had been dropped from the force over the course of the year. Before the first full year of the dry experiment was out, State Prohibition Director Frank L. Boyd also resigned his position in frustration, telling reporters that Prohibition enforcement in New York was "a hopeless and thankless task."[21]

The corruption and irresponsible conduct displayed by Prohibition agents during the early years of Prohibition virtually destroyed any chance of winning compliance with the Eighteenth Amendment from New Yorkers. Yet the dry laws remained on the books, begging to be enforced. With the Bureau of Prohibition so out of favor and its agents thoroughly discredited, the dry lobby turned to the New York City Police Department in an effort to revitalize Prohibition enforcement efforts.

Under the Volstead Act, the obligations of the NYPD to enforce the dry mandate were unclear. According to the letter of the law, the Bureau of Prohibition was clearly meant to take the lead in dry enforcement by investigating violations of the Volstead Act and referring them to the United States Attorney for prosecution. But from the beginning it was also evident that the bureau's top administrators expected a significant degree of assistance from state and local authorities. In 1921 the nation's first Prohibition commissioner, John F. Kramer, went so far as to claim that "the matter of enforcing the law will be primarily in the hands of the local [authorities]."[22]

Essentially, the bureau and its dry watchdogs were relying on the idea of concurrent enforcement. Because the Eighteenth Amendment stated that "Congress and the several states shall have concurrent power to enforce this article," drys expected state and local authorities to pass laws that would match if not exceed the scope of the federal dry laws. Yet nothing in the phrasing of the Eighteenth Amendment compelled states to enforce Prohibition, and the vague wording of the amendment opened the possibility that state legislation might weaken or even nullify federal dry policy. In 1920 the question of what "concurrent power" actually meant wound up before the Supreme Court, whose ruling gave equal weight to federal and state enforcement laws. Essentially, the high court's ruling left state and federal enforcement efforts on parallel tracks, meaning states could meet, exceed, or opt out of federal Prohibition enforcement efforts but not nullify federal law.[23]

Whatever the vagaries of the law, the suggestion that the NYPD play an active role in Prohibition enforcement did not sit well with New Yorkers. Given that Prohibition was a federal law, critics of the Eighteenth Amendment argued, city and state agencies had no business playing any role in its enforcement, no matter what problems the Bureau of Prohibition faced. They did not want to see their tax dollars or city resources going to uphold a reform agenda that had been imposed on New York and that already seemed unlikely ever to succeed.

Some of the most vocal opponents of the idea of local enforcement of the dry laws were the New York City police officers themselves. Since the beginning of wartime Prohibition, city police officers had endured numerous run-ins with agents from the Bureau of Prohibition and had quickly come to regard them as unprofessional and reckless. They resented the suggestion that they should share their beats with the bureau, and they knew that being required to enforce the dry laws in the city would significantly increase their workloads. City prosecutors were equally wary of having the NYPD get involved in Prohibition enforcement efforts. As scandals and corruption tainted the bureau's work, its agents were no longer regarded as credible witnesses, their arrests failed to stand up in court, and case files and evidence were known to disappear frequently from the bureau's offices. If the same were to happen to the NYPD, the effects on law enforcement in the boroughs would be devastating.

There were also political reasons for the NYPD to stay away from Prohibition enforcement. Most of the department's upper brass were closely connected to Tammany Hall and felt no obligation to contribute the department's resources or manpower to a dry cause that Tammany strenuously opposed. In addition, the department's top officials knew well that the members of the city's overwhelmingly Irish Catholic police force despised Prohibition and dry leaders like William Anderson. Still, the political pressure exerted by the Anti-Saloon League to drag the NYPD into Prohibition enforcement was formidable. As a result, when the Eighteenth Amendment went into effect in 1920, the city's Corporation Counsel and the Police Department negotiated an agreement calling for federal agents to take the lead in enforcing Prohibition, while the NYPD would intervene when overt violations of the Volstead Act were encountered. The two forces also agreed to share information on Prohibition violations and the liquor traffic in the city.[24]

Despite this agreement, many of the department's officers and their superiors showed a clear unwillingness to assist in the enforcement of the Volstead Act. Most of the city's policemen had grown up in the world of ethnic saloons; some had been bartenders or saloon owners themselves, and many more had family members or relatives who owned or worked in saloons. With the onset of Prohibition, police officers were now being asked to break their long-standing ties with neighborhood saloons and, worse, to turn in their families, friends, and neighbors. One member of the department was sufficiently dismayed by the dry mandate to send an anonymous hate letter on NYPD stationery to Representative Andrew Volstead, calling the author of the federal dry law "an infinitely despicable specimen of the genus vermin."[25]

Nor were the city's police officers inclined to obey the dry laws themselves. In station houses around the city, police kept caches of liquor seized in raids for their own consumption. Investigative reports filed with the Committee of Fourteen in the early years of Prohibition regularly described uniformed policemen and plainclothes detectives, both on and off duty, drinking in speakeasies, saloons, and waterfront bars, where they chatted with owners and bartenders, finished their paperwork, or mingled with longshoremen, laborers, prostitutes, and other customers. Drinking by police officers proved so blatant that in 1920 Police Commissioner Richard Enright was compelled to issue a warning to his officers that anyone found guilty of drinking on duty would be suspended from the force. Still, after the Police Lieutenants' Benevolent Association held its annual dinner at the Commodore Hotel in 1921, a newspaper report described the dining room as filled with "a cheerfulness . . . greater than any one-half of 1 percent could have produced . . . which entered the banquet hall in suit cases, handbags, and paper wrappers." When a retired police lieutenant present at the banquet was arrested later that night for disorderly conduct and intoxication, William Anderson unleashed a tirade in the press against Mayor Hylan and Commissioner Enright, who both attended the dinner. Calling Hylan "a blatherskite monument to the political folly of the electorate of New York City," Anderson asked how the mayor and commissioner could in good conscience preside over a "drunken orgy."[26]

Whatever William Anderson's feelings might be, most members of the NYPD found that the most practical approach to Prohibition violations was to ignore them. Many officers simply refused to see drinking as an offense worthy of their attention. They viewed Prohibition enforcement as a headache more than a serious matter of law enforcement, and so they did their best to avoid getting involved in it, even if it meant ignoring direct orders. As one bartender told a Committee of Fourteen investigator, "The cops know we are selling whiskey but they don't bother us." Unless the liquor trade took on an overt criminality, resulting in violence or other illegal activity, the police took a hands-off approach. Most adopted the view of August Flath, a veteran detective who dismissed Prohibition by saying that "the thing could never be enforced."[27]

The reluctance of the Police Department's rank-and-file to take up the task of Prohibition enforcement quickly became a sore point within the department. When the upper brass ordered a crackdown on speakeasies in Greenwich Village in April 1921, ten officers assigned to the Charles Street Precinct were brought up on charges for ignoring Prohibition violations occurring on their beats. In response, Commissioner Richard Enright ordered any precinct captain whose officers racked up more than five complaints for neglecting dry violations to be charged with dereliction of duty. A year later, Enright was still hammering the same point, stating in an open letter to the force that "negligence upon the part of any member of this department in connection with the proper enforcement of this law is at an end, and there must be no misunderstanding upon this score."[28]

Try as Enright might to discipline the force, the general disregard for the dry agenda within the NYPD continued, fueling a statewide political battle. As a city agency, the Police Department was primarily accountable to New York City's Democratic leadership, which strongly opposed Prohibition and was content to keep the NYPD out of Prohibition enforcement. At the same time, the Anti-Saloon League, Republican Governor Nathan Miller, and dry supporters in the State Assembly grew increasingly upset with the department's failure to enforce the dry law in the city.

Commissioner Enright found himself at the center of this political storm. As a former officer who had served as president of the Lieutenants' Benevolent Association before being appointed commissioner in 1918, Enright generally enjoyed strong support from the rank-and-file of the department. Now he was at odds with his own force, and local political leaders, over the issue of Prohibition. Personally, Enright was highly skeptical of Prohibition and concerned about the additional burden it would place on the police force. Nonetheless, he believed strongly that, like any other law, the dry amendment needed to be enforced to preserve the integrity of the department and maintain public respect for law enforcement in the city. As he explained in the Police Department's 1921 annual report, "The Police Department of this City . . . will have an extremely uphill fight in exacting obedience to the [Prohibition] law. It will, however, be done."[29]

Commissioner Enright's determination to enforce the law, even over the opposition of his own force, was not enough to satisfy a critical dry lobby, however. With dry proponents refusing to own up to the shortcomings of their agenda, criticizing the NYPD became a convenient way to explain the sorry state of the Prohibition experiment in the city. In an April 1920 speech to the West Side YMCA, William Anderson complained bitterly that the officers of the NYPD had undermined all that the Anti-Saloon League had worked for by refusing to do their jobs. Federal officials also expressed annoyance with the half-hearted efforts of NYPD officers to take part in Prohibition enforcement. From the bureau's standpoint, the NYPD, with its 13,000 officers and ample resources, had the power to determine whether Prohibition would succeed or fail in the city. Bureau Supervisor James Shevlin went so far as to complain that a lack of cooperation from the NYPD was making his work impossible. On another occasion Frank Boyd, the bureau's New York director, complained about the lack of coordination between the two forces. He told the *New York Sun,* "Of course I would be glad to have the cooperation of the police, for I have only 200 employees to make the State dry, including my office staff and my girl stenographers. You can see what I am up against." The United States Attorney for Brooklyn, William Ross, similarly complained, "We have had to proceed without any cooperation upon the part of the police."[30]

Out of frustration, the dry lobby looked to compel the NYPD to take a greater share of the burden of dry enforcement, ultimately returning to pressure politics and legislated mandates to force a solution to the problem. Banding together with Governor Nathan Miller and dry allies in the state legislature, the Anti-Saloon League's William Anderson pushed for the passage of a strong state enforcement law that would require the NYPD to take a more aggressive role in enforcing Prohibition. Once again taking advantage of the majority held by upstate Republicans in the state legislature, William Anderson again got his way, just as he had in the battle for the ratification of the Eighteenth Amendment.

On April 5, 1921, Governor Miller signed the Mullan-Gage Enforcement Law, a strict state-level equivalent of the Volstead Act, which drastically stepped up the legal consequences for violating the dry mandate in New York. Actually a compilation of four bills, the Mullan-Gage Law not only mirrored the Volstead Act by outlawing the manufacture, sale, and transportation of alcohol in the state; it also made it a crime to carry liquor on one's person without a permit and shifted to the accused the burden of proof as to whether liquor was owned legally. (That provision was later ruled unconstitutional.) According to commentary in the press, the Mullan-Gage Law essentially made carrying a hip flask in New York the legal equivalent of carrying an unlicensed handgun. The Mullan-Gage Law had far-reaching effects on the way Prohibition cases were tried in New York. Over the opposition of nearly every district attorney in the state, who rightfully feared they would be inundated with liquor cases, the measure as initially passed required Mullan-Gage violators to be tried before juries in the Court of General Sessions, the state's main criminal court.[31]

The passage of the Mullan-Gage Law significantly raised the NYPD's stake in Prohibition enforcement. Upon signing the law, Governor Miller issued a strong warning to Commissioner Enright, telling the press, "I want the Police Commissioner of New York to understand . . . that the law cannot be made a joke." Arguing that "every policeman will know where liquor is being sold on his beat," Miller hinted that he would replace Enright if the new laws were not enforced: "The Police Department . . . with the right head would prevent what is now a public disgrace in the city of New York." The new mandate of the Mullan-Gage Law placed an enormous burden on Commissioner Enright. With Governor Miller's thinly veiled threats to replace Enright exposed, the *New York Times* commented, "No doubt Governor Miller haunts Mr. Enright's dreams."[32]

Aside from the praise offered by William Anderson, who later called it "the most amazing state enforcement law in the country," the newly passed Mullan-Gage Law received a mostly negative reaction in the city. The *New York Evening Post* commented that if the Mullan-Gage Law had any positive side, it was only that it would demonstrate that the Prohibition laws were unenforceable and badly in need of revision. The *New York Times* unequivocally opposed the law, arguing that the Mullan-Gage proposal would "require the placing of a policeman in every saloon." In addition, the editors warned that the new law would do little more than exhaust Police Department resources that would be better spent pursuing car thieves and violent criminals.[33]

Put on the spot, Commissioner Enright responded to Albany's demands and ordered an immediate police crackdown on alcohol sales beginning April 6, 1921, at 8:00 A.M. With begrudging approval from Mayor John Hylan, Enright dispatched the police force to go after any and all Prohibition violators. In Greenwich Village, police officers on motorcycles with sidecars began stopping in the same cafés two or three times a night, peering into coffee cups for booze and frisking patrons for bottles. In the Theater District, police moved to arrest the "walking saloons" who sold shots of liquor out of hip flasks on the street. Midtown speakeasies closed to wait out the crackdown, and on the Lower East Side, police pressure raised the average price of a drink to two dollars. Raids on Coney Island left the amusement area "absolutely dry," and headlines declared the first Sunday after the crackdown "the dryest day the city ever knew." Within one week of the passage of the Mullan-Gage Law, the New York City police had made more than 400 arrests and seized over a million dollars worth of liquor. This aggressive campaign against alcohol delighted the Anti-Saloon League, thus prompting General Counsel Wayne Wheeler to write a rare letter of praise to Commissioner Enright. "Allow me to congratulate you upon the manner in which you are enforcing the State Prohibition Law," Wheeler wrote. "The whole country is watching with great interest your splendid efforts."[34]

Under the Mullan-Gage Law, the NYPD kept the pressure on the liquor trade for several months. By the end of 1921, the NYPD had made 10,062 arrests for Mullan-Gage violations and seized 98,594 bottles of liquor worth $15 million. But like every other effort to enforce Prohibition, the crackdown was having numerous unintended and undesirable consequences for the police force. The law put extreme demands on police staffing owing to Enright's decision to station police officers in cabarets and nightclubs that had repeatedly violated the dry law. As a result, Enright had hundreds of officers doing nothing but watching for liquor sales for entire eight-hour shifts. This policy in particular angered New Yorkers and prompted one state judge to complain: "It is demoralizing for the police force. Men are being stationed in restaurants to see no one steals a drink, while around the corner a hold-up man is breaking into a jewelry shop." Public animosity toward the police force grew substantially with these aggressive attempts to enforce Prohibition, and Mayor Hylan's office was inundated with complaints about arrests, raids, and improper searches.[35]

Mayor Hylan, who had given his initial blessing to the Mullan-Gage crackdown, quickly pulled an about-face. Now worried about the political costs of dry enforcement, the mayor expressed his displeasure to Commissioner Enright and urged him to take steps to rein in his men. As public complaints against the police force escalated, the city's Corporation Counsel joined Hylan in backing away from dry enforcement. Abandoning Enright, the counsel announced that the city would not defend police officers in any court action related to illegal searches stemming from Mullan-Gage enforcement. The counsel added pointedly, "New York is still at the mercy of the Federal enforcement crew . . . but it need not also be at the mercy of its own police."[36]

In addition to stoking public ire against the police, the effects of the Mullan-Gage law on the mechanics of law enforcement were even more worrisome. By Commissioner Enright's own estimate, the new law doubled the work of the Police Department. It distracted officers from their regular duties, tied them up in court cases and paperwork, and swamped the department's laboratories with liquor samples waiting to be tested as evidence. The city sheriff's office, responsible for storing seized property, was inundated by the increased volume of liquor seizures. It suddenly had more than $7 million worth of confiscated liquor to store as evidence at a cost of $20,000 a month, though it had neither the space to store it all nor the funds to procure additional storage space, nor enough guards to watch over the rapidly growing stockpile. Faced with these costly demands, Commissioner Enright went to the Board of Estimate to request a $100,000 budget increase and 1,000 additional officers to meet the added burden of enforcing Mullan-Gage. The board flatly rejected his request, suggesting he simply reassign the 750 officers he had stationed in cabarets if he found the NYPD in need of additional manpower.[37]

Ironically, the Mullan-Gage Law was now undermining the contention long held by drys that Prohibition would actually decrease the cost of law enforcement in major American cities by reducing criminal activity related to drinking. The case of New York instead offered concrete proof to the nation that the Prohibition experiment was actually substantially increasing the cost of law enforcement in its cities, while the federal government was reluctant to commit additional funds for enforcing the Eighteenth Amendment, the Volstead Act, or local enforcement laws.[38]

Politically, the Mullan-Gage Law put both Commissioner Enright and Mayor Hylan in difficult situations. As the city's top law enforcement official, Enright felt obligated to uphold the law. Yet in his annual report for 1921, Enright expressed the opinion that the Mullan-Gage Law was nothing more than a political tool of the dry lobby "prepared and passed for the sole purpose of embarrassing [the Hylan] Administration." Furthermore, Enright acknowledged that the Mullan-Gage Law was irrevocably damaging the public standing of the police in the city. He concluded his report by noting that "if a serious attempt were made to enforce [Prohibition], the effect on public sentiment would be to everlastingly damn those responsible for the attempt."[39]

Enright's bleak assessment reflected his understanding that within a matter of months the Mullan-Gage Law had made daily work for police officers infinitely more difficult. Like Prohibition agents, they now found themselves routinely attacked by bar patrons when they tried to uphold the dry laws; on occasion they were greeted by flying chairs, glasses, and bottles. Before Mullan-Gage, such violent resistance had usually been directed only at Prohibition agents. As the most disliked government employees in the city, the bureau's agents had been chased, bombarded with bowling pins, assaulted by women and children, and knocked unconscious by angry New Yorkers caught in raids. With the NYPD's reluctant entry into Prohibition enforcement, its officers were now susceptible to the same attacks. This increase in violence confirmed the fears of Prohibition's critics, who had forecast that the imposition of such a far-reaching moral reform on a resistant population would ultimately undermine respect for law enforcement in general, potentially creating an even bigger problem than the one Prohibition was meant to address.[40]

In addition to the daily threat of violence, local enforcement efforts were undermined by the ever-changing ways New Yorkers found to disguise and dispense illegal liquor. Faced with added pressure from the NYPD, New York's bartenders simply developed a more elaborate repertory of skills to avoid being caught. They concealed liquor in teapots and coffee cups, or kept alcohol locked in safes that required search warrants to open. Some took great care to sell liquor only to known or properly referred customers. In some establishments, liquor was kept in wide-mouthed pitchers by a trough of running water. In the case of a raid, the pitchers would be knocked over and the liquor washed quickly down the drain. Other bars kept trays of already poured shot glasses behind hidden doors and stashed bottles in back rooms, on other floors, or even in nearby buildings, where they would be safely hidden in case of raids. In one Polish speakeasy on the Lower East Side, whiskey bottles were kept near the window. As the proprietor later recalled, "When the cops would come in, we'd throw the whiskey into the yard. They knew we were doing it but they were never smart enough to catch us." These constantly changing methods to evade the law stymied police officers and Prohibition agents, forcing one to conclude, "We are just about a hundred jumps behind the violators of the law all the time."[41]

The economics of the illegal liquor trade factored heavily in the evolution of these increasingly elaborate methods of evading the dry laws, as New Yorkers, and especially working-class New Yorkers, sought to get a piece of the liquor economy. In Bay Ridge, Brooklyn, for example, working-class Italian families in need of extra cash knew they could earn fifteen dollars a day from crime boss Frankie Yale by keeping illegal stills in their homes. Teenagers in Greenwich Village earned ten dollars a week making night deliveries for bootleggers, while younger boys earned extra money opening taxi doors in front of nightclubs or acting as "spotters" for speakeasies, keeping an eye out for police. Eventually, as one sociologist estimated, "the liquor business in one form or another [became] the chief new source of employment or income for residents of the area."[42]

In its zeal to impose its vision on the urban environment, the Anti-Saloon League failed to recognize that many New Yorkers embraced the illegal liquor trade as a chance to escape the reality of working-class poverty. For many, dabbling in the liquor trade was simply a way to supplement the family income. Cigar store owners, bootblacks, barbers, tailors, and grocers were all known to sell small quantities of liquor to their customers in order to augment their modest incomes. One tailor, who offered a Prohibition agent a flask of whiskey, explained that he did it only because he wanted to keep his regular customers coming back. Few of these merchants were looking to make it rich. Rather, they simply hoped to improve business or raise their economic standing. As one Lower East Side resident explained, his mother's decision to convert her restaurant into a speakeasy "was the only way we could exist."[43]

The same factors that drew many working-class New Yorkers to the illegal liquor trade had a similar effect on the officers of the NYPD once the Mullan-Gage Act became law. In the early 1920s, New York's police officers on average earned a modest salary of $1,900 a year. Still, the corrupting influence of Prohibition on the force had been limited while the Police Department played only a secondary role in the enforcement of the Volstead Act. The passage of the Mullan-Gage Law in 1921 changed all that, for it exposed almost all the members of the NYPD to the lures of corruption. Before the final passage of the bill, an anonymous Police Department official warned that "every crooked policeman in New York City is praying that the law will be passed." He added, "When it is passed everyone will buy his wife a hat or a gown, for he certainly will be able to afford it. It opens up pathways to graft which no other law on the statute books could uncover." True to those predictions, soon after the Mullan-Gage Law went into effect, police officers were being charged with petty larceny and extorting payments from bar and saloon owners in exchange for protection from dry raids.[44]

With their extensive knowledge of the communities they patrolled and the places where liquor was sold, police officers on all levels of the force now found themselves in a position to cash in, and they quickly did. At the highest levels of the bureaucracy, Charles "Lucky" Luciano, one of the city's biggest bootleggers, was reputed to be sending $10,000 to $20,000 in weekly payoffs to police headquarters. Some speakeasy owners went directly to precinct commanders and paid them handsomely for assurances that they would not be raided. On the lower levels of the force, saloon and speakeasy owners regularly paid police officers protection fees ranging from $50 to $500. Neighborhood patrolmen made extra money by agreeing not to tip off their superiors to the presence of speakeasies or saloons, and even traffic cops took payments to look away when liquor deliveries were made to local bars.[45]

Though one bartender complained that bribing the police "costs us heavy," such payments were a necessary precaution for those who wanted to keep their businesses running smoothly. Most bartenders and saloon owners accepted the cost of this "protection" and often threw in free drinks or food for police officers as well. As one speakeasy owner told a journalist, "the first day we opened up the police came right in, four of them, to be stood drinks, and I've had these four cops on my side in this business from that day on." Protection arrangements of this kind were "universal," according to reformer Mary Simkhovitch, who personally knew of a wine-vending Italian restaurant in Greenwich Village where "one could find on a Sunday a policeman dining with his family in innocent domesticity at the proprietor's expense." The glamorous, high-profile speakeasies hosted law enforcement officers, too. Peter Kriendler, whose brother Jack and cousin Charlie ran the upscale 21 Club in midtown, recalled that the local precinct captain was a regular guest whose presence reassured patrons of the club's immunity from raids throughout the 1920s.[46]

With the increased involvement of the police in protection schemes under the Mullan-Gage Law, Commissioner Enright worried that the corruption engendered by the law would have the long-term effect of discrediting the Police Department as a whole. Once the public accepted that the police were engaged in illegal activity, Enright feared, other types of criminal activity in the city would increase, as respect for law enforcement eroded. To prevent this outcome, he desperately tried to maintain discipline on the police force, threatening officers with suspensions, sanctions, demotions, and docked pay if they failed to stay in line. True to his word, Enright suspended thirty-five officers and patrolmen in July 1921, and fined them from one to five days' pay for failing to report saloons to their commanding officers.[47]

Despite these efforts, staunching the corrupting influence of Prohibition on the police force proved impossible. By 1923, the deleterious effects of the Mullan-Gage Law on the NYPD had grown so pronounced they prompted City Magistrate Joseph E. Corrigan to complain that the law had "debauched the police force of this city and caused an orgy of graft, perjury, and corruption." William O'Dwyer, a future mayor of New York who served on the police force during the Prohibition era, recalled that the Mullan-Gage Law ushered in an "era of fabulous fortunes in many sections of the Police Department." Before long, the NYPD was embroiled in scandals rivaling those that haunted the Bureau of Prohibition.[48]

In one case, investigators from the Committee of Fourteen reported that a corrupt group of police officers on the Lower East Side had set up shop in Mingo's speakeasy on East Fourth Street, where they met regularly to fix cases and "straighten out" problems with local criminals in exchange for

cash. Like Prohibition agents, some police officers also began selling confiscated liquor to saloons and restaurants. Others became partners in bootlegging schemes, riding with drivers on beer and liquor trucks to protect them
from seizure. As William O' Dwyer recalled, "a policeman would ride in the
truck in uniform, so that in the event he was stopped by someone else, he'd
say 'He's my prisoner, I'm taking him to the nearest station house.'" By
O'Dwyer's estimate, "these things went on at an extraordinary rate."[49]

As was the case with the Bureau of Prohibition, the Police Department
saw its officers increasingly accused of using excessive force, planting evidence, and conducting illegal searches and seizures. In one such incident in
July 1921, Detective Charles Tighe went on a one-man rampage in a Ninth
Avenue saloon. Outraged at four men who shrugged off his announcement
of a raid and went back to following baseball scores on the news ticker in
the bar, Tighe went berserk and began smashing up the saloon and beating
customers with his nightstick. When a crowd gathered on the avenue to investigate the commotion, Tighe went out onto the street and began beating
people at random before locking them in the back room of the saloon. According to eyewitnesses, Tighe appeared intoxicated as he allegedly choked
a seven-year old girl, knocked a shoeshine man off his crutches, and struck
five women, including one with a baby in her arms, before his superiors arrived from the Forty-seventh Street Precinct House to subdue him. At the
local courthouse, an irate magistrate sternly reminded Tighe that there was
nothing illegal about following baseball scores and immediately released all
those whom Tighe had arrested. Detective Tighe was summarily brought
up on charges of assaulting forty people and sentenced to two years in Sing
Sing for his rampage.[50]

Episodes like these demonstrated the destructive effects of Prohibition
on law enforcement in the city. Just two years into the dry experiment, the
inability of the Bureau of Prohibition and the NYPD to enforce the dry
laws or control their officers had completely undermined the viability of
the noble experiment, diminished public respect for the law, and made a
mockery of the dry mission. Yet the dry lobby, and the Anti-Saloon League
in particular, failed to acknowledge the unintended consequences of the
dry experiment. Refusing to consider the impracticality of translating its

moral vision into a workable law, it held fast to its reform agenda, insisting on stricter provisions to make Prohibition work.

With enforcement efforts in New York falling far short of their goals, the judicial system stood as the dry movement's last hope for the successful implementation of Prohibition in the city. In many regards, the prosecutors and judges who presided over the trials of Prohibition violators were the most important participants in the campaign to enforce the dry laws. The courts had the power to determine how much leeway to give law enforcement officers in their efforts to dry up the city, and at the same time influenced public regard for the dry law through their sentencing of Prohibition violators. Harsh sentences, drys believed, would deter further Prohibition violations, whereas lighter sentences would limit the sting of the law. Dry lobbyists also made the point that district attorneys could shape public compliance with the law in their determination of which cases warranted prosecution and which were unworthy of the court's attention.

The Anti-Saloon League, still capable of flexing its political muscle, had high hopes that the judiciary would be able to shore up the dry experiment in the city. But again dry expectations contrasted sharply with the practical considerations of enforcing Prohibition. Though New York's judges and prosecutors had substantial power to influence how Prohibition was enforced in the city, they did not see themselves as beholden to the dry crusade. From the very beginning of the Prohibition era, both federal judges and city magistrates working in New York openly voiced their skepticism of the Eighteenth Amendment and its enforcement, on both philosophical and practical grounds.

Within two weeks of the enactment of Prohibition, one city magistrate told the press that he saw the Eighteenth Amendment as an unnecessary and ill-advised alteration of the Constitution. Other judges in the city bluntly declared that the dry experiment would never work, and two city magistrates went so far as to call Prohibition "a joke." Some jurists criticized the dry laws as a departure from the American tradition of federalism and argued that Prohibition gave far too much police power to the federal government to regulate private behavior. On the federal level, Judge Learned

Hand of the U.S. District Court in Manhattan readily expressed his opposition to the Eighteenth Amendment, especially its effect on federal caseloads. Complaining that the burden of Prohibition enforcement demeaned the federal court system, Hand stated that the dry experiment had turned the federal judiciary "into so much of a police court as to be thoroughly disgusting."[51]

Politics no doubt played some part in these judges' harsh words for Prohibition, especially on the local level. The city magistrates who presided over the lowest level of the court system owed their jobs to Tammany Hall and thus would have been reluctant to oppose Tammany's wet leadership under any circumstances. But even with their political obligations taken into consideration, many judges who opposed Prohibition did so simply because it offended their sense of justice. From the cases coming before them on a daily basis, they saw that the law was not being enforced evenly, and that Prohibition enforcement efforts in the city clearly discriminated against Jews, Catholics, and ethnic minorities. They also saw class discrimination in the way Prohibition was being enforced; particularly disturbing were the many cases they heard involving poisoned or impure alcohol, which often resulted in debilitating injury. (Among the many provisions of the Volstead Act was the requirement that poisonous denaturants be added to industrial alcohol to prevent it from being used for beverage purposes, though large quantities of this denatured alcohol made it onto the black market and into the glasses of unsuspecting drinkers anyway.) City Magistrate Harry Dale complained in his courtroom that Prohibition had only "deprived the poor workingman of his beer and . . . flooded the country with rat poison." Another magistrate at the Essex Market Court, faced with the case of nine laborers who had passed out in Cooper Square after drinking denatured alcohol, lamented, "See what Prohibition has done—driven hard working, honest men to drinking wood alcohol." Other justices marveled at the petty nature of many of the Prohibition cases that came before them. While presiding over the trial of Brooklyn laborer Domito Recci, who had been arrested for carrying a half-pint of wine in his lunch box, U.S. District Judge Harlan B. Howe, a native of Vermont, exclaimed, "Why up in my country they would not indict a case like this." Incensed that the federal courts were being tied up with such petty violations of the law, Judge Howe released the defendant after imposing a five-dollar fine.[52]

In contrast to the open hostility many drys expressed toward urban immigrants, many of New York's judges were distressed by the treatment of immigrants under Prohibition and warned that the biases inherent in dry enforcement would undermine immigrants' faith in the American legal system. In his 1920 annual report, the city's chief magistrate, William McAdoo, voiced his concern that immigrants would lose all respect for the American legal system if they continued to be singled out under an unevenly enforced dry law. He argued that they "get their first and lasting impressions of our government—whether it is just or unjust, honest or otherwise—from the way they are treated here."[53]

As onerous as Prohibition was to many justices on philosophical grounds, the practical implications of dry enforcement concerned them even more, for the effects of Prohibition on the judicial system proved worse than anyone expected. In the first two years after the enactment of the Eighteenth Amendment, federal judges assigned to the Southern District of New York were surprised to find Volstead Act violations suddenly making up more than two-thirds of their criminal caseloads. State and city courts were similarly flooded. As the number of liquor-related arrests multiplied, the federal and state court systems grew hopelessly congested. By September 1920, the federal courts had already accumulated a one-year backlog of Prohibition cases. On the local level, the Manhattan District Attorney's office reported in January 1921 that it had handled 16,197 Prohibition cases during the first full year of the dry experiment, and 6,275 cases remained pending. With new arrests for Prohibition violations continuing at the rate of sixty a day, the District Attorney warned that the courts would need to enlist more than 18,000 jurors in the coming year if each defendant demanded a jury trial.[54]

In the spring of 1921, the courts were further inundated with liquor cases as a result of the Mullan-Gage Law. With the NYPD pressured to step up its enforcement efforts, the number of pending cases shot skyward, resulting in 600 new cases in the first week alone. Noting that the state criminal courts usually handled only 300 jury cases a year, one New York newspaper calculated that each week of arrests under Mullan-Gage created a two-year back-log of Prohibition cases. The paper joked that "at this rate . . . defendants in any action might rest easy. There would be small chance that the court could get around to weigh their guilt or innocence before . . . they had been gathered to their fathers."[55]

The backlog of court cases ensured Prohibition defendants that they would not have to appear in court for at least a year, a fact that only encouraged them to return to their illegal activities until their cases came to trial. Many simply never showed up for their court dates, knowing that the sheer volume of Prohibition cases made it unlikely that they would ever be tracked down. At the same time, prosecutors found it increasingly difficult to win convictions in Prohibition cases owing to sympathetic juries, unreliable witnesses, and illegally seized or missing evidence. But the sheer volume of arrests posed the biggest problem. Of the more than 10,000 arrests made by the police in the first year under Mullan-Gage, 3,089 cases were dismissed, 92 defendants were acquitted, and only 239 of the accused were convicted. The nearly 7,000 cases remaining were simply added to the enormous backlog swamping the state courts.[56]

The provision of the Mullan-Gage Law that required alcohol cases to be handled by jury trials proved especially problematic. Because of the unpopularity of the dry laws, prosecutors had trouble finding jurors for cases related to Prohibition violations. In one case involving a Brooklyn bartender in April 1921, sixty-nine potential jurors had to be called before a jury could be seated, after fifty-seven jurors were dismissed for declaring their opposition to the dry laws. In response to the pleas of judges and prosecutors to intervene in this legal quagmire, Governor Nathan Miller was forced to call a special session of the State Supreme Court during the summer of 1921 to address the backlog of Mullan-Gage cases. This extraordinary session, called the "rum court" by the local papers, treated Mullan-Gage violations not as felonies but as misdemeanors that carried felony penalties. This meant that defendants in Mullan-Gage cases could be tried quickly and without juries. Though this special session disposed of hundreds of Prohibition cases with a 70 percent conviction rate during its brief seven-week term, 300 cases remained untried when it ended, and the backlog continued to grow on a daily basis.[57]

Overworked and demoralized, angry judges and magistrates grew more vocal in their criticisms of Prohibition and the Mullan-Gage Law. They were especially incensed by the disregard for constitutional rights and proper search procedures shown by police officers and Prohibition agents. In July 1921, after a police officer arrested a man for having four ounces of liquor in his Harlem candy store, Magistrate William Sweetser yelled at the arresting officer, "What's the trouble with you? Don't you read the paper? Don't you know you can't enter a man's business or home and search for liquor without a warrant? . . . I'm going to write the Police Commissioner personally about you." The officer angrily responded that he was simply doing his job. But when he refused the magistrate's orders to return the confiscated liquor to the defendant, the magistrate had the officer held for contempt of court.[58]

In a similar case that same year, a city magistrate criticized police officers for a warrantless search of a druggist's home that resulted in the confiscation of 137 bottles of whiskey and gin. Calling their search "outrageous and unwarranted," the magistrate dismissed all charges against the defendant. Another magistrate in the Washington Heights Court was so tired of police violating proper search guidelines that he fined two officers for disorderly conduct for conducting a liquor raid without a warrant.[59]

Some magistrates, unwilling to accept the dry lobby's demand that Prohibition be enforced in New York at any cost, gave up completely on the dry mandate. After denouncing another case of "outrageous" police conduct, one judge at the Tombs Court said he would gladly give up his eight years as a magistrate "for just one day on the bench of the Supreme Court to pass judgment on this law." Even the grand juries charged with indicting Prohibition violators began speaking out in frustration. In 1921 a grand jury in Brooklyn threw out 121 of the first 129 Prohibition cases presented to it as warrantless. Similarly, a grand jury in the Bronx, so discouraged with the Prohibition cases it heard, subpoenaed Police Commissioner Enright to explain personally the tactics of his officers. In October 1921, its members publicly recommended that the Mullan-Gage Law be repealed.[60]

With Prohibition enforcement in New York failing and tension running high between the various parties charged with enforcing the dry laws, New York City's judges and prosecutors still had to resign themselves to one unfortunate fact: though they may have had serious misgivings about Prohibition, they were nonetheless compelled to enforce it. In a search for an expedient solution to their judicial quandary, many prosecutors and judges turned to the plea bargain as the solution to their dilemma.

By the 1920s, plea bargains had become a mainstay of American judicial practice on the state level, but Prohibition made them common practice on the federal level as well. With liquor violations composing up to two-thirds of the federal criminal court dockets, the speedy resolution of these cases proved to be of paramount importance in keeping the federal judicial system functioning. To alleviate their massive caseloads, federal justices came to accept plea bargains as the only practical way to deal with the immense backlog of Prohibition cases. Under this new understanding, Prohibition violators who pleaded guilty and spared the court a time-consuming jury trial could avoid prison time and be released with fines as little as one dollar. By contrast, if defendants chose to go to trial and were ultimately convicted, they were guaranteed harsher penalties, including jail sentences of up to six months.[61]

Understandably, many defendants in Prohibition cases gladly took advantage of the offer to enter into plea bargains. After U.S. District Judge Learned Hand announced to his courtroom that he would impose fines without jail time on any defendant who entered a guilty plea to Prohibition violations committed before June 7, 1920, the date on which the Supreme Court upheld the Eighteenth Amendment, the court collected more than $20,000 in fines in one day. (The only defendants who avoided entering guilty pleas, according to the *New York Times,* were saloon and speakeasy owners, who risked having a police officer stationed in their establishments after a conviction or having a federal injunction brought against them for maintaining a nuisance.) The majority of defendants, usually petty violators such as bartenders and waiters, happily paid the fines and got on with their lives.[62]

The plea bargain system was not without flaws, however. Because of differences in opinion and temperament, the federal judges handling Prohibition cases in New York could issue wildly disparate sentences to Prohibition violators, sending conflicting messages to the public. Some justices, like Federal Judge Edwin Garvin, avoided using plea bargains altogether and

insisted on handing down the harshest possible penalties to Prohibition violators. One federal judge had a tendency to fine all liquor law violators
$250, while other judges were remarkably inconsistent in their application
of fines to plea bargains. In one case, a defendant was fined $25 for possess-
ing a gallon of whiskey, while another defendant was fined $75 for the same
offense. Possession of two gallons of whiskey warranted a $30 fine in one
instance and a $75 fine in the next, while possession of a gallon of wine
might bring only a $5 fine. Not even multiple offenses were certain to bring
stiffer fines. One bartender was fined only $50 after pleading guilty to his
fifth Prohibition offense.[63]

As the sheer volume of dry cases made plea bargains an acceptable alternative to jury trials, prosecutors developed their own system of legal triage
to deal with the demands of Prohibition enforcement. Cases involving wine
were often dismissed outright by prosecutors as unimportant, while women
and elderly defendants generally won lenient treatment from prosecutors,
who noted in their files time and again, "the case is trivial and not worth
prosecution." Other cases were dropped owing to misconduct on the part
of the NYPD or Bureau of Prohibition. Any time an arresting police officer
or Prohibition agent was dismissed from the force, prosecutors quickly
dropped all pending cases involving the implicated officer, acknowledging
that convictions would be impossible to obtain. After being forced to drop
multitudes of cases because of official corruption, some prosecutors argued
that no dry case was worth prosecuting unless two officers of unimpeachable standing could substantiate the charges. The United States Attorney's
office was forced to dismiss even more cases because evidence had been improperly or illegally seized, or, on occasion, because evidence and case files
had disappeared from the Bureau of Prohibition headquarters.

Even when the evidence was in order, prosecutors found that proving
cases against Prohibition violators was a tricky business. Cases against saloon
and restaurant owners frequently fell apart because the owners claimed that
they had not been on the premises at the time of a raid and had no knowledge that their bartenders and waiters were selling liquor. In dismissing
one such case, the United States Attorney admitted that "the evidence is
such that it would be impossible to prove [the owner's] knowledge of the
sale." Defendants similarly escaped possession and transportation charges by

claiming that they had not known what they were transporting. Anthony Solitore, a wagon driver charged with possessing and transporting one barrel of wine on a coal wagon, had the charges against him dismissed when he claimed in court that he had not known what was in the barrel. The United States Attorney conceded in the case file, "The government has no evidence . . . that he knew what he was carrying. There are no marks on the barrel to indicate that it was liquor or wine."[64]

With prosecutors and judges struggling to find practical ways to keep the justice system functioning under the burden of the Volstead Act, the Anti-Saloon League and other dry lobbyists complained that judges and prosecutors were treating Prohibition cases too leniently. William Anderson griped that judges who entered into plea bargains that released Prohibition violators with mere fines were "lacking a conception of their duty to the public." He argued that by not sentencing defendants to jail, the courts were essentially giving the public license to disregard the Prohibition laws. Yet the justices and prosecutors laboring to keep up with the league's mandate paid little attention to Anderson's complaints. With neither resources nor jail cells at their disposal to sentence every dry offender to prison, judges and prosecutors dealt with Prohibition violations as effectively as they could with plea bargains, reduced sentences, and dismissal of questionable cases. Considering that most defendants in Prohibition cases were not career or hardened criminals but bartenders, waiters, and petty violators, many members of the judiciary concluded that it was unreasonable to devote any more of the judicial system's resources to Prohibition cases with more serious criminal cases pressing.[65]

By mid-1923, city, state, and federal authorities were receiving annually close to 50,000 complaints of Prohibition violations, while the District Attorney's office reported that it was handling between 15,000 and 20,000 Prohibition cases each year, with only a fraction resulting in jury convictions. At the same time, arrests for public intoxication, which had dropped off sharply in the first months of Prohibition, began climbing rapidly. On the first anniversary of Prohibition in 1921, both the Jefferson Market Courthouse in Greenwich Village and Essex Market Courthouse on the Lower East Side reported that cases for public intoxication had reached record numbers. By 1922, the number of arrests for drunkenness in the city had climbed to 11,402, up from a low of 7,028 in 1919, suggesting that drinking in the city was increasing, not diminishing, in the face of Prohibition enforcement. Despite all efforts to deter them, New Yorkers were violating the dry laws in growing numbers.[66]

In the meantime, public anger over the dry laws mounted, as did the political consequences of supporting the dry mandate. In the fall of 1922, only a year and a half after the passage of the Mullan-Gage Law, Governor Nathan Miller was voted out of office. By a record margin of 386,000 votes, his wet predecessor Alfred E. Smith was returned to Albany, despite strong opposition from the dry camp. With Smith back in office, wet Democrats led by State Senate Majority Leader James J. Walker immediately began preparing a bill to repeal the immensely unpopular Mullan-Gage Law.[67]

Once returned to the governor's office, Al Smith realized that taking on the Anti-Saloon League, which had invested a great deal in Mullan-Gage, was not a matter to be taken lightly, and that challenging the dry lobby could have great political consequences. When the state legislature passed Senator Walker's bill repealing Mullan-Gage in May 1923, Smith initially hesitated to sign it, despite his long-standing reputation as a wet. Smith had serious presidential aspirations and was concerned that repealing the law, though a welcome move in New York, could damage his national political standing and fragment the Democratic Party. His fears were compounded when his fellow New York Democrat, Assemblyman Franklin D. Roosevelt, warned Smith, "It is going to hurt you nationally a whole lot to sign the repealer bill." Newspaper publisher Frank Gannett added to Smith's fears when he told colleagues, "If he should sign this bill I don't see how it would be possible for us to lend him any support in the future." The leaders of the Anti-Saloon League and other drys also chimed in, predicting an apocalyptic combination of the Civil War and Judgment Day should the Mullan-Gage Law be repealed.[68]

For nearly a month, Governor Smith delayed his decision on the repeal bill as wets and drys anxiously waited to see if he would sign it. Smith finally was prevailed upon by the most persuasive voice in state politics, Tammany Hall leader Charles Murphy. At a meeting at Murphy's Long Island home, Murphy was reported to have bluntly told the governor, "Al, you will sign this bill or I will never support you again, either for the Presidency or the Governorship."[69]

Worried about alienating his closest allies, Governor Smith signed the bill repealing the Mullan-Gage Law on June 1, 1923. In a carefully prepared statement, Smith reminded his constituents that in no way was he legalizing drink or negating the Eighteenth Amendment. He simply explained that the state had never been obligated to carry out the enforcement of national Prohibition, and that its attempts to do so under Mullan-Gage had failed. Governor Smith insisted that New Yorkers were still legally obligated to obey the Eighteenth Amendment and added that he was merely shifting the burden of dry enforcement back to the federal authorities, where, he noted, "it will be where it rightfully belongs."[70]

Smith's decision, as drys feared, made national headlines. President Warren Harding spoke out against Smith's decision, calling it a political "blunder." The announcement that the most populous state in the nation would no longer enforce Prohibition on the state level dealt a serious blow to the dry cause and served as a remarkable challenge to the power of the Anti-Saloon League, which had insisted that Smith veto the repeal act. Instantly, Smith had emerged as one of the most visible wet leaders in the nation, praised in some camps and damned in others.[71]

Six days after the repeal of the Mullan-Gage Law, the Washington Heights Magistrate's Court had only one bootlegging case on its docket. Throughout the city, court caseloads were said to have been "considerably reduced" as police dropped their Prohibition enforcement efforts. Though Prohibition had not ended, Governor Smith's repeal of the Mullan-Gage Law marked a fundamental turning point in the course of the dry experiment in New York. The state and the city had essentially conceded defeat, admitting that Prohibition enforcement had proved too large and too complicated a task for local authorities to undertake. Despite the combined efforts of the Bureau of Prohibition, the NYPD, and the judicial system, the sheer volume of resistance to Prohibition in New York had been enough to make enforcement of the Eighteenth Amendment impossible, while unintended consequences in the form of corruption, violence, and abuse of power had done even more damage to the city in the name of the dry crusade. At the very least, the repeal of the Mullan-Gage Law would soften some of Prohibition's most injurious effects.[72]

The repeal of Mullan-Gage in 1923 left Prohibition enforcement in New York in a state of limbo. Federal agents still attempted to enforce the law, occasionally with help from the local police, but for now their efforts would be far less aggressive, much to the satisfaction of wet New Yorkers. Yet as much as the dry experiment had been weakened by the repeal of the Mullan-Gage Law, it still remained entrenched in the Constitution, a factor that led many New Yorkers, including Police Commissioner Enright, to conclude that Prohibition would "not be repealed in our day and generation." The situation presented a quandary to wets and drys alike. With the dry experiment being neither enforced nor repealed, the debate over the Eighteenth Amendment had seemingly reached a stalemate.[73]

4

The Brewers of Bigotry

In May 1921, seventy-seven-year-old Nora Kelly appeared in a New York City courtroom, charged with possessing a one-dollar flask of whiskey. When taken before the judge, the elderly resident of West Seventeenth Street pleaded that she needed the liquor to maintain her health. "I am old and weak and I take a little drop to brace up my strength," she explained to a city magistrate, "especially early in the day." Her plea fell on deaf ears. The magistrate sentenced Kelly to five days in jail. Before the proceedings ended, however, Kelly spoke out against Prohibition for what it was doing to people like her. "It is on the poor people it drives hardest," she said. "Those that are rich can have what they want, with [no one] to interfere with them."[1]

The Eighteenth Amendment to the Constitution was clearly meant to apply to all Americans, regardless of class, race, or ethnic background. But as Nora Kelly's complaint indicated, in practice the moral reform agenda embodied in Prohibition was directed disproportionately at the country's working class. From the moment of its enactment, Prohibition in New York was marked by blatant displays of religious intolerance, class bias, and outright bigotry. As the dry experiment took shape in the early 1920s, the city's Irish, Italian, and Eastern European immigrants, its Catholics and Jews, and the masses of other ethnic Americans who populated New York found that the main objective of the dry lobby was to police the habits of the poor, the foreign-born, and the working class.

No one who had followed the rise of the dry movement in the United States should have been surprised that the Eighteenth Amendment would become a vehicle for such prejudices. The history of American temperance movements was riddled with examples of bigotry toward and paternalistic disdain for nonwhites, immigrants, Catholics, and Jews. While many prominent drys did try to reach out across racial, ethnic, and religious barriers for the sake of building a stronger temperance movement, their work could be undone by an off-the-cuff comment, such as that of Purley Baker of the Anti-Saloon League, who declared that Germans "eat like gluttons and drink like swine." Dry leaders like William "Pussyfoot" Johnson and Bishop James Cannon, Jr., did little to hide their racist or anti-Catholic views, while key temperance organizations like the Woman's Christian Temperance Union and the Knights of the Good Templars suffered deep schisms over the question of whether to allow African Americans to participate in the temperance movement.[2]

Though the American temperance movement had its benevolent side, for decades strong nativist sentiments had lurked beneath its surface. In New York, as in every other major American metropolis, these issues were made more pronounced by the presence of large ethnic populations. Dry advocates had long presented the temperance crusade as part of an inevitable conflict between native and immigrant cultures. Prohibition supporters viewed the passage of the Eighteenth Amendment as a key victory in that conflict because they believed it would help force the ethnic inhabitants of America's cities to give up their alien habits and preserve the cultural dominance of "respectable" Americans.

American drys and many of their Progressive allies shared deep suspicions of ethnic urban populations, and they rarely hesitated to criticize ethnic Americans, especially New Yorkers, in the harshest terms. Fearing that their very presence would undermine traditional American values and erode the moral standards of the Protestant middle class, they especially emphasized what they perceived as the inherent criminality of ethnic Americans, which they often linked to the abuse of alcohol. One Progressive-era pamphlet, for example, described New York's Italians as "Dagos, who drink excessively, live in a state of filth and use the knife on slightest provocation." A journalist surveying New York's Little Italy for the Progressive *Century Magazine* described the neighborhood by saying that "all the criminals are here." In similar fashion, a journalist writing for *Scribner's* at the turn of the twentieth century vividly described New York's saloons as the haunts of the Irish "ugly drunk" and the "despised dago," whose generally temperate demeanor could be transformed in a moment into knife-wielding passion. According to one historian, this distrust of urban immigrants, and especially of Italians, was so intense that in 1904 the New York City Police Department built its new headquarters at Centre and Grand Streets, in the heart of Little Italy.[3]

American distrust of the foreign-born was not new to the Progressive era, as virulent displays of nativism had accompanied nearly every major wave of immigration in the nation's history. But when the Progressive and dry movements converged in the 1910s, the xenophobia and nativism of both movements inevitably came to the surface. As the dry lobby gained momentum, it staked its success on its ability to depict foreigners, Catholics, Jews, and city dwellers as threats to everything genuinely American. At the height of its power, the Anti-Saloon League in particular appealed to a prevailing contempt for ethnic city dwellers by condemning New York as full of "ignorant and vicious" immigrants badly in need of the moral and social reforms promoted by drys and Progressives. This nativism became more pronounced after the dry reforms went into effect. Unable quickly to create the dry utopia they had hoped for, and unwilling to reflect upon the flaws in their own program, drys scapegoated ethnic Americans, Catholics, and Jews for the failure of the dry experiment.[4]

New York City was the natural target of the dry crusade's anger because of the obvious dilemma it presented to the dry experiment's implementation. Temperance leaders working in New York had long understood that the immigrant and ethnic communities of the city had deeply rooted customs involving alcohol, but they nevertheless insisted that these New Yorkers would be made to abide by the Eighteenth Amendment and, by extension, the values championed by the dry lobby. Immediately after the amendment's passage, Reverend Rollin O. Everhart of the Anti-Saloon League told reporters, "We expect New York to be the most difficult of all places, particularly because of its foreign population." Everhart argued that though "these people are difficult to reach through propaganda, example works splendidly with them. Even though they have learned to drink in their own countries, the vast majority of them will quit when they have to go 'ramming around' for illicit alcohol instead of getting it easily, comfortably and legally."[5]

Relying on example would prove very difficult given the demographics of the city. Long before 1920, New York City had emerged as the most culturally diverse urban environment in the United States. With the city's population hovering just below six million, New York had nearly two million foreign-born residents, and over two million more inhabitants born of immigrant parents. Seventy percent of the city's churchgoers were Catholic, and nearly a third of all New Yorkers were Jews. The city had by far the largest Italian community in the United States: nearly 800,000 residents, half of whom were foreign-born. New York was also home to over 670,000 German Americans, 400,000 Irish Americans, another 200,000 first-generation Irish immigrants, and over 800,000 Eastern European immigrants. Additionally, more than 150,000 African Americans and tens of thousands of members of other ethnic groups including Puerto Ricans, Greeks, Chinese, and Spaniards lived in New York and contributed to the city's polyglot nature.[6]

New York City's diversity in the 1920s was so striking that the Prohibitionist literature of the era was apt to describe New York not as one city but as a collection of "many little foreign cities." A publication of the World League against Alcoholism, for example, depicted the Lower East Side as a "distinctly Jewish city." It described Mulberry Street as "to all the world like a section of Naples," while in parts of Harlem "the German atmosphere dominates so completely that one wonders at times if this is New York or Germany." One report went so far as to cite New York as "the least American part of the United States."[7]

Yet the dry preoccupation with the "foreignness" of the city as the root of the problem with Prohibition enforcement was misplaced. In the cosmopolitan city, Prohibition violations could be found as easily in the Yale Club as in a working-class saloon, and as easily on Park Avenue as in a Brooklyn tenement. But the drys were far less concerned with policing old-stock Americans than with enforcing the dry agenda in the ethnic quarters of New York.

In essence, the dry crusade divided New York into opposing camps of "dry Americans" and "wet foreigners." In doing so, it indiscriminately lumped together first-generation immigrants with more assimilated second- and third-generation ethnic Americans; looked at Catholics and Jews as if they were members of the same wet cult; and classified New Yorkers of any number of ethnicities, races, and cultures under the collective label of "un-American." This haphazard grouping created an "us against them" mentality that defined the dry crusade to many urban Americans in the 1920s.

Until the advent of Prohibition, drys had invested their efforts in the ideology of "anti-saloonism," from which the Anti-Saloon League derived its name. Though nativist sentiments ran deep in the dry movement, saloons had been the main enemy, along with those who ran them, those who supplied them, and those who used them as a base from which to corrupt city politics. The drinker had been seen not as the focal problem but instead as an unwitting victim in the whole affair. With the enactment of Prohibition, however, the saloon could no longer serve as the rallying point for drys, as it no longer legally existed. The brewers and distillers who had drawn the ire of drys were also out of the picture. So when compliance with the Eighteenth Amendment was not as automatic as drys had hoped, the Anti-Saloon League, the Woman's Christian Temperance Union, and other dry organizations and reform groups shifted their focus to the working-class ethnic drinker as the "un-American" enemy of their agenda. With this shift, enforcing Prohibition in the ethnic quarters of the nation's cities emerged as a top priority of the dry crusade.

The dry movement's determination to police "foreign habits" was met with strong opposition in the city's ethnic quarters. Despite their relative silence during the wartime era, when drys had equated opposition to Prohibition with treason, New York's ethnic communities defied the Eighteenth Amendment as soon as wartime Prohibition took effect in 1919. Their resistance to Prohibition was not simply about the illegality of booze. To ethnic New Yorkers, resistance to the dry laws became a form of protest against the cultural authority of Protestant drys who presented themselves as the defenders of all things genuinely American. Confronted with the choice between being "dry Americans" or "wet foreigners," ethnic New Yorkers accepted neither characterization. By defying the dry mandate, they asserted their own identity as ethnic Americans while defending their cultural traditions.

Whether Irish, Italian, or Jewish, many ethnic New Yorkers resisted Prohibition by simply ignoring it. In neighborhoods throughout the city, hundreds of ethnic saloons went about their business in the early 1920s as if the Prohibition amendment had never passed. Their numbers were diminished, their business slower, and their trade necessarily disguised from the street, but saloonkeepers defiantly kept at their trade. While dry advocates continuously repeated the cliché that the Eighteenth Amendment meant the end of the "old-fashioned saloon," reports compiled by the Committee of Fourteen throughout the 1920s described illegal barroom scenes in working-class neighborhoods that were remarkably like those of pre-Prohibition days. The décor and atmosphere in these places remained largely intact, down to the signs advertising New York's best-known breweries: Doelger, Ehret, Hupfel, and Ruppert. Saloon patrons still drank beer and whiskey, though of unknown origin and questionable quality, while reading the afternoon papers and playing cards or billiards. Noting little more than that these establishments were alive and well, the undercover investigators usually closed their reports with the cursory note "Nothing disorderly was observed."[8]

This defiance of Prohibition could be seen all over the city. In Little Italy, Greenwich Village, East Harlem, and sections of the Bronx, Italian workers still gathered in cafés to drink wine. In Jewish neighborhoods, cafés and restaurants freely sold wine, beer, and liquor to their patrons. In Harlem, grills and cafés remained open for business, with the traditional walnut or mahogany screens still covering their plate-glass windows to obscure the goings-on inside. One reporter argued that the only discernible difference between these Prohibition-era saloons and their legal predecessors was that the traditional free pretzels had been replaced by potato chips. Their dingy interiors—complete with cigar smoke, long bars, brass rails, sports tickers, and free food—were a direct link to the saloons of the past. Beer, wine, whiskey, and gin were still sold and consumed openly, though at times disguised in teapots or coffee cups. Just as they had before Prohibition, one observer noted, these places still "seem[ed] to constitute the club rooms of the neighborhood."[9]

These establishments persisted into the 1920s, despite their illegality, for the simple reason that they still served important social functions. Within the city's ethnic enclaves, bars, cafés, and saloons had been centers of the immigrant social world for decades, and in working-class neighborhoods filled with crowded tenements, the saloon and its many variants served as the living rooms and parlors that neither immigrant families nor their single male boarders could afford.[10]

The evangelist Charles Stelzle, a well-known temperance reformer who grew up on the Lower East Side, was one of the few Prohibitionists who understood the role the saloon played in New York's poor neighborhoods, and consequently why ethnic New Yorkers were so reluctant to give up the saloon in the 1920s. In his memoirs, Stelzle recalled the neighborhood saloon as the place where "the working men . . . held their christening parties, their weddings, their dances, their rehearsals for their singing societies, and all other social functions." It was where workers had "the opportunity to play billiards, pool and cards, and often there was a bowling alley." Certainly beer and whiskey were a major part of the attraction, but as Stelzle showed, the saloon provided its patrons with much more. It was a place for celebration, conversation, and amusement. As Stelzle put it, "The saloon was in a very real sense the social center for working men in practically every community."[11]

Saloons reflected the life and rhythm of the neighborhood as few other institutions could, from dawn into the late evening. They opened at five or six in the morning so working men could have their "eye-openers"; provided free lunches at noon; occasionally catered to neighborhood women in the afternoon; and filled up with men again when the work day was done. Children were commonly sent to them to retrieve growlers of beer to bring home for dinner. In the late nineteenth century, when both drinking water and fresh milk were of questionable quality, the saloon's beer was seen as a cheap, nutritious, and safe component of working-class diets. In the city's German communities especially, beer was seen as such an integral staple of the diet that it was nicknamed "liquid bread."[12]

The saloon also played an important role in ethnic identity. Though patrons of any given saloon might come from diverse ethnic and racial backgrounds, most saloons maintained a clear ethnic identity and served a dedicated patronage from within that community. Irish pubs and German beer gardens, for example, enjoyed universal patronage, but their owners made open displays of their ethnic backgrounds and culture. Irish saloons displayed scenes of Ireland, harp motifs, and other nationalist symbols. One Irish barkeeper preserved a sense of ethnic identity for his patrons by keeping a thirty-year-old block of dry sod from County Leitrim above the cash register. German beer gardens and saloons replicated the décor, music, and foods of the homeland with such accuracy that one 1901 report described a German establishment on Avenue A that was said to evoke "an ancient German tavern." Norwegian saloons on Hamilton Avenue in Brooklyn displayed Norwegian flags in their windows. Language was also part of the scene. For Bohemians, Romanians, Poles, and Czechs, saloons were places where they could speak their native languages and sing songs in their native tongues. To outside observers, the foreign trappings of saloons were often their most distinguishing characteristics. Within ethnic immigrant communities, one reformer noted, "the saloon becomes a kind of national headquarters."[13]

Even the drinks consumed in saloons were expressions of ethnic identity. Whether it was German lager, Italian wine, Irish whiskey, or some other variant of alcohol, New York's ethnic communities all had a drink, if not several, that was held in esteem as a valuable part of cultural heritage. In Committee of Fourteen reports, for example, investigators noted that many Greek and Turkish establishments served neither scotch nor rye but only a liquor that reporters described variously as "mastika" or "Mahaska," while in Romanian Jewish cellars on the Lower East Side, wine was the drink of choice for young and old. In ethnic neighborhoods, the choice of drink, where one drank, and even how much one drank became expressions of ethnic identity as much as belonging to a mutual aid society or marching in an ethnic parade.[14]

In part, the strong sense of ethnic identity fostered by these establishments, and the sense that they were beyond the reach of traditional American culture, were what made them appear so threatening to the dry movement. Contrary to the insistence of drys, however, these saloons were not refuges where working-class ethnics avoided assimilation into American culture. Rather, they served as bridges between the old world and the new, places where newly arrived immigrants could learn from their predecessors and begin the often painful process of adapting to a new homeland. Almost all ethnic saloons served as invaluable orientation centers for new arrivals to the city, whether from Eastern Europe or the Southern United States, by offering a sense of community identity and belonging for transplanted migrants. The saloon allowed them to assimilate into American culture and the hectic pace of New York life on their own terms, by introducing them to American language and culture in bits and pieces, without forcing them to give up their heritage altogether. Saloons allowed immigrants to drink their national drinks, speak their native languages, and associate with members of their native ethnic groups while also hearing English, learning about American culture, politics, and sports, and mixing with working-class patrons of other ethnicities.[15]

The neighborhood saloon also provided an important social forum where working-class men could settle their differences, discuss community issues, and hold meetings for trade unions and other associations. While reformers argued that these working-class associations would be better off meeting in settlement houses or community centers, saloons offered their spaces at much more affordable rates. When one New York union official considered moving his group's weekly meetings from a saloon to a settlement house, he was shocked to learn that the settlement house charged $150 a year for the use of its space. His local saloon had charged him only $40 a year for the use of its meeting hall. The popularity of saloon meeting halls was self-evident in the numbers of associations that met in them. One East Tenth Street saloon, the Casino, was reported to host twenty-eight separate groups each week.[16]

While drys often depicted saloonkeepers as exploiting the poor, working-class patrons were just as likely to see them as social benefactors. Saloonkeepers traditionally used their political ties to the police and fire departments to arrange jobs for their customers and their customers' children. They furnished bail money when it was needed, gave more freely to their needy neighbors than did relief groups or community charities, and attached fewer strings to their generosity. Recalling his own childhood on the Lower East Side, Charles Stelzle remembered that when his widowed mother was evicted from her apartment with her young children, the local saloonkeeper lent her the money to move into a new apartment. "He did it out of pure generosity," Stelzle wrote, "because mother wasn't one of his customers."[17]

Saloons also provided practical services to working-class communities. They readily cashed paychecks for workers at more favorable rates and more convenient hours than banks. Saloon owners might keep valuables for local residents in their safes; provide short-term loans; and quickly take up collections for funerals and other financial emergencies. Saloons also served as unofficial neighborhood post offices, accepting packages and mail for local residents. Bartenders would read letters for their illiterate or non-English–speaking patrons. Saloons were also sources of news, ranging from local sports scores to updates from the homeland, and generally kept a variety of newspapers on hand for their customers. One reformer acknowledged that in poor neighborhoods without indoor plumbing, the saloon "served the public by being often the only place where a glass of water could be asked for and retrieved without fear of intrusion." As modern technology transformed America, saloons were often the first establishments in a neighborhood to have electric lights, and were usually the first if not the only places to have a public telephone. The saloon charged nothing for these conveniences. It asked only for the regular and continued patronage of its customers.[18]

The central role of the saloon in the everyday lives of working-class New Yorkers naturally elevated the saloonkeeper to a position of community leadership. While Prohibitionists condemned saloonkeepers as parasites who fed off the miseries of the poor in working-class neighborhoods, they were more likely to be admired in their own communities as entrepreneurs who had risen to positions of prominence, respectability, and middle-class security through hard work and business acumen. This was the opinion of Charles Stelzle, who argued that many of the saloonkeepers he had come across in his career were models of propriety. The best of them, he argued, were devout religious men who showed a strong sense of family obligation, disavowed swearing and gambling, and took measures to prevent intoxication in their establishments by keeping a close eye on their patrons. One such saloonkeeper was the legendary John McSorley of McSorley's Ale House, who neither smoked nor drank, closed his Seventh Street saloon promptly at midnight, and had no tolerance for drunks. His saloon was described in one 1913 profile as a "working-class temple" with a decidedly "moral atmosphere." In recognition of saloonkeepers like McSorley, Stelzle argued that "prohibition agitators who pictured the saloon-keeper as a low-browed brute simply did not understand his relationship to the average workingman."[19]

Given the role the working-class saloon played in the everyday lives of ethnic New Yorkers, it is no wonder that these communities vehemently opposed the final arrival of Prohibition. To many of them the Eighteenth Amendment meant much more than just a ban on alcohol. It was an assault on their ethnic traditions, a blatant example of class-based paternalism, and an imposition on the daily rhythm of city life. The enormous gulf between dry reformers' and working-class New Yorkers' views of Prohibition revealed a fault line that the dry crusade would never be able to breach.

Though the city's immigrant and ethnic communities had been slow to voice their opposition to the dry laws during the wartime campaign for the ratification of the Eighteenth Amendment, by 1919 they had begun to speak out against Prohibition publicly. The Italian paper *Il Cittadino* protested that Prohibition solved no social ills but simply punished honest, hard-working laborers by taking away wine, their "beverage of daily habit and . . . a quasi-absolute necessity." At the same time, an advertisement placed in *Il Progreso* by a Mott Street wine merchant promised "Guerra alla Proibizione" (War on Prohibition), and urged customers to resist the dry crusade by stocking up on wine. On the streets of Little Italy and Greenwich Village, Italian immigrants derided "la Proibizione" as a hypocritical farce, especially considering the number of policemen they saw drinking in neighborhood restaurants.[20]

Italian New Yorkers, who saw nothing immoral or criminal about a daily glass of wine, took matters into their own hands and made their own wine, according to one observer, "as they would make bread if the bread shops were suddenly closed." In the early years of Prohibition, social workers serving Italian neighborhoods estimated that Italian households spent anywhere from $50 to $300 every year on wine-making supplies, while court records revealed numerous instances of Italians' producing in their basements hundreds of gallons of wine, which they drank at home or sold to neighbors for three to five dollars a gallon. Wine-making was so common in the Italian quarters of New York that every fall the gutters in front of tenements and storefronts would be stained red by the dregs from the process, and the women who worked in the local grocery stores would apologize for their grape-stained hands.[21]

While the Italian response to Prohibition was a practical one, rooted in the desire to hold onto wine as a part of daily life, in New York's German and Irish communities, opposition to dry reformers took on more political overtones. In the *American Monthly,* a magazine published for New York's German community, editor George Viereck called Prohibition a hypocritical violation of the principles of self-determination and freedom that the United States had promoted during World War I. Another German paper, the *New Yorker Staats-Zeitung,* argued that Prohibition was "the work of political cliques and a demonstration of contempt for the will of the people." The *Irish World* offered a similar argument, contrasting the coercive Prohibition laws with the American tradition of liberty. Imagining how refugees who had fled war-torn Europe in search of freedom in the United States might view the dry experiment, the *Irish World* asked, "Will they, who have come here from under a rule which oppressed them in so many things but left them free [to drink] . . . still think of America as the land of personal liberty and human equality? Or will they listen to the 'Reds' who tell them America is a land of as little liberty as Europe?"[22]

Thousands of New York City's immigrants had a more dramatic reaction to the dry mandate. Seeing the prospect of living under Prohibition as unthinkable, they responded to the enactment of the Eighteenth Amendment by leaving the United States and returning to their native countries. In striking contrast to the great waves of immigrants who came to the United States before World War I, in the first months of 1920 more than 61,000 immigrants returned to Europe, far outpacing new arrivals. Though the end of World War I certainly played a major role in this mass exodus, Congressman Isaac Siegel of the House Immigration Committee argued that Prohibition was the primary reason for their departures.[23]

An article on the immigration situation printed in the *New York Times* came to the same conclusion. Noting that thousands of working-class Poles, Czechs, and Yugoslavians were returning to Europe, a reporter for the *Times* argued that three-fifths of them were returning "because, they declare, America has gone dry." They were of the opinion "that after ten or twelve hours of work a workman should be permitted to buy his beer or other drink." A report in the *New York Herald* also attributed the rush of immigrants back to Europe largely to Prohibition. "Most of the aliens are lovers of wine," explained the article, "which they are unable to get under present conditions." As a result, the *Herald* concluded, "they are changing their minds about America being the free country they thought it was and are going back now where they will be able to get their wine and beer unmolested."[24]

Immigrants did not take the decision to leave the United States lightly, and the fact that Prohibition played such a large role in this decision showed how significant the issue was in the city's ethnic communities. For many, the decision was not just about drink; it reflected a larger disillusionment with the United States. Gustavo Tolentino, a New York wine merchant, outlined his decision to return to Europe in a letter to the *New York Times*. After he had fled the Austrian occupation of Trieste in the 1880s, Tolentino explained, "the blessed country of America offered justice and liberty, and I decided to make the United States my home." Thirty-four years later, Tolentino had become a citizen, participated in Liberty Loan drives, and supported the war effort. "In return for loyal services," Tolentino wrote, "I am now without work, and shall be forced to return to Trieste." He angrily closed his letter: "America is mocking the symbolic Statue of Liberty. It would be better to return the glorious statue to France, which has always championed its principle." For immigrants like Tolentino, it was impossible to reconcile the dry crusade's vision for the nation with American ideals of liberty.[25]

Another common thread that bound many ethnic New Yorkers together in opposition to Prohibition was the economic impact of the law. When the dry era arrived, the city's working-class communities blamed the dry lobby for cavalierly destroying the livelihoods of brewery workers, bartenders, waiters, and teamsters without showing the slightest concern for their survival. In the *Daily News,* one reader protested, "It is a wonder to me that the Prohibitionists can sleep. They have thrown thousands of honest men out of work and caused great hardships. Many of the men in breweries had families to support. Now they are hunting jobs."[26]

In their single-minded determination to outlaw alcohol, drys had offered no proposals to aid those whose jobs had been eliminated by the Volstead Act. Saloon owners in particular were left in disbelief as their once respectable careers were transformed into criminal enterprises. When Brooklyn saloon owner Joseph Logan found himself in federal court for violating the Prohibition laws, he refused to accept that his trade had been outlawed. Upon being sentenced to twenty days in jail for illegally selling liquor, Logan exclaimed, "Can't a fellow make a living for his wife and kids?"[27]

While many of New York's saloon owners and bartenders tried to stay in business in spite of Prohibition, the law eventually caught up with them. One Bronx bartender, William Nienstadt of East 204th Street, had his saloon raided twice in the summer of 1920. A bartender for thirty-five years, Nienstadt had in April of that year taken over the small saloon where he worked, hoping that despite its illegality, saloon ownership would provide him with financial security as it had done for generations of saloonkeepers. Neinstadt's aspirations were short-lived. After two arrests for Prohibition violations, the sixty-year-old Nienstadt gave up his saloon and his bartending career. At a hearing in federal court, a repentant Nienstadt told the judge that since his second arrest, he had taken a job as a sandwich maker to support his wife and father-in-law, working from 7 P.M. to 7 A.M. for thirty dollars a week. Sparing Nienstadt jail time, the court fined him $100 for violating the Volstead Act, the equivalent of three weeks' pay.[28]

Sometimes the law caught saloonkeepers even as they tried to comply with the dry mandate. Thomas Kalishes of 40 Madison Street, a Lower East Side saloonkeeper, was converting his former saloon into a grocery store when he ran afoul of the law. As police officers entered the dismantled barroom one evening in the fall of 1920, they interrupted Kalishes and his family as they ate dinner. Seeing a pitcher of wine on Kalishes's dinner table and finding three more bottles of wine in his cellar, the police arrested Kalishes and charged him with operating a nuisance, although he insisted that he had given up his barkeeping trade and that the wine was for his personal consumption. Though federal charges against Kalishes were eventually dropped, his experience exemplified many of the fears and resentments that ethnic New Yorkers harbored in regard to Prohibition. They felt harassed and spied upon, saw their livelihoods threatened, and found the privacy of their homes violated under a set of laws designed to make them conform with the social ideals of middle-class drys.[29]

What made the experiences of people like Joseph Logan, William Nienstadt, and Thomas Kalishes even more irksome to working-class New Yorkers was the sense that wealthier New Yorkers were accorded preferential treatment, if not left alone entirely, under the dry laws. In the summer of 1920, the relative immunity from the Volstead Act that accompanied wealth was demonstrated in a highly publicized incident at the exclusive Lamb's Club on West Forty-eighth Street. On the evening of August 8, 1920, a violent brawl broke out in the club between actor William Boyd, comedian John Slavin, and John McGraw, the part owner and manager of the New York Giants. According to press accounts of the incident, the brawl started after McGraw had consumed four bottles of whiskey in the Lamb's Club, at least one of which he allegedly purchased at the club. Despite appearances, the managers of the Lamb's Club vehemently denied that any liquor had been sold on the premises. A spokesman insisted that "any liquor in this club could have been brought in only in a bottle or in the members' stomachs."[30]

The suggestion that liquor was being sold in the Lamb's Club sparked public demands for the Bureau of Prohibition to investigate. Though the club pledged to cooperate with any investigation and insisted that liquor was not allowed on the premises, the following night police officers arrested two Lamb's Club employees and seized fifteen cases of liquor from the club. Again the club's managers professed innocence, arguing that if any liquor was present, it was the fault of the employees. James Shevlin, the district supervisor for the Bureau of Prohibition, initially exonerated the club, telling the press that he believed the Lamb's Club had nothing to do with the liquor involved in the McGraw incident. McGraw, however, soon confessed to the District Attorney's office that he had bought all four bottles in the club on the evening of the brawl. According to press accounts, McGraw admitted, "I had bought four bottles of whiskey. I remember there was one bottle of Old Grandad, one of Midvale and one of Melville. The last bottle I bought after a boy in the club had come to me and asked me if I didn't want to buy more." McGraw's disclosure prompted the NYPD to arrest a night clerk who worked at the Lamb's Club, but Shevlin continued to defend the club's administration and its members, maintaining that "if there is no evidence that the club knew of the reported sale of liquor, that will end the matter." Finally a federal investigation of the Lamb's Club led to the seizure of more liquor and an admission from Shevlin that alcohol was knowingly sold at the club, though it took more than three weeks for the bureau to take decisive action against the club's owners.[31]

The Bureau of Prohibition's reluctance to intervene in the Lamb's Club case was seen on the street as a blatant example of the double standard inherent in Prohibition enforcement. Editors for the *New York American* complained that "if the evidence involves an East Side café, the owner is arrested with his bartender. He is arraigned in court, the newspaper announcements of the capture are issued, and ultimately a fine is imposed on the owner of the café and a jail sentence on the bartender." Noting the Lamb's Club case, the editors argued that "if the evidence involves a West Side Club, with a more or less respectable membership, the whole procedure is different. Instead of arrest, there is deliberation; instead of prosecution, there is investigation; instead of announcement of the facts, there is silence or meaningless words." Considering that fifteen cases of liquor had been seized at the Lamb's Club while Yorkville bartenders were going to jail for selling single glasses of whiskey, the *American* argued, the social standing of the Lamb's Club members clearly influenced the way the case was handled by the Bureau of Prohibition.[32]

Though there were certainly instances in the early 1920s when the Bureau of Prohibition and the federal courts made examples of wealthy defendants, by and large upper-class New Yorkers could violate the Volstead Act as they pleased. With the dry lobby insisting on strict enforcement in ethnic communities, anti-vice groups like the Committee of Fourteen, the Bureau of Prohibition, and the NYPD all focused the bulk of their enforcement efforts on working-class establishments. Even when efforts were made to enforce Prohibition in wealthier circles, practical considerations complicated matters. For one, surveillance of elite private clubs like the Lamb's Club, the

Yale Club, and other elite midtown establishments proved nearly impossible. Investigators from the Committee of Fourteen found it difficult to gain access to such businesses, and reports on them rarely made their way into the committee's voluminous surveys of saloons and speakeasies in New York. Because private clubs were closed to the general public and needed none of the licenses required of dance halls, cabarets, or other nightlife establishments, they were never scrutinized as closely by the Bureau of Prohibition or the NYPD as were public establishments. Whereas Prohibition agents might raid as many as one hundred Lower East Side saloons on a single night in 1920, establishments patronized by the elite were largely left alone, targeted only from time to time when a point had to be made.

The ability of wealthy Prohibition violators to afford more effective legal counsel also had very clear implications for Prohibition enforcement. When wealthy defendants faced Prohibition charges, they could afford skilled lawyers to steer them safely through the legal system. Working-class defendants either resorted to hiring "shyster lawyers" in court hallways for ten dollars, or threw themselves at the mercy of the court and opted for plea bargains as the most expedient way to end their legal troubles.[33]

When an Italian-speaking immigrant named Giuseppi Conti did happen to secure the services of a lawyer, his counsel, Francis X. Hennessy, described to the court how daunting the system appeared to immigrants charged with Prohibition violations. Hennessy explained that his client had already appeared once at a hearing without legal representation, and was "unfamiliar with the practice in said court and is not sufficiently familiar with the English language to fully and completely understand and appreciate the matter set out in the indictment upon which he was arraigned." Through the efforts of his lawyer, Conti had the case against him dropped, but most working-class defendants were not so fortunate; those who could not afford the services of a lawyer simply accepted fines or short jail sentences. Others were encouraged to enter guilty pleas by bargain lawyers who feared that their immigrant clients would not be able to pay for more extensive legal representation.[34]

For their part, dry advocates expressed little concern that class bias had come to characterize Prohibition enforcement so clearly. Believing whole-heartedly that Prohibition's main purpose was to regulate the intemperate behavior of "foreign" groups and uplift the laboring classes, they looked at the law's disproportionate impact on the working classes as an indicator of its success rather than a cause for concern. To drys and other reformers, the effectiveness of Prohibition was to be measured by standards other than its fairness. Industrialists, professional associations, and charities expressed satisfaction in their belief that the dry experiment had reduced Monday absences, industrial accidents, illness, and other alcohol-related problems among the working class. Many industrialists clearly never thought the dry laws applied to them in the same way they applied to their employees. The journalist Matthew Josephson famously noted this irony after listening to the Chicago meatpacking magnate Louis Swift discuss the benefits of Prohibition for the working class while holding a cocktail in his hand. To Josephson, his exchange with Swift indicated that under Prohibition a two-tiered legal system had emerged in the United States in which Americans of higher social standing were exempt from the dry laws, while working-class Americans were expected to abide by the Volstead Act.[35]

Ironically, some of the reformers most devoted to helping New York's working class were also the most supportive of the class bias inherent in Prohibition's enforcement. Lillian Wald, the founder of Henry Street Settlement, acknowledged that Prohibition's effects were uneven in class terms, yet she defended the dry experiment because she felt it provided enormous benefits for the working classes among whom she worked on the Lower East Side. Under Prohibition, Wald argued, workers no longer spent their entire paychecks in saloons, which she believed would allow families to save more of their earnings and partake in the consumer bounty of the 1920s. Another settlement director, Dr. John Elliot of the Hudson Guild, made similar claims about Prohibition's effects in Chelsea. Having long regarded alcohol as a major problem in Chelsea's working-class community, with its concentration of dockworkers, longshoremen, and sailors, Elliot concluded that with the advent of Prohibition, "there is no question the Chelsea District is incomparably better than it was years ago." Dr. Maximilian Schulman of Manhattan's Vanderbilt Clinic made a similar observation. Noting a decrease in alcoholism cases at his clinic, Dr. Schulman argued that "whatever prohibition may have done for the idle rich, it certainly has done well for the laboring poor."[36]

Many New York employers supported the idea that Prohibition enforcement efforts should focus on the working class. These employers did not seem to care whether Prohibition was effective nationally (nor did they necessarily adhere to it themselves), but they were eager to see it enforced within their employees' communities. To aid Prohibition enforcement efforts, they guided investigators to speakeasies and saloons near their workplaces, which generally brought quick responses from the Bureau of Prohibition, the Police Department, or the Committee of Fourteen. The famed Prohibition agent Isidore "Izzy" Einstein later recalled that he spent a considerable amount of time responding to employer complaints about employee drinking, which resulted in raids near Mount Sinai Hospital, at the street car depots on upper Third Avenue, at the Staten Island shipyards, and at other employer-selected locales around the city.[37]

Einstein, generally regarded as one of the most comical figures of the era for his outlandish use of disguises and sense of humor, unwittingly reflected the biases that shaped Prohibition enforcement in New York. His recollections of enforcing the dry laws in New York show that from his first raid in a working-class saloon in Brooklyn to his last, the overwhelming focus of his job was to police drinking in the ethnic neighborhoods of the city. He recalled in his autobiography: "I got results . . . because I was able to pose as a foreigner in places where foreigners were catered to. I could speak German, Polish, Hungarian, Bohemian, Yiddish, and some Italian, and I knew the old world ways."[38]

Despite continuous surveillance and constant enforcement pressure, working-class resistance to Prohibition in New York remained insurmountable in the early 1920s. The best indicator of the widespread nature of this resistance came from the records of the Committee of Fourteen, which dedicated considerable resources during the Prohibition era to investigating the city's illegal saloons, speakeasies, bars, and cabarets. In its aggressive pursuit of evidence concerning prostitution, drinking, homosexuality, and other forms of illegal or immoral activity, the committee compiled thousands of reports that constitute one of the only comprehensive examinations of the underground drinking culture of New York in the 1920s.[39]

Using undercover investigators who spoke Yiddish, Russian, and Hungarian, among other languages, the Committee of Fourteen infiltrated a great variety of drinking establishments: the Russian Casino on Eldridge Street; the Odesser Café on Stanton Street; the Ruvo del Monte on West Ninth Street; nameless "black and tan" saloons in Harlem; and an abundance of dancehalls and ballrooms in midtown. Taken together, the Committee of Fourteen's reports detailed a thriving ethnic and working-class drinking culture in the city. They documented establishments that catered exclusively to Russians, Germans, or Italians, and others frequented by a mixture of Turkish, Spanish, Arabian, and Greek patrons. In some places, prostitution and other vices were openly proffered with booze, while others came across as innocent beer or cider halls. Taken as a whole, they collectively demonstrated not only that Prohibition had failed to dry up New York but also that drinking in the city was as entrenched as ever.[40]

The Committee of Fourteen's work had a direct bearing on the way Prohibition was enforced in the city. Though there were no official connections linking the committee and the Bureau of Prohibition, the committee's findings combined with the political pressure exerted by the Anti-Saloon League ensured that efforts to enforce the dry laws in the city in the early 1920s rarely strayed from the ethnic working class. The Bureau of Prohibition denied that it targeted ethnic drinking spots (and ethnic drinkers) any more than establishments in midtown or the theater district, but the press coverage of the bureau's efforts suggested that was not the case. Almost daily, New York's newspapers featured headlines like "Federal Dry Agents Raid Greek Cabaret" or "Find Oriental Rum in Chinatown Raid." Accounts of a 1921 sweep of working-class haunts along Eighth and Ninth Avenues identified twenty of those arrested in the raids as Irish, eight as Italian, five as Jewish, and eleven as German. A 1922 sweep of forty-eight establishments yielded similar results. Of those rounded up, nineteen had identifiably Irish surnames, ten were German, and five were Italian. Even when the Bureau of Prohibition did shift its focus to establishments catering to wealthier New Yorkers in more upscale neighborhoods, the arrests still fell upon the working-class Irish, Italian, or German waiters and bartenders. No matter where Prohibition was enforced in the city, it seemed ethnic and working-class New Yorkers were the ones most likely to end up in trouble with the law.[41]

The court records of the era invariably reflected this inherent bias in Prohibition enforcement. Despite claims from drys and Prohibition administrators that the law was being applied evenly to New Yorkers, the voluminous federal court records indicate that the large majority of defendants in Prohibition cases lived in ethnic working-class neighborhoods, and that the great majority of these defendants faced charges for small if not insignificant violations of the Volstead Act. In instance after instance, defendants who were otherwise law-abiding citizens were caught in trivial cases involving a bottle of wine or a shot of whiskey.[42]

The minor nature of these offenses was not lost on the federal judges, who were angered to see so many trivial cases involving minority defendants and so few cases involving major bootlegging syndicates or large-scale criminal enterprises. While the well-known racketeers and gangsters were amassing fortunes from the city's beer and liquor trades, Federal Judge Julian W. Mack considered the case of Mack McKinney, a black porter charged with selling a ten-cent glass of beer. Frustrated by the petty nature of the case, Mack released McKinney with a one-dollar fine. Afterward, Mack lamented that the law seemed to apply only to small offenders: "It seems a pity we cannot get some of the big fellows . . . It is too bad that the officers will only bring in poor fellows like Russian Jews, Greeks, Negroes and Italians on these violations."[43]

As tens of thousands of Prohibition cases wound through New York's federal district courts, the names on the docket might as well have come from the entry records at Ellis Island—Koenig, Plopinger, Pieratti, Murphy, McQuiston, Manzoni, Blumenstock, Shapiro, Bruno, Hochfelder, and Fitzgerald. The defendants were male and female, foreign-born and native, and from a wide range of occupations and trades. They were by no means innocent, and many openly admitted breaking the Volstead Act. (One defendant, an Italian restaurant owner named Joseph Saleo, yelled defiantly in court, "Lock me up . . . every wop around here is selling drinks, why can't I?")[44]

As they traded guilty pleas for reduced sentences and fines, they came to understand Prohibition as a distortion of the American principles of equal justice. Ethnic New Yorkers were clearly bearing a disproportionate burden of the dry experiment, yet drys paid little attention to this inequity. In response to complaints from labor groups that foreign-born workers were unhappy with Prohibition and the manner in which it was being enforced,

Prohibition Commissioner Roy Haynes asserted that "foreigners" in New York City were four times more likely to violate Prohibition laws than "citizens." William Anderson shared the same view. Angered by the lack of respect for the Eighteenth Amendment shown by ethnic and working-class New Yorkers, Anderson attributed the resistance to Prohibition in the city to "unwashed and wild-eyed foreigners who have no comprehension of the spirit of America." The Board of Temperance, Prohibition, and Public Morals of the Methodist Church similarly dismissed complaints of an unfair emphasis on ethnic drinking in Prohibition enforcement. It issued a statement saying, "If it is true that foreign-born laborers are rebellious against the country because of Prohibition, it may be said that the country is not being run for their benefit. If they do not like the way things are being done let them go back to Europe."[45]

The tension between ethnic New Yorkers and dry reformers grew even more contentious when religion entered the debate. Though Protestant drys made a show of trying to win support from Catholic and Jewish leaders before the ratification of the Eighteenth Amendment, by the early 1920s Catholics and Jews frequently found themselves demonized by influential Protestant organizations. At the center of the controversy was the issue of sacramental wine.

Under the initial terms of the Volstead Act, all households in the United States were entitled to an annual allowance of ten gallons of sacramental wine for religious use. This provision was written into the law at the request of Catholic and Jewish leaders, but from the outset it troubled dry advocates, who suspected that the provision would be abused. Rather than acknowledge the legitimate use of wine for religious purposes, William Anderson and other dry leaders argued that Catholics and Jews should substitute unfermented grape juice for wine as Protestant churches had done under Prohibition. This brought angry responses from Catholic clergy and Jewish leaders. The Catholic weekly *America,* for one, rejected the suggestion that drys had the right to dictate to Catholics how to practice their religion. The paper blasted Anderson for "telling Catholics, His Holiness included, what the Pope can do in regard to the Mass."[46]

As tensions between New York's Catholics and drys intensified, the dry lobby adopted an increasingly anti-Catholic tone. William Anderson in particular unleashed a torrent of anti-Catholic rhetoric, blaming "certain Catholics" for "endeavoring to break down Prohibition enforcement." In a letter addressed to the Protestant clergy of New York, Anderson further accused the Catholic Church of mounting an "assault on law and order" by working in conjunction with Tammany Hall to nullify the Prohibition laws. Arguing that Catholic Church officials were "indignant over what they consider a Protestant victory," Anderson accused the Catholic Church of taking part in "efforts to destroy [the Prohibition] victory and bring back the saloons."[47]

Anderson's widely publicized outburst provoked a heated response from New York's Catholic community. The spiritual leader of the city's Catholics, Archbishop Patrick J. Hayes, denounced Anderson as a "sinister figure in American politics . . . who sinks so low as to play the un-American role of a brewer of bigotry." Hayes angrily dismissed Anderson, adding, "Better for America that he had never been born." Catholic papers in New York and around the nation similarly protested Anderson's statements. The editors of *America* argued that Anderson and his fellow drys were using Prohibition to launch a new wave of religious persecution in the United States, while the Philadelphia-based *Catholic Standard and Daily Times* lamented that Anderson's comments represented "narrow-minded, stupid bigotry."[48]

With Catholic and non-Catholic writers expressing concern that the dry lobby was reviving the nativist campaign of the 1880s against "Rum, Romanism, and Rebellion," Anderson made no effort to reconcile with New York's Catholics. Instead, he rejected claims that he had unfairly criticized the Catholic Church, insisting that the Church was "in politics up to its neck" and that he would not be intimidated by efforts to keep him from speaking out against it. He insisted that he would not retract his comments about the Church's intent to undermine Prohibition unless Archbishop Hayes personally disavowed all attempts to legalize beer and wine and promised to oppose any changes to the federal Prohibition laws.[49]

The New York press corps was aghast that Anderson would make such demands of the archbishop, and they condemned Anderson's tirade. Many drys, by contrast, praised Anderson for standing up to the Catholic Church and, in some cases, took his comments further. The minister W. M. Hess of

Trinity Congregational Church defended Anderson, arguing that the Anti-Saloon League leader was simply stating "a simple truth that every intelligent person knows": that the Roman Catholic Church was the "most bigoted church in America." Explaining that a Catholic-Tammany conspiracy undoubtedly aimed to undermine Prohibition, Reverend Hess asked, "Will you tell me what else Tammany Hall has been during the last forty years, but a combination of Rum and Romanism?" He continued, "Is it not about time for the real Americans to drive the low-down, grafting, Irish Catholic rum-sellers and 'rummies' out of city politics?"[50]

With comments like these fueling greater animosity between New York's Catholics and drys, William Anderson's tirades against the Catholic Church would soon become the distinguishing characteristic of his tenure as state superintendent of the Anti-Saloon League. At one point, the Catholic weekly *Brooklyn Tablet* even argued that the Anti-Saloon League under Anderson had supplanted the Ku Klux Klan as the leading anti-Catholic organization in New York State.[51]

In 1923, Anderson further secured that reputation with a speech to a Methodist congregation in Kingston, New York, in which he commented on the recent resurgence of the Ku Klux Klan in the state: "I am not losing sleep grieving over the increase in the membership of the Klan," Anderson stated. He explained that Catholic priests and groups like the Knights of Columbus had made the Klan's reappearance inevitable, "since these anti-Protestant political forces directly kicked the Protestant churches in the face on the Prohibition issue." The Klan's resurgence, Anderson argued, was simply a natural and welcome response to Catholic opposition to the Eighteenth Amendment and "the aggression of these wet anti-Protestant forces." While Anderson's sensational comments exposed the dry leader's true character, they also revealed a deeper truth about the dry crusade as a whole. Its inability to impose its moral agenda by legislative means had brought out its nativism and an obsessive demonization of ethnic Catholics that would overshadow the rest of its agenda.[52]

Like the city's Catholics, New York's Jews also found themselves coming under attack by drys owing to conflicts between their religious practices and Prohibition. Initially, Jews had tried to stay out of the fray during debates over the Eighteenth Amendment because they feared persecution if they appeared to resist the campaign for Prohibition. As the reform rabbi Louis Wolsey argued, "Prohibition is an Anglo-Saxon Protestant issue that we Jews ought to keep out of." Privately, however, many of New York's Jews harbored the same fears that Catholics did—that Prohibition would serve as a vehicle for Protestant extremism, and that the nativism associated with the Eighteenth Amendment would result in the public persecution of Jews.[53]

Once the dry laws were enacted, however, criticism of the Prohibition experiment emerged as forcefully in the Jewish community as it had in the Catholic community. Both the *Jewish Daily Forward* and the *American Hebrew* expressed doubts about the wisdom of the Eighteenth Amendment, and Louis Marshall of the American Jewish Committee voiced his concerns that the Volstead Act showed little understanding of or respect for Jewish culture in the United States. Mostly, Marshall feared that Prohibition would lead to the vilification of American Jews as inassimilable "foreigners" beyond the reach of American law.[54]

As was the case with Catholics, the issue of sacramental wine was at the center of these concerns. Before the dry experiment began, reformers and temperance advocates had generally characterized Jews as temperate, law-abiding people who rarely frequented saloons. But as Jewish leaders like Louis Marshall had predicted, the arrival of Prohibition brought about a drastic change in attitude. As scandals and misunderstandings over the use of sacramental wine eclipsed any good will that had existed previously between Jews and the dry lobby, Jews were attacked as criminals looking to take advantage of the dry mandate.

At the root of the problem were federal provisions that failed to take into account how Jews used sacramental wine. Unlike Catholics, who generally used sacramental wine in a church mass under the direction of a priest, Jews commonly used wine in religious observances at home, meaning that sacramental wine circulated more widely in the Jewish community than it did in the Catholic community. To make matters worse, whereas the bureau was accustomed to dealing with the clearly delineated hierarchy of the Catholic Church, it was less comfortable working with rabbis, who belonged to no such formal organization. Because they found it difficult to verify the credentials of rabbis who applied for permits to distribute sacramental wine to their congregations, bureau officials grew suspicious, especially of rabbis of Eastern European origin.[55]

Unable to discern between legitimate and illegitimate requests for sacramental wine, the bureau found itself frequently duped early in the Prohibition experiment by fraudulent rabbis who inflated the sizes of their congregations to get more wine; sold wine to saloons; forged wine permits; took kickbacks from wineries; set up elaborate schemes to import wine illegally; or sold wine to gentiles using fake Jewish names.[56]

These abuses resulted in a flurry of negative press that proved highly embarrassing for New York's Jewish community. Sensational newspaper headlines announcing "Dry Agents Plan War upon Illicit Rabbis," "Jewish Rabbis Reap Fabulous Sums by Flouting Dry Law," and "Big Illicit Pools Selling Sacramental Wine" scandalized the city. The most newsworthy stories involved a Bronx rabbi who unsuccessfully tried to procure permits to buy $100,000 worth of champagne, vermouth, and sherry as sacramental wine, and the case of the Menorah Wine Company, a front set up by an olive oil dealer on the Lower East Side to import 750,000 gallons of fortified Malaga wine with a forged Bureau of Prohibition permit.[57]

Officials with the Bureau of Prohibition complained bitterly about these incidents, arguing that Jews had been given favorable treatment under the law only to take advantage of it. Assistant Prohibition Commissioner James E. Jones complained that these rabbis were "worse than ordinary bootleggers" for "violating the law in the name of religion," while Assistant Secretary of the Treasury Lincoln C. Andrews later complained that the sacramental wine problem was "almost exclusively on account of the Government's efforts to satisfy the Jewish faith." The problem existed, according to Andrews, because "the Jewish faith is not organized as our hierarchical churches are. There is no discipline and no control."[58]

The bureau responded to the sacramental wine problem in its own backhanded way. In the spring of 1921, New York's Jews discovered that their legal right to procure sacramental wine did not automatically guarantee the cooperation of the Bureau of Prohibition. When a New York paper headline announced, "Jews of City without Wine for Passover," the city's Jewish communities learned that no licenses had been issued to New York rabbis to allow them to distribute wine to their congregations for the Jewish holidays because of what the bureau termed "an administrative oversight." When more than one hundred rabbis protested about the shortage, the deputy commissioner of the Bureau of Prohibition acknowledged there had been an administrative foul-up, but argued that he could do nothing about it. Assistant District Attorney Joab Banton complained that the bureau's apathetic response demonstrated little regard for Jewish New Yorkers and proved that the authors of the Prohibition law "had in mind only the Christian faith."[59]

As Jewish leaders had feared, an anti-Semitic backlash accompanied the stories of bootlegging rabbis and sacramental wine scandals. Paralleling the resurgence of the Ku Klux Klan, anti-Semitism was already on the rise in the United States in the 1920s, and the stories emanating from New York about sacramental wine abuses and bootlegging rabbis only strengthened American perceptions of Jews as criminals. When Louis Marshall of the American Jewish Committee testified to the House Immigration Committee in 1922, he experienced the prejudice firsthand. As Marshall urged legislators to consider the effects of immigration restriction on European Jews, a congressman interrupted him to remind him that Jews were among the nation's foremost violators of the Volstead Law.[60]

Even more extreme was the vilification of Jews as Prohibition violators in the infamous *Dearborn Independent,* a Michigan newspaper published by Henry Ford. In a 1921 article, the *Independent* claimed that "bootlegging is a 95 percent controlled Jewish industry in which a certain class of rabbis have been active." Mocking the provisions of the Volstead Act that allowed the use of sacramental wine, the paper insisted that "'rabbinical wine' is a euphemism for whiskey, gin, Scotch, champagne, vermouth, absinthe, or any other kind of hard liquor." It concluded that "the illicit liquor business has always been Jewish, and it is not a cause for shame among the majority of Jews, sad to say; it is rather a cause for boast." To many of New York's Jews, these diatribes simply confirmed the biases lying beneath the surface of the Prohibition movement. They worried that continued dry agitation along these lines would breed a lasting and virulent anti-Semitism in the United States and result in further immigration restriction, quotas, and other measures against Jews.[61]

Fearing that the issue of sacramental wine would irreparably stigmatize the Jewish community, many Jewish leaders pledged to cooperate with the Bureau of Prohibition to crack down on the illegal trade in sacramental wine. Some Jewish leaders even argued, at least for the sake of appearance, that Jews should forgo sacramental wine altogether. In 1922, Cyrus Adler of the Jewish Theological Seminary and the Central Conference of American Rabbis publicly announced that the practice of Judaism did not require the use of sacramental wine. At a convention of Jewish leaders in 1923, the philanthropist Julius Rosenwald agreed that American Jews had no need for sacramental wine and argued that they should replace it with unfermented grape juice as Protestant churches had done. At Rosenwald's urging, the Union of American Hebrew Congregations passed a resolution stating that "fermented wines or spirituous liquors are not necessary for Jewish religious observance." These efforts to accommodate Prohibition enforcement won praise from dry leaders like William Anderson but caused a stir among orthodox rabbis in New York, who worried that giving up sacramental wine would be a dangerous break from religious tradition for the sake of accommodating Protestant extremists, in essence capitulation to the bullying of the dry lobby.[62]

The scapegoating of ethnic New Yorkers, Catholics, and Jews early in the Prohibition era ultimately had one overwhelming effect, which ran completely opposite of what drys like William Anderson had anticipated. The constant depiction of ethnic New Yorkers as delinquents who neither understood nor respected American culture and laws naturally prompted these people to reexamine their place in American society. Rather than accepting William Anderson's characterization of them as "unwashed and wild-eyed foreigners" and criminals, ethnic New Yorkers turned the assertions of the dry movement upside down, and began using their opposition to Prohibition to emphasize their own identities as ethnic Americans. Arguing that drys were actually the ones who failed to comprehend the spirit of America, ethnic New Yorkers began invoking American ideals of religious freedom and personal liberty in their defense, and derided Prohibition as nothing more than a determined effort by a vocal moral minority to deny them their rights as Americans.

As New Yorkers found a political voice to speak out against Prohibition, Representative Andrew Volstead of Minnesota, the author of the Volstead Act, became a primary target of their ire. At his office in Washington, Volstead found anonymous letters and postcards pouring in from New York City, expressing contempt for Volstead's role in crafting the mechanism of their oppression. One Lower East Side resident sarcastically wrote to Volstead, "Keep the good work up—the country is safe so long as ignorant bigots of your stripe direct things at Washington." In another letter to Volstead, penned in red and blue pencil for patriotic effect, a New Yorker attacked Volstead for his "drastic dry bone fanatical jackass laws." William Anderson received his fair share of criticism, too. A letter to the *Daily News* suggested that the country would "accomplish a great deed" if rather than deporting immigrants it were to deport "a few Prohibitionists like Anderson and his narrow minded ilk."[63]

It was just a start, but by trading barbs with the drys, ethnic New Yorkers began to challenge the nativism and political power of the Prohibitionists. Rather than remaining passive targets of reform, they now became active participants in the debate over Prohibition. For the remainder of the 1920s, they would grow increasingly vocal about claiming their stake in America as they opposed the dry laws. In the pages of newspapers, through civic associations, and in public demonstrations, ethnic New Yorkers began to present themselves as "real Americans," arguing that they exemplified American ideals better than old-stock Protestant drys did. Recasting Prohibition as a bigoted and unwise experiment, they began laying the groundwork for a political uprising against the dry movement.

On a hot July 4, 1921, one of the first clear signs that ethnic opposition to the noble experiment could be channeled into organized political activity came as thousands of New Yorkers marched against Prohibition in a protest parade up Fifth Avenue. Organized by the American Liberties League, the march featured Irish hansom cab drivers, members of the Sons of Italy and Garibaldi Association, representatives from German societies, and a division of African-American marchers, all carrying American flags and signs with slogans like "We're American Citizens, Not Inmates," and "We Prefer Brewers of Beer to Brewers of Bigotry." The parade combined displays of ethnic identity with traditional American political references, demonstrating that one could be ethnic, American, and a Prohibition opponent at the same time. Just as important, the parade gave ethnic New Yorkers the opportunity to show that they were not alone in opposing Prohibition, as they were joined along the parade route by Mayor Hylan, veterans groups, a contingent from the Grand Army of the Republic, and thousands of other "blue-blooded" Americans who opposed the dry laws just as vehemently as they did. It would take several more years for any truly effective political opposition to the Eighteenth Amendment to take shape, but the seeds for such a movement had been sown. In the meantime, drys would have their hands full trying to keep a defiant population of New Yorkers in check.[64]

The idea that resisting Prohibition could be an expression of Americanism had an infectious, liberating effect on the city. There was no telling where or when someone would be overtaken by the urge to strike a blow for liberty by defying the dry mandate. One Sunday afternoon in 1921, a few weeks before the July 4 parade, a Lower East Sider named Malkan Yelka led a much smaller, but just as remarkable, rally against Prohibition in his own neighborhood. Having just returned from a three-year stint in Wyoming, where he had worked as a cowpunch and a guide in Yellowstone Park, Yelka reunited with a group of old friends on the corner of Grand and Orchard Streets. Dressed up as an all-American cowboy in sheep-hide pants, a flannel shirt, bandana, and sombrero, Yelka launched into an impromptu speech against Prohibition. When a crowd gathered to see what Yelka was up to, he told the assembled group a little of what he had learned about personal liberty out West. He explained, "When we want something out in the big country, we get it." He then added, "A feller can get his beer in the big country and I'm going to get mine." Yelka then directed 200 onlookers, newly indoctrinated with the American cowboy spirit, in a march down Grand Street toward the Bowery. After chanting "We want beer" and letting out wild cowboy yells for a few city blocks, the marchers were dispersed by two bewildered patrolmen. The march disappeared as quickly as it had formed, but its message was clear. There would be no telling these Lower East Side cowboys that they were "foreigners." If the drys meant to push the issue, they would be in for a fight.[65]

More important, the gradual but unmistakable response of ethnic New Yorkers to the dry laws, and the resistance to the Eighteenth Amendment that had become a part of their daily lives, highlighted a fundamental flaw of the dry crusade. While purporting to advance a social agenda that would apply to all Americans, it had in fact promoted a campaign that singled out the urban, ethnic working class. It had done so not out of noble sentiments but out of distrust and fear of those who did not fit in to the dry crusade's vision of America. In the end, the nativism and moral inflexibility of the drys would provoke a resistance that would render the dry experiment untenable.

5
The Itch to Try New Things

On any given night during the Prohibition era, a crowd of actors, writers, dramatists, celebrities, and hangers-on would gather at Tony's, a popular Forty-ninth Street speakeasy known for its crowded bar, white cotton tablecloths, inedible Italian food, and plentiful supplies of liquor of questionable quality served in coffee cups. Tony's was stuffy and had no music, but the regulars loved it anyway for its $1.25 drinks and its host, Tony Soma. A former hotel waiter who got started in the speakeasy business with a supply of bootleg liquor procured from a dentist, Tony treated his patrons well, especially the actors and actresses who showed up nightly. He sang for them, encouraged pranks and merriment of all sorts, and took care to see that the ladies didn't drink too much. Tony took his responsibilities as host seriously, as he explained years later: "I was doing a service to humanity, to the intelligentsia."[1]

According to legend, the humorist Robert Benchley stood at Tony's bar one evening in the early 1920s, turned to his best friend, Dorothy Parker, and cracked, "Let's find out what all the fuss is about." He then stunned his friends by downing a gin-and-juice concoction called an "Orange Blossom." Though Benchley had frequented the midtown speakeasy scene with his colleagues from *Vanity Fair* and the *New York World* for several months, he had to this point studiously avoided alcohol. While his friends indulged themselves with round after round of bootleg liquor, Benchley had consumed only juice and soft drinks. Now, at age thirty-one,

Benchley gave in to the allure of the speakeasy and took the first drink of his life.[2]

Like much of the lore of the Prohibition era, the details behind the story of Benchley's first drink are unclear. By another account, Benchley had his first cocktail in 1921 in a speakeasy with playwright Robert Sherwood and Zelda and F. Scott Fitzgerald. Another version has writer Donald Ogden Stewart offering Benchley his first drink at the Yale Club. Yet another has Benchley drinking a Manhattan at a dinner party thrown for him by *Vanity Fair* editor Frank Crowninshield. The exact facts of the story, however, matter much less than what they illustrate. Regardless of when and where Robert Benchley took his first drink, until Prohibition came along he had, in spite of the company he kept, embodied the traditional middle-class Protestant dry. Something about the dry experiment changed Benchley's attitude toward alcohol. He became emblematic of a cultural rebellion against Prohibition that rejected the dry crusade's moral vision for America.[3]

The scale of Benchley's transformation was striking. Born in 1889 and reared in Worcester, Massachusetts, by a mother who made no secret of her distaste for alcohol, Benchley grew up constantly reminded of the menace of demon rum. Liquor was forbidden in the Benchley household, and young Robert heard of its dangers firsthand as an adolescent when the temperance firebrand Carry Nation spoke at his Sunday school. While a student at Harvard, Benchley dutifully shunned alcohol despite the beer- and liquor-infused revelries of his classmates. In a paper for his government class, he praised Worcester's dry laws for improving the moral, social, and economic well-being of his hometown. In 1915, Benchley campaigned for the Prohibition Party's gubernatorial candidate for Massachusetts, and in 1916 he wrote an editorial for *Collier's* in support of Prohibition. When the Eighteenth Amendment was ratified in 1919, Benchley joyously noted in his journal, "I never thought I'd live to see this . . . it is almost too good to be true."[4]

After the enactment of the Eighteenth Amendment, Benchley briefly remained true to his Prohibitionist rearing. He chided his friends and coworkers in New York's publishing circles about their drinking, telling them it was bad for their health and made people act unlike themselves. In an early visit to a speakeasy with friends, Benchley tasted a cocktail, scowled, and joked, "I hope this place is closed by the police." Yet in a short time, all vestiges of the Prohibitionist in Benchley vanished. Like many of his friends and fellow writers, Benchley began drinking heavily and would continue to do so for the duration of the Prohibition era. By the mid-1920s, his daily routine consisted of a late breakfast, a writing stint in his hotel room, a late lunch at the Algonquin Hotel, various errands, meetings, and afternoon phone calls, all followed by up to ten hours of drinking and socializing with writers, editors, publishers, and theater personalities, interrupted only by dinner and the Broadway performances Benchley reviewed. He became a fixture at Tony's, Jack and Charlie's, the Savoy, Polly Adler's, Dickie Well's, the Nest, and countless other speakeasies and nightclubs around New York City. His appetite for alcohol, and the New York nightlife that accompanied it, became the stuff of legend. By one account, Benchley once visited thirty-eight speakeasies and clubs in a single night, yet according to his friends he held his liquor so well that only rarely did he display signs of intoxication.[5]

Some of Benchley's drinking was strictly business: the socializing that went on in speakeasies was a central part of the literary and theatrical world that Benchley inhabited. His book deals with his publisher and Harvard classmate Henry Holt, for example, were cemented by late nights spent together at Jack and Charlie's, where each would drink from his own bottle of booze. Liquor also fueled Benchley's witty essays and aphorisms, which became hallmarks of American humor in the 1920s. Yet as with so many others of his generation, Benchley's drinking eventually and tragically caught up with him. A hard drinker to the very end, the one-time Prohibitionist ultimately died from complications of cirrhosis of the liver in 1945.[6]

Prohibition-era converts to the wet life like Benchley were myriad. Within his immediate circle, Benchley's friend Dorothy Parker had never smoked and had rarely drunk before Prohibition, complaining that the taste of liquor made her sick. Yet Prohibition transformed her into a drinker as legendary as Benchley. Throughout the 1920s, Parker imbibed prodigious quantities of bootleg whiskey, which she nicknamed "White Hearse," and matched Benchley and other companions drink for drink as they made their nightly rounds of the city's speakeasies. The famous cocktail parties in her room at the Algonquin Hotel attracted such social luminaries as Irving Berlin, Tallulah Bankhead, and Harpo Marx. Parker ultimately suffered

Benchley's fate as well, succumbing to alcoholism years later in a slower, though equally tragic, fashion.[7]

For every Robert Benchley and Dorothy Parker, there were thousands of less-notable New Yorkers who also took to drinking, and drinking heavily, precisely during the one period in American history when it was illegal. Part of the trend was undoubtedly tied to the end of World War I; heavy drinking was a reaction to the catastrophic devastation of a conflict whose savagery caught so many Americans off guard. The sense of social liberation that followed the end of the conflict reflected Americans' desire to leave behind the horrors of the war. Robert Benchley's son Nathaniel later offered a simpler but equally valid explanation: "It was fun to drink and fun to mock the law and it was considered rude not to accept a drink that was offered to you."[8]

Most of all, New Yorkers drank during Prohibition despite knowing that it was illegal and bad for them (especially given the often abysmal quality of bootleg liquor) because drinking was a form of cultural rebellion against the heavy-handed moralism of the dry lobby and its insistence that all Americans adhere to the same social mores. Buying bootleg liquor, frequenting speakeasies, risking being caught in a nightclub raid, and drinking all became ways to reject the moral standards that Prohibitionists had forced into the Constitution. New Yorkers, even New Yorkers who had once been sympathetic to the dry cause, now opted to embrace metropolitan culture and the new set of values being forged in the city in the 1920s.

On the surface, the significance of New Yorkers' cultural rebellion against Prohibition might be hard to discern. The emphasis placed on drinking and dancing could easily be dismissed as a shallow form of weekend escapism that was destined to fade with the memories of a few wild evenings. But the cumulative effect of New Yorkers' resistance to the dry laws was tremendous, as it ultimately doomed national Prohibition. By the mid-1920s, New Yorkers were growing bolder in their defiance of the dry laws and the paternalism of the Anti-Saloon League. As the cultural rebellion against Prohibition expanded to encompass an ever-widening cross-section of the city's populace, it not only drew away the middle-class New Yorkers whom the dry movement had counted on as stalwart supporters, but also gave the rebellion against the dry laws an air of "smartness" and sophistication rather than criminality. For middle-class New Yorkers especially, refusing to comply with the federal Prohibition laws became a form of self-liberation and a way to reinvent oneself within the context of the urban culture of the 1920s. By opposing the dry ideal, the inhabitants of the city were now giving notice that they refused to live under any vision of America other than their own.

As the Prohibition experiment entered its middle years, a new set of questions emerged that redefined how New Yorkers experienced the dry laws: *Are you cosmopolitan? Are you sophisticated? Are you a modern New Yorker?*

By the mid-1920s, Prohibition had reshaped myriad aspects of the city, and New York's response to the dry experiment continued to play a major role in defining the culture of the era. As New Yorkers from all levels of society delved deeper into the city's nightlife, listening to jazz and drinking plentifully, they also mixed more readily with people from different social backgrounds. In doing so, they created a more cosmopolitan social environment than could have existed a generation earlier. Although the Anti-Saloon League and other dry proponents had always insisted that Prohibition would create a stricter social order in the city, the noble experiment seemed instead to be dissolving the traditional boundaries that had defined city life as New Yorkers lost themselves in a search for spectacle, amusement, and personal liberation.

This reformulation of city culture was not the sudden product of the 1920s, brought about spontaneously by the mixing of illegal liquor, dancing, and jazz. New York had been building toward this moment for a generation. Well before the final arrival of Prohibition, New Yorkers from all walks of life had begun to explore new ideas, identities, and modes of behavior. As they did so, they also learned to move about the city's environs more freely, exploring nightclubs, cabarets, bars, theaters, and other public and semi-public spaces where traditional class boundaries and social roles seemed to matter less and less. As different classes and social groups came together more frequently, city culture in the 1920s became less about keeping people in their place and much more about challenging the social boundaries of previous generations.[9]

In defiance of the Eighteenth Amendment, nightclubs, cabarets, and speakeasies sprung up in response to New Yorkers' desire to explore the city's nightlife. It seemed that the Anti-Saloon League's attempt to stamp out the sale of alcohol in the city, and all forms of urban amusement linked to it, only made New York's nightlife more varied and alluring. Ironically, the dry reformers who had intended to assert absolute control over the city's night-life through the dry laws now found that their actions instead fostered the creation of an extensive underground culture of drinking, dancing, and un-regulated amusement that was much faster paced and far more daring than anything the city had seen before.

Mapping the world of speakeasies and nightclubs that emerged in New York City during the Prohibition era presents a difficult challenge. While some clubs basked briefly in fame or notoriety, most of the tens of thou-sands of illegal establishments that hid in the shadow of the Eighteenth Amendment came and went unnoted. For obvious reasons, the owners of these clubs, the bartenders who plied their trade in them, and the bootleg-gers who supplied them kept no detailed records of their illegal enterprises. Without the tax receipts or business records generated by a legal trade, it is impossible to know how many New Yorkers they served or how much money they made. It is equally difficult to determine how many of New York's six million inhabitants participated in this underground culture in the 1920s. Though arrest records and court proceedings detailed the legal travails of tens of thousands of New Yorkers who ran afoul of the dry laws, most New Yorkers who defied the Eighteenth Amendment never saw the inside of a courtroom or a jail cell. Nonetheless, both dry and wet observers alike could not help noticing the effects of the cultural rebellion they em-bodied.

Beginning in the early 1920s, New Yorkers' attitudes toward alcohol were clearly changing because of Prohibition. New Yorkers could never be said to have opposed drinking, but the consumption of alcohol under Pro-hibition suddenly took on greater social significance and a cachet that it had not had in previous generations. As early as 1921, the *Irish World* noted that "one of the most surprising results of our new policy is that many who were entirely indifferent to alcohol have begun to drink it out of a sort of defiance of that kind of legislation, and because it requires secrecy and smartness." Rather than dampening New Yorkers' interest in alcohol, the dry experiment only increased its appeal. In 1927 George Schuyler, a columnist for Harlem's *Amsterdam News,* noted how widely accepted that drinking had become in spite of the dry laws. "Now that the social taboo is off the booze," he wrote, "people are drinking more and more people are drinking." The best explanation of the trend, according to Martha Bensley Bruère, a veteran of the city's reform circles, was that Jazz Age New Yorkers were embracing "a much more cosmopolitan way of life." Regardless of the dry lobby's efforts to dictate its moral and social standards to the city, New Yorkers were exhibiting "a greater toleration of other ways, as well as an itch to try new things."[10]

This "itch to try new things" did not mean that drinking itself was novel. But the *way* New Yorkers were drinking in the 1920s was certainly new. With the onset of Prohibition, procuring a drink had turned into a game of cunning and wit. Men would surreptitiously ask for "ginger ale" in bars, hoping the bartender would respond with a wink and the query, "Imported or domestic?" "If the customer wants imported ginger ale, and he is the right kind of customer," an article in the *Literary Digest* explained, "he gets a regulation pre-Prohibition highball."[11]

At Broadway roof gardens and fashionable nightspots, well-dressed gentlemen took to carrying hip flasks. To accommodate them, the establishments they patronized did a brisk business in "set ups," bringing glasses, a bucket of ice, and ginger ale or soda water to the table. Neither party needed to mention the alcohol. It was understood by all what the "set up" was meant for, and just as clearly understood that any alcohol present would remain out of sight.[12]

As a columnist for the *New Republic* argued in 1922, the defiant response to the dry mandate in the city was creating both a new New York and a new New Yorker. In a piece entitled "New York's Cocktail Hour," H. I. Brock explained that New Yorkers of the 1920s were in no mood for the rules and regulations proffered by Prohibitionists and other moral reformers. Having been subjected to a ban on alcohol, a ban on smoking in the subway, a ban on women's smoking in hotel dining rooms, and a ban on walking on the grass in Central Park, New Yorkers had "reached the limit of patience with being told not to do things [that are] obviously good for everybody to do." As a result, Brock argued, New Yorkers had grown more determined to skirt all these prohibitions, especially the prohibition of alcohol.[13]

In fact, one's ability to defy the dictates of the "Forbidden City" became a hallmark of New York identity in the 1920s. To be sophisticated or "in the know," one had to master the art of dodging the manifold prohibitions that reformers had attempted to impose on city residents. To illustrate his point, Brock admiringly recounted an exchange he witnessed in a restaurant between a waiter and two patrons. When the diners requested two highballs, the waiter asked, "Do you know anybody?" The one guest pointed at his companion and replied with a smile, "I know him, and he knows me." With that, Brock noted, "the waiter fetched the drinks," for "these, unmistakably, were true New Yorkers, qualified to be served."[14]

Initially, the dining and drinking culture of the city had difficulty keeping up with New Yorkers' demands. The fact that so many New Yorkers insisted on the freedom to drink as they pleased posed a quandary for many of the city's old-guard dining establishments, which were overrun by patrons who expected to be served alcohol, illegal or not. The fashionable Delmonico's at Fifth Avenue and Forty-fourth Street was a case in point. Renowned as one of New York's most lavish and civilized gathering places since the Civil War era, Delmonico's remained popular into the Prohibition era with patrons determined to be served alcohol. In fact, when a party of Prohibition agents and a "fashionably dressed" female companion visited one of the restaurant's Saturday afternoon tea dances in 1921, they found a crowd of well-dressed parties waiting over an hour for a table. Once the parties had paid their cover charge and been seated, the agents saw why. They matter-of-factly told their waiter, "We'll have a round of Scotch and gin," and were promptly served the drinks.[15]

The proprietors of Delmonico's had no choice but to serve liquor. Their competitors at Mouquin's, Shanley's, and Maxim's were all serving alcohol as well. If they didn't, the discerning New Yorkers who patronized these establishments would take their business elsewhere. In this sense, Prohibition gave many of New York's highest-profile gastronomic institutions the choice of a quick death or a slow death. Economically, they were doomed to fail without the revenue derived from alcohol sales, but if they defied the dry law, the authorities were bound to catch up with such high-profile offenders. Of the most famous, Mouquin's went the quickest, lasting only six months into Prohibition. Sherry's closed soon after. Delmonico's, by contrast, lasted until 1923, though it too finally succumbed to Prohibition, no longer able to compete as a legitimate business.[16]

The demise of these *grande dames* of New York dining by no means marked the end of New York City nightlife. Instead, the city experienced more of a changing of the guard. When the pressures of Prohibition made survival impossible for fancy hotels, restaurants, and lobster palaces, the nightlife of New York simply evolved. Institutions like Delmonico's and Shanley's gave way to newcomers who emphasized drinking and dancing more than dining, and speakeasies and nightclubs became the city's preferred gathering spots.[17]

By the mid-1920s, journalist Stanley Walker explained, the city had different expectations of its nightlife. New York's "new children of the night wanted a gay show, swift dance music, and no curfew." That, along with plenty of liquor, was what they got in the form of the Palais Royal, the Moulin Rouge, the Bal Tabarin, the Beaux Arts Café, the Montmartre, the Tent, the Monte Carlo, and the scores of other nightclubs that opened in the middle years of the Prohibition era, each of which in its own way reflected the urban sensibility of a city opposed to the dry experiment.[18]

In February 1925, a new magazine landed on New York City's newsstands. It was *The New Yorker.* In its first issue, a columnist writing under the name "Van Bibber III" asked, "Have you observed, of late, how fastidious everyone has become in the matter of liquor? Not only a particular brand, but a definitive vintage and especially shaped bottle are now almost always demanded." Drinking had become not simply an act of defiance in New York, Van Bibber noted, but a mark of social status. "We sniff and scrutinize with the utmost care," he added. "What a change from the first year of the Eighteenth Amendment, when cocktails were manufactured out of anything liquid, and whatever had a kick passed muster."[19]

Brash, sassy, and humorous, *The New Yorker* came onto the scene in the middle years of the Prohibition era as a magazine uniquely in tune with the changing city and its rebellion against the noble experiment. Famously pronounced by its editor Harold Ross as "the magazine which is not edited for the old lady in Dubuque," *The New Yorker* was meant to be "a reflection in word and picture of metropolitan life." As Ross phrased it, *The New Yorker* would be published expressly for a "metropolitan audience" and speak the language of city life.[20]

While Ross clearly wanted *The New Yorker* to attract a sophisticated readership, accomplishing this task proved harder than anticipated. The first issue of the magazine was met with stinging criticism by publishing industry insiders, who found it provincial and insular, as if written for an audience so "in the know" that it may as well have numbered in the dozens. The magazine's small staff struggled to come up with material to fill the publication, and by August 1925, *The New Yorker*'s circulation had plummeted from an initial 15,000 to a mere 2,700. At that point, publisher Raoul Fleischmann planned to cease publication of the magazine, but spared it after a last-minute change of heart.[21]

Part of *The New Yorker*'s problem was that it had not yet found its identity or its audience. Ross paradoxically wanted *The New Yorker* to have the feel of a village newspaper while at the same time reflecting the smart, sophisticated, urban culture of 1920s New York. If the challenge for the new magazine was to find a way to connect with New Yorkers, Ross stumbled onto the answer, or at least part of the answer, as the magazine cemented its reputation as a chronicler of New York City nightlife.

In November 1925, *The New Yorker* published a piece by the young socialite Ellin Mackay entitled, "Why We Go to Cabarets: A Post-Debutante Explains." In it Mackay, the twenty-two-year-old daughter of American Post and Telegraph Company president Clarence Mackay, raised eyebrows by explaining why young society women like herself were so enthralled with the city's cabaret scene. Having already earned notoriety in New York society circles for her romantic involvement with the composer Irving Berlin (whom she would marry a few months later), Mackay shocked high society by pronouncing society parties, and young society men in particular, unbearably dull, and voicing her preference for the more unpredictable cabaret, where she could dance and talk (and drink) with whomever she pleased.[22]

Ellin Mackay's piece on cabarets captured exactly the tone *The New Yorker* had been striving for—iconoclastic, honest, sophisticated, and funny.

The issue sold out on the newsstands, and Mackay's article gave the fledgling magazine a badly needed commercial boost. Some staffers credited it with saving the magazine, and as a token of his gratitude Harold Ross gave Mackay a lifetime subscription to the magazine.[23]

More important, Mackay's piece paved the way for what would become a central part of *The New Yorker*'s appeal in the mid-1920s: its unflinching coverage of what went on in the city after dark. After Mackay's success, Ross assigned staff writer Charles Baskerville to "report [on] what you think amusing." The result was a weekly column entitled "When Nights Are Bold," which gave New Yorkers a cheeky look into New York's nightclubs, speakeasies, and cabarets, the people who ran them, and the people who frequented them. Ross paid Baskerville a pittance for the column, but Baskerville, writing under the pen name "Top Hat," was delighted to have the opportunity to explore the city's nocturnal amusements on Harold Ross's dime. A few months later, Baskerville's duties were transferred to Lois Long, a twenty-two-year-old theater critic and editor hired from *Vanity Fair*. Renamed "Tables for Two" and printed under the byline "Lipstick," Long's column gave readers spirited accounts of city life between dusk and dawn and set *The New Yorker*'s standard for nightclub reporting.[24]

"This town is night club mad," Baskerville wrote in one of his 1925 columns, and reporting on the city's nightclub madness proved to be a task for which *The New Yorker* was ideally suited. With its weekly quota of pages to fill and its desire to cater to the "metropolitan interest," *The New Yorker* was uniquely positioned to capitalize on the city's nightlife. It quickly became the must-read publication in New York's "smart" circles, and by the end of the decade sales of *The New Yorker* grew to constitute 35 percent of all weekly magazines sold at newsstands in neighborhoods like Greenwich Village. By the end of the decade, its circulation had surpassed 100,000. In terms of advertising pages, it had become one of the top three magazines in the country, evidence of its influential role in shaping the tastes of the city, if not the nation.[25]

"Night club mad" New Yorkers were fortunate to have a resource like *The New Yorker*. Without it, navigating the city's nightlife would have been impossible. Even with it, probably no more than a fraction of the nightclubs, speakeasies, cafés, cabarets, barrooms, grills, and hotel lounges that provided the backdrop for the city's nightly revelries were covered. Though Baskerville or Long might mention ten to twenty establishments a week in their columns, by some estimates there were more than 5,000 illegal speakeasies in Manhattan at the height of the Prohibition era, and another 10,000 at least in Brooklyn. At one point, the Police Department estimated the number of illegal drinking establishments in the city to be as high as 35,000, with 2,200 in the Wall Street area alone. No one knew for certain. Given what Baskerville described as the "mushroom-like" proliferation of speakeasies and nightclubs in the city, even the most skilled observers of New York nightlife had trouble keeping track.[26]

The variety of New York's Prohibition-era drinking spots was mind-boggling. The most prolific form, however, was the speakeasy. Likely derived from the "speak-softly shops" of nineteenth-century England, where smuggled, untaxed liquor could be bought cheaply, the term "speakeasy" served in New York as a catch-all phrase for illegal bars ranging from cellar dives peddling twenty-five-cent beers or fifty-cent glasses of "smoke," to fancy townhouses in midtown outfitted with multiple bars, dining areas, game rooms, and live entertainment. Speakeasies could easily be hidden in storefronts, office buildings, or apartment houses. An early survey of speakeasies published by *Variety* in 1921 noted that "they nest in empty lofts, former dancing studios, the lower floors of old English basements and high stoop houses, in flats and wherever one can imagine." Another article noted that they could be "found in every conceivable place, from a cellar to the fashionable blocks of the 50s and 70s." They could be found high, like the exclusive Cloud Club nestled at the top of the Chrysler Building, or low, like the basement speakeasies that dotted the business district. In fact, part of the appeal speakeasies held for New Yorkers seemed to be the unpredictable nature of their locations. Whether these gathering places were tucked away in construction sites, hidden in apartment back rooms, disguised behind receptionists' desks in office buildings, or brazenly situated across from police precinct houses, New Yorkers delighted in discovering the locations of speakeasies as if it were all part of a game. The journalist Stanley Walker recalled an apocryphal case in which a well-to-do young man slowly realized that the speakeasy he had been drinking in for hours one evening was "vaguely familiar." It slowly dawned on him that the bar in which he found himself was in fact located in his childhood home, and that he was standing in what had once been his nursery.[27]

New York's speakeasies were as remarkable in their mood, tone, and décor as they were in their location. Unlike old-fashioned saloons, which had always been comforting in their familiarity, speakeasies were full of surprises. Some evoked the fancy cocktail bars of the previous generation. As if witnessing a mirage, *The New Yorker* columnist Morris Markey described entering one Wall Street speakeasy and being transported back in time by the apparition of "six white-coated fellows . . . flinging the shakers up and down lustily to the tune of rattling ice . . . while the faintly sweet aroma of gin floated back through the crowd pressed against the rail." It was, he rejoiced, "the most friendly sight."[28]

Others went far beyond mere "friendly sights." The Park Avenue Club, one of the city's grandest nightclubs, boasted an interior by the famed Viennese designer Joseph Urban and featured an octagonal bar and floor-to-ceiling mirrors. The Country Club featured a miniature golf course. The Marlborough House, described by some as the "crème de la crème" of New York's speakeasies, sported a pearl entry buzzer, silver leather banquettes, and a hammered brass ceiling in its upstairs cabaret room. Symbolically, their excess catered to New Yorkers' desire for spectacle as it simultaneously rejected the dry movement's desire to foster an American culture based on respectability, sobriety, and restraint.[29]

At the other extreme were speakeasies that completely lacked charm or any sense of taste. These were bare-bones affairs devoid of ritual or feeling, and only modestly equipped to dispense liquor until the law caught up with them. Given the high costs of bootleg liquor and "protection," such places offered none of the generosities—meaning no free lunches and no free drinks—that had been mainstays of working-class saloons. Even these low-end speakeasies charged two to ten times more for drinks than pre-Prohibition saloons had, and the quality of the booze they served was far inferior. Their "gin" was often industrial alcohol mixed with glycerin and oil of juniper, while their "scotch" was made from grain alcohol colored with prune juice, creosote, or Moxie. Further, as one European observer noted, the food, if they served food at all, was "almost always poor, and the service deplorable." Still, even in their ramshackle squalor, they served as a rejection of the dry movement's ideals just as effectively as did the high-end night-clubs.[30]

Whether high-end or low-end, all speakeasies were vehicles of self-expression for the individuals or groups of patrons who frequented them. The owners supplied the décor, the bartender, and the booze, but the patrons provided the character. *The New Yorker's* copy editors, for example, seeking refuge from their tight deadlines, would take over John Peron's early in the morning to curse their editor, Harold Ross. Their presence, and their drinking schedules, gave the place its personality. Catering to college students, bars like the Pre-Catalan and Matt Winkle's enjoyed a popularity with visiting Ivy Leaguers that was boosted by favorable mentions in the Yale and Harvard student papers. For artists and writers, there was the aptly named Jack Bleeck's Artists and Writers, located conveniently next to the offices of the *New York Tribune*. Other speakeasies catered to lawyers, judges, teachers, songwriters, musicians, politicians, or criminals, each accommodating the drinking habits of its patrons. In short, whether seedy or sophisticated, a speakeasy was available in New York for everyone. Taken together, they represented a wide cross-section of New York and a collective statement that the city refused to abide by the dry agenda.[31]

The variety of experiences to be found after dark in New York increased exponentially as one moved from speakeasies, where the emphasis was primarily on drink, to nightclubs and cabarets, where the emphasis was on a combination of entertainment and drink. Though the difference was subtle, nightclubs and cabarets occupied a different place in the city's nightlife. Unlike speakeasies, which were illegal in a theoretically dry nation, and were therefore forced to maintain a level of secrecy in their operations, nightclubs and cabarets could brazenly claim to be legal entertainment ventures because the revues and musical performances they presented nightly helped legitimate their existence. Still, illegal liquor could be had in them just as easily as in speakeasies, depending on whom you asked and how.

Because they were legal, nightclubs and cabarets tended to be harder to shut down and, thus, lived longer than did speakeasies. This allowed their owners to invest more in entertainment and décor, which produced a dazzling array of venues scattered throughout the city, each offering a unique nightlife experience and a bold statement against Prohibition. As "Lipstick" and "Top Hat" mapped out the terrain of the city's nightclubs and cabarets for *The New Yorker,* they illuminated a world ranging from bohemian haunts in Greenwich Village to gaudy party palaces in midtown to mixed-race "black and tans" in Harlem to exclusive Fifth Avenue social clubs. Their variety was a critical part of their appeal. By stepping into one of New York's nightclubs, one could suddenly be transported to an ocean liner, a Hungarian village, a pirate's den, an antebellum plantation, an old-fashioned Parisian café, an ultra-modern European casino, a bohemian tearoom, or a luxurious country club. Some, like the Mayfair Yacht Club, offered propriety, while the Club Pansy offered female impersonators. The entertainment could range from Fred and Adele Astaire dancing at the Trocadero, to scantily clad dancing girls at the Club Richman, to "filthy" songs at the Nest, to the Drool Inn in Harlem, where, it was said, "the fun was excruciatingly lowdown."[32]

In terms of themes and décor, club names alone indicated that nothing was too over the top or too esoteric for a New York nightclub. There was the Aquarium with its giant fish tank, the Club Alabam, Baghdad-on-the-Roof, the Circus, Frau Greta's, Cowboy, and the Cave of the Fallen Angels. There was the Wing Club on Fifty-second Street, a favorite with airline pilots. Some clubs were living monuments to the celebrity of an owner or entertainer: Jimmy Durante had his Club Durant, Harry Richman had Club Richman, Helen Morgan had Helen Morgan's, and racketeer Larry Fay had in succession El Fey, Del Fey, and Fay's Follies. Raids, renovations, and a steady stream of openings and closings kept the mix constantly changing.

In spite of their variety, most of New York's nightclubs and cabarets still shared a few common characteristics. Because high-end establishments undoubtedly set the standard for the nightclub trade, nearly all clubs participated in a culture within which lavish displays of wealth, profligate spending, and conspicuous consumption were the norm. The most reliable indicators of this excess were the prices charged by nightclubs, which ranged from high to astronomical. At a time when the average American earned about $100 a month, membership fees at New York City nightclubs ranged from $10 at the Embassy Club to $100 at the more exclusive Regent Club. At Charlot's Rendezvous, the cover charge was $5, while the Lido and Heigh-Ho both charged $15, and the Montmartre $20. A bottle of ginger ale in a nightclub might cost a dollar, and a pitcher of water two dollars. A pint of whiskey cost $10 at many clubs, and at Larry Fay's clubs a quart of champagne ran $20. Patrons, however, hardly batted an eye at these prices, as paying ungodly sums of money to be entertained while drinking bootleg liquor was part of the experience. As Stanley Walker explained it, paying exorbitant sums was to some an aphrodisiac, and to others "a form of exhibitionism." Many professionals simply brushed off the expense of nightclubbing as part of city life, a necessary expense in the course of courting clients and entertaining associates. No one seemed to complain, as it was all part of the "smart" culture of the mid-1920s. After a particularly lavish night spent in Larry Fay's club, one patron explained to Walker, "It was $1,300 for the evening for me and my four or five friends. But I was glad to pay it. It was worth it. I had a hell of a good time."[33]

The level of spending in 1920s nightclubs presented one of the greatest contrasts to the pre-Prohibition drinking culture of the city. Before the Eighteenth Amendment, nickel beers and ten-cent whiskeys in saloons had been the norm, and there had been nothing pretentious or extravagant about them. While the elite had cultivated a taste for more elaborate cocktails during the Gilded Age, their tastes had by no means set the standard for the drinking culture of the city. But to New Yorkers of the 1920s, the newest nightclubs, cabarets, and speakeasies defined urban sophistication, and if New Yorkers had to spend large sums of money to be a part of the scene, many were willing to do so.

In spite of the expense, or perhaps because of it, New Yorkers gravitated to the nightclub culture as a way to leave their everyday lives behind and reinvent themselves. The spectacular décor, the entertainment, and the exhilarating experience of breaking the law in a nightclub or cabaret attracted a mixture of people from all levels of society. Whether midtown clerks, Fifth Avenue socialites, Irish politicians, street toughs, plumbers, or housewives, patrons were transported by the sense of freedom and possibility brought about by dancing and drinking in an unregulated environment with unfamiliar people.

As a cosmopolitan atmosphere was critical to a nightclub's success, the primary challenge for nightclub owners was to maintain the appearance of exclusivity while still drawing an interesting mixture of people. Nightclub owners knew very well that absolute exclusivity was boring. Without a daring mix of people in their clubs, their patrons might as well drink at home. From a commercial standpoint as well, total exclusivity was a financial impossibility. There were simply not enough wealthy New Yorkers to keep the city's thousands of clubs in business. Savvy club owners realized, as columnist Helen Lowry noted in a 1922 profile of clubs in the *New York Times,* that "Woolworth money is quite as good as Cartier's."[34]

The best (and most profitable) nightclubs were the ones that somehow achieved the right mixture of people and spectacle, bringing together the ritziest and grittiest elements of the city in the right proportions. One such place, described in a 1929 *Ladies' Home Journal* article as a "typical, smart night club in New York," collected a dazzling range of New Yorkers under its roof. They included "cool, cruel faces, gray with the night-club pallor. Red, bloated faces, indicative of overstrained hearts. Brown faces of outdoor men and alabaster faces of indoor ones. Faces of women . . . young faces and old ones, ugly and beautiful, stupid and daring. Keen, sophisticated faces beside blandly innocent ones." The resulting environment was "a rich and shaded brilliancy, a hard confusion of sounds, an atmosphere tense and expectant." It was a chaotic mixture that was at once unnerving and electrifying. But it was also successful.[35]

The nightclubs' most ardent champions, New Yorkers were not merely entertaining themselves but also taking part in something unprecedented in the history of American society. A 1927 article on New York's nightclubs in the magazine *Smart Set* claimed that "never before has there been such a meeting ground of the very highest and very lowest of human society." Some went as far as to argue that nightclub culture was easing social barriers in a manner that would ultimately result in a more democratic society. In the *American Mercury,* for example, journalist Benjamin de Casseres described Joel's, a favorite midtown café well known for its defiance of the Volstead Act, as the embodiment of a new American cultural pluralism. Calling it "the melting pot of all nations and races," de Casseres declared Joel's an "ultra-democratic, ultra-New York, ultra-cosmopolitan" refuge from the dry experiment.[36]

In their exuberance, those who sang the praises of the democratic nature of New York's nightclub culture may have gone too far. Nightclubs may have brought together a cross-section of the city, but the scene was hardly as democratic as de Casseres and others imagined. The high prices charged in most clubs, for example, ensured that many New Yorkers had only fleeting access to the most cosmopolitan playgrounds of the Prohibition era. And while nightclubs and speakeasies were indeed remarkable for the different types of people they brought together, in reality their social interactions were often fraught with tension. The different classes of New Yorkers who came together in clubs and speakeasies may have shared the same desire to drink and be entertained, but in the end they often shared little else.

After observing the culture of the speakeasies, clubs, and cafés of 1920s Greenwich Village, sociologist Caroline Ware concluded that the interactions between their various groups of patrons produced more contempt than empathy. In Harlem, African-American locals often resented the well-heeled outsiders who saw their patronage of the neighborhood's speakeasies and clubs as "slumming." The tension was also present in the interaction between the working-class employees and wealthy patrons of nightclubs. While well-to-do clientele were often thrilled to be in the rough and exciting environment of an Italian speakeasy, waiters, Ware noted, were as likely to curse their presence, muttering insults such as "May you drop dead, signor" in Italian and under their breath.[37]

If New York's nightclub culture fell short of the new "ultra-democratic" environment that de Casseres envisioned, it nevertheless altered significantly the social character of the city and the sensibilities of its citizens. New Yorkers from various walks of life and social strata may not have completely embraced one another, but they had come in closer contact and been made more aware of one another's presence. In regard to their attitudes toward alcohol, the effects of the exuberant nightclub scene had left no ambiguity. Nightclub culture in the mid-1920s served as a powerful antidote to years of dry propaganda, attaching to drinking a newfound cachet that made highly unlikely the probability that New Yorkers would ever abide by the Prohibitionists' moral crusade. As one English observer noted, the rebellious culture of the Prohibition era had "raised drunkenness in America from a vice to the dignity of a sport."[38]

As speakeasies, nightclubs, and cabarets redefined New Yorkers' relationships to urban culture, they also transformed middle-class New Yorkers' relationship to the dry movement. During the two decades the Anti-Saloon League had spent promoting Prohibition in New York as a reform that would improve the lives of the working class, it had always trusted that the "respectable" tiers of society would set an example for the less fortunate with their own compliance to the dry laws. Instead, Prohibition had now convinced middle-class New Yorkers to turn their backs on the dry lobby and to embrace drinking, even heavy drinking, as the height of urban sophistication.

As early as 1921, *Variety* observed with amazement that "homes that never had over a case of liquor at a time, if even that, are now loaded up with it; visitors are asked to drink, and get drunk every time they call." A year later, the magazine noted the growing acceptance of illegal liquor, which could be found "everywhere, in the pocket, in the car, and in the office." As Benjamin de Casseres recalled, dinner guests in middle-class homes would "assemble at four o'clock for a seven o'clock dinner . . . and for three hours they sosh up on cocktails." While dinner was served, the guests, "plastered to the dome," would discuss liquor prices, bars, and cocktail recipes. At midnight, more guests would arrive with fresh bottles for the post-dinner party.[39]

The ubiquitous presence of alcohol in Prohibition-era New York all but eliminated its criminality. Even being arrested, once the ultimate social disgrace in respectable circles, became a badge of honor when it involved breaking the dry laws. Joseph Madden, the son of a famous horse breeder, was arrested in 1921 for carrying a hip flask in the Pre-Catalan, a favorite club of college students. After leaving a city courtroom, he remarked, "Well, I'm still a gentleman, I suppose. This Prohibition offense seems to be the only law you can get arrested on and still retain your self respect." This sentiment, widely shared by New Yorkers, was echoed by a writer in the *Atlantic Monthly* who noted that "those who violate [Prohibition] . . . are not condemned at all. Rather is their cleverness applauded."[40]

This unmistakable shift in "respectable" New Yorkers' attitudes toward alcohol was not simply a knee-jerk reaction to the Eighteenth Amendment. Rather, it was rooted in a much broader transformation of American culture that took place in the 1920s. During that decade, Americans embraced a new "culture of abundance" fostered by the postwar economic boom, and placed a greater focus on consumer bounty and leisure as a part of modern, urban life. These pursuits reflected an emerging "pleasure ethic" that significantly tempered the traditional American preoccupation with work and the Victorian values that the dry lobby promoted.[41]

With drinking at the center of New Yorkers' "pleasure ethic," the status of alcohol as a consumer good skyrocketed in the 1920s. Expensive bootleg liquor, despite its illegality, became a luxury item that no savvy New Yorker could be caught without, and having the right whiskey carried the same cachet as owning a fur coat, a fancy automobile, or a piece of diamond jewelry. As Carl Van Vechten noted in a 1925 issue of the *American Mercury,* modest social gatherings that in previous decades would have made do with one bottle of champagne or six bottles of beer now required more and better supplies of liquor. "When a contemporary hostess plans a party," Van Vechten remarked, "she calls up her bootlegger and orders two cases of scotch with the current fashionable label." New York's bootleggers, eager to satisfy, did what they could to meet these demands. They conspicuously circulated flyers and price lists with recognizable brands—Johnny Walker scotch, Martell cognac, Booth's gin, Bacardi rum, and Veuve Cliquot champagne—catering to customers who refused to settle for anything less.[42]

The consumer demand for particular brands of liquor carried over to demands for the right drinking accessories as well. In the mid-1920s, for example, *The New Yorker* carried advertisements for "dashing, smart" bars for the home, complete with chrome railings, either for rent or for sale. The *Ladies' Home Journal* also picked up on the trend, noting that middle-class housewives were ordering bars and designing "whoopee rooms" resembling private speakeasies for their homes, indicating that the "pleasure ethic" of the Jazz Age was creeping from the nightclub into the living room.[43]

Home bars were just the beginning of the trend. A 1926 article in the *New York Evening Post* marveled over the variety of cocktail shakers (euphemistically described as "beverage mixers"), crystal bar sets, and $175 silver hip flasks available in the city's finest department stores. The author added that "staid and respectable old Fifth Avenue shops, which would shudder at the thought of selling pistols, blackjacks, jimmies and other such implements designed for the breaking of the laws, proudly display the anti-Volstead set and implements on the most prominent positions among all their Christmas stocks." *Outlook* reporter Ernest Mandeville noted that sporting goods shops and some of the "best stores" in the city were also marketing flasks and other drinking accessories. Another article on the liquor trade in New York noted that a Manhattan store of "unquestionable standing" was doing brisk business selling "traveling cocktail sets" for businessmen. These goods were literally the accoutrements of an illegal drug trade, yet New York consumers flaunted them nonetheless as conspicuously as they would a fine pair of shoes or a fancy set of cufflinks.[44]

In 1919 the Prohibition experiment had come to pass because Americans, including a surprising cross-section of New Yorkers, had embraced "the dry fashion." They had jumped on a bandwagon proclaiming that the vision of a United States free from the problems associated with alcohol was too appealing to resist. By the mid-1920s, however, New Yorkers had clearly found a new vision, or a new fashion, more to their liking. Captivated by the liberating and spectacular experience of the nightclub and speakeasy culture that was sweeping the city, even the most respectable New Yorkers on whom the dry lobby had counted most lost all interest in the dry agenda. Consumed by the "itch to try new things," they now found the cultural rebellion against Prohibition far more compelling than the dated and intolerant logic of the dry movement. From Robert Benchley's drinking, to *The New Yorker*'s coverage of nightlife, to the nightly goings on at the Club Richman, New Yorkers were seduced by a new sense of what it meant to be cosmopolitan. With the wet fashion having supplanted the dry, the Prohibitionists' crusade lost even more ground. The dry lobby and its supporters might still attempt to prop up the Eighteenth Amendment through the use of brute force, but they would find the momentum of the Jazz Age working squarely against them.

6

Vote as You Drink

At three o'clock in the morning on July 3, 1926, a raiding party of Prohibition agents and officers from the NYPD entered Texas Guinan's 300
Club at 151 West Fifty-fourth Street. Acting on evidence gathered over the
previous nights by policewomen dressed as flappers and detectives dressed
in evening wear, the late-night raiders seized four bottles of liquor and arrested a seventeen-year-old floor dancer for performing an "objectionable
dance."

More than four hundred patrons were crowded into the club when the
raid commenced, including two United States senators and twenty members of a Georgia delegation traveling with golfer Bobby Jones, who had
just returned stateside after winning the British Open. The 300 Club's patrons made their displeasure with the raid plainly visible. According to the
New York Times, "Some of the patrons became very boisterous and . . . several men offered to 'fight it out man to man' with the [raiders]." Twenty patrons complained that the agents acted "roughly" as they forcefully ejected
them from the club. Others challenged the raiding officers to arrest them.
Guinan and her father, Michael, the manager of the club, insisted to the
Times that no liquor had been found in the raid, and they confirmed that
"many patrons had expressed indignation at what they termed an 'unwarranted intrusion.'"[1]

In the early years of the Prohibition experiment, it had been common for
working-class drinkers to stand up to, and even assault, Prohibition agents

and police officers. As the decade progressed, however, the trend toward verbal and physical resistance to Prohibition enforcement efforts moved up the social ladder to establishments that served middle-class and wealthy drinkers. The incident at the 300 Club, one of the city's most celebrated nightspots, was not an isolated one. On numerous occasions in the mid-1920s, speakeasy and nightclub patrons grew bellicose when Prohibition agents interrupted their drinking. Raids on midtown speakeasies frequently degenerated into violent melees, complete with flying chairs, thrown bottles, and fisticuffs. On many occasions, patrons jeered at or threatened police officers and federal agents. In one case, a defiant café patron stood up during a raid and berated a group of Prohibition agents. He told them that he was the secretary to a high city official and that he would have all the raiders dismissed from their jobs.[2]

Such open resistance to Prohibition enforcement efforts among the city's "better classes" contributed significantly to the eventual demise of the noble experiment. The Anti-Saloon League had firmly believed that even in American cities, middle-class support for the dry laws would shore up the Eighteenth Amendment against any initial resistance. But the rebellion against Prohibition in New York and other large cities escalated as the decade progressed, showing that a significant segment of America's urban middle class no longer shared the Prohibitionists' vision or their ideas about morality and respectable behavior. No one had expected to read in the papers that white-collar professionals were throwing bottles at policemen, or that college women, businessmen, and politicians were defying the orders of Prohibition agents. Their increasingly wet behavior cast serious doubts over the long-term success of the Prohibition experiment in the nation's largest city, which in turn raised further questions about whether Prohibition could survive on the national level.

Incidents like the one at the 300 Club made a difficult situation even worse for the city's law enforcement agencies. High-level officials of the Bureau of Prohibition and the NYPD, who had counted on middle-class supporters of Prohibition to set an example for the rest of the city, were instead shocked to see New York's middle class increasingly involved in the city's drinking culture. As early as 1921, National Prohibition Commissioner

John Kramer complained, "I do not marvel so much at the lower element in the community violating the law, but it is an amazing thing to have the so-called good citizens lending their aid and their comfort and their support in word and in deed to those who are engaged in violating the law." In 1923 Police Commissioner Richard Enright echoed Kramer's sentiments when he expressed his displeasure with the "men who have always represented the highest standards of honor and integrity, [who now] carry their private flasks and maintain their private supply of intoxicating liquors at their office, home or club."[3]

The problem that Kramer, Enright, and other dry enforcement officials faced went beyond the fact that professionals, college students, career women, and other "respectable" New Yorkers had invested themselves in the city's nightlife and drinking culture so deeply. Equally daunting were the indications that the rebellious character of the city's nightlife was being celebrated in the magazines, popular songs, advertising, and motion pictures of the 1920s, thus transmitting New Yorkers' attitudes about Prohibition to the rest of the nation, and with devastating effect.

Pining for liquor, for instance, became a common motif of the popular music of the era, beginning with songs like "How Are You Going to Wet Your Whistle (When the Whole Damn World Goes Dry?)," "I Must Have a Little Liquor When I'm Dry," and Irving Berlin's "You Cannot Make Your Shimmy Shake on Tea." In magazines like *Collier's* and *Ladies' Home Journal,* which often supported Prohibition on their editorial pages, advertisements for mixers, home bars, and Jazz Age fashions straight out of nightclubs targeted middle-class readers, while cigarette ads featuring fashionable men and women drinking from cocktail glasses further undermined the dry mandate.

The advent of motion pictures with sound made even stronger impressions on middle America. Movies like *The Jazz Singer, Lights of New York, Queen of the Nightclubs,* and *Night after Night* captured not only the sights of New York nightlife but also, for the first time, the music and sounds as well, thus bringing the full experience of the New York nightclub to life for the nation's moviegoers. Amplifying the effects of popular songs and advertisements, these motion pictures heightened the thrill and romance of the rebellion against Prohibition. With their glamorous depictions of speakeasies, drinking, and, as one film advertisement promised, "beautiful jazz babies, champagne baths, [and] midnight revels," motion pictures showed seventy-seven million Americans a week that New Yorkers were not only defying the Eighteenth Amendment openly but also having a great time doing it.[4]

The proliferation of mass media celebrating New York's drinking culture did not go unnoticed by the dry lobby. In 1925, D. Leigh Colvin of the Methodist Board of Temperance accused the motion picture industry of making the Prohibition amendment look "ridiculous" by highlighting the allure of drinking. Another statement issued by the Board of Temperance accused New York of "bombarding the West with 'wet' propaganda" that made fun of or otherwise encouraged disrespect for the noble experiment.[5]

Dry officials could hardly contain their anger at the abundance of media images in the mid-1920s depicting middle-class drinking. With motion pictures and magazines broadcasting the image of "respectable drinking" to the rest of the country, spokesmen for the Bureau of Prohibition and the U.S. Attorney's office denounced middle-class revelers for breaching their responsibilities as both citizens and moral leaders. Speaking at a citizenship conference at Manhattan's Marble Collegiate Church in 1923, Federal Prohibition Commissioner Roy Haynes took "respectable drinkers" to task for believing themselves to be "above and superior to law." Haynes argued that middle-class drinkers who disobeyed the dry mandate had become "dangerous to the life of the nation," not to mention an embarrassment. "Of them much is expected," he complained, "for they represent the very best in American traditions, and the nation naturally looks upon them as representative of the finest in American life." He continued: "Non-observance on their part makes it easier for the foreigner unfamiliar with our customs and ideals, to violate the law." U.S. Attorney William Hayward echoed Haynes's criticism of "non-observers" when he accused middle-class professionals who drank of hypocritically depending on law enforcement agencies to protect their homes, property, and businesses, while engaging in social behavior that undermined public respect for the law.[6]

But speaking out against "respectable drinkers" did nothing to counter the middle-class rebellion. The widespread disregard for Prohibition by "respectable" New Yorkers instead forced the Bureau of Prohibition to reconsider its enforcement strategies. Having incorrectly assumed that the example set by "the so-called higher groups" would help quash working-class drinking, federal authorities now reluctantly concluded that they would have to take more aggressive steps to enforce Prohibition in middle-class circles. In the mid-1920s, the Bureau of Prohibition and other authorities resorted to spectacular sweeps of midtown speakeasies to hit the "respectable" drinking spots as well.

When the bureau shifted its strategy, it did so in typically heavy-handed fashion. Raiding twenty, forty, or as many as seventy midtown establishments in a twenty-four-hour period, the bureau aimed to publicize as conspicuously as possible its new determination to enforce Prohibition on all levels of society and to counter the idea that "respectable" drinking was just sophisticated fun. Aware that they were now trying to reach a different audience with a different message, the bureau invested its midtown raids with the pageantry of finely orchestrated media events. After a raid on Jack's, a popular midtown restaurant at Sixth Avenue and Forty-third Street, federal agents dramatically marched case after case of confiscated liquor in front of newsreel crews to allow them to record the event on film. Parading the evidence through busy midtown sidewalks sent a clear message to New Yorkers that the so-called respectable places would no longer be left alone, as they had been earlier. A crowd of one thousand people watched as the liquor was carted away, showing that the bureau had also learned a thing or two about the value of Jazz Age spectacle. A *New York Times* reporter noted that, as intended, the raid had captured the attention of the grumbling spectators, but, he noted further, "the majority appeared not to be in sympathy with what was taking place."[7]

Well-publicized, high-profile raids aimed at shutting down the speakeasies and restaurants that catered to "the so-called higher groups" were no more successful than the efforts targeting New York's working class. Most resulted in relatively minor seizures of liquor and the arrests of waiters, bartenders, and the occasional proprietor. They failed to have a larger impact on the city, however, in part because they carried too few consequences for the "respectable" patrons caught in them. Regardless of how much alcohol was found in a speakeasy or nightclub, it was technically still not illegal to drink under the Volstead Act, so middle-class drinkers themselves were rarely held. While more aggressive police captains and Prohibition agents might arrest speakeasy and club patrons *en masse* on the lesser charge of disorderly conduct, weary city magistrates almost always dismissed the charges against them. In 1926, for example, when police arrested 150 patrons at the Miami Inn on Greenwich Avenue and Christopher Street and brought them to the neighboring Jefferson Market Courthouse, a frustrated city magistrate quickly released all 150 after reminding police officers that holding a drink in one's hand was not a crime.[8]

In the end, the Bureau of Prohibition's attempt to use raids to stop drinking among the city's "better classes" only furthered the cat-and-mouse game of Prohibition enforcement. If raided, many speakeasies reopened within a matter of days. When their liquor supplies were seized, they simply bought more booze. If enforcement pressure in midtown forced speakeasies to close for a few days, patrons looked for their drinks in other parts of the city, moving from midtown to Greenwich Village to the Upper West Side, only to return to their favorite locales after agents had passed on.

Speakeasies continually devised new ways to stay ahead of federal agents. In addition to the membership cards, passwords, peepholes, and hidden entrances that disguised speakeasies from the street, proprietors began to buy neighboring buildings in which to hide their liquor supplies. As adjoining addresses were rarely included in search warrants, liquor supplies cached next door could remain safely off limits to investigators. Speakeasies also engineered elaborate systems of chutes and slides that could empty a bar of evidence at the push of a button by dropping bottles to a hard basement floor below, breaking them to let the liquor drain harmlessly into the sewer. The drop left only shattered glass behind for investigators to find.

In the end, these escapades illustrated that opposition to Prohibition was becoming more determined and more elaborate as the nightclub and speakeasy trades attempted to cater to a growing number of wet New Yorkers. No longer able to count on the support of middle-class New Yorkers to help stem the illegal liquor trade or the culture associated with it, the dry lobby angrily came to accept that Prohibition enforcement efforts would remain a struggle for years to come.

With new ways of evading the dry laws constantly evolving, federal authorities were hard pressed to come up with a more effective method of stopping the city's liquor trade. For a brief while in 1925, it seemed that the new United States Attorney for the Southern District of New York, Emory C. Buckner, had found the answer—the padlock. A former political aide to Mayor John Purroy Mitchel and formerly Assistant U.S. Attorney, Buckner took office in March 1925 with bold promises to "debunk" Prohibition enforcement efforts in New York. Buckner's plan was simple. His office would collect evidence of liquor sales in New York's nightclubs and speakeasies independently, bypassing the Police Department and Bureau of Prohibition. Once armed with evidence of liquor sales, Buckner would file for injunctions in federal civil court to have offending establishments padlocked as public nuisances. Under Buckner's plan, there would be no more need to arrest petty violators and no need for jury trials. Civil cases against violators would be presented to federal judges, who could quickly rule on requests for injunctions. If an injunction was issued, Buckner's office would move to padlock the establishment immediately, closing it for up to one year.

Buckner hoped that the use of civil injunctions rather than criminal proceedings would break the endless cycle of arrests, plea bargains, and fines that had come to define Prohibition enforcement in New York City. By targeting the owners of illegal clubs rather than those who worked in them, and by threatening owners with financial losses rather than throwing bartenders in jail, Buckner planned to "pinch the pocketbook of the man higher up."[9]

Buckner expected his campaign to send ripple effects through the entire nightclub trade. He anticipated that waiters and bartenders would look for other lines of work under the constant threat of a one-year furlough. He also expected commercial landlords to reconsider the risks they faced by renting space to liquor law violators. Under the provisions of the padlock procedures, if a nightclub was padlocked for liquor violations, the rental space would remain shuttered for the entire duration of the injunction. Buckner told reporters that "this would compel the owner of the real estate to look sadly upon his locked premises for twelve months, and be deprived of rental." Buckner estimated that landlords could lose up to $50,000 per club, and added that "there are not many landlords with $50,000 establishments who will desire to risk such a stake in a padlock action."[10]

Buckner also believed his padlocking campaign would ease the burden that Prohibition enforcement had placed on the federal judicial system as a whole. Because the evidence used in civil cases would be collected independently by the U.S. Attorney's office, it would be free from the taint of corruption that plagued both the Bureau of Prohibition and the Police Department, and thus more likely to result in a successful injunction. Because no arrests would be involved, no additional strain would be placed on the already overcrowded prison system. Hearings would take the place of criminal trials, and thus Buckner expected federal judges to be able to dispose of ten to fifty padlocking cases a day, enormously reducing the federal backlog of 15,000 criminal Prohibition cases already on the New York dockets, which Buckner estimated would otherwise take ten years to bring to trial. Optimistically, Buckner enlisted the support of Judge John C. Knox to set up a special federal court calendar to handle 200 initial padlocking proceedings. With this special court at his disposal, Buckner expected to resolve the first round of padlocking cases within a month's time.[11]

Buckner launched this ambitious campaign with great fanfare in March 1925, making headlines with his announcement that he had begun padlocking proceedings against more than one thousand New York establishments that were selling liquor. He promised that this effort would constitute a fresh start for Prohibition enforcement in the city. He predicted that the padlock strategy would work so effectively, in fact, that the public would soon forget the earlier failures of the Bureau of Prohibition and the NYPD. He even encouraged the public to take an active role in the padlocking campaign, inviting anyone who had witnessed an illegal liquor sale in a café or nightclub to fill out an affidavit against the offending establishment and mail it to Buckner's office.

One of the most distinctive characteristics of Buckner's campaign was that for the first time since 1920, the main focus of Prohibition enforcement was taken off the city's working class. In order to maximize the impact of his campaign, Buckner opted to target high-profile, well-known nightclubs and speakeasies in Manhattan's theater district, rather than the ethnic, working-class saloons that had been singled out by the Bureau of Prohibition under pressure from the dry lobby. By focusing on prominent nightclubs, Buckner hoped to hold the city's more cosmopolitan social circles accountable for their drinking.

With Buckner at work, the possibility of a dry New York seemed real for the first time during the Prohibition era. Even the skeptics of the New York City press corps, who had derided virtually every previous effort at dry enforcement, believed that Buckner was on the verge of success. One reporter predicted that "New York will be on a strict 'water diet' within sixty days." Another noted that Buckner's new effort to dry up New York had resulted in "one of the most abrupt changes in Prohibition climate on record."[12]

The campaign to institute Prohibition by padlock had an immediate impact on the city's nightclub scene. Within six weeks, Buckner had succeeded in padlocking all fourteen clubs he had initially targeted, including the Crillon, the Club Borgo, the Beaux Arts, Owney Madden's Silver Slipper, and the El Fey Club, owned by racketeer Larry Fay. None of the clubs offered any significant resistance to the civil proceedings against them, and several owners voluntarily consented to padlocking before their court hearings took place, accepting reduced closures of one month to six weeks in exchange for pledges never to sell liquor again. In accordance with Buckner's plan, padlocking proceedings took precedence over all other Prohibition enforcement efforts, and liquor arrests in the city dropped precipitously.[13]

From these auspicious beginnings, Buckner expanded his padlocking campaign to include Greenwich Village, Harlem, and other parts of the city, where he padlocked nightclubs, speakeasies, pharmacies, and groceries for violating the Volstead Act. Yet Buckner's foremost goal remained "making Broadway dry." By removing liquor from the theater district, Buckner hoped to change the cultural atmosphere of midtown and diminish the appearance that drinking was a vital part of Broadway tourism and entertainment. If Buckner's plan worked, it would show that drinking would no longer be tolerated as an acceptable part of New York City nightlife.[14]

Despite its impressive beginning, U.S. Attorney Buckner's plan to institute Prohibition by padlock proved less effective than he had hoped. Though Buckner had 500 establishments padlocked in the first six months of 1925, the nightclubs and speakeasies of New York proved remarkably resilient. Larry Fay's padlocked El Fey Club, for example, was reborn nearby as the Del Fey Club, until it, too, was padlocked. The Lido-Venice, one of the city's most expensive nightclubs, was closed for one year for Volstead violations, but, according to *Variety,* its owners took the padlocking in stride. They continued paying their $32,000 annual rent and simply planned to reopen when the injunction against them expired. Other club owners fell back on similar strategies, shrugging off padlockings and reopening as soon as possible at new locations, proving the pockets of the nightclub owners were deeper than Buckner had imagined. One speakeasy even succeeded in using its padlock as a cover, using a rear entrance to stay open for business while hiding behind a padlocked facade.[15]

Rather than destroying New York's nightclub culture, Buckner's campaign only fostered the further evolution of nightclubs in terms of location, atmosphere, and even architecture. With the threat of the padlock shortening the average lifespan of nightclubs and speakeasies, owners began to shun extravagant interiors and lavish decorations that could be lost in a fifteen-minute raid. The trend during the Buckner era, according to *The New Yorker,* was toward inexpensively decorated clubs that appeared to be "the product of the informal conjunction of a back parlor and a pot of paint." Business partners invested less capital in their clubs and focused instead on maximizing short-term profits. Clubs grew smaller, more anonymous, and more secretive in order to extend their brief lifetimes. Owners closed and reopened clubs with greater frequency to stay ahead of the law, changing names and moving around, according to *Variety,* like pieces in a game of checkers. Such resilience prompted *The New Yorker* to observe that "each day brings new victims of Buckner's spies, but a . . . rise of new places keeps up the supply." The *New York Times* agreed: "The bigger the batch of places padlocked one month, the bigger is sure to be the hatch of their successors the next month."[16]

Once the initial shock of Buckner's campaign had passed, padlocking only increased the allure of New York's nightclubs. If anything, the padlock became a part of the spectacle of New York nightlife, instantly producing the best kind of notoriety and ensuring that throngs of tourists and thrillseekers would soon descend upon the club to see and be seen in it before it was shut down. The leading lady of New York's nightlife, Texas Guinan, went so far as to adopt the padlock as her personal trademark. Guinan, who had a penchant for serenading and blowing kisses to Prohibition agents as they made their way through a packed house, had survived several run-ins with the Prohibition authorities. She began wearing a charm bracelet made of tiny gold padlocks in a spirited show of defiance, and then staged an irreverent revue entitled "The Padlocks of 1927" at her 300 Club. Guinan's audacity and persistently rebellious manner not only made her a national celebrity but also showed that Bruckner's plan to shore up Prohibition enforcement was no match for either the economics of the liquor trade or the city's cultural attachment to Prohibition-era nightlife.[17]

In 1925 *Collier's* published a poll indicating that middle-class Americans were tiring of Prohibition, not just in New York City but across the country. Sixty-eight percent of the more than 260,000 respondents queried expressed dissatisfaction with conditions under Prohibition, with similar levels of discontent being voiced by both men and women. The poll results reflected a growing trend that even U.S. Attorney Buckner had to acknowledge. Despite his zeal for padlocking, Buckner expressed his own misgivings about the dry experiment. When asked by reporters to publicly state his own views on Prohibition, Buckner replied frankly that he had little interest in it "except as a legal problem." He refused to categorize people who bought liquor as criminals, saying that "such a man, presumably, is dissatisfied with a particular condition imposed upon him by society and is making his protest against it." "As long as he is frank about it," Buckner added, "I have no quarrel with him."[18]

Like many of the dry experiment's staunchest critics, Buckner expressed dismay over the unintended social effects of Prohibition and conceded that the dry experiment had "afflicted American life with a miserable sore" by furthering crime and corruption. He also worried that the dry laws could never be effectively enforced until Prohibition agents were paid living wages and the court system reorganized for the task. When pressed, Buckner even admitted in an interview with *The New Yorker* that he had not given up drinking himself until January 1925, when he was first nominated for the position of United States Attorney.[19]

Though Emory Buckner's prominent role in Prohibition enforcement normally would have provoked the ire of New Yorkers, his candor actually endeared the U.S. Attorney to the city's residents. They found Buckner's honesty admirable and a welcome break from the hypocrisy, corruption, and bombast that had come to characterize so much of Prohibition enforcement in the city. Ironically, drys, not wets, were Buckner's harshest critics. Despite the fact that he had enforced Prohibition more aggressively and more effectively in eight months on the job than any of his unfortunate predecessors, Buckner's honesty about Prohibition and its shortcomings irritated dry leaders to no end. The Anti-Saloon League's counsel Wayne Wheeler, for example, harshly criticized Buckner for refusing to arrest petty violators of the Volstead Act. He took great exception to Buckner's comment about "having no quarrel" with small-time liquor buyers and argued that Buckner was allowing New Yorkers to drink without fear of reprisal. Wheeler eventually took his complaints against Buckner to the nation's highest-ranking dry, President Calvin Coolidge, who directly rebuked Buckner in a statement reminding all federal officials of their obligation to prosecute every Prohibition violation, large or small.[20]

Damned by drys and praised by wets, Buckner's high-profile campaign against liquor dealing in New York City ultimately failed. No one in New York had gone without a drink because of Buckner's efforts, despite the fact that he had closed hundreds of establishments throughout the city. But Buckner was successful in another regard: he challenged New Yorkers, especially the "respectable classes," to come clean about where they stood on Prohibition, not just as a cultural issue but as a political one as well. In speeches to Rotary Clubs, Masonic Temples, churches, synagogues, and in his statements to the press, Buckner repeatedly admonished New Yorkers not to be hypocrites. If they supported Prohibition and wanted it, then he promised he would enforce it through more aggressive measures. If they didn't want it, as their private and public behavior clearly suggested, then they were compelled to do something about it. Buckner offered his solution in a speech to the Rotary Club in July 1925. Emphasizing his own "respectable" middle-class background, he told the Rotarians, "When I was a boy in the Middle West there was a slogan in the churches during certain campaigns: 'Vote as you pray.'" In 1925, Buckner insisted that the time had come for New Yorkers to adopt a new slogan: "Vote as you drink."[21]

With those words, Buckner prompted a major shift in the relationship between politics and Prohibition in New York City. Until the mid-1920s, no one had successfully challenged the political identification of middle-class Americans with the dry movement. It was widely understood that "respectable" Americans, the "good citizens" for whom dry organizations had always claimed to speak, would offer either genuine support for the dry agenda or tacit support for it while drinking on the sly and treating Prohibition as a moral reform that applied to other people more than it did to them personally. Buckner's admonition to "vote as you drink" now threatened to end that understanding. Buckner reminded New Yorkers that Prohibition was not simply part of the status quo of life in the city but also a political issue on which they would have to take sides. If they were unhappy about the dry experiment, they would need to make Prohibition a central issue in politics.

Though slow in coming, political opposition to Prohibition was finally maturing in the mid-1920s. In contrast to the climate of the late 1910s, when it was clearly a political liability, opposing the dry experiment was now becoming a source of political capital, especially in wet centers like New York. Signs that a wholesale political realignment was in the works over the issue of Prohibition extended back to 1922, when New York voters, shifting away from the dry movement, returned the wet Democrat Al Smith to the governor's office in the place of the dry (and by many accounts inept) Republican governor Nathan Miller. Smith was elected by one of the largest margins in state history, and his return to Albany signaled that wet voters, especially urban, ethnic voters, were beginning to flex their political muscle. By 1925, further signs of this realignment could be seen in neighboring New Jersey, where the wet Democratic candidate for governor, Harry Moore, defeated the dry Republican Arthur Whitney. In New York City, the most obvious sign that the issue of Prohibition was spilling into politics could be seen in the political ascendance of James J. Walker, New York's popular "nightclub mayor."

The well-known story of James J. "Jimmy" Walker's elevation from the State Senate to the Office of Mayor in 1925 serves as a curious example of American municipal politics in the 1920s. In many respects, Walker's election was not an election at all but a coup staged by Tammany Hall to unseat the incumbent Democrat, Mayor John F. Hylan. After eight years in office, Hylan, a Brooklyn party stalwart supported by the publisher William

Randolph Hearst, had lost favor with the Tammany machine. Grim, humorless, and widely viewed as ineffective, Hylan was a poor public speaker known for pandering to moral reformers and focusing single-mindedly on the five-cent subway fare. Such an uninspiring figure seemed ill suited to serve as mayor of such an energetic metropolis as 1920s New York, and public support for the mayor dwindled as the decade progressed. As one observer of the period noted, Tammany's plan to oust Hylan was helped by the fact that "the people were tired of Mr. Hylan."[22]

In the summer of 1925, Tammany Hall threw its support behind the more flamboyant Walker to replace Hylan as the Democratic candidate for mayor. Although Hylan retained the support of Hearst and Democratic Party leaders in Brooklyn, Queens, and Staten Island, without Tammany's support, he had no chance at securing the nomination. In September of that year, Walker trounced Hylan in the Democratic primaries, beating him by 100,000 votes. Having won the primary, Walker was virtually guaranteed election in the overwhelmingly Democratic city, and in the November 1925 general election, he soundly defeated the Republican challenger, fountain pen tycoon Frank Waterman, by 400,000 votes, the second largest margin in the city's history.[23]

The significance of the 1925 mayoral election lay not in Walker's victory over the Republican Waterman, which was almost a given, but in Walker's political style and its relation to Prohibition-era culture. An energetic, boyish-looking, and impeccably dressed dandy, Walker embodied the cosmopolitan ideal of 1920s New York. As an adoring portrait of Walker in the *American Mercury* illustrated, his style was more movie star than politician. The magazine described Walker as "just turned forty-five, [but with] the appearance of a man still in his early thirties. His hair is black, thick and unruly. His eyes are dark and restless. He has the slim build of a cabaret dancer, of a gigolo of the Montmartre. He dresses in the ultra advanced fashion redolent of the tenderloin. He is a native New Yorker, smokes cigarettes continuously, has a vast contempt for the Volstead Act, and reads nothing but the sporting pages." Even better, reporter Henry Pringle noted, "he knows the speakeasies, the hotels and the nightclubs." "If Alfred E. Smith . . . comes from the sidewalks of New York," Pringle concluded, "Jimmy Walker comes from the dance floors."[24]

Walker was a social man with strong ties to the worlds of show business and sports. In contrast to his staid predecessor, he designed his own flashy suits, was said to change his clothes three times a day, and loved to frequent New York's nightclubs and speakeasies with his mistress while his wife stayed at home on St. Luke's Place. Comfortable in the world of celebrity, Walker could claim George M. Cohan, Irving Berlin, boxer Jimmy Johnston, and Giants manager John McGraw as some of his closest friends and political supporters. He posed for campaign photos with Babe Ruth and had earned his own share of fame even before entering politics, when he penned the minor 1908 hit "Will You Love Me in December as You Do in May?"[25]

Walker was, as a profile in *The New Yorker* noted, not a profound thinker. He claimed to have read only six books since graduating from law school. But despite his playboy image, he was an undeniably skillful politician. After entering politics in 1910, Walker proved himself a gifted public speaker, and earned a reputation during his tenure in the state assembly as a champion of social welfare and housing improvement.

But Walker's willingness to take on moral reformers, or as he called them, "the side-burned shock troops of reform," cemented his place in New York politics. A constant defender of working-class leisure and entertainment, Walker had fought to lift the state's ban on Sunday baseball games, sponsored a law to legalize boxing in New York, and campaigned against movie censorship. When Republicans in the Senate proposed a Clean Books Bill in 1923, he famously ridiculed it, telling his fellow Senators, "I have never yet heard of a girl being ruined by a book."[26]

Most of all, Walker was an outspoken foe of Prohibition. He had fought vehemently against the state's ratification of the Eighteenth Amendment in 1919, prophetically declaring that Prohibition was a "measure born in hypocrisy, and there it will die." He dismissed the dry cause as being rooted in bigotry and political blackmail, and lampooned Republican legislators who had come under the influence of William Anderson and the Anti-Saloon League. On one occasion, Walker challenged a fellow senator's reluctant dry stand saying, "Your body belongs to the Anti-Saloon League, but I hope your soul still belongs to yourself."[27]

Though he was unable to prevent the ratification of the Eighteenth

Amendment by the state assembly, Walker made himself a constant annoyance to New York's dry leaders after its enactment. He sponsored a state bill legalizing beer in 1920, which passed but was struck down as unconstitutional by the Supreme Court. In 1923 he masterminded the repeal of the Mullan-Gage Law, managing to see the measure pass by a one-vote margin before being signed by Governor Smith.

Though Walker's opposition to Prohibition and moral reform endeared him to his constituents, his opponents tried to turn these issues against him in the 1925 mayoral race. Mayor Hylan, for instance, insinuated that Walker's political stances and personal conduct made him unfit to serve as mayor. If Walker were elected, Hylan proposed, he would turn New York into a "wide-open town" of illegal drinking and other vices. Ella Boole of the Woman's Christian Temperance Union, a vocal Hylan supporter, issued her own dire warnings about Walker, whom she referred to as the "leader of the liquor forces."[28]

But Walker's wide margin of victory in 1925 demonstrated that New Yorkers were excited about the prospect of a "nightclub mayor," and that Walker's identification with drinking and nightlife was a benefit, not a liability, for the mayor. Like his mentor, Governor Smith, Walker was known to drink as he pleased in spite of Prohibition, and he was generally admired for it. If Emory Buckner's admonition to "vote as you drink" was going to be taken to heart by New Yorkers, then Jimmy Walker would be the beneficiary.

At Walker's inauguration on the morning of January 1, 1926, cheering crowds who had been up all night toasting the New Year gathered in the cold in front of City Hall to greet the "nightclub mayor" with horns, noise-makers, and raised flasks. With the *American Mercury* proclaiming that "the jazz age is in office in New York," New Yorkers saw in Mayor Walker a kindred spirit. For his part, the new mayor embraced that image.[29]

Walker's political stance, style, and dynamic personality made him an immensely popular mayor. In Walker, New Yorkers of every ethnic group saw a politician who embodied the variegated culture of the city. Raised in Greenwich Village by an Irish-born father and an Irish-American mother, Walker was embraced by the immigrant working class as one of their own. At the same time, his reputation as a nightclub denizen appealed to the self-styled "cosmopolitans" of the middle class and the elite. Always a "New Yorker's New Yorker," Walker could win praise simultaneously as "a regular guy" and an urban sophisticate.[30]

A great deal of Walker's appeal was rooted in his understanding of leisure, nightlife, and drinking as part of the cosmopolitan way of life. As mayor, Walker saw no reason to deny anyone what he considered legitimate urban pleasures, and in that regard he made a strong impression on his constituents. One Lower East Sider remarked of Walker, "We all had a good saying about him: he lived and let live." His realistic view of the urban culture of the 1920s contrasted starkly with the staunch idealism of the drys, and his tolerance of legal and illegal amusements prompted *The New Yorker,* one of the mayor's biggest fans, to proclaim that "he understands the simpler human motives . . . as do few in politics."[31]

Walker remained true to his wet reputation as he set a course for his administration. Arguing that the city and the nation were tired of the Eighteenth Amendment, Walker immediately pulled the police away from the aggressive campaign to enforce Prohibition in the city. He replaced Mayor Hylan's limelight-loving police commissioner, Richard Enright, with the more matter-of-fact George McLaughlin, a former state superintendent of banking. McLaughlin, a man with a notable distaste for publicity, discouraged police involvement in high-profile Prohibition cases. As one of his first acts in office, McLaughlin immediately dismantled Enright's oft-criticized Special Service Squad as an anticorruption measure, claiming that "the nature of their work subjected them to temptation from all sides."[32]

Contrary to his critics' fears, Walker did not adopt an "anything goes" attitude to governing the city. As a wet who did not consider drinking a crime, Walker saw no need for the police to take an active role in Prohibition enforcement, other than to reign in particularly excessive Prohibition violations or to respond to a newsworthy crime linked to Prohibition. During his fifteen-month tenure, Police Commissioner McLaughlin similarly demonstrated that the city had not abandoned law enforcement. Rather, the NYPD had shifted its priorities to reflect the wishes of New Yorkers, taking a much more practical view of policing the city rather than heeding the demands of the dry lobby.

Walker's approach to regulating city nightlife could best be seen in the cabaret law he sponsored in 1926. The law, which Walker had proposed during his mayoral campaign, mandated a closing hour of 3:00 A.M. for the city's nightclubs and cabarets, and required a license for "any room, place or space in the city in which any musical entertainment, singing or dancing or other similar amusement is permitted in connection with the restaurant business or the business of directly or indirectly selling food or drink." Broadway supporters who knew the mayor's social habits were stunned that Walker would sign such a law, and they believed the mayor was only responding to Republican assertions that Walker would turn New York into a "wide-open" town. But Walker defended his cabaret law, arguing that it only set reasonable limits on New York nightlife. The 3:00 A.M. curfew, Walker contended, would give New Yorkers and tourists plenty of time to enjoy themselves on the town. Moreover, it left generous loopholes by exempting large hotels and private clubs from the law, as well as by allowing membership clubs to remain open as late as they pleased, provided they admitted no new patrons after 3:00 A.M. Most important to Walker, the license requirement gave the city a means to shut down establishments that blatantly violated the law or otherwise created nuisances.[33]

The cabaret law was Mayor Walker's way of regulating without regulating. It appeased Walker's critics who wanted stricter surveillance of clubs and cabarets, but it did nothing to dampen the spirit or quality of New York's nightlife; nor did it do much to strengthen Prohibition enforcement. The law was enforced sparingly, and Walker even suspended the curfew on New Year's Eve, 1926, arguing that he had no desire to be a "spoilsport." Liquor violations were in fact of little consequence in terms of maintaining a cabaret license. Most clubs that ran afoul of the cabaret law were punished with a paltry twenty-five-dollar fine, and in 1928, seventy-six cabarets had their licenses renewed by the Department of Licenses despite having complaints filed against them with the Police Department. In 1929 only one licensed cabaret in New York had its license revoked for liquor violations, while thirty-two had their licenses suspended, mostly for curfew violations.[34]

It has been argued that Walker's cabaret law was later used to regulate jazz clubs and, in particular, interracial dancing in Harlem clubs, but there is little evidence that this was the case during Walker's administration. Though

Police Commissioner Joseph Warren and other city officials would express concern over racial mixing in nightclubs later during the Prohibition era, the cabaret law was enforced so sporadically and imprecisely under Walker that it served almost no purpose other than to encourage a modicum of self-restraint in the nightclub trade. In many regards, the law was Walker's way of taking back the regulation of city nightlife from the Bureau of Prohibition and allowing the city to set its own priorities rather than follow the federal agenda.[35]

Walker's run-ins with the Bureau of Prohibition were much more indicative of his attitudes toward the dry mandate than were his half-hearted efforts to enforce the cabaret law. Walker feuded openly with federal officials over Prohibition, especially with Assistant U.S. Attorney General Mabel Walker Willebrandt, who was in charge of Prohibition enforcement. During the 1928 presidential election, Willebrandt accused the NYPD and Mayor Walker of dereliction of duty in their efforts to enforce the law. Needling the mayor for his reputation as a playboy, Willebrandt urged Walker to consider taking charge of the investigation of speakeasies himself, given his extensive personal knowledge of what went on in them. In response to these complaints, Walker protested to Willebrandt that the Police Department had forwarded 29,000 liquor complaints to the Bureau of Prohibition since he had taken office, and that it was the responsibility of the bureau, not the city, to act on these complaints. The failure of Prohibition enforcement in New York, Walker added, was due to the bureau's own incompetence rather than to neglect on the part of the NYPD. Walker pointedly reminded Willebrandt that, "regrettably as it may seem, the 18,000 policemen [of New York] are not . . . available at all hours of the day and night to cope with the flood of illegal beverages prohibited by the Volstead Act." Walker's letter was followed by one from Police Commissioner Joseph Warren, who explained to Willebrandt in no uncertain terms that if conditions in New York were not to her liking, she should blame the Bureau of Prohibition, not the NYPD. Commissioner Warren acknowledged that federal authorities faced difficulty enforcing Prohibition in the city, but added: "I am not willing to have the men of the Department, to whom our citizens look for protection of life and property, make an intensive crusade to enforce a Federal Act, particularly when such high Federal officials as yourself have only considered New York's interest since the beginning of the national political campaign." As far as Warren was concerned, Willebrandt's fuss was nothing more than an attempt to curry favor with the Republican nominee for president, Herbert Hoover, in hopes that she might be rewarded with a high position in his administration should he prevail in the 1928 election.[36]

Undoubtedly, Walker's constituents shared the mayor's view that Prohibition was a federal problem, not an issue that warranted the expenditure of city resources. Many New Yorkers wrote letters to Mayor Walker in support of his decision to keep the NYPD out of Prohibition matters. They congratulated the mayor on his refusal to be bullied by the dry movement. (One 1926 letter urged the mayor to "let the federal government do their own work." The correspondent added, "I . . . see no reason why the police should bother . . . enforcing Prohibition and other minor matters when robbers and murderers are to be looked after.")[37]

The letters of support Walker received further signaled Prohibition's increasing importance as a political issue. Walker's popularity as mayor of New York demonstrated, both locally and nationally, that taking a firm stance against Prohibition, something most American politicians had been afraid to do for fear of the dry lobby, was not only possible but could have political rewards. Walker's opposition to Prohibition, combined with his personal conduct, made him a controversial figure and polarizing presence in national politics. The national press was as fascinated by him as the local press was, and reported on Walker just as it did on other elements of New York's rebellion against the Eighteenth Amendment. Being identified as "the nightclub mayor" made Walker one of the city's most popular mayors of the twentieth century. Even years after he left office plagued by corruption and scandal, polls consistently showed Walker to be more popular than his successor, the far more capable and honest Fiorello LaGuardia.[38]

Walker's immense popularity was based on several factors. His Irish Catholic background, his allegiance to Tammany Hall, and his generous distribution of patronage and city contracts through the political wards of New York all made him popular with loyal Tammany Democrats. His willingness to embrace ethnic groups all over the city virtually assured him of the adoration of working-class voters. But Mayor Walker's popularity extended far beyond the ethnic working class, and here the growing importance of Prohibition to American politics becomes clear. In addition to his working-class support, Mayor Walker also enjoyed the support of middle-class New Yorkers in the 1920s, even though there was a great deal about Jimmy Walker that should have made "respectable" voters wary. They supported him because they were "voting as they drank," just as Emory Buckner had urged them to do.

Walker's drinking and nightclubbing, beloved traits in a city that hated Prohibition, apparently allowed New Yorkers to forgive flaws that normally would have turned respectable voters against him. Though some credited Walker with hard work during his first few months in office, after that, the mayor conducted himself in a manner that under any other circumstances would certainly have cost him his job. For one, there was the married mayor's barely disguised affair with stage actress Betty Compton. Walker also vacationed extensively, missed work frequently, and raised his own salary from $25,000 to $40,000. He indiscreetly gave a friend, Sidney Solomon, the lease to the Central Park Casino as a political favor, and then took an active role in promoting the casino as one of the ritziest nightspots in Manhattan, where liquor flowed freely. Walker was caught in a gambling raid at the Montauk Island Club, mistress at his side, and unsuccessfully tried to sneak out disguised as a waiter. He engaged in numerous improper financial arrangements as well, receiving money through brokerage accounts set up in his name by political supporters. Yet as his administration was slowly consumed by scandal through the late 1920s and early 1930s, support for the mayor remained strong across the city. In 1929, when Congressman Fiorello LaGuardia campaigned against Walker as a reform candidate for mayor, he justly attacked Walker for allowing graft and corruption to thrive in his administration. Yet New York voters returned Walker to office by a humiliating margin of 500,000 votes, and were unfazed by LaGuardia's criticism of the mayor or by Walker's own corruption.[39]

If Walker was such a corrupt and irresponsible mayor, why did such large numbers of New Yorkers continue to vote for him, and support him even after scandals forced him from office in 1932? The answer is not simply rooted in Walker's opposition to Prohibition, because LaGuardia was as much of a wet as Walker. Rather, Walker's political longevity was rooted in his symbolic role as the "nightclub mayor." His cosmopolitan style, his taste for nightclubs and champagne, his personal flair, and his dapper appearance were as seductive to New Yorkers in the 1920s as was the city nightlife itself. He was, as Edward Robb Ellis wrote decades later in a popular history of New York City, "a symbol of their way of life." Whether in the Irish slums or on the pages of *Vanity Fair,* which remarked that Walker "loves . . . sophisticated society (and is loved by it)," all of New York seemed to believe that Walker embodied the spirit of the city in the Jazz Age. He had become a political and cultural hero to everyone who opposed the dry crusade.[40]

James J. Walker's rise to power as "the nightclub mayor" provided a startling contrast to the cataclysmic decline in support for drys and reformers in New York that occurred at the same time. Half a decade after the Anti-Saloon League's brilliant victory with the ratification of the Eighteenth Amendment in New York, the dry movement had grown myopic, insular, and increasingly irrelevant. With the Prohibition experiment failing to attain its noble goals, its one-time supporters grew disillusioned, lost interest, and looked to cast their political support elsewhere.

In New York, the decline of the dry movement was drastic and sudden. William Anderson, once the hero of the Anti-Saloon League for his exploits in New York, had already caused a stir with his caustic comments about Catholics and inopportune statements in support of the Ku Klux Klan. While these statements predictably brought a slew of criticism to bear on the Anti-Saloon League, the group lost even more favor in 1923, when Anderson was indicted for doctoring the organization's failing finances and siphoning funds from the league for his personal use. With these revelations, donations to the Anti-Saloon League dropped precipitously, and the state organization went deep into debt. Anderson was reprimanded by the league's national leadership and disowned by all but a few key allies. His downfall was complete in 1924, when he was convicted of forgery and sentenced to two years in prison. Dry supporters claimed that Anderson had been railroaded by Tammany Hall, but regardless, with his fate sealed, the Anti-Saloon League's credibility in New York was destroyed. Upon his release from Sing Sing, where he served nine months, Anderson ventured further into the realm of extremism. He formed a new organization called the American Protestant Alliance, which pledged to work closely with the Ku

Klux Klan in an effort to keep New York's dry movement alive and to restrict immigration to the United States.[41]

William Anderson's dramatic fall and Jimmy Walker's spectacular rise symbolized the simultaneous demise of the drys and ascendance of the wets in New York politics. Whereas drys had once been winning allies and pulling off surprising victories, they were now mocked as throwbacks to a bygone era. A *New York Telegram* article summarily dismissed them all, from the Anti-Saloon League to the Committee of Fourteen to the Methodist Board of Temperance, as no different from the Ku Klux Klan. "If they are not naïve . . . and zealous to the point of incredulity," its author scoffed, "they are bigoted and tyrannical." Rather than commanding the respect they had at the height of the Progressive era for their moral vision and political clout, New York's dry reformers were disparaged in the mid-1920s as cranks, fanatics, or reactionaries.[42]

As the "nightclub mayor," Jimmy Walker offered New Yorkers a political alternative more in tune with the urban culture of the 1920s. His political ascendance and the popularity he commanded in spite of his many shortcomings were indicative of the widespread rejection of moral reform by New Yorkers during Prohibition. Just as drinking an "orange blossom" in a speakeasy had been Robert Benchley's way of redefining his social identity, supporting Mayor Walker became a way for New Yorkers to reinvent their political identities. Having aligned themselves with a new wet politics, New Yorkers waited to see whether the call to "vote as you drink" would transform the rest of the nation as well, steering it away from the unrealistic dry agenda and toward a more cosmopolitan ideal.

7

I Represent the
Women of America!

As the rebellion against the Eighteenth Amendment raged on in the 1920s, women would come to play a pivotal and surprising role in the demise of the noble experiment. That role was rooted in the transformation of the relationship between women and the American temperance crusade, as women moved from the traditional role of moral guardians and reformers in service to the dry lobby to rebels against the double standards of Victorian morality. In the end, women would become pioneering political leaders in the movement to repeal the Eighteenth Amendment. By the end of the Prohibition era, these women, roused by a broader campaign for women's rights in the 1910s and 1920s, and caught up in the anti-Volstead culture of the Jazz Age, would completely redefine themselves and their relationship to the dry cause.

In 1920s New York, the emergence of Jazz Age speakeasy culture thrust women into uncharted terrain. As the nation entered the dry era, the prevailing assumption, rooted in the public lore surrounding characters like Carry Nation or in the well-known activism of the Woman's Christian Temperance Union, was that women had always been, and would always be, devotees of the dry cause. But for women in cities like New York, this expectation became increasingly unrealistic as the Jazz Age took root. Once welcomed into the world of the speakeasy, women in New York embraced the new culture, shattering the idea that women and the dry movement shared an unbreakable bond.

From the outset of the Prohibition experiment, drys who had expected women to set a moral example for the rest of the nation were profoundly disappointed with what they found in New York City. The drys' expectations for women, naive as they were, were based on middle-class notions of morality and "respectability" that were particularly out of touch with the women who lived and worked in the ethnic, working-class communities of the city. This became apparent in the early 1920s, when working-class women began appearing in court alongside men to face a variety of liquor charges. Cases involving women appeared with greater regularity as the era progressed, laying to rest the notion that women would be unquestioning supporters of the Prohibition experiment.[1]

In New York, Prohibition cases involving women generally fit the same pattern. The defendants were working-class women from Italian, Irish, or Eastern European backgrounds. Despite occasional claims that the supplies of alcohol they were caught with were for personal consumption, most of the women caught were part of the underground economy of illegal liquor trade. Like many working-class New Yorkers, they hoped that the money they earned from bootlegging would augment their meager incomes, keep them above the poverty line, or maybe even make them rich. Considering their economic backgrounds and the continual harassment of ethnic New Yorkers under the Volstead Act, it should come as no surprise that these women showed no regard for the dry agenda.

As the 1920s progressed, cases of a different nature began to appear in the press and on the court dockets. On April 15, 1925, the *New York Times* reported that Frances French, "an attractive young woman living at 73 Clermont Avenue, Maspeth, Queens," had appeared in federal court in Brooklyn the previous day to face charges of violating the Volstead Act. According to the *Times,* French's arrest came after she had sold Patrolman James Dolan a fifty-cent shot of whiskey out of a pint bottle concealed in her beaded handbag. French was unapologetic as she testified in court. She freely admitted selling the whiskey to Patrolman Dolan, explaining to the court that she was bootlegging to help pay her business school tuition.[2]

The image of an aspiring young professional woman like Frances French selling shots of whiskey from a pint bottle hidden in her beaded handbag challenged prevailing notions about what types of women were likely to be arrested for Prohibition violations in New York. The same could be said for Claire Fiance, a twenty-four-year-old legal stenographer from West 156th Street who was stopped on the street one afternoon by detectives inquiring about the suspicious looking package she carried under her arm. According to a newspaper report, when Fiance was asked what she was carrying, she replied, "with a bright smile and a shake of her bobbed hair," that the package contained a bottle of whiskey. The detectives then arrested her and took her to a midtown stationhouse.[3]

Frances French's beaded handbag, Claire Fiance's bobbed hair, the women's brazen defiance of the Eighteenth Amendment, and the jaunty self-assuredness they both demonstrated in their encounters with the law were indications that they belonged to the new generation of young, headstrong women whose fashions and unrestrained behavior captured the imagination of the American public in the 1920s. In some of the numerous articles printed about them in American magazines and journals, these "flappers" were noted for their economic independence, their disregard for traditional gender roles, and their penchant for "shaking off the shreds and patches of their age old servitude." In an article in the *New Republic,* Bruce Bliven wrote admiringly that the flappers of the Jazz Age were "highly resolved that they are just as good as men, and intend to be treated so." He added, "They don't mean to have any more unwanted children. They don't intend to be debarred from any profession or occupation which they choose to enter. They clearly mean . . . that in the great game of sexual selection they shall no longer be forced to play the role, simulated or real, of helpless quarry."[4]

As part of her independent and unconventional nature, the flapper of the 1920s also developed a taste for alcohol, and the cocktail became a motif as central in her popular depiction as bobbed hair, short skirts, and rolled stockings. So vital was the cocktail to the experience of 1920s urban women that even beauty parlors and dress boutiques were expected to dispense alcohol to their female clients. One woman commented on the trend, "A nice place! A girl goes for a manicure and gets a nip, goes for a wave and gets a splash." By the end of the decade, journalist Margaret Culkin Banning would definitively declare in *Vanity Fair* that "the lifting of the glass" had been embraced by the young women of the 1920s as "one of the modern gestures." Journalist Stanley Walker expressed a similar point, though less delicately, at the end of the era: "After 1920 great, ravening hordes of women began to discover what their less respectable sisters had known for years—that it was a lot of fun, if you liked it, to get soused."[5]

The flapper's drinking and her rebellious nature when it came to confronting moral double standards had a great impact on the debate over the Eighteenth Amendment. Until the arrival of the flapper in the 1920s, American women had been expected to campaign actively for temperance and Prohibition. Those women who failed to live up to this expectation were considered immoral, eccentric, or beneath the American standard of womanhood.

This belief was rooted in the extraordinary role that American women had played in the temperance movement of the late nineteenth and early twentieth centuries. The Woman's Christian Temperance Union was perhaps the most visible temperance organization in the United States, and it engaged more women in political activity than any other group, eclipsing even the suffrage movement. Guided by the WCTU's president, Frances Willard, 150,000 women members embraced the group's motto of "Do Everything" as they worked on projects ranging from temperance education to the construction of public drinking fountains. From the 1880s through the ratification of the Eighteenth Amendment, the WCTU encouraged American women to take part in myriad campaigns from labor reform to legislative efforts for the protection of children. The WCTU's work was one of the main vehicles through which women challenged the male dominance of American politics from the late nineteenth century into the Progressive era.[6]

By the 1910s, the women's temperance movement had grown so strong politically that liquor and brewing interests campaigned actively against women's suffrage out of fear that women voters would force Prohibition on the nation. As it turned out, women helped ratify the Prohibition amendment before most of them could even vote, giving credence to the belief that American women were best equipped to convince men of the merits of the dry experiment.[7]

In the early 1920s, however, assumptions about a women's consensus on Prohibition began to fall apart, especially when they concerned urban, working-class women, who were among the first to voice their opposition to the dry experiment. In 1919, Rose Schneiderman of the Women's Trade Union League in New York argued that the 50,000 women of her union stood together against the Eighteenth Amendment. She estimated that half a million additional women nationwide shared their sentiments, though the dry movement dismissed their views as unrepresentative of American womanhood because their ethnicity and their participation in the labor movement called into question their "respectability."[8]

The emergence of the flapper presented an even more difficult problem for temperance forces. A far cry from the ethnic immigrant woman of the working class, the flapper appeared as genuinely American as anyone could be in the 1920s. Yet her break from the traditional definition of American womanhood, including her stand on Prohibition, was so complete as to revolutionize ideas about women and their place in American society, while also opening the way for women's political involvement in the campaign for repeal.

The flapper, like many other social developments of the 1920s, was not a completely new creation of the Prohibition era. The flappers of the Jazz Age had been preceded by the "New Women" of the 1910s, a similarly independent and ground-breaking generation that had made great strides toward elevating the place of women in American society, by campaigning for the right to vote and for legal protections to safeguard women's personal and political freedom.[9]

The flapper extended the limits of women's personal freedom even further than the "New Woman" had, taking advantage of an era that saw moral restrictions relaxed for both women and men. Scoffing at the double standard of Victorian sexual morality, flappers insisted that when it came to social behavior, women of the 1920s should stand on equal footing with men. Their determination to drink, date, and socialize as they pleased prompted Bruce Bliven to comment, "They think a bachelor girl can and should do everything a bachelor man does."[10]

By insisting that women had the right to enjoy themselves socially as much as men did, whether through drinking, sex, or indulging in the pleasures of urban nightlife, flappers offered an alternative to the stereotype that women were to be thought of first and foremost as reformers and moral guardians. Their goal of social emancipation of women stood in stark contrast to the demands of the dry movement, which believed that women should both abide by and support the Eighteenth Amendment. It was fitting then, that at the same time that American women were enjoying new political freedom in the form of the vote, they were simultaneously standing up to the moral restrictions imposed upon them by drys and other reformers. The extreme demands of Prohibition were a kind of last straw for American women, who used the wider cultural rebellion against Prohibition as an opportunity to reject their moral subjugation in all its forms.

Flappers and booze, then, became inextricably linked during the Prohibition era as drinking became a new way for women, like men, to express their "smartness" and sophistication. But it was not simply the flapper's drinking that made her noteworthy. Rather, it was her effect on a drinking culture that had until this point remained solidly masculine (despite the occasional presence of women), as well as her role in furthering the cultural and political rebellion against the dry crusade.[11]

As the urban drinking culture of the 1920s moved away from the traditional saloon and toward ever more spectacular co-ed nightclubs and cabarets, women became an integral part of the new culture. The décor of New York's drinking establishments reflected this change in a new sense of flair, color, and polish designed to appeal to their female clientele. Tony's, for instance, drew a predominantly female crowd with its rose-colored walls and Italianate décor. The Park Avenue, done up in a regal red and gold theme, and the Aquarium, dominated by a mammoth illuminated fish tank, were also favorites with women. Other clubs went out of their way to hire attractive male bartenders and waiters to draw women customers. Even the drinks of the era reflected the feminization of drinking culture. As the era of whiskey shots and beer faded, sweeter and more colorful cocktails took their place, in part because they appealed more to women's palates (and in part because they masked the harsh flavors of bootleg liquor). At the Aquarium, for example, a drink called the Goldfish, made of equal parts goldwasser, gin, and French vermouth, emerged as a favorite with women, while at Zani's, women preferred the Zani Zasa, a combination of gin, apricot brandy, egg white, lemon juice, and grenadine.[12]

In New York, this trend toward accommodating women drinkers had its roots in the years before World War I, when the city's fancier restaurants and cafés courted upper-class women. Segregating female patrons from lone male drinkers, and catering to them specifically with sweet, colorful drinks, these establishments especially valued women's patronage in the slower afternoon hours, when they were encouraged to come in after shopping or attending Broadway matinees to enjoy a drink in the company of fellow shoppers or their daughters. The Aquarium and Zani's simply followed in that tradition, not letting the small matter of federal law get in the way of what appeared to be a natural progression toward a modern drinking culture that included women on their own terms.[13]

As women increasingly found their way into New York's nightclubs and speakeasies, the customs that had traditionally regulated the city's drinking culture fell by the wayside. The rapidity of the changes brought about by Prohibition caught many men off guard, however. Some male drinkers were initially shocked to see women reveling in the alcoholic excesses of the era, matching men drink for drink. *The New Yorker* columnist Lois Long, who leapt headfirst into the city's nightlife, left her editor, Harold Ross, stunned after he joined her for a night on the town. "It worried Ross that I was only twenty-two," she recalled. "He was one of those Protestant Westerners who was certain that no woman who drank, smoked, or cursed could be truly respectable. One night I took him with me on my nightclub tour and he never got over the shock."[14]

The new world of co-ed drinking did in fact produce some shocking scenes of women passing out in bars or reeling in the streets as they discovered the highs and lows of drunkenness, especially in the early years of the Prohibition experiment. Dry reformers were particularly upset to see their notions of respectable feminine behavior demolished. In one sermon, Reverend Dr. John Roach Straton lamented that, while engaged in a fact-finding mission in New York bars, he had encountered "many young women who were tipsy . . . and three young women who were reeling and hilarious." He added that he had also seen "noisy and boisterous" drunken women in front of restaurants and witnessed "indecent dancing, and women who were badly underdressed" in the clubs he visited. Such scenes were a sign to Straton that women, and young women in particular, were drinking more than ever before and behaving in a radically new fashion.[15]

The flapper's drinking and larger defiance of traditional gender roles in the 1920s prompted a mixture of astonishment and admiration. As H. I. Brock noted in a 1922 *New Republic* article, women in New York were conducting themselves nonchalantly in ways that would have been shocking a generation earlier. He noted "women smoking in hotel dining rooms, bare female legs on the public beaches . . . taking the lady's arm instead of letting her take yours." Along with drinking, Brock argued, these were all signs that the old rules regulating women's behavior no longer seemed to apply in the modern city of the 1920s.[16]

As Prohibition took hold, the perceived link between the flapper's drinking and her sexuality became a topic of public interest, regarded with consternation in some circles and enthusiasm in others. To moral reformers of the day, the relative sexual openness of the era posed as great a threat to Victorian morality as drinking did. With newspapers like *Variety* noting that New York's flappers were "as free with their persons as longshoremen," fear spread among moral reform circles that the combination of free-flowing liquor and sexual openness indicative of the era had the making of a moral calamity.[17]

The combination of sex and drink in the 1920s was not a new social development, as most reformers were well aware. Since the mid-1800s reformers had waged a constant crusade against alcohol in part because of its links to prostitution and other sexually "deviant" behaviors, in particular homosexuality and interracial sex. In the 1920s, the new sexual openness in style, speech, and attitude personified by the flapper and her male counterpart lent a new sense of urgency to the reformers' efforts.

Because New York's speakeasies were nearly impossible to police, they allowed displays of sexuality in the 1920s that would have been possible only in the most disreputable saloons a generation earlier, fostering a rebellion against restrictions on sexual behavior as much as on drink. Homosexuality, transvestitism, and interracial relationships were all becoming more visible elements of the city's speakeasy culture. Once discreetly hidden and accessible only to those who actively sought them out, such displays of sexuality now became part of the amusement for every thrillseeker who ventured into the city's nightlife.

Nightclub reviews in *Variety* and other publications confirmed that speakeasies and clubs provided a backdrop for all sorts of displays of sexual openness as part of the cultural rebellion of the 1920s. Downtown, *Variety* commented, were gay-oriented bars where "the women sing bass . . . and the men sing soprano," while certain Times Square speakeasies developed reputations as the haunts of "pansies." In Harlem, numerous clubs toyed with patrons' preoccupations with sexuality and race. At times, even the permissive editors of *Variety* were tested by the unrestrained and "nasty" behavior found in some clubs. According to the editors, one club brought out so much "indecent dancing, bootlegging, flask carrying, open love-making and the presence of professional 'vamps'—some as young as 15," that it deserved the six raids it had endured in the span of four weeks.[18]

The sexual openness that characterized the period proved exhilarating for many New Yorkers, but it had its costs, too, especially for women. Of her nights spent on the town for *The New Yorker*, Lois Long recalled, "You never knew what you were drinking or who you'd wake up with." She noted that the unrestrained sexuality resulted in numerous unplanned pregnancies. Long added, "We wore wishbone diaphragms that weren't always reliable. There was a woman doctor who handled abortions for our crowd. She would take a vacation at Christmastime to rest up for the rush after New Year's Eve."[19]

While reformers looked at the sexual promiscuity of New York's drinking culture with dismay, prostitution concerned them even more. Reform groups like the Committee of Fourteen were adamant that the city's speakeasies and nightclubs were responsible for a new surge in prostitution and "deviancy" in New York City, and in the 1920s the committee labored extensively to find out which of New York's drinking establishments were harboring prostitutes and pimps. It argued that the owners and managers of speakeasies and wine cellars in working-class neighborhoods commonly used prostitution as a way to augment their incomes in the increasingly competitive and risky liquor trade. In some of these places, waitresses and hostesses told investigators they were forced not only to ply drinks on male patrons but to prostitute themselves as well. One seventeen-year-old hostess working in a Greek speakeasy summarized her situation to a Committee of Fourteen investigator by saying, "Either you lay or out you go." She said she had looked for work in at least three other speakeasies, but found that the situation in them was the same.[20]

The Committee of Fourteen was so concerned about prostitution in New York's speakeasy culture, and so confident in its conclusions, that in 1926 it pushed for a citywide crackdown on prostitution. Claiming that 360 of the 392 speakeasies it had investigated that year harbored prostitutes, and that 544 of the 998 hostesses encountered in these clubs had solicited investigators with offers of sex for money, Committee of Fourteen chairman Frederick Whitin demanded that Mayor Walker commit city funds to such an effort. The committee elaborated in internal reports, arguing that "low class clubs and speakeasies are virtual prostitution mills." It especially emphasized the danger such clubs posed to young women from outside New York who were being lured into jobs as hostesses in the city only to find themselves exploited as prostitutes.[21]

But few New Yorkers accepted the findings of the Committee of Fourteen at face value. In the social climate of the city in the mid-1920s, the claims of moral reformers and drys were regarded with more suspicion with each passing year. The Committee of Fourteen in particular was seen as an alarmist relic of earlier times. Though prostitution undoubtedly existed in nightclubs and speakeasies, critics argued that the committee's findings were ridiculously out of proportion, and that it was finding only what it wanted to find. *Variety* dismissed the committee's investigations of nightclubs as the work of amateurs committed to a predetermined conclusion. "If they decided a place was vicious and did not find it was, their immediate object appeared to create the viciousness," the editors commented. They added that the committee's efforts had become more outlandish and irrelevant with each passing year: "Neither the police nor the magistrates have much regard for the Committee, its members or investigators. Its methods are often reprehensible."[22]

Like the Anti-Saloon League, the Committee of Fourteen found itself scorned because it was committed to a strict moral vision that was increasingly out of sync with the urban culture of the 1920s. Part of the problem stemmed from the committee's inability to distinguish among prostitution, the relative sexual openness of the 1920s, and the many types of behavior that fell in between. In wavering statements about hostesses who appeared to be "occasional or professional prostitutes," the Committee of Fourteen claimed to find prostitution in the nightclubs it investigated, even if the evidence was flimsy. In a surveillance report on Peter's Restaurant on West Ninety-seventh Street, for example, the committee described "twenty unescorted women" in the restaurant, noting that they "were smoking cigarettes and some of them appeared to be under the influence of liquor." When the investigator witnessed single women moving from table to table exchanging addresses and phone numbers with men, he concluded that "most of them appeared to be probable prostitutes," though he admitted that his attempts to procure the services of a prostitute through the manager of the restaurant were unsuccessful.[23]

While committee investigators were intent on finding commercial prostitution in New York nightspots, they were far more likely to find women casually looking to take advantage of interested men to supplement their incomes. In a Rockaway Beach restaurant, for example, an investigator who bought drinks for two women was told by one of them that she was a telephone operator who was only making eighteen dollars a week, and that she might be interested in making some extra money on the side if he was interested. Far more numerous were the so-called charity cases involving women who exchanged sex for drinks, a night on the town, or even "gifts" of extra spending cash or money to help pay the rent.[24]

Although these "charity cases" had been part of working-class culture in New York since the turn of the century, Prohibition had increased the number of opportunities for this sort of interaction. With more single women frequenting bars, police surveillance of speakeasies limited, and the sexual standards of the 1920s far more open than they had been in previous generations, single women were free to engage in any sort of sexual transaction they wished, either for personal gratification or for profit. But this was not the explosion of commercial prostitution at which the Committee of Fourteen had expressed such alarm. In fact, evidence suggests that commercial prostitution actually declined in New York during the Prohibition era, in large part because the sexual openness of the era fostered more frequent and casual sexual exchanges between men and women, thus rendering commercial sex less necessary.[25]

In the context of the 1920s, dry groups like the Anti-Saloon League and moral reform organizations like the Committee of Fourteen shared a paternalistic concern that if women diverged from their traditional gender roles, they would become unsuspecting victims of alcohol abuse, prostitution, or both. These reformers seemed unable to grasp the possibility that women might actually take advantage of the social world created by the noble experiment to assert themselves and their desires. Indeed, many women in New York showed a daunting command of all aspects of the new culture, whether social, sexual, or economic. Women who worked in nightclubs, bars, and dance halls, rather than being victims, were especially bold opportunists willing to assert control over these realms. In the era of free-spending "suckers" and "butter and egg men," women saw taking advantage of such men as a normal part of the social scene, if not an added thrill of the nightclub era.

In fact, one of the most highly developed skills of nightclub hostesses in New York was their ability to fleece unsuspecting customers. Trained by their bosses "to get as much information as possible from prospective suckers regarding their bank accounts and business," hostesses came on to male patrons with the express goal of "mounting the check." "After enough money is spent," one hostess recounted to a Committee of Fourteen investigator, the goal is to get "the sucker drunk and the works [will] follow." Hostesses plied drinks on single male patrons at three or four dollars apiece, had patrons buy them drinks (which were watered down by the management), and danced with them for ten-dollar tips. Before long the "sucker" was broke and drunk to the point of helplessness. According to a hostess working at the Rendezvous, a West Eighty-fourth Street club owned by the gangster Red Sheehan, "any sucker who comes in here never walks out conscious. When his pockets are emptied or check obtained from him, he is carried out from here into a taxi, driven by a chauffeur who we know."[26]

In some lower-rate dance halls, these unwitting patrons were nicknamed "fish" by the hostesses, who sought to take them "hook, line, and sinker." Hostesses squeezed them for dances, drinks, and an evening's entertainment, then often ditched them before any sexual exchange was demanded. Other times, the racket was to blackmail men by getting them into compromising situations with women other than their wives. In fancier establishments, where sex was less a part of the equation than flirtation, hostesses were chosen for their good looks and had their talents rated on their ability to empty a male patron's wallet while making him enjoy it enough to come back another night. For their efforts, these hostesses earned tips and commissions on the checks they mounted, often as much as one-third of the total, which could bring them from $150 to $400 a week.[27]

Professional hostesses were not the only women who exploited male patrons this way. They had to compete with amateur women who were just as skilled in taking advantage of single male patrons in nightclubs. A Committee of Fourteen investigator discovered this one night in a Bronx nightclub. In his search to expose prostitutes, he was repeatedly taken by women who feigned interest in his solicitations, accepted drinks from him, and promptly disappeared into the crowd. No record indicates whether the investigator learned a lesson from these escapades, but the experience clearly showed that the women of the Prohibition era felt no compunction to adhere to the behavioral constraints and moral demands of the dry crusade.[28]

Perspectives on the relationship among speakeasies, sex, and liquor in New York City during the Prohibition era varied widely. While reformers tended to view speakeasies as places where innocent young women, lured by drink, could be exploited by men, the women who worked in them could be just as dangerous to unwitting patrons. But the experience found in most nightclubs resembled neither extreme. Despite the alarms raised in dry quarters, defenders of New York nightlife maintained that the integration of women into the drinking culture of the city was the best thing ever to happen to the city's social scene. Newspaper columnist Helen Lowry, for one, credited the flapper with permanently enlivening the city's club scene. "She is the first woman in history that has not been checked at home when man went forth alone in search of his pleasures," she wrote in the *New York Times*. "And because of her we have with us the most merry, the least jaded night life yet."[29]

Lowry and many others saw little reason to be concerned about the "naughtiness" and open sexuality that were part of the speakeasy and nightclub scene. Though copious amounts of illegal liquor consumed in New York's nightclubs could certainly lower the inhibitions of men and women, any observer could tell that the sexually charged atmosphere of the clubs was a big part of their appeal. As a cigarette girl working in the Orange Grove Club on Longwood Avenue in the Bronx explained to a Committee of Fourteen investigator, the young men and women in the club were there not just for alcohol but also for social companionship. From her perspective, "mostly everyone is anxious to be picked up."[30]

Despite the sexually charged atmosphere of the average nightclub, most New Yorkers insisted that the dangers found in clubs, cabarets, and speak-easies were grossly exaggerated. Certainly dangerous places existed in the city, but New Yorkers with any common sense could easily steer clear of them. As Helen Lowry acknowledged, the city's nightclubs were expected to provide "a sprinkling of expensive naughtiness" for their patrons, but overall they were safe and, in some cases, rather wholesome. In fact, Lowry argued, the greatest danger found in most clubs was posed by the shocking sight of exuberant young flappers who danced too wildly. This was a danger patrons would have to live with, explained one club owner, who asked Lowry, "How can I send the head waiter up to an innocent looking little girl whose mother lives on East Seventieth Street, and tell her to cut that sort of dancing?"[31]

In spite of the insistent chorus of reformers that nightclubs and speakeasies needed to be regulated for the moral protection of women, their calls were drowned out by more realistic voices like Lowry's. In fact, women emerged as some of the staunchest defenders of the city's nightclub culture in the 1920s. Many of them argued that nightclubs were growing more respectable all the time, and that they marked the refinement, not the decline, of urban culture. Lois Long, for one, scoffed at the notion that serious dangers, moral or otherwise, lurked in the New York night. Complaining of the people who asked her to direct them to "a really rowdy and terrible place," she declared, "When a few alarmists stop writing articles that give people the idea that New York is full of joints where hundred dollar bills are casually tucked into garters of entertainers by aristocratic gentlemen in full evening dress; where notorious gunmen roam about looking threatening in a nice way; where the management starts a little blackmailing to amuse the guests; where half-dressed young women dance on the tops of tables and rush about kissing the male members of the audience in picturesque abandonment; this town will be better off." "Sin and iniquity do not flourish in full view of the casual night club goer," she concluded. In regard to the sexual openness of the era, she added that, "as far as New York is concerned, the orgy's place is in the home."[32]

By the end of the Prohibition era, the idea that women could not only fend for themselves in speakeasies but also enjoy them on their own terms would become ingrained in American culture. For a new generation of women, speakeasies were places where "smart women" could feel at home and enjoy the company of other sophisticated men and women. More important, women had shattered the stereotype that all American women were temperance supporters. Whereas reformers like Carry Nation and Frances Willard of the WCTU were once thought to embody the American woman's stance on temperance, now women who rebelled against the moralism of Prohibition were becoming equally visible cultural icons. In particular, a trio of New York nightclub hostesses—Belle Livingstone, Helen Morgan, and Texas Guinan—emerged in the mid-1920s as the counterparts to the great women drys.[33]

As the reigning queens of New York's nightlife in the mid-1920s, Livingstone, Morgan, and Guinan were three of the city's most prominent opponents of the Eighteenth Amendment, male or female, and they won adulation for it. Livingstone, a former showgirl, ran some of the city's most luxurious nightclubs. At the height of her popularity, she commanded a five-story resort on Park Avenue at Fifty-eighth Street, described as a "riot of decoration," complete with a miniature golf course and ping pong tables. Though federal authorities raided Livingstone's clubs repeatedly, she defiantly reopened them each time, much to the delight of her patrons, who lauded her as a wet heroine. Only after she was convicted of Volstead violations in 1931 and sentenced to thirty days in jail did Livingstone quit the trade.[34]

Singer and celebrity hostess Helen Morgan was another of New York's martyrs for the wet cause, especially after she suffered a particularly egregious example of abuse of power at the hands of the Bureau of Prohibition. When federal raiders under the direction of Major Maurice Campbell burst into her popular nightclub, Chez Morgan, and seized twenty-five bottles of liquor in December 1927, they took the liberty of smashing the club's glassware, ripping out its plumbing and wiring, and carting away the furniture, causing approximately $75,000 in damage. Rather than sending a message to the defiant city, Campbell's tactics infuriated Unites States Attorney for New York Charles Tuttle, who was a stickler for procedure, and prompted a public outcry. Campbell was vilified for his reckless tactics, and Morgan was cleared of any wrongdoing in federal court in absence of any proof of liquor sales. In a strange shift of gender stereotypes, the city newspapers likened Campbell to a hysterical Carry Nation, while Morgan was praised as a hero for standing up to the federal government.[35]

While Livingstone and Morgan were admired for defying the Volstead Act and its enforcers, by far the greatest anti-Prohibition heroine the city produced was Texas Guinan, whose standing in Prohibition-era New York prompted journalist Stephen Graham to write, "Jimmy Walker rules New York by day; Texas Guinan by night." Between 1924 and 1931, Guinan ran a succession of the city's most spectacular midtown nightclubs—the Texas Guinan Club, the Salon Royal, the El Fey, the Del Fey, the Club Intime, the Argonaut, and the 300 Club. The "gay, lighthearted, irresponsible" atmosphere of her clubs attracted patrons who reveled until 5:00 A.M. as they threw felt snowballs at each other and had showgirls dangle cherries into their mouths. Patrons watched with rapt attention as the dynamic and irreverent Guinan introduced scantily clad dancers with her trademark line, "Give this little girl a great big hand." Guinan personally loved to bait big spenders as part of an evening's entertainment, calling out to them in her deep voice, "Hello, Sucker!"[36]

Born Mary Louise Cecilia Guinan in Waco, Texas, in 1884, the one-time B-movie star entertained editors, baseball players, senators, diplomats, and millionaires in her nightclubs, reminding them all to check their society addresses at the door. She presided over her clubs, according to Stephen Graham, "like a gorgeous tamer who has just let herself into a large cage of pet tigers." She welcomed strangers like they were old friends and made it a point to greet customers by name. Even Prohibition agents took note of her legendary hospitality and her talent for "making people feel at home, [and] acting the part of a very good hostess." When Prohibition agent James

White swore a deposition against Guinan in 1928, he recalled how well she had treated him on a late night at the Salon Royal at 310 West Fifty-eighth Street. Despite having met White only once previously, Guinan came over to his table and insisted, "You folks must come to my party tomorrow night. I am giving a party . . . and if you come I will have a table reserved for you." When White responded that he had been to the Salon Royal on other occasions and had been unable to get a table, Guinan replied, "Well, why didn't you call for me? I would have had an extra table put in for you." She promised White, "Any time you come here and cannot get seats, just call for me." This kind of treatment kept patrons coming back to Guinan's clubs night after night, despite the club's exorbitant prices, which, according to Prohibition agents, included a nine-dollar cover charge, nine dollars for a round of ginger ale, ten dollars for a pint of whiskey, and twenty-five dollars for a quart of champagne.[37]

Guinan rose to the top of New York's competitive nightclub trade on a wave of social and financial success. At the height of her popularity, *Variety* estimated her income to be $7,000 a week, while Stanley Walker reported that Guinan once earned $700,000 in one ten-month period. Guinan also demonstrated some of the most brazen and public resistance to Prohibition enforcement the city had ever seen. The Bureau of Prohibition raided her clubs repeatedly, but she greeted each raid with humor, having her band play "The Prisoner's Song" as she was taken away to the stationhouse. Guinan accepted periodic interruptions by law enforcement as part of her trade, but she also saw them as excellent publicity, especially when U.S. senators or police officers were caught in the raids.

To New Yorkers, Guinan possessed an astonishing resilience. She endured padlockings, indictments, and injunctions yet quickly returned to work each time. Though summoned to federal court in two criminal cases and nine civil cases during the noble experiment, Guinan was never convicted of a crime. As she neither owned her clubs nor personally sold liquor to her patrons, she successfully argued in each case that she was merely a hostess who had broken no law.[38]

But Guinan was definitely more than a hostess. As the "Queen of the Nightclubs," she not only showed New Yorkers a good time but also acted as one of their symbolic leaders in the rebellion against Prohibition. She

mocked the Volstead Act simply by going to work every night, and her refusal to give up her trade despite dozens of raids demonstrated that Prohibition enforcement would remain an impossibility in the city as long as
people like her were willing to defy the Eighteenth Amendment. As a successful businesswoman and entertainer who challenged the conventions of
society and the law, Guinan, like Mayor Walker, stood out as someone who
understood the place of leisure and entertainment in modern urban life.
She knew what her customers wanted, and endeavored to provide it to
them regardless of interference from the Bureau of Prohibition.

The fact that Guinan was a woman was even more important in terms of
her crusade against Prohibition. The press depicted her as the archrival and
long-awaited antidote to Brooklyn's Ella Boole, who became the national
president of the Woman's Christian Temperance Union in 1925. The much
older Boole, born just before the Civil War, seemed to embody all that was
old-fashioned about the temperance movement. The wife of a Methodist
preacher, Boole was active in several reform causes but was often bitter
and vindictive in her comments about wets. Compared with Guinan, she
seemed to have no understanding of New Yorkers' desires to embrace the
cosmopolitan culture of the city. The contrast between the two women,
both New Yorkers, was highlighted vividly in a 1933 *Vanity Fair* cartoon by
Miguel Covarrubias that depicted Guinan and Boole sitting at a nightclub
table discussing the pros and cons of Prohibition. By virtue of her visibility,
Guinan offered the highest-profile challenge yet to the temperance movement's ideal of womanhood, and her example sent a message to the country
that there were plenty of women in American cities who were bold and
brash enough to defy Prohibition and have a good time doing it.[39]

While the flappers, women journalists, and nightclub hostesses of 1920s
New York drastically altered long-standing ideas about American women
and their place in the debate over alcohol, the revolution in women's social
behavior that they embodied also had clear political ramifications. Indeed,
the change in women's attitudes toward drinking led to equally important
developments in the realm of women's politics.[40]

Women's agitation against Prohibition emerged in the mid-1920s as a
reaction to the incessant droning of temperance leaders that *all* Ameri-

can women stood steadfastly behind the noble experiment. Organizations like the Woman's National Committee for Law Enforcement, the Anti-Saloon League, the WCTU, and the Salvation Army consistently called upon women to uphold the dry experiment, despite clear signs that many women were tiring of the demands of the drys. The widespread assumption that American women uniformly supported the dry cause was epitomized by the WCTU's Ella Boole, who famously opened her statement to a 1928 congressional panel on Prohibition by proclaiming, "I represent the women of America!"[41]

Throughout the 1920s, there had been plenty of indications that the political alliance between the temperance movement and women was falling apart. In 1920, for example, women delegates at the New York State Democratic Convention expressed strong opposition to Prohibition, demanding its repeal and urging state legislators to legalize beer and wine. In 1924, after women drys made several speeches at the Republican National Convention goading the party to stand by the noble experiment or face the wrath of women voters, a letter to the *New York Times* proclaimed, "It is absurd to state that the women of America are 'dry' as a whole because a few prohibition organizations send their delegates to speak." The writer, a woman, continued, "These women do not represent the women of their country, but only the women of the temperance societies to which they happen to belong."[42]

As their resentment of the dry movement grew, women began to form political organizations opposed to the Eighteenth Amendment. Among the first were the Molly Pitcher Clubs, organized in several Northeast states beginning in 1922 as women's auxiliary branches of the Association against the Prohibition Amendment (AAPA), the Delaware-based lobbying group dominated by prominent industrialists. Though the Molly Pitcher Clubs enjoyed a brief moment in the spotlight, highlighted in New York by demonstrations in favor of the repeal of the Mullan-Gage Law, to many women they appeared to be an afterthought of the AAPA and had only limited political influence. The Molly Pitcher Clubs attracted only a few hundred members by 1924, and then disbanded in 1928.[43]

Women's opposition to Prohibition advanced more rapidly when women's groups organized independently of men's repeal associations. M. Louise

Gross, a suburban New Yorker with close connections to Governor Al Smith, organized the first such group in 1926 when she transformed the remnants of a local Molly Pitcher Club into her own repeal group, the Women's Committee for the Modification of the Eighteenth Amendment. In a statement for the group, Gross announced, "The time has now come when we must organize a strong militant national women's anti-prohibition organization to offset the activities of the WCTU and other drys." In a magazine article profiling the group, Gross explained that her goal was to bring housewives, professional women, and society women together to join forces against Prohibition and to educate American women about the negative effects of the Eighteenth Amendment.[44]

Women temperance leaders saw Gross's efforts as a serious threat to their political standing and responded with strong criticism. One WCTU member called Gross an "insult to our country and womanhood" and pledged, "We certainly will fight this." Nevertheless, Gross, who received threatening letters from drys around the country, stood her ground. She responded forcefully to her attackers, writing to one critic, "I am rather suspicious that the various letters I receive like yours . . . are part of an organized campaign of the Drys or the WCTU or Anti-Saloon League . . . which is getting annoyed because some decent, honest, patriotic American women . . . are working against prohibition." Gross insisted that there were plenty more "decent, honest, patriotic American women" like her who shared the desire to join a movement for repeal.[45]

Gross's efforts eventually stalled. Though women, particularly in New York, were receptive to her message, by the end of 1928 the group had only $285 in its treasury. In addition, Gross's organization changed names three times in the span of a few years, suggesting either disorganization or a lack of direction within the group. Worse, Gross's ideological messages were muddled and constantly shifting, alternating between calls for education, political action, and even armed rebellion in the fight against Prohibition. On some occasions, she urged Democratic and Republican supporters to steer their parties toward repeal, while at other times she called for the formation of a third party dedicated to repeal.[46]

Though unsuccessful, Louise Gross's early efforts spearheaded a women's campaign that would only grow stronger in the late 1920s. By publicizing the fact that many women had lost faith in dry reform, Gross opened the way for a larger non-partisan, grassroots repeal campaign organized by women. She also helped uncover the language that women would use in that repeal campaign. She injected patriotism into their efforts, arguing that her ultimate goal was the "Restoration of the Bill of Rights," thus shielding women repeal advocates from accusations that they were only interested in legalizing cocktails. To counter the dry movement, she also successfully urged other groups like the New York City Bar Association and the Brooklyn Democratic Club to come out against the Eighteenth Amendment in the hopes that their public statements would make it easier for other wets to express their political views.[47]

Gross also showed the repeal movement how to borrow tactics from women drys. Like the WCTU, she sent delegates to lobby members of Congress, wielding the threat of organized women voters as the drys had always done. After noting that many of the hate letters she received were adorned with stickers bearing dry slogans like "Give Prohibition Its Chance! The Liquor Traffic Had Its Day," Gross printed stickers for her group's correspondence that read, "Vote for Wet Congressmen—End Prohibition."[48]

More than anything else, Gross demonstrated that growing numbers of American women had changed their minds about Prohibition and were ready to turn to politics to prove it. At a time when Caroline Ware noticed women New Yorkers registering to vote in greater numbers and getting more involved in political clubs, women from all over the country were joining the board of Gross's Women's Modification Union. Gross noted receiving letters from women in Iowa, Nebraska, and Colorado requesting information on how to set up local repeal organizations of their own.[49]

Gross's work came as national polls showed that an increasing number of women who had initially supported Prohibition were expressing doubt about the noble experiment, if not disavowing it altogether. A 1928 poll on Prohibition in *Outlook,* for example, showed that while 70 percent of women still supported Prohibition, the number of women under the age of forty-five who opposed it was growing. Martha Bensley Bruère, who analyzed the poll for *Outlook,* pointed out that the number of professional and urban women who opposed Prohibition was even higher. A similar poll conducted by the Women's National Republican Club a year later showed much greater defections of women from the dry ranks. Of the 1,500 women polled, 1,393 expressed a desire to see the Eighteenth Amendment repealed or modified, while only 103 respondents voted to keep Prohibition as it stood.[50]

In 1929, the emerging women's campaign for repeal would be galvanized by Pauline Morton Sabin, one of the many American women who had reversed her stand on Prohibition. A wealthy New York socialite and heiress to the Morton Salt fortune, Sabin in many regards made an unlikely repeal leader. Though she came from a family active in Republican Party politics, including a grandfather who had been the governor of Nebraska and a father who had served as secretary of the navy to President Theodore Roosevelt, Sabin did not express interest in politics until the early 1920s. She had not participated in the women's suffrage movement or campaigned for the Eighteenth Amendment, and she entered politics in the 1920s only because she believed that her work with New York City charities would be more effective if she carried more political influence. Once involved in politics, however, Sabin quickly rose through the ranks. After becoming active in the New York Republican Party in the early 1920s, Sabin was named to the Republican National Committee in 1923.[51]

Sabin, like many women of her social standing, had originally been a supporter of the Eighteenth Amendment. As she explained in 1932, "I felt I should approve of it because it would help my two sons . . . I thought a world without liquor would be a beautiful world." Yet the failure of Prohibition to accomplish any meaningful change in the United States unsettled Sabin, who felt that alcohol had become a greater problem during Prohibition than it had been before the noble experiment. She was particularly disturbed by the hypocrisy of Americans who claimed to support Prohibition but did not abstain from using alcohol personally. Like many American women, Sabin also grew to resent the insistence of temperance leaders that all American women unfailingly supported the noble experiment. For Sabin, the last straw came in 1928, when she heard Ella Boole of the WCTU state to Congress, "I represent the women of America!" Upon hearing this, Sabin later told an interviewer, she remarked to herself, "Well, lady, here's one woman you don't represent."[52]

Sabin kept her doubts about Prohibition in check through the 1928 election, when she campaigned actively for Herbert Hoover without protesting the Republican Party's support for the Eighteenth Amendment. Only after Hoover's inauguration did she entertain the thought of actively campaigning against Prohibition. She resigned her position on the Republican National Committee in April 1929, announcing at a Women's Republican Luncheon, "I want to devote my untrammeled efforts towards working for a change in the Prohibition law." Within weeks, Sabin was busy forming the Women's Organization for National Prohibition Reform (WONPR), a national, bipartisan women's group dedicated to repeal.[53]

Initially, Sabin's anti-Prohibition efforts reflected her lofty social standing, as the first WONPR gatherings were attended solely by women from the highest echelons of East Coast society. On May 29, 1929, when Sabin met with fifty women in Chicago to elect officers for WONPR, the membership roster featured some of the most prominent family names in the country—Whitney, Sloan, Pratt, Nicoll, Van Rensselaer, Mather, and Pierrepont. As Grace Root later wrote in the organization's official history, Sabin and her colleagues "were determined that the women representing WONPR should be outstanding in their respective communities as women of unimpeachable integrity, and known for their interest in public welfare and good citizenship." They were also fantastically wealthy.[54]

While the aristocratic standing of its founding members gave WONPR instant recognition, it also gave temperance groups plenty of ammunition for their initial attacks on the group. Harping on the elite social status of WONPR's core members, dry leaders dismissed the group as a cadre of libertine socialites. One evangelical paper criticized WONPR by saying, "These wet women, though rich most of them are, are no more than the scum of the earth, parading around in skirts, and possibly late at night flirting with other women's husbands at drunken and fashionable resorts." Clarence True Wilson, secretary of the Methodist Board of Temperance, dismissed WONPR as a "little group of wine-drinking society women," while Dr. Mary Armor, president of the Georgia WCTU, referred to

WONPR as "Mrs. Sabin and her cocktail-drinking women," and pledged, "We will outlive them, out-love them, out-talk them, out-pray them and out-vote them."[55]

Drys were mistaken in dismissing WONPR as merely a group of wealthy socialites, however. After several years of observing flappers, celebrities, writers, and nightclub hostesses like Texas Guinan challenge the dry status quo, the nation had grown to appreciate iconoclastic women as part of the zeitgeist of the 1920s. The media especially had become fond of daring, newsworthy women, and they welcomed Sabin and the women of WONPR onto the national scene as the latest incarnations of the smart and sophisticated women of the era. Glowing profiles in *The New Yorker, Vogue, Vanity Fair,* and other magazines praised Sabin as a "charming aristocrat," "alive with vitality, beautifully dressed, vastly interested in the world's goings on and equipped with a ready, sophisticated tongue with which to talk matters over."[56]

The women of WONPR were by no means flappers. They did not dance or dress like flappers, and they insisted that they did not drink like flappers. But the press portrayed them as having the same spirit, daring, and energy as flappers, which gave them considerable appeal. In contrast with the women of the WCTU, a reporter for *Time* argued, the women of WONPR were "more charming than churchy," while photographic comparisons in the press of the graceful Sabin and the WCTU's dowdy Ella Boole visually reiterated the same point.[57]

Like Texas Guinan, Pauline Sabin became a symbol of the independent woman of the 1920s, the difference being that Sabin translated Guinan's model of independent social behavior into a model of independent political behavior. Sabin, in essence, showed American women that they were no longer bound to support the Prohibition movement politically, just as flappers had shown women that they were not obligated to uphold outdated social mores. This message had enormous appeal for American women, especially in New York and other urban areas. Far more successfully than Louise Gross had, Sabin made repeal a central issue of women's politics in the late 1920s. Her efforts through WONPR destroyed any remaining notion that the women of the 1920s shared a uniform code of political behavior, or that they were obliged to support the dry cause.

With Sabin working to open up a gulf between women wets and women drys, the influence of the flapper on women's politics became obvious. The media found it impossible to separate WONPR members' politics from their style, and though Sabin did not tacitly encourage such treatment, the women's repeal movement benefited from stories on "the Sabine women," which paid as much attention to their dress, jewelry, and style as to their political goals. In *Vanity Fair*, for example, Jefferson Chase described the WONPR leaders as "beautiful, cultured, and practical to their fingertips," adding, "They . . . are invoking all the social and personal arts of their sex to win Congress to a more balanced view of [Prohibition]." Yet the focus on style did not obscure WONPR's political accomplishments. Chase marveled that WONPR had "set up one of the most amusing and effective lobbies which the Capitol has ever seen," and noted that "it uses the full force of social blandishments and sex appeal upon the Senators and Congressmen." By emphasizing women wets as feminine, cultured, and smart, the press seemed to have discovered "flapper's politics." Political opposition to Prohibition now became as essential to the identity of the sophisticated modern woman as bobbed hair or a beaded dress had been earlier in the decade.[58]

Taking advantage of this positive treatment in the press and using her formidable skills as a political organizer, Sabin quickly built WONPR into the leading repeal organization in the United States. In New York, where the organization was based, WONPR passed the 50,000-member mark by 1930, overtaking the 45,000 women enrolled in the state chapter of the WCTU. By the end of 1931, the number of women enrolled in WONPR nationally had grown to more than 400,000, surpassing the 381,000 women enrolled nationwide in the WCTU. Soon, WONPR membership surpassed 1.3 million, making it by far the largest repeal group in the country and making Sabin the de facto leader of the national repeal movement.[59]

As WONPR's membership grew, women's dry organizations desperately sought to hold onto their waning authority. They accused Sabin of dishonest recruiting tactics and asserted that the millionaire husbands of WONPR board members were financing the organization. They also sought to emphasize WONPR's connection to New York City, insisting that the organization reflected the views of Park Avenue socialites, not average American women. Sabin fought back by challenging the WCTU leaders and other prominent women drys to public debates in the city, asking them to back up their claims about their supporters and the supposed benefits of Prohibition. At one event sponsored by the American Women's Association, Sabin humiliated drys by challenging the WCTU to produce a list of 1,000 New Yorkers who had been reformed by Prohibition.[60]

With the contest over repeal becoming more heated, WONPR campaigned aggressively to win the endorsement of prominent women political leaders in New York and across the country. As WONPR broadcast the message that it was acceptable for women to change their minds about Prohibition and speak out publicly against it, the WCTU scrambled to preserve its eroding base, reaching out to women leaders for support and insisting that the Prohibition experiment could succeed with better enforcement. In 1930 two prominent women drys, Mamie White Colvin and Charlotte Wilkinson, lobbied New York's first lady, Eleanor Roosevelt, to express her support for Prohibition. In a letter, Wilkinson urged Roosevelt to defend the Eighteenth Amendment in order "to establish the fact that the leading and most prominent characters in this country believe in the good of prohibition." At the same time, WONPR member Elizabeth Lovett also lobbied Roosevelt, informing her of WONPR's growth and urging her to join the groundswell of support for the repeal movement. (Roosevelt remained unenthusiastically in the dry camp for the time being. She wrote to Wilkinson, "I believe in Prohibition but I can see some difficulty in its enforcement. I am not sure, however, just what changes should be made to better the situation.")[61]

Through Sabin's work, repeal became the dominant women's political issue of the late 1920s, and WONPR quickly gained the upper hand in the battle for the support of American women. From its headquarters in New York, WONPR took the repeal message nationwide, appealing to women not to let themselves be spoken for by the dry lobby. As a measure of their success, Sabin made sure that every prominent defection to the repeal campaign was well publicized, and she emphasized the enthusiasm that college, urban, and professional women were showing for repeal. At a time when many American women were said to have little interest in politics, Sabin found the level of women's commitment to the repeal issue inspiring, and she rejoiced as the movement attracted women of all classes, ethnicities, and races, making it far more welcoming than the dry movement had ever been. She told her supporters, "I know of nothing since the days of the campaign for woman's suffrage to equal the campaign which women are now conducting for repeal of the Eighteenth Amendment."[62]

By the close of the decade, the relationship between women and the dry camp had almost completely reversed. No one denied that American women had been a central force in enacting Prohibition, but now women repeal advocates made Ella Boole's proclamation that "the Nineteenth Amendment will safeguard the Eighteenth Amendment" appear hopelessly out of touch. As journalist Margaret Culkin Banning observed in a 1930 *Vogue* article, women's social and political behavior had changed significantly during the 1920s. Banning noted that "most American women of the last decade or so had been brought up to consider drink their natural enemy . . . The entire female sex was supposed to have a complaint against alcoholic beverages, and all but a few unfortunate women . . . kept pretty well away from it." But Prohibition had changed all that, Banning argued, adding that women of the 1920s no longer saw drinking as a sign of disrepute, just as they no longer held up Prohibition as an example of a worthy moral reform.[63]

The full effects of women's changing stance on Prohibition would not become apparent until 1932, when a national repeal movement gained momentum. But even before then, many American women were rejoicing in the sense of political liberation that Sabin and her colleagues had generated. Journalist Grace Robinson joked in *Liberty* magazine that the new wave of women's political activism on the issue of Prohibition had caught male politicians off guard. She mocked men's long-standing assumption that "women might be as flighty and disorganized as an army of fluttering hens on most issues . . . but on the subject of drink they were undoubtedly of one great herd mind. They would vote a mighty 'No!' on all questions pertaining to alcoholic beverages." The new generation of women, she noted, had in fact taken the repeal issue much further than men had.[64]

While the Prohibition era yielded numerous surprises, few were as startling as women's rebellion against the noble experiment. The temperance cause in the United States had always been linked to women, supported by women, and promoted as benefiting women and families, but in the 1920s, New York saw a new generation of women transform their relationship to alcohol socially and politically. Having been told by drys and other moral reformers for so long what constituted respectable behavior for women and what their position on alcohol had to be, women responded by defying the outdated and unrealistic demands put upon them. Young, urban women in particular abandoned the dry cause and, in doing so, enjoyed newfound social and political freedoms. By the end of the 1920s, the Prohibitionists, deprived of what had been their most reliable core of support, found their world turned upside down.

8
Hootch Joints in Harlem

Harlem emerged in the 1920s as the most vibrant African-American community in the nation. Dubbed the "Mecca of the New Negro," Harlem in the Jazz Age bustled with excitement. As a result of the Great Migration of the 1910s, the community was filled with tens of thousands of black migrants from the American South. An additional influx of immigrants from the West Indies pushed the population even higher, transforming what had once been a predominantly German-Jewish area into an almost entirely African-American one. The Harlem Renaissance was in full flower, and black writers and intellectuals garnered international attention, as did the singers and musicians of Harlem's vibrant jazz scene. Rents were high. Jobs—especially high-paying jobs—were hard to find, and abject poverty clashed with ostentatious displays of wealth. In *The Messenger,* writer Ira Reid described a community that was "throbbing, pulsating, and vibrating." The excitement was palpable, and in the 1920s African Americans looked at Harlem with pride and a sense that they were building "the greatest Negro City in the world."[1]

Yet the liquor question troubled Harlem, too. In the summer of 1923, the *Amsterdam News* warned its readers that a "death-dealing fluid" was ravaging the area. Under the headline "Liquor, Liquor, Everywhere!" the paper's editors warned that the foremost African-American community in the nation was about "to lose nearly all of its drug stores, cigar stores, bootblack parlors and delicatessen shops, as nearly all of them are engaged in the sale of alcoholic liquors." Ladies' department stores in the district hawked whiskey and gin under code names like "red stockings" and "white stockings." The Seventh and Twelfth Magistrates' Courts in Harlem were fingerprinting more defendants in intoxication cases than almost any other district court in Manhattan. From their pulpits, Harlem ministers deplored the high levels of public drunkenness witnessed in the neighborhood, and the *Amsterdam News* complained that "hootch joints in Harlem continue to be as busy as ever . . . drunken men may be staggering out of these dens of poison at all hours of the day." Most troubling of all, the editors complained, was the fact that one man, the English-born gangster Owney Madden, controlled 90 percent of the storefront liquor traffic in the district. Madden, they argued, had turned Harlem into a modern-day plantation for white thrillseekers.[2]

Newcomers and old-timers quarreled vehemently over the place of liquor and drinking in Harlem. While the community's moral guardians, described by some as "Black Victorians," called for efforts to staunch the area's supply of bootleg liquor, just as many residents looked for ways to get a piece of the profitable alcohol trade. While liquor fueled the jazz scene and flowed freely in the literary salons that were a source of community pride, in churches, ministers blamed "hootch joints" for a decline in the moral standards of the district. In speakeasies and dance clubs, more optimistic souls wondered if liquor and jazz might finally bring the white and black races together socially, even if only for a few hours at a time. Despite the numerous cultural changes that defined the era, the writers, ministers, moralists, and workers of Harlem often came back to the question of liquor.

The debate over the Eighteenth Amendment raged in Harlem just as it did in every other part of New York City during the Prohibition era, with one major distinction: in Harlem the Prohibition debate was also a debate about race. As residents knew all too well, race complicated all social and political issues in 1920s America. It determined where one lived and worked, and where and with whom one socialized. It altered relations involving sex, money, and politics. Now, with the controversy over alcohol already enveloping the entire city, the issue of race raised the stakes and made the debate over Prohibition in Harlem even more contentious.

The emphasis that the dry movement placed on "respectability," combined with the long history of racial prejudice within the temperance movement, infused the Prohibition issue with great symbolic meaning for African Americans seeking to improve their place in society. Many African Americans looked to Prohibition as an important opportunity to prove the decency and "respectability" of their race. If they showed respect for the dry laws, this logic held, they would be accorded better treatment from the nation as a whole. Others in the community disagreed, arguing that Prohibition was a racist and paternalistic intrusion into their lives. The double standards already visible in the enforcement of the Eighteenth Amendment suggested to many skeptics that African-American communities would be unfairly targeted to satisfy reformers. Others wondered if the city's booming trade in nightlife and liquor would yield opportunities for African Americans or lead to their exploitation. At a time when American interest in the "New Negro" subjected everything African American to greater scrutiny, the black community debated what exactly the noble experiment would mean for the relationships between blacks and whites, both in the city and in the nation as a whole.

The most immediate influence of the Prohibition debate in Harlem was the way it highlighted the growing gap between a traditional generation of post-Reconstruction leaders, who saw in Prohibition an opportunity for blacks to prove themselves as citizens, and a younger generation, more attuned to modern urban culture, who embraced the cultural rebellion of the Prohibition era as a sign of a less moralistic and possibly more tolerant nation.

Harlem's Black Victorians, the old guard of civic leaders, ministers, and moral reformers, had been vocal supporters of Prohibition since the early years of the dry movement. In the pages of the *Amsterdam News*, Harlem's leading newspaper, they promoted the temperance ideal both to Harlem residents and to the paper's substantial national readership. Kelly Miller, a Howard University sociology professor who wrote a weekly column for the paper, and fellow columnists Edgar Grey and Ernest Rice McKinney used the pages of the *Amsterdam News* to voice their opposition to drinking, speakeasies, and bootlegging, but for slightly different reasons than those of their white counterparts. Arguing that the issue of Prohibition carried the same moral gravity for the black community in the 1920s that slavery had in the nineteenth century, they insisted that the temperance movement provided African Americans with a critical opportunity to demonstrate the "respectability" of their race to the rest of the nation.

The fervent support for Prohibition demonstrated by figures like Miller, McKinney, and Grey contrasted sharply with the racist reputation of much of the dry movement. Though a few of the nation's leading temperance organizations had made efforts to reach out to African Americans, more notable were the alliances that drys had forged with the Ku Klux Klan and other nativist organizations. The belief in many dry circles was that temperance was an Anglo-Saxon ideal that would have to be imposed on supposedly intemperate African Americans, just as it would have to be imposed on immigrants. This link between Prohibitionists and the ideology of white supremacy was addressed in African-American journals like *The Crisis,* which in 1929 criticized the Anti-Saloon League's Bishop James Cannon, Jr., by noting bluntly that "Bishop Cannon dislikes liquor and Niggers."[3]

In spite of sentiments like these, Black Victorians embraced the Eighteenth Amendment enthusiastically. As Kelly Miller assured his readers in the *Amsterdam News,* "The cause of Prohibition promises [to deliver] more beneficial results for the race than any other movement." Echoing Progressive arguments that Prohibition would foster prosperity and the moral renewal of the nation, Miller insisted that the Eighteenth Amendment would do even more for African Americans by strengthening their political power, increasing black homeownership rates, decreasing death and crime rates, and reducing the number of lynchings and race riots nationwide.[4]

Miller and his colleagues insisted that African Americans had a solemn duty to obey Prohibition as part of the Constitution. They argued that the strict enforcement of the Eighteenth Amendment would only bolster their calls for the enforcement of the Fourteenth and Fifteenth Amendments, which guaranteed civil rights and voting rights for African Americans. As an *Amsterdam News* editorial put it, "The best interest of the Negro will be found in the enforcement of the Constitution . . . and for this reason he ought to be willing to be denied whiskey, wine and beer if such a denial will give backbone to the supreme law of the land." One African-American politician in neighboring Jersey City went so far as to suggest that if the

Eighteenth Amendment were ever repealed, it would open the possibility for a repeal of the Thirteenth Amendment and a return to legal slavery in the United States.[5]

Black Victorians leveled harsh criticism against African Americans who refused to abide by the Volstead Act, condemning them as "race traitors." Believing as white Prohibitionists did that women were the most important supporters of the dry experiment, Kelly Miller further singled out for derision African-American women who failed to defend Prohibition. In one of his columns he wrote that "any Negro woman who votes against [Prohibition] votes against both her race and her sex."[6]

With so much at stake in the Eighteenth Amendment, the old guard expressed great disappointment when the noble experiment failed to take root within the city's black enclaves. They believed that the African-American community of New York was squandering a long-awaited opportunity to present itself as orderly, respectable, and temperate. "Perhaps the whites can afford this sort of thing," Ernest Rice McKinney wrote in the *Amsterdam News* in 1925. "I know the Negroes cannot afford it." Embarrassed by this failure, editors in *The Crisis* lamented, "We are a drunken land today and a drunken race."[7]

A younger, more modern Harlem population responded to the Black Victorians' impassioned pleas for African Americans to support the Eighteenth Amendment. While the old guard called for temperance, Theophilus Lewis, a young theater critic and columnist for the *Amsterdam News,* quipped that drinking was so widespread in Harlem that gin was considered the new "Aframerican national beverage." (Lewis's assessment stood in stark contrast to the paternalistic claims of white reformers like Martha Bensley Bruère, who naively asserted that "Negroes as a whole are not drinking . . . for them personally Prohibition works.") Lewis's colleague George Schuyler, a thirty-year-old writer who contributed to *The Nation, American Mercury,* and *The Messenger,* echoed the more realistic assessment that African Americans were not finding many good reasons to join the dry crusade. Despite pleas from the old guard for temperance, Schuyler observed that drinking continued unabated in the black neighborhoods of Manhattan, Queens, and Brooklyn, and on all levels of African-American society—working class, middle class, and elite.[8]

Schuyler's observations about the reluctance of African Americans in New York to obey the Eighteenth Amendment were apt. Even Harlem church groups were drinking in defiance of the Prohibition laws, and on several occasions in the 1920s, excursions and picnics planned by African-American churches ended in raids, drunken skirmishes between revelers and police, and arrests for alcohol sales. In one case, a day trip to Bear Mountain organized by a group from Harlem's Mother AME Zion Church ended with police confiscating 250 bottles of liquor, including 42 bottles from one enterprising member of the congregation who hid them in her baby bag to sell to other picnickers. The incident demonstrated that even groups that should have been most receptive to the pleas of Black Victorians were disobeying the Volstead Act in unceremonious fashion.[9]

This disparity between what the Black Victorians hoped for from Harlem residents and how they actually lived their lives revealed the old guard's resistance to the vast cultural changes ushered in by the 1920s. They reacted to the intemperance of the era with a paternalistic fury similar to the anger expressed by white temperance reformers at the failure of the dry agenda. Just as William Anderson of the Anti-Saloon League had lashed out at the social behavior of immigrants and Catholics, Black Victorians now assigned blame for the failure of the Volstead Act in Harlem to the unwillingness of the African-American community to discipline itself.

The outspoken African-American leaders who denounced drinkers and bootleggers as "race traitors" and insisted on strict adherence to the Eighteenth Amendment were sadly out of touch with the majority of black New Yorkers. Their fears of the consequences should African Americans disregard the dry laws were not unfounded, however. As part of the generation of black leaders who had come of age during the post-Reconstruction era, with its emphasis on racial uplift and self-improvement, they had seen first hand the difficulties African Americans had faced in claiming their rightful place in American society, and they were wary of any behavior that would endanger the social standing of blacks. But they now encountered a younger population, more than 66 percent of whom had migrated from the American South. These newcomers cared little about the moral preoccupations of the old guard. They viewed the migration northward as an opportunity to escape the rigid social restrictions that had defined their lives in the Jim Crow South. For these transplants, who had come looking for work and a way to escape violence and segregation, Harlem was a place to explore new personal freedoms that had been denied them in the South, including the freedom to drink, dance, dress, and socialize as they pleased. Faced with the moral outrage expressed by reformers like Kelly Miller, many recent migrants to New York came to regard the Black Victorians as an obstacle to their personal liberation.[10]

Money, or more precisely economic survival, factored into the equation as well. Many black New Yorkers embraced the Prohibition-era liquor trade as a new and badly needed economic opportunity. Despite the common perception of the 1920s as a decade of prosperity, life was still fraught with economic hardship for African Americans in New York. They faced great difficulty finding jobs; as the *Amsterdam News* frequently commented, many white-owned businesses in Harlem employed no African Americans at all. The paper calculated that in 1928 the district's eighty-five chain stores together employed a total of only twelve African Americans, while another study estimated that 59 percent of Harlem businesses in the 1920s employed whites only. The most desirable union jobs were all but off limits to blacks, a reality George Schuyler noted in 1925 when he wrote that "the unions control many industries and it is next to impossible for the dark brother to get admitted to many of them." "Fact is," he continued, "the Negro of New York state is very largely restricted to working as porter, cook, elevator operator, messenger, laborer, musician, chauffeur, laundress, maid, cook, dishwasher, stevedore, waiter, and janitor. Negroes doing other kinds of work are the exception."[11]

With limited employment opportunities, the average black family in New York City brought home only $1,300 annually, compared with the citywide average of $1,570. Poor housing conditions and rent gouging by landlords in Harlem made the economic situation even more difficult. The average annual rent in Harlem in 1928 was $480, well above the average rental price of $316 for the rest of Manhattan. Families in Harlem not only spent upwards of 33 percent of their income on housing costs but also lived in substandard conditions despite the inflated prices they paid. As a result, African-American families commonly took in boarders to meet rent costs. According to one district resident, the housing crisis in Harlem meant that "a four or five room apartment was . . . often crowded to capacity with roomers. In many instances, two entire families occupy space intended for only one. When bedtime comes, there is the feverish activity of moving furniture about, making down cots or preparing floor-space as sleeping quarters."[12]

Faced with such conditions, African Americans in New York looked to the illegal liquor trade during Prohibition, as well as to employment in Harlem's nightclubs and speakeasies, as important sources of economic opportunity. Even black drys were forced to accept that Prohibition offered the promise of financial gain, if not the dream of outright riches, for many African Americans. On the most basic level, black Americans found small-time bootlegging a profitable venture that required little more than a bottle of liquor and the courage to defy a laxly enforced federal law. Surveillance reports compiled by the Committee of Fourteen and federal court records from the era show that many Harlem men entered the bootlegging trade simply by selling shots of whiskey to nightclub patrons from pint flasks hidden in their coat pockets. Black women also joined the city's liquor trade. The *Amsterdam News* reported on African-American women in Harlem and Brooklyn who sold illegal or homemade liquor out of their homes or opened apartment speakeasies in working-class tenement buildings to augment their household income. *Amsterdam News* reporter Walter Lifton wrote about a five-story tenement in an African-American neighborhood in Brooklyn that had at least one apartment speakeasy on each floor. To solicit business, the proprietors simply called out to locals and passersby from the front stoop or an apartment window.[13]

For many black New Yorkers, small-time liquor peddling was a practical way to deal with the costs of living in overpriced housing. Over time, exorbitant rents and financial hardship in Harlem gave birth to the ubiquitous "rent parties" of the day, which promised live music, food, dance, and plenty of homemade corn whiskey or gin to guests who paid a nominal admission charge. By hosting parties a few days before the rent was due, or even on a weekly basis, renters could be sure to collect enough to pay the landlord or bill collector. According to Frank Byrd, a reporter for the New Deal–era Federal Writers' Project, hundreds of Harlem residents opened their apartment doors on weekend nights at the height of the rent-party craze, admitting neighbors and strangers in order to provide "a partial solution to the problem of excessive rents and dreadfully subnormal incomes."[14]

While the liquor was obviously a big draw for party goers, the parties served a social need as well, supplying badly needed and inexpensive amusement to working-class porters, servants, and laborers, many of whom were recent arrivals to New York looking for the opportunity to meet people, reconnect with friends, and court suitors. Despite police raids and attempts by organized crime to capitalize on the craze by staging simulated "rent parties" of their own, the rent party remained a Harlem institution into the Depression era. Similar parties kept cash-strapped labor or community associations funded through the sale of liquor, especially after the stock market crash of 1929.[15]

For those who were reluctant to enter the liquor trade themselves, Prohibition opened up numerous, less risky economic opportunities within the speakeasy and nightclub trade. Bartenders, for example, could easily make two to three times what most Harlem laborers made, and musicians, waiters, dancers, hostesses, chefs, and busboys all found a steady market for their services in speakeasies and nightclubs. These economic opportunities were so plentiful that even the most fervent dry advocates were forced to admit that the nightclub trade offered many African Americans a better chance for financial gain than most industries. In a column for the *Amsterdam News,* Edgar Grey put aside his usual Prohibitionist leanings and reluctantly acknowledged that "in Harlem, thousands of people earn a living from the activities of the community after dark." By his own estimate, Harlem's eighteen licensed nightclubs, which invariably but discreetly sold liquor, employed more than 600 African Americans at an average annual salary of $1,428. One club alone, he noted, employed over 70 Harlem residents, while an additional 172 black chauffeurs relied on the nightclub trade for their livelihoods. As much as he opposed the liquor trade, Grey conceded that these jobs were essential to the economic well-being of Harlem.[16]

The paychecks from these nightclub jobs, or the additional income derived from selling homemade whiskey out of an apartment, did not translate into riches for most black New Yorkers. At best, they prevented evictions or helped pay the bills. Nevertheless, an enterprising few parlayed the trade in illegal liquor into substantial wealth. For African Americans looking to get started in business, bootlegging and speakeasy ownership were risky routes to entrepreneurship, but they were also two of the few business opportunities plainly open to members of their race. The African-American writer Alain Locke, for example, noted that he personally knew many black entrepreneurs in the 1920s who had been "shut out" from traditional business paths on account of their race. They turned to the illegal liquor trade as "the 'only chance' to get a start" and raise the capital they needed as entrepreneurs.[17]

For some, the risks were worth taking. In his reports from African-American districts in Brooklyn, journalist Walter Lifton argued that Prohibition had indeed proved a "commercial blessing" for some of the city's black communities. As a result of the wealth that black bootleggers and speakeasy owners had earned in the liquor business, Lifton explained, they could now "buy homes, have large bank accounts and even buy automobiles." He noted that several bootleggers had turned small initial investments into fabulous sums of money in very short periods of time. Some of them stuck with bootlegging as a career; others made their money and got out, using their profits to move into legal trades. The African Americans who did stay in the business expressed the same pride in their work that any small entrepreneur would, boasting that though they generally charged higher prices than many of their Italian and Jewish competitors, they offered their patrons superior-quality liquor made with the purest ingredients. Though few African-American bootleggers ever attained the stature or notoriety of New York's most famous Jewish or Italian liquor traffickers, they too reached a comfortable standard of living replete with all the trappings of Jazz Age wealth.[18]

While the economic realities of life in Harlem played a large role in undermining the effectiveness of Prohibition in the district, numerous cultural factors also worked against the dry crusade. The drinking, jazz, and nightclubs of 1920s Harlem appealed to every sector of African-American society. Like its white counterpart, the city's African-American middle class came to accept drinking, partaking in the thrills of nightlife, and jazz culture as badges of urban sophistication.

This trend dismayed the community's moral guardians. In one of his columns for the *Amsterdam News*, Edward Rice McKinney wrote, "What intrigues me is the inroad that hooch [has] made into the homes, the stomachs and the good graces of many supposed respectable and upright citizens." He added with displeasure, "It seems that there can be no social affair worth attending unless the host or hostess passes out the word that there will be plenty of gin or whiskey. Good church members, upstanding business and professional men take their wives, sons and daughters to these gin and whiskey fests."[19]

The journalist Walter Lifton confirmed McKinney's observations. His reports from Brooklyn indicated that though many well-to-do black families still kept dry homes, more and more elite households were stockpiling supplies of the high-quality liquor that connoted status. Lifton saw this as a clear sign that drinking among "respectable" African Americans, including women and youth, was on the rise. Novelist Dorothy West's observations also confirmed that "respectable types" and Harlem's well-to-do were enthusiastically joining the drinking culture. At one cocktail party, West recalled, professors, heirs and heiresses, and college-educated professionals from "good families" were all "lapping up" their hostess's liquor without reservation.[20]

West's recollections indicated that within the world of Harlem society, the desire to appear "smart" and sophisticated had replaced concern for respectability and moral righteousness. In a 1925 *Messenger* essay on Harlem culture, George Schuyler substantiated West's claims. Noting a new emphasis on "wealth and ostentatious display," he described the rich and poor of Harlem competing to maintain "smart appearances" in public. "Large numbers of the Negroes go to the extreme in following the fashions," he wrote. "Attention is given by everyone to personal appearance." The result was dazzling displays of finery. In Schuyler's words, "a stroll on Seventh Avenue on Sunday afternoon or any evening is unforgettable. In the parade one sees the handsomest girls and women to be found anywhere, and there are no better dressed people in the city. Many of these Negroes will go without proper nourishment in order to present a 'front' to the promenaders, the members of her club, or the sisters of the church. To dress shabbily here is to lose caste—and the peculiar economic situation facing the Negro here makes him lay more stress on social prestige." This social atmosphere, which

Schuyler conveyed as "one continual round of dances, socials, picnics, excursions, parties and liaisons," was plainly visible to all comers as one of the hallmarks of new Harlem society.[21]

The increasing preoccupation of Harlem society with the nightclub scene, jazz, and drinking as elements of "smartness" did not sit well with the Black Victorians, who worried that the new trends were undermining the moral fabric of the community. In editorials in the *Amsterdam News,* they complained bitterly about the changing nature of urban culture in Harlem. One proclaimed that "even a vulgar moron must see, if he has half an eye, that the present nightclubs are a decided moral liability to the community." Another denounced jazz with equal vehemence for being "as intoxicating as morphine or cocaine [and] just as harmful." Another editorial claimed that "Jazz is killing some people . . . some are going insane; others are losing their religion. The young girls and boys who constantly take jazz every day and night are becoming absolutely bad, and some criminals." Still another complained that drink, jazz, and nightclubs were creating a new "high Negro sassiety" dominated by "keepers of shady houses, women of questionable reputation, degenerates of every description, men with no visible means of support, professional gamblers and drunkards." As these types took over Harlem society, the Black Victorians argued, "the thousands of decent people living here . . . who do not consider the hip flask of poisonous liquor indispensable to social intercourse" were made irrelevant.[22]

Contrary to these admonitions, these "decent people" were the ones joining the rebellion against Prohibition. Disregarding the warnings issued by moral guardians and clergymen, Harlem's black professionals in the 1920s flocked to their favorite nightclubs and resorts like Tabb's, the Cape Cod, and Connie's Inn. The Queens neighborhoods of Corona and Jamaica, described in the black press as home to a "better class of Negroes," experienced similar changes. According to press reports, the number of clubs and speakeasies in each district increased steadily in the mid-1920s, a sure indication that drinking was becoming more acceptable among the black middle class in the outer boroughs.[23]

The change in social mores could also be seen at the gatherings of several core institutions of the black bourgeoisie, such as the YMCA, the Urban League, and the National Association for the Advancement of Colored

People (NAACP). These well-respected early supporters of Prohibition now shied away from their commitment to the dry agenda. Despite occasional pronouncements from these groups about the dangers that alcohol posed to the community, fundraisers hosted by the NAACP and the Urban League were held in cabarets where liquor was quietly served. At a 1924 benefit for the NAACP at Happy Rhone's cabaret, the intelligentsia drank, danced, and rubbed shoulders with the charity's benefactors as well as with patrons of the Harlem Renaissance and nightclub stars.

Events like these brought sharp rebukes from the dry-leaning editors of the *Amsterdam News,* who wondered how the supporters of charitable and civic groups could gather in "the rendezvous of the sporting element." They insisted that the cabaret "can play no part in a program of social service." Nevertheless, the allure of belonging to the smart set prevailed, and Harlem nightclubs filled up night after night with, as George Schuyler noted, "respectable people who would not have been seen dead in them a few years before."[24]

As resistance to Prohibition became more established in New York's African-American community, it seemed that even the ministers who had spoken out against nightclubs, speakeasies, and jazz culture could not be trusted to uphold the dry agenda. In 1927, the *Amsterdam News* criticized a Harlem minister for trying to obtain a job for his son at Connie's Inn in exchange for a promise not to denounce the nightclub from his pulpit. The newspaper hinted that other ministers were accepting money from nightclubs in exchange for similar pledges of silence. As this kind of hypocrisy came out in the open, cartoons in the African-American press began to parody ministers for publicly preaching against drinking, jazz, and dancing while frolicking and drinking cocktails with flappers behind closed doors. At the same time, attendance at black churches declined in the 1920s, a situation that some ministers attributed to the unrealistic moral positions taken by the black clergy.[25]

In the *New York Age,* Reverend W. Spencer Carpenter offered a partial explanation for the decline of the churches' standing in Harlem: his colleagues were placing too much emphasis on "dead issues" and behaving like hypocrites. He noted, "We ministers denounce the dance halls and those who see no sin in going to an occasional dance but we are as tight lipped as a corpse when the 'big member' of our church gives a parlor dance in honor of some out of town guest." "We raise the devil about the painted-face flapper who parades the street of our town," he continued. "But when our wives and daughters, made up like Indians, and with knee-high skirts, walk down the aisle of our church, we argue that we want our girls to be stylish." Carpenter also berated ministers who condemned cabarets yet freely accepted donations from their owners. He concluded: "We praise the Volstead Act to the skies. But some of us take our glass of beer or wine when we feel that we are with the 'right parties.'" From Carpenter's perspective, African-American religious leaders, who themselves appeared less than fully committed to the dry agenda, were in danger of losing their urban flock unless they "ceased abusing and banging at our members" and learned to accept some of the pleasures of city life.[26]

This notion of accepting drinking and some degree of vice as inevitable parts of modern city life helped shape a more cosmopolitan vision of urban life in the 1920s that immediately resonated with Harlem's residents. Though this new perspective had many proponents among the younger generation of Harlem writers, few were as entertaining and effective in promoting it as the writer George Schuyler. In his weekly "Shafts and Darts" column for the *Amsterdam News*, Schuyler offered an antidote to the moralism often found on the paper's editorial page. With wit, a sharp tongue, and a heavy dose of realism, he dismissed Harlem's self-appointed moral guardians as "puritans and . . . disagreeable ninnies." In response to claims that Harlem was suffering a severe moral decline in the 1920s, Schuyler simply argued that Harlem had never been morally pure and never would be. Closing every cabaret in the district would still not rid the area of vice, he insisted.[27]

Schuyler argued that modern urban life was shaped by both "puritan" and "pagan" elements, and that only the presence of both in Harlem would give residents, in Schuyler's words, the opportunity to "live a complete life." Schuyler apparently understood what Kelly Miller did not, namely, that the residents of Harlem in the 1920s valued personal freedom more than moral discipline, and that the urge to explore the full range of social and cultural experiences was natural. He argued, "From all indications, both churches and cabarets seem to be flourishing side by side, and often with much the same patronage." Rather than condemning churchgoers for drinking, as Kelly Miller did, Schuyler accepted that "one can come directly from church and get a substantial drink of intoxicant, or one can leave the [YMCA] and walking half a block descend into the realm of unrestrained jazz." Rather than expressing shock or dismay at such conditions, Schuyler professed joy. "This is what makes Harlem the civilized community it is," he explained. Without cabarets, he argued, Harlem would be "as dull as the wastes of the Bronx or the desert of Washington Heights." Speakeasies, bootleggers, and nightclubs only complemented "the boisterousness and exuberance of our black population." They were a central part of life in Harlem in the 1920s.[28]

Schuyler's opinions found a receptive audience in the readers of the *Amsterdam News*. One reader pleaded with the *News* to print more from Schuyler and less "rot by Edgar Grey and foolish stuff by Kelly Miller." Still, in the face of such criticism, the Black Victorians did not yield. Rather, they opened an even more contentious debate over Prohibition culture and its effect on race relations in 1920s New York. While Harlem residents had clearly rejected the argument that jazz and drinking were bad for them, it was harder to dismiss the old guard's argument that the proliferation of nightclubs and speakeasies in that district was exploiting blacks for the benefit of white thrillseekers. Edgar Grey, for one, argued in a 1927 *Amsterdam News* column that whites who came to Harlem were doing so only to "engage in vices which they would not attempt in their own communities." In Grey's opinion, the slumming craze of the 1920s was turning Harlem into a "devil's playground" run for the benefit of "depraved" whites in search of illicit pleasures.[29]

At the heart of Grey's comments were concerns that speakeasy culture had increased the likelihood of interracial sexual relations within the unregulated and uninhibited spaces of Harlem nightlife, and that those relations were exploiting the men and especially the women of Harlem. The topic of interracial sex had been taboo for generations, but public interest in the topic was on the rise in the 1920s as large numbers of African Americans moved into Northern cities during the Great Migration. With the nightclubs and speakeasies of the Prohibition era, the social mingling of the races became more widespread than at any time since the Civil War.

In New York, the Black Victorians' concern over interracial relationships was heightened by the sensational story surrounding the 1925 marriage of Leonard "Kip" Rhinelander, a wealthy young New York real estate heir, and Alice Jones, a biracial chambermaid. Though Rhinelander and Jones had courted for years before eloping, Rhinelander filed for divorce one month after their marriage under pressure from his family, who claimed that young Kip had not known Alice Jones's racial identity. The case outraged African-American New Yorkers, not only because of Rhinelander's flimsy claim not to have known his wife's racial heritage, but also because of the public humiliation of Jones, who was forced to disrobe in the courtroom as her lawyers tried to prove that Rhinelander must have known her race. The Rhinelander case fueled larger fears that "slumming" whites were exploiting blacks to satisfy their own sexual curiosities, prompting *Amsterdam News* editors to complain that "the Insanity Bug is running wild among the white folks." Upset by the public spectacle of the Rhinelander case, the editors complained, "We don't believe particularly in interracial marriages; neither do we believe in the exploitation of the virtue of our women."[30]

Though they, too, were disturbed by the Rhinelander case, many young Harlem cosmopolitans found the Black Victorians' protests against interracial relationships indefensible. They dismissed warnings against interracial marriage as no different from the arguments put forward by white supremacists who wanted to maintain the strict separation of the races. George Schuyler, who would himself marry a white woman writer in 1928 after a six-month courtship carried on nightly in the Savoy Ballroom, staunchly defended interracial marriage. In spite of the Rhinelander case, he refused to budge from his commitment to the idea that the presence of mixed-race couples dancing in nightclubs was bringing people together across the color line. He saw interracial mingling as a positive development that would yield long-term benefits both for New York and for American society as a whole. He argued, "The joy and gaiety they dispense certainly marks them as more of a promise than a menace, despite the fervent yawping of our distressed puritans." Chandler Owen concurred, writing in *The Messenger* that "certain Negro leaders" were colluding with the Committee of Fourteen to "secure the adoption of segregation in the cabarets." Their motivation, he explained, was that "it hurts such gentlemen to see white and colored people dance and drink together."[31]

The controversy surrounding the Rhinelander case may have given old guard moralists a new boost in their condemnation of the "slumming" nature of Harlem's nightclub culture. But it did nothing to dampen the unbridled optimism of Schuyler and many other black writers that nightclubs and speakeasies, rather than fostering exploitation, constituted a new type of liberated space that brought blacks and whites together. By allowing members of different races to mix socially in ways that were rare before the 1920s, they hoped the racial animosity of the urban environment would dissipate. Schuyler made this point in one of his columns when he stated that "people who chat, dance and drink together are not apt to harbor ignorant and unreasonable prejudices, or to indulge in lynching orgies." Theophilus Lewis agreed, arguing in the *Amsterdam News* that interracial dancing was "one of the quickest, as well as the most enjoyable and innocent ways of bringing about understanding between individuals." It was also "one of the best ways of reducing friction between the races." He added, "This is why the night clubs have done more to improve race relations in ten years than the churches, white and black, have done in ten decades."[32]

Chandler Owen of *The Messenger* was even more optimistic. He argued that in the long run the nightclub would help break down the barriers of both race and class in the United States. "It is breaking down the color line," he argued. "It is destroying the psychology of caste. It is disseminating joy to the most humble and the most high. It is the dynamic agent of social equality." In another essay, Owen called the "black and tan" cabaret, which catered to whites and blacks, "America's most democratic institution." Describing nightclubs as refuges from racial hatred, Owen explained, "It is here that white and colored people mix freely." He insisted that "all classes of people go there, rich and poor, learned and ignorant, white and colored, prominent and unknown. Besides, they get along." More than any other social institution, "these black and tan cabarets establish the desire of the races to mix and mingle." By encouraging the pursuit of pleasure, and by showing that whites and blacks shared this universal desire, Owen hoped the clubs would usher in a new era of racial tolerance by promoting "general understanding through general contact."[33]

Whether the Black Victorians or the cosmopolitans were more accurate in their perceptions of the effects of Prohibition-era nightlife in Harlem remained to be seen. There were plenty of examples to support Grey's view that Harlem had become the "devil's playground," but Schuyler's view that the district served as the site of a great social experiment in improving race relations was also compelling. The historical evidence is clear on one account: Social interaction between the races was undoubtedly a common part of the nightclub and speakeasy culture of Harlem in the 1920s, and plenty of black and white observers took this as a sign that racial barriers were coming down, at the very least within the confines of the nightclub.

Variety reviews of cabarets and nightclubs where blacks and whites socialized commented often on how effortlessly the races interacted. One review of the Black Bottom, a black and tan cabaret near Times Square, noted that the general rule for dancing in the club was, "When the spirit moves, just grab anybody. No color line here." At other midtown cabarets like the Seven-Eleven and Harlem establishments like Small's Paradise, *Variety* noted, "whites and blacks rub shoulders and celestials dance with either race." When Connie's Inn, one of the most well known Harlem jazz clubs, first opened, it prominently placed the phrase "ALL ARE WELCOME" in its newspaper ads, inviting patrons of all races.[34]

The Committee of Fourteen also took note of the mixing of the races in nightclubs, but for very different reasons. What Schuyler, Lewis, and Chandler celebrated as an indication of positive social interaction, the Committee of Fourteen condemned as a sure sign of illicit sexual activity. For example, at the Astoria Restaurant on 134th Street, a committee investigator warily noted that "colored and white couples were sitting at the same tables and white women under the influence of liquor were conversing with colored men who invited them to drink with them." At Baron Wilkin's Club on 134th Street, another reporter described seeing more than fifty couples, black and white, patronizing the establishment at one o'clock in the morning. The reporter noted with alarm that "colored men and white women [were] sitting at the same tables."[35]

Reports from the Police Department and the Bureau of Prohibition also took note of race mixing in Harlem. Raids at establishments like the Actors Inn on 131st Street, the Shuffle Inn on 131st Street, the Nest Club on 133rd Street, and the Elks Restaurant on 141st Street all netted black and white patrons, while court records and reports of raids on the Pullman Café, the Black Gold Cabaret, Edmond's, the Oriental, the Capitol Palace, and dozens of other clubs and speakeasies overwhelmingly indicated that race mixing was common in most of Harlem's nightspots.[36]

The nature of the social interactions that occurred in these nightclubs and speakeasies can hardly be determined from brief descriptions outlined in the surveillance reports of reformers or in summaries from the police blotter. In some cases, no doubt, investigators witnessed the very types of social interaction that Victorians, black and white alike, feared most. But by no means should the interracial socializing in Harlem's clubs be interpreted solely as the hallmark of a vice district. The sheer numbers indicate that many black and white New Yorkers comfortably patronized the same establishments, dancing and drinking together in the 1920s on a scale that would have been inconceivable a decade earlier.

In most cases, the evidence rarely lived up to the exaggerated fears of the moral reformers who took pains to present any interracial interaction in the most negative light. They insisted that the white presence in Harlem was never innocent, and they continued their campaign to convince Harlemites that the liquor-infused nightlife of the district provided nothing more than an opportunity for whites to exploit African Americans culturally, sexually, and economically. Underneath their bombastic pronouncements, however, their concerns were not entirely unfounded. Just as drys were genuinely concerned about alcohol abuse, Black Victorians were sincere in their apprehension about what the African-American journalist Rudolf Fisher called the "contagious interest in everything Negro" cultivated by New York's white elite in the 1920s. Even the novelist Wallace Thurman, who had almost nothing in common with the Black Victorians, at times echoed their fears. Remarking on the interactions of whites and blacks in Harlem at night, he cautioned, "Tomorrow all of them will have an emotional hangover."[37]

Some white patrons, writers, and scenemakers contributed to the notion that Harlem had become a playground for white thrillseekers. On the dance floors of several of the area's most notable nightclubs, they crafted voyeuristic, exploitative, and sensationally racist visions of Harlem and its residents to suit their desires. The Cotton Club was the most famous example to fit this pattern. The club, owned by gangster Owney Madden, strictly maintained the color line in the 1920s, presenting light-skinned black entertainers to white audiences and excluding black patrons with an unwritten but well-known door policy. The Plantation Club provided another notorious example of a racist vision brought to life in the middle of Harlem for the sake of white audiences. Decorated with slave cabins and real-life mammies, the Plantation Club re-created the bygone era of the antebellum South for white audiences. In terms of admission policies, the message to Harlem residents was clear. As the *Amsterdam News* explained, "the majority of these cabaret owners do not go so far as to deny admission to the residents of the community, but they give instructions to their colored patrons in such a way as to discourage them frequenting the cabarets."[38]

For tourists and thrillseekers who wanted a taste of "Negro culture" in a strictly controlled and segregated environment, the Cotton Club and Plantation Club satisfied their curiosities. Still other denizens of the nightlife sought to explore Harlem's pleasures for themselves, hoping for a more "authentic" experience. The journalist Stephen Graham, for example, recounted an evening trip uptown to Harlem with several colleagues, which he described in the exotic language of an urban safari. Graham marveled at the sounds of a jazz band "trumpeting like enraged elephants in battle" and described "a gay Negro populace, dressed to the last limit in finery . . . swarming in dance." On the dance floor, he encountered "tall elegant negresses with carven faces, held by bellicose fighting bulls, sun bonneted mammas with crazy rustic boys, mightily hipped hostesses keeping time by contortioning their buttocks in unison with the males who gripped their waists." Graham admitted that he and his white companions were "interlopers" in this realm who "really did not belong," but he was delighted by the sights and sounds of the Harlem night, of "white men dancing with coloured girls, and Negroes dancing with white women." In search of the genuine Harlem experience, Graham and his white companions feasted on barbecued ribs and drank gin and ginger ale, while one of the revelers told jokes about "some white man [who] comes down here, gets very drunk and finds himself dancing with his wife's coloured maid . . . or when a white woman discovers that she has 'got off' with the elevator boy from the apartment house where she lives." The evening ended at dawn, Graham recalled, with the group bundling into a taxi, which then "crossed the Congo, 125th Street, leaving the black compound to enter once more the domain of civilization."[39]

Graham's descriptions of the Harlem night showed the Prohibition era's infatuation with black New York at its worst. Describing his "experimental" attempts to dance with "an elephantine coloured girl," Graham noted, "You change into a bit of a Negro when you join the dance or you do not enjoy it; some of the black comes off on you, none of the white comes off on them." Though Graham expressed smug satisfaction that he had shocked a white Southern couple watching him dance from a nearby table, in the end he felt that his experiment had failed. "It was like dancing with a big black wooden doll," he concluded, denying his dance partner her very humanity.[40]

Graham's exploits embodied the idea that whites could find any vice they sought in Harlem, a reputation that proved difficult to overcome by the late 1920s. The district, according to *Variety*, was becoming known as a place where whites could "get away with plenty" and generally behave in any manner they pleased. By then, even George Schuyler, the champion of the cabaret, was disgusted with the way whites carried on in Harlem. "The efforts of the Nordics to be carefree are grotesque," he wrote, "the so-called emancipated whites being the worst of the lot." He continued, "No group of Negroes anywhere could be louder or rowdier than [whites] are in their efforts to impress the neighborhood with the fact that they are having a good time."[41]

As whites flooded into Harlem in search of Prohibition-era pleasures, African Americans grew increasingly resentful of their presence. Socializing, drinking, and dancing with whites had been one thing, but their domination of Harlem was another. African Americans increasingly viewed the white presence in Harlem not as a challenge to the color line but as a form of voyeurism. In 1927, Edgar Grey pointed out the irony of white New Yorkers' nocturnal invasion of Harlem, describing how "well dressed and bejeweled white men and women are seen entering these cabarets, and at dawn, just before their colored maids have turned over for their final morning naps, they hurry to their homes, drunk and well amused."[42]

The increasing control of Harlem's clubs by white owners who forced their black competitors out of business irritated critics even more. As gangsters like Owney Madden took over resorts like the Cotton Club, organized crime came to control a substantial percentage of the liquor trade in the district, giving credence to the complaint in the *Amsterdam News* that "white racketeers are making Harlem a huge plantation with white overseers." The *New York Age* similarly complained that "the men of other races who come into Harlem seeking financial profit . . . are actuated [solely] by avarice and are not concerned in either the moral or physical well-being of the people." By the end of the decade, the white domination of the liquor and nightclub trades was almost complete. According to a Committee of Fourteen report, a sample of eighty-five speakeasies in Harlem revealed that 90 percent were white-owned, 5 percent were owned by black/white partnerships, and only 5 percent were owned by blacks.[43]

By the late 1920s, sorting out the social and economic situation that had evolved in Harlem proved difficult. The assertions of Harlem's moral guardians that the nightlife of the 1920s presented a liability to the community were not altogether inaccurate. The presence of figures like Madden, and the "slumming craze" demonstrated by the likes of Stephen Graham, made it easier to accept the criticism that whites had indeed turned the district into a "devil's playground." But the moral reformers who criticized the white exploitation of Harlem also took positions that seemed backward and out of date. They continued to issue prudish comments about the immorality of jazz and the "filthy" content of blues songs performed in clubs; and they argued that no "permanent good comes to the girl who is a habitué of public dance halls—white, colored, brown or yellow." In an alarmist fashion, the *Amsterdam News* issued a laundry list of complaints, blaming Prohibition culture for leading the youth of Harlem to engage in such behaviors as "promiscuous sex experiences, imbibing bootleg liquor, dropping out of school and adopting careers of crime or shame."[44]

The Black Victorians' position on racial segregation was as inconsistent as it was out of date. While Kelly Miller and Edgar Grey criticized the blatant separation of the races in establishments like the Cotton Club, they also complained that race mixing in clubs was a threat to the respectability of African Americans. Though they urged African-American youths to stay away from immoral whites, they responded angrily in the *Amsterdam News* when the *Daily News* printed an editorial opposing race mixing in New York City dance halls. Adopting a confusing and contradictory stance, the *Amsterdam News* argued that "the average, rational individual of any race, civilized and uncivilized, superior and inferior, is able to pick out his own associates, even in a dance hall," but added as a caveat, "Mind you, we are not putting up any argument for cheek-to-cheek or lip-to-lip dancing."[45]

Even the issue of Prohibition enforcement resulted in paradoxical twists of logic on the part of Harlem's old guard. Both the *Amsterdam News* and the *New York Age* advocated stricter Prohibition enforcement in Harlem, and the *Age* went so far as to regularly print open challenges to U.S. Attorney Emory Buckner, listing the addresses of dozens of Harlem speakeasies and asking why Buckner had not moved to close them. Both papers also called for stricter enforcement of anti-vice laws and a crackdown on numbers running, complaining that lax law enforcement in Harlem was politically designed to concentrate vice in the black districts of the city. They also enthusiastically championed the efforts of Richard Warner, Jesse Harvey, and Joshua Dixon, the city's only African-American Prohibition agents. Yet when Prohibition laws were strictly enforced in Harlem, the *Amsterdam News* and the *New York Age* both complained that the police and the Bureau of Prohibition were being "unjust and unfair" in their efforts. The papers accused them of targeting black-owned resorts or establishments with a racially mixed clientele.[46]

With their shows of support for Prohibition enforcement, calls for racial purity, and warnings of a moral calamity in Harlem, the old guard proved too extreme to be taken seriously. Though black and white critics agreed that exploitation and degradation existed in Harlem nightspots, claims that the district had become a cesspool of vice and a "devil's playground" that catered only to white slummers were exaggerated, especially compared with what was happening in other sections of New York during Prohibition. Nightlife columnists in *Variety* and *The New Yorker,* for example, argued that the cabaret scene in Harlem was a far cry from what Kelly Miller or Edgar Grey depicted, or, for that matter, what Stephen Graham described to his readers.

One *New Yorker* column described the pleasantness of some of the "less pretentious and more African resorts" of Harlem, where the number of white sightseers was minimal and the crowds danced in an ecstatic but "orderly" fashion. The African-American owner of the club told the reporter from *The New Yorker* that he ran the place "for the working people of the community, but visitors under control are welcome." *Variety,* which with *The New Yorker* provided more thorough coverage of nightlife than any other publication in the city, also disputed the contention that Harlem was as wild and licentious as reformers imagined. One columnist argued that Harlem in no way resembled its reputation. He added that "this *Variety* reporter can show twenty white night clubs within the Times Square precincts, any one of them wilder at four in the morning than all the combined cabarets or black and tans in Harlem." In contrast, he argued, the typical Harlem clubs clustered around 137th, 138th, and 139th Streets that catered to black professionals and business owners were "peaceful" and safe establishments, unmolested by the antics of white troublemakers. Their presence directly contradicted the sensationalistic image of Harlem as a place where all moral standards had been erased and anything could be had for a price.[47]

The only way to reconcile these different interpretations of Harlem during the Prohibition era is to accept that they all had some basis in fact. Prostitution existed in Harlem resorts, at least as far as the records of the Committee of Fourteen show, but it was not omnipresent. Discrimination and segregation were real, too, in the Cotton Club and other well-known nightclubs, but they were not the norm. Of the hundreds of speakeasies, nightclubs, and cabarets that thrived in Harlem during Prohibition, only a handful maintained the strict racial segregation openly practiced at the Cotton Club. There were certainly places where blacks were not welcome, just as there were many places in Harlem where white thrillseekers were not welcome, but report after report from Harlem at night shows that blacks and whites were mixing socially, without incident, in environments ranging from the lowest dives to the most respectable establishments in the district.

Defining the character of Prohibition in Harlem thus becomes an exercise in cutting through the mythology of the era, whether in the form of the colorful exaggerations of Stephen Graham or the moral rantings of Kelly Miller and Edgar Grey. In reality, the nightlife of the district was characterized by a remarkable social environment in which whites and blacks mixed, not always harmoniously, but in a clear departure from earlier social standards. At the very least, Harlem was a place where strict taboos on interracial social behavior weakened briefly during the Prohibition era. What went on in Harlem gave some credence to Chandler Owen's idea that social interactions between blacks and whites in 1920s nightclubs and speakeasies could in the long run help break down racial barriers.[48]

Whichever interpretation of the racial dynamic of 1920s Harlem prevailed, the one observation that remained beyond dispute was that Prohibition enforcement failed as drastically in Harlem as it did in every other section of the city. Despite claims by contemporary critics that Prohibition was enforced differently or more strictly in Harlem because of the issue of race, aside from isolated remarks from police captains or reform investigators, there is little evidence to suggest that race figured prominently in the way Prohibition was enforced in the district.

While the *Amsterdam News* and the *New York Age* both argued at times that Harlem was unfairly targeted by Prohibition enforcement efforts, not a single nightclub in Harlem was padlocked until September 1928, when the Nest Club was closed for Volstead Act violations. When Police Commissioner Grover Whalen ordered a massive citywide crackdown on speakeasies in 1929, only 45 of the 786 clubs raided were in Harlem, a figure that suggests Harlem was neither ignored nor specifically targeted. Contrary to assertions that popular white-owned and white-patronized clubs were left alone by the authorities, when police raided nine clubs in Harlem in 1926 for violating the city's cabaret laws, they hit every extreme from the whites-only Cotton Club and the popular Happy Rhone's to the lesser-known black-owned clubs. For the most part, Harlem nightclubs found it as easy to violate the Eighteenth Amendment as did clubs in other sections of the city, but they were not exempt from the sporadic waves of enforcement that swept the city, either. If anything, illegal payoffs and political connections were a far bigger factor in a club's survival than was race. No pattern in the raids suggests that they had any racial subtext.[49]

There is no evidence that the Bureau of Prohibition or the police ever attempted to target black bootleggers more forcefully than they did white bootleggers in New York. Doing so would have proved difficult, as bootleggers seemed to draw few racial distinctions themselves when choosing their business partners. Examples of black-white bootlegging partnerships showed up with regularity in Prohibition enforcement records, suggesting that the promise of making money in the illegal liquor trade was a strong incentive in itself to cross the color line.[50]

Nor did the problem of official corruption in Prohibition enforcement make any distinction when it came to race, as the case of the Bureau of Prohibition's three African-American agents demonstrated. When Agents Richard Warner, Jesse Harvey, and Joshua Dixon began working for the bureau, they initially won commendations for their work and were praised by the *Amsterdam News* and *New York Age* for their efforts to enforce Prohibition in New York's African-American districts. In time, however, they proved as susceptible to the temptations of bribery and corruption as were other Prohibition agents. In 1927 the three men were relieved of their duties after being caught in a bribery scandal and charged with systematically collecting protection payments from a number of Harlem speakeasies and nightclubs, including Connie's Inn and the Club DeLuxe. In the trial that followed, the agents' defense argued that the bureau was trying to purge its only black agents from the force, and added that their supervisor had threatened to torture a witness in the case to force him to testify against the three defendants. At the end of the trial, Agent Dixon was acquitted, but Agents Harvey and Warner were convicted of conspiracy and bribery and sentenced to thirteen months in federal prison, embarrassing those who had supported the agents as role models for the community.[51]

The underlying message behind the story of Agents Dixon, Warner, and Harvey and their fall from grace was that those who claimed to present some sort of moral superiority in the Harlem of the 1920s seldom lived up to their claims. Columnists offering wholesale condemnations of nightclubs, ministers ranting against jazz and drinking, and professors heralding the dry experiment as a means to uplift the race appeared so far removed from the reality of modern city life that most Harlem residents concluded they were either delusional, hypocritical, or both.[52]

Harlem residents of the 1920s ultimately sided with a view of the city that was more complex and realistic than the one the old-guard leaders offered. By the late 1920s, it was universally acknowledged in Harlem that the Eighteenth Amendment had promoted neither sobriety nor thrift. It had not fostered new respect for the Fourteenth and Fifteenth Amendments, nor had it increased the political power of African Americans. In these respects, African Americans who had supported Prohibition were shown to be unmistakably wrong. As the decade closed, even the *Amsterdam News* acknowledged that its readers desired repeal by a margin of five to one, and conceded that it was "high time to have a referendum on the whole subject." The Black Victorians had been silenced.[53]

But the many defenders of the nightclub who challenged the Black Victorians were also forced to ask themselves if their promises had been fulfilled. Chandler Owen, George Schuyler, and Theophilus Lewis had all insisted that cabarets and dancing in Harlem would usher in a new era of interracial social interaction that would change race relations in the city forever. But when the stock market crashed in 1929 and cast a sudden pall over the city's nightlife, they could not be certain that anything had improved. There was no doubt in any New Yorker's mind that whites and blacks had interacted socially in unprecedented numbers during the 1920s, but there was ambivalence in the African-American community over what such interaction had actually achieved. In the *American Mercury*, Rudolf Fisher asked with uncertainty, "Maybe these Nordics have at last tuned in to our wavelength? Maybe they are at last learning to speak our language?" Fisher's questions went unanswered, and even some of George Schuyler's readers found Schuyler unduly optimistic about the potential of the nightclub to break down racial barriers.[54]

If possibilities for better social interactions between the races had emerged in Harlem during Prohibition, they would vanish with the arrival of the Depression, leaving George Schuyler and his colleagues feeling that a great opportunity had been lost. Decades later, Schuyler still refused to back away from his belief that the 1920s had opened opportunities, sadly missed, to challenge the color line. Reminiscing on the Prohibition era in 1962, Schuyler noted that the social environment that emerged in Harlem in the 1920s had presented more opportunities for interracial socialization than had existed ever before, and possibly more than have existed since. When challenged on this premise by an interviewer, Schuyler simply responded, "There were many more white people who came to Harlem then than come to Harlem now."[55]

In the end, the experience of Harlem during the noble experiment offered another example of how the economic realities and cultural trends of New York City in the 1920s continually thwarted the dry crusade's unrealistic hope that New Yorkers would eventually accept Prohibition as law. Like many New Yorkers, Harlem residents looked to the liquor trade as a potential source of income and embraced Prohibition-era nightlife as an essential part of modern city life. At the same time, the issue of race made the Prohibition experiment doubly complicated for black New Yorkers. Positioned between the demands of dry reformers who insisted that African Americans adhere to the Eighteenth Amendment to demonstrate their "respectability," and the curiosity of white "slummers" who saw in Harlem an exotic and liberating culture, black New Yorkers found themselves caught between two irreconcilable ideals, neither of which reflected the reality of life in Harlem during the Jazz Age.

9

Al Smith, the Wet Hope of the Nation

After nearly a decade of excessive drinking, farcical police raids, and end-less cycles of nightclub openings and closings, the excitement that had characterized the cosmopolitan rebellion against the Eighteenth Amend-ment in New York City slowly gave way to weariness. The gaiety that New Yorkers found in speakeasies could not obscure the fact that the noble ex-periment had become a national embarrassment. The United States, which had preached the virtues of Prohibition internationally, ended the decade not as a model of temperance but as the world's largest importer of cocktail shakers. One New York City paper lamented, "We mix more cocktails than any other nation . . . that's why the world laughs at us." Senator James J. Wadsworth, the prominent wet Republican from New York, expressed sim-ilar dismay in a letter to a colleague. "This Prohibition business has gotten us into a ridiculous mess," he wrote. "How the world must despise us for making such asses of ourselves!"[1]

While these sentiments were not surprising coming from an avowed wet like Wadsworth, by the late 1920s even those charged with enforcing the Eighteenth Amendment agreed with the senator. In 1927, U.S. Attorney Nat Harben told reporters he suspected that 65 percent of New Yorkers were violating the Prohibition laws, thus forcing him to conclude that the noble experiment would never achieve its purpose in New York City or anywhere else in the nation. He told the press that "this tragic farce has lasted long enough. The time has come for the people to put an end to Prohibition together with its army of paid spies, snoopers, grafters, fanatics, bootleggers, poisoners and murderers. They have no place in an American democracy."[2]

New Yorkers had tired of the cat-and-mouse game of Prohibition, but they were less certain of what could be done about it. They could drink with impunity and obtain any form of alcohol they desired at virtually any hour of the day, almost anywhere they liked, but they were no longer content to accept Prohibition as the status quo. Though they enjoyed the raucous atmosphere of their nightclubs and speakeasies, the secondary costs of the Eighteenth Amendment—alcoholism, crime, corruption, and gangland violence—were mounting. The federal budget for Prohibition enforcement had ballooned from $4.75 million in 1921 to $12.4 million in 1929 to no apparent benefit. Public defiance of Prohibition was undermining the rule of law in the city and creating a national culture of hypocrisy, while federal law enforcement agencies menaced the public with increasingly aggressive and violent measures to uphold the Eighteenth Amendment. It was time, a great majority of New Yorkers agreed, to look for a way out of the Prohibition experiment.[3]

As New Yorkers began to contemplate a solution to the mess that Prohibition had become, their thoughts turned increasingly to politics. In 1926 the *New York Times* had raised the possibility of a serious political campaign against Prohibition, noting that the drys had used national politics to their advantage in a masterly fashion. The editors suggested that "if politics got Prohibition into the law, it is not illegitimate to use political means to get it out." They urged patience for what would surely be a protracted battle. "If this be politics," they noted, "make the most of it." A 1931 editorial in the *Irish World* confirmed this new emphasis on the need to use politics to advance the wet cause. "There is but one way of curing this condition," the paper noted, "by driving out of public office all who are allied with and responsible for conditions which are a disgrace to the United States of America."[4]

But the task was not that simple. Driving every dry politician in the United States out of office would not have accomplished anything beyond giving wets the satisfaction of revenge. The real challenge facing opponents of Prohibition was a much more daunting one—repealing a constitutional amendment. Both wets and drys alike acknowledged that the idea of repealing an amendment to the Constitution was impossible to fathom. Dry stalwart Morris Sheppard, the United States senator from Texas, put it best in 1930 when he declared, "There is as much chance of repealing the Eighteenth Amendment as there is for a humming-bird to fly to the planet Mars with the Washington Monument tied to its tail." Frederick C. Whitin, the general secretary of the Committee of Fourteen, similarly dismissed talk of repealing the Eighteenth Amendment by simply saying that "it cannot be undone," while Prohibition Agent Izzy Einstein wrote in his autobiography, "The day Prohibition is repealed will not be in our lifetime. And I'm not looking forward to dying soon." Even Chief Justice of the Supreme Court William Taft weighed in on the matter. Although personally opposed to Prohibition, Taft resigned himself to the notion that the Eighteenth Amendment would remain national law indefinitely. "There isn't the slightest chance that the constitutional amendment will be repealed," he told opponents of the noble experiment. "You know that and I know it."[5]

With historical precedent squarely against them, New Yorkers hoping to repeal the Eighteenth Amendment needed to make their dissatisfaction with Prohibition a matter of national importance. They slowly came to realize that they could succeed only by channeling their opposition to Prohibition into politics, mobilizing wet voters around the country, and taking leading roles in a national repeal movement.

But in 1928 there was no such movement. Through most of the 1920s, wets had offered no significant political opposition to the Eighteenth Amendment except on the local level, and mounting an organized challenge to the noble experiment had proved much more difficult than anyone expected. The Supreme Court, by striking down every legal challenge to Prohibition it considered, had given wets little reason to hope. To make matters worse, few politicians dared to oppose the Anti-Saloon League and its dry allies, even as the organization declined in power. Nearly ten years after the Eighteenth Amendment was ratified, the political movement for repeal was moribund.[6]

The dry movement, in contrast, had weathered the increasing unpopularity of Prohibition and maintained a core of supporters who zealously defended the Eighteenth Amendment. Though donations to dry organizations had dwindled and membership rolls were down by the late 1920s, Prohibitionists could still threaten legislators with enough dry votes to bounce them from office. Senator Wadsworth had learned this the hard way when the Anti-Saloon League endorsed an independent dry candidate in the 1926 New York Senate race. The move cost Wadsworth 215,000 votes, which threw the election to Democrat Robert F. Wagner in a three-way race. The drys had not gained anything, for Wagner was no more a friend of Prohibition than Wadsworth was, but by playing the spoiler in the race the drys had punished Wadsworth for years of opposing their cause and again sent the message that their pressure politics could determine the outcome of elections.[7]

From Wadsworth's experience, elected officials who wavered in their public commitment to the noble experiment knew that they, too, could quickly find themselves unemployed. As a result, many politicians continued to vote dry, not because they believed in Prohibition, but because they still feared the Anti-Saloon League. While polls in the late 1920s and early 1930s indicated that as many as two-thirds of the members of Congress privately hoped to see Prohibition modified or repealed, as long as the Anti-Saloon League, the Woman's Christian Temperance Union, and the Methodist Board of Temperance remained at work in a political arena devoid of any formidable wet organizations, the Eighteenth Amendment would remain safely ensconced in the Constitution.[8]

Until the late 1920s, a national movement for repeal had failed to materialize because opponents of Prohibition had been unable to do what the drys had done in 1919: build a unified political coalition and get it to the polls. Considering the clear unpopularity of Prohibition and the widespread disregard for the dry laws throughout the country, the inability of American wets to harness opposition to the Eighteenth Amendment for nearly a decade should stand out as one of the great political failures of the twentieth century.

The best example of the failure of the wet movement to rally public support for repeal during the 1920s can be seen in the Association against the Prohibition Amendment (AAPA), a national repeal organization based in Wilmington, Delaware. Founded in 1918 by Captain William H. Stayton, a retired naval officer and lawyer, the AAPA had originally attempted to block the ratification of the Eighteenth Amendment as an unwarranted and unconstitutional expansion of the powers of federal government.

Stayton's conservative, almost libertarian, opposition to Prohibition as a form of governmental intrusion attracted mainly conservatives and business world luminaries to the AAPA. After procuring an initial donation of $10,000 from John A. Roebling, the grandson of the famed engineer who built the Brooklyn Bridge, Stayton recruited a number of prominent industrialists and political figures to the AAPA, among them Pierre S. DuPont, the chairman of General Motors and the DuPont Company; his brothers Lammot and Irénée; John J. Raskob, the treasurer of the DuPont Company; Henry Joy, the president of the Packard Motor Company; Senator Wadsworth; real estate baron Vincent Astor; and the philanthropist Edward Harkness. This "little group of millionaires," as *Life* called them, brought considerable financial resources to the AAPA, with the core members of the board each contributing between $10,000 and $45,000 annually to the organization to fund its lobbying efforts.[9]

But despite its financial resources and the publicity generated by the high social standing of its members, the AAPA never developed into an effective force for repeal. Relying predominantly on the wealth and influence of its small core of directors, the AAPA was plagued by poor decision making and missteps that obscured its anti-Prohibition message. For one thing, the AAPA accepted thousands of dollars in contributions from brewers and brewing trade associations, despite a provision in the group's by-laws that prohibited representatives of the alcohol trades from holding voting membership in the group. When these contributions were made public under the Corrupt Practices Act of 1925, which required lobbying groups to make a public accounting of all political contributions of $100 or more, Prohibitionists blasted the AAPA as a tool of the nation's brewers and distillers. The group faced more negative publicity in 1930, when Senator Arthur Robinson of Indiana excoriated prominent AAPA members for attempting to privately lobby Supreme Court justices on the issue of Prohibition. While not illegal, these lobbying efforts gave dry critics even more reason to argue that the AAPA's directors were using their positions of privilege and wealth to undermine a duly ratified constitutional amendment.[10]

Undoubtedly, the AAPA's most fundamental flaw was its elitism, for throughout the 1920s, the association failed to recognize the potential for a popular movement against Prohibition. The leading members of the AAPA, for example, took an overwhelming interest in the drinking habits of their employees and the negative effects of Prohibition on the nation's labor force, but the multimillionaire industrialists showed almost no desire to build any political alliance with their working-class employees, despite their mutual opposition to Prohibition.

In the area of recruitment, the AAPA was similarly shortsighted. Although membership in the AAPA was open to anyone who contributed one dollar annually, the organization made few efforts to enroll large numbers of supporters. A 1929 report issued by the group explained that it preferred to recruit wealthy members, whose influence and resources would directly further the AAPA's lobbying efforts. Summarizing the group's recruitment agenda, the report stated, "We are to incline away from dollar-a-year members in great numbers and toward sustaining members and more substantial annual contributors. The ultimate objective in this field to be ten thousand contributors averaging $100 each, with a resulting annual total contribution of a million dollars." To attract these wealthy contributors, Irénée DuPont underwrote subscriptions to the AAPA publication *Freedom,* which he sent to country clubs and golf courses in New Jersey, Pennsylvania, and Delaware, ignoring popular sentiment against Prohibition in American cities.[11]

With the AAPA more interested in building an elite membership than in cultivating a grassroots repeal movement, it is not surprising that the overall membership figures for the organization were weak. In the early 1920s, Captain Stayton had optimistically predicted that two million members would join the AAPA, and early membership totals for the organization did in fact rise to the impressive number of 400,000. But by 1928, ten years after the association was founded, enrollment had dropped below 190,000 despite increasing public opposition to the Eighteenth Amendment. Of those members on the rolls, only a few thousand made regular contributions to the organization, leaving the DuPont brothers to make up for the shortfall in the group's operating budget by each contributing more than one hundred thousand dollars annually to the AAPA.[12]

The AAPA's consistent espousal of libertarian politics, its small-government brand of conservatism, and its elitism greatly undermined its political potential. By appealing largely to the highest echelons of the American business community, the group never attained the political power that a grassroots wet organization could have commanded, and thus never mounted a serious challenge to the dry movement during its fifteen-year existence.

Like the AAPA, the nation's two major political parties also failed to exploit the Prohibition issue for most of the decade. Both the Democratic and the Republican parties meticulously avoided taking a stand on the Prohibition issue during election years throughout the 1920s, lest they incur the wrath of the dry crusade. Though adamant wets of both parties kept the repeal issue alive, neither party's leadership dared inject the issue of Prohibition into national politics.

As the dominant party of the 1920s, the Republicans sought to accommodate the dry crusade as a matter of expedience; the Democratic Party leadership, by contrast, feared that the issue of Prohibition would divide Southern drys and Northern wets, splitting the party as it tried to mount a challenge to Republican rule. The evasiveness of both parties especially angered wet New Yorkers, who considered such behavior hypocritical and cowardly. Exasperated by the failure of either party to offer a serious challenge to national Prohibition, the *Gaelic World* griped, "A majority of the rank and file of both parties are opposed to it, and the leaders of both parties who shout loudest for it are whiskey drinkers in private." U.S. Representative Fiorello LaGuardia, a rare example of a politician who spoke up loudly and frequently in opposition to Prohibition, was also dismayed by the absence of challenges to the Eighteenth Amendment. He complained that "with both Parties half wet and half dry . . . the issue will never be decided."[13]

With no national movement against Prohibition to rally behind, New Yorkers relied on local political representatives to express their opposition to the Eighteenth Amendment. Just as New Yorkers had played a pivotal role in leading the cultural rebellion against Prohibition, local figures from both major parties now moved to spark a national movement for repeal. By the end of the decade, several New Yorkers would emerge as the nation's most outspoken opponents of the dry laws, and their efforts would ultimately force the repeal question to the top of the national political agenda.

For New York's Republicans, expressing support for a repeal movement proved particularly difficult. As the leading national party of the 1920s, and the party in control of the federal mechanisms for enforcing the Eighteenth Amendment, Republicans were generally identified more with Prohibition than with the wet cause. But as the decade came to an end, two of New York's most prominent Republicans, Columbia University President Nicholas Murray Butler and Representative Fiorello LaGuardia, emerged as leading dissenters on the subject of Prohibition. Arguing that the party's stubborn adherence to the dry cause would prove disastrous in the long run, they pushed the party to abandon its alliance with the dry movement and embrace the wet agenda, which was quickly becoming more politically viable than the fruitless continuation of a failed experiment.

Butler, an esteemed university president who for a time was considered a possible presidential candidate, lent instant respectability to the wet cause within Republican circles. In 1923, he began to cultivate his position as a repeal leader with numerous speeches and comments critical of Prohibition. "We seem to forget the government is the servant of the people and not the master," Butler told a reporter in 1925, complaining that federal Prohibition policy was a sign that the United States was "drift[ing] towards absolutism." In other comments, he attacked dry leaders as "the cowards, the hypocrites, the ignorant, [and] the fanatics," and urged, "Let us repeal the Volstead Act and return to decency." By the late 1920s, Butler was convinced that national sentiment against Prohibition was increasing, and he repeatedly pushed the Republican Party to break free of what he saw as a doomed relationship with the dry lobby.[14]

Butler's outspokenness on the issue of Prohibition predictably provoked angry responses from drys across the nation. His critics sent protest letters to his office at Columbia University in which they questioned his fitness to serve as a university president entrusted with the moral guidance of young people given that he did not support the Eighteenth Amendment. But Butler adeptly turned these protests against him to the wet advantage, using them to illustrate the fanaticism running rampant in the dry movement. In a letter to a colleague, Butler noted that the "ill written and anonymous" letters he received "record the conviction that I have been captured by the Pope as part of a plan to undermine American institutions." The hate letters only strengthened Butler's belief that Prohibitionists represented a "persecuting spirit" that had taken over the United States in the 1920s. On one occasion he remarked that "the amount of bigotry and intolerance that exists in our American lives is unbearable and doubtless the chief danger which confronts us as a nation." Highlighting the extremism of the dry crusade, Butler contended that the Republican Party was "violently wrong" for not severing its ties with dry organizations, and he insisted that the party's reluctance to break away from the dry movement would create a serious political dilemma for Republicans in the future.[15]

Whereas Nicholas Murray Butler's critique of Prohibition from the halls of the Ivy League lent respectability to the wet cause, Fiorello LaGuardia gave the burgeoning repeal movement passion. A child of immigrants, LaGuardia had entered politics in 1916, when he represented East Harlem in the United States House of Representatives. LaGuardia opposed Prohibition from the very beginning, warning his colleagues in Congress that "this law will be almost impossible of enforcement . . . it will create contempt and disregard for law all over the country." LaGuardia remained a vocal critic of the Eighteenth Amendment throughout the 1920s, relentlessly criticizing the nation's dry leaders as hypocrites, charlatans, and bigots.[16]

As the sole wet on the House Committee on the Alcohol Liquor Traffic in the mid-1920s, LaGuardia was a vocal opponent of federal Prohibition policy. He was especially critical of the Bureau of Prohibition, the United States Coast Guard, and the Customs Service for their role in dry enforcement, accusing them of abuse of power, corruption, and squandering government funds in their work. He once quipped that "it would take 75,000 Coast Guardsmen to protect the Florida coastline alone—and then we'd need 75,000 more to watch *them*." In 1926, LaGuardia blew the cover off the Bridge Whist Club, a lavish midtown Manhattan speakeasy run by the Bureau of Prohibition as a sting operation to trap bootleggers. Generously outfitted at taxpayer expense, the Bridge Whist Club was supposed to catch liquor traffickers in the act of delivering bootleg liquor to the establishment.

It was also outfitted with recording equipment to capture the conversations of its patrons as evidence in Volstead cases. In six months of operation, however, the Bridge Whist sting managed to catch only one mid-level bootlegger, despite expending $45,000 of bureau funds. LaGuardia was incensed to learn that the bureau was selling liquor in order to catch those who were selling liquor, and apparently not having much success doing it. He made a public mockery of the operation and succeeded in having it shut down.[17]

The highlight of Fiorello LaGuardia's anti-Prohibition activism came in 1926, when the congressman gave a public demonstration in his Capitol office of how Americans could make legal beer by mixing alcohol-free "near beer" with flavored malt tonics. In front of twenty reporters and a bevy of photographers, LaGuardia announced, "Gentlemen . . . you needn't feel anxious. There will be at least a little for all of us." He then produced half a dozen samples of Pilsener, Wurtzberger, and stout, which cooperative reporters in LaGuardia's audience described as "delicious," "splendid," and "like pre-Volstead brew." LaGuardia explained that his purpose in staging the demonstration was "to show how a palatable beer . . . can be made without violating the law." Insisting that the beer he made was not just harmless but "refreshing, pure and wholesome," LaGuardia added, "If the Prohibition people think it is a violation of the law to mix two beverages permitted under the law and that a person doing so can be arrested, I shall give them a chance to test it." If the American public could easily make beer with commonly available ingredients, LaGuardia argued, then 2.75 percent beer should be legalized as well.[18]

LaGuardia's demonstration delighted wets around the nation and produced a rush on malt tonics, but it infuriated the Anti-Saloon League's Wayne Wheeler, who demanded that LaGuardia be prosecuted for violating federal law. LaGuardia defiantly responded to Wheeler's threat by taking his home-brewing show to his home district of East Harlem, where he mixed more of his legal beer outside Leo Kaufman's drugstore on Lenox Avenue at 115th Street. When a police officer arrived to investigate why the crowd had gathered outside the drugstore, LaGuardia and Officer John Mennella had the following exchange:

LAGUARDIA:	"I'm making beer."
PATROLMAN MENNELLA:	"All right."
LAGUARDIA:	"Why don't you arrest me?"
MENNELLA:	"I guess that's a job for a prohibition agent if any-body."
LAGUARDIA:	"Well, I'm defying you. I thought you might ac-commodate me."

Mennella then shrugged and walked away. Comic elements aside, LaGuardia's mocking of the Eighteenth Amendment made a clear point. By publicly flouting the Prohibition laws, and using the press to highlight his defiance, LaGuardia hoped to inspire Americans to stop griping about Prohibition in private and make their opposition to the dry mandate public.[19]

LaGuardia was not a single-issue politician; nor was he a big drinker. Though he was known to take an occasional Old-Fashioned in a modest lower Manhattan speakeasy, to LaGuardia the Prohibition issue was not about drinking. He found issues like urban poverty, housing reform, and immigration policy far more important than the Eighteenth Amendment, but he also knew that his working-class constituents in East Harlem experienced the ethnic and class biases inherent in the Prohibition experiment as acutely as they experienced these other urban problems. In particular, LaGuardia was outraged at the way Prohibition enforcement targeted the "foreign element" in American cities. For instance, in 1927, when Prohibition Administrator Chester Mills ordered churches and synagogues to register the names and addresses of all members who received sacramental wine, LaGuardia denounced the action as a violation of religious freedom and a sign of Mills's prejudice against Catholics and Jews. When Assistant Secretary of the Treasury Lincoln C. Andrews complained that sacramental wine abuses in New York were the result of the lack of hierarchical organization in the Jewish faith, LaGuardia retorted that Andrews should "reorganize his own department before attempting to reorganize the ancient Jewish faith."[20]

LaGuardia thought it was ridiculous that Prohibition administrators were so obsessed with the minor issue of sacramental wine. He did not regard excessive drinking as a problem in his district, and he pointed out in his autobiography that the 250,000 people he represented in East Harlem often had a hard time affording food, never mind liquor. Yet Prohibition enforcement efforts consistently targeted his working-class constituents while leaving New Yorkers in wealthier districts free to drink unmolested.[21]

To LaGuardia, Prohibition represented a cultural vendetta against American cities, directed by a dry lobby that hated ethnic Americans. For proof that Prohibition was rooted in bigotry, all LaGuardia needed to do was thumb through the daily correspondence he received from drys, who attacked him and his constituents on the basis of their ethnicity. One critic from Maine blasted LaGuardia by saying, "He's from New York, where there are few real Americans." The tirade continued: "He has the commonest of all foreigners for his constituents—Italian wine-bibbers who have sent him to Congress to recover for them their lost beverage."[22]

In addition to exposing the bigotry of drys, LaGuardia demonstrated that politicians could turn "wetness" into a source of political strength. Frustrated by the lack of courage shown by so many politicians on the issue of Prohibition, LaGuardia pledged that he would support wet candidates of any party, and he urged wet voters everywhere to do the same. His own success with the voters of East Harlem further demonstrated to wets that opposition to Prohibition could be a great political asset. In a city where Democrats outnumbered Republicans two to one, and where a strong Democratic machine had a virtual stranglehold on city politics, LaGuardia's ability as a Republican to attract supporters who otherwise voted straight Democratic tickets showed that opposition to Prohibition, combined with the right stands on other issues, could convince urban voters in the 1920s to cross party lines. He demonstrated better than any other American politician at the time that urban ethnic voters were angry about the Eighteenth Amendment, and that political strength could be found by tapping into the widespread resentment toward the Prohibition experiment.

LaGuardia's political success cannot be attributed solely to his stance on Prohibition. But his status as a wet was a large part of his popularity, and his undeniable success as a wet Republican in an overwhelmingly Democratic city and district brought home two of the fundamental political lessons of the dry era—that the issue of Prohibition was waiting to be exploited by ei-

ther party, and that politicians like LaGuardia who had the courage to oppose the dry agenda publicly could win broad support from wet voters. In
an era when voters by and large saw few differences between Democrats
and Republicans, Prohibition was one of the few major political issues that
regularly divided candidates, and it was beginning to play a significant role
in an age of otherwise unspectacular politics.

The example set in New York, where elected officials like Mayor Jimmy
Walker and Representative Fiorello LaGuardia demonstrated how to parlay
opposition to Prohibition into political strength, offered the first indication
that a wet tide was building that would eventually wash over the entire
United States.

As wet leaders of both parties looked to take advantage of the issue of
Prohibition, the Democratic Party remained at a distinct advantage. Although nationally the Democratic Party remained divided over Prohibition,
with Southern Democrats preventing the party from abandoning the dry
cause, New York Democrats emerged as the wettest in the nation. Governor Alfred E. Smith and Mayor Walker were at the head of New York's wet
contingent, and their prominence as public officials made New York the
center of wet political agitation in the United States. By the end of the
1920s, Smith and Walker's reputations as wet crusaders prompted the Anti-
Saloon League to describe New York as "the wet hope of the nation."[23]

Though Mayor Walker's liberal view of drinking as a legitimate urban
pleasure made him the darling of the city's wets, it was Governor Smith
who would stake his political career on Prohibition and become the Democratic Party's national leader on the repeal issue. In 1920, Smith had been
ousted from the governor's office by the dry Republican Nathan Miller, an
uninspiring candidate whose narrow victory rested more on Warren Harding's coattails in the presidential election than on Miller's appeal. After
working in the private sector for two brief years, Smith reentered politics.
In 1922, he reclaimed the governor's office after campaigning against Governor Miller on numerous issues, including revising the State Constitution,
reforming the state budget, and opposing censorship laws and loyalty tests.
Though Smith had not intended to make Prohibition an issue in the 1922
campaign, when Republicans attacked him on his wet stance, he responded

by openly stating his opposition to the Eighteenth Amendment, while accusing Republicans of trying to appear wet to wet voters and dry to drys.

As the election neared, New York's voters embraced Smith's wet politics. *Variety* argued that the Prohibition issue had given the Democratic Party a big boost that year, and predicted that wet voters, especially women, would make the difference in the election. When every major paper in the city endorsed Smith (except Joseph Pulitzer's *New York World* and the *American,* owned by Smith's enemy William Randolph Hearst), he retook the Executive Mansion by a margin of 387,000 votes, the largest in a state gubernatorial race at that time. Once back in office, Smith confirmed his wet leanings. He made little effort to hide his personal fondness for highballs and vowed not to be a coward or a hypocrite about it, openly offering liquor to guests at the Executive Mansion in Albany. In policy matters, he made his repeal position clear by stating that "the present condition is intolerable" and calling for the immediate legalization of wine and beer. Smith's 1923 repeal of the Mullan-Gage Law, the state's Prohibition enforcement statute, only further clarified his stand on Prohibition for the voting public.[24]

Now back in the governor's office, Smith began a decade-long flirtation with the presidency. His repeal of the Mullan-Gage Law proved to be a pivotal moment in his political career, prompting humorist Will Rogers to comment, "We will see now whether he lands in the White House or the ash heap." After expressing initial reservations that his wet position might hamper his political advancement, Smith comfortably eased into his role as a wet leader and began actively lobbying against Prohibition from Albany. Having risen to national prominence in Democratic politics, Smith now corresponded with senators and representatives of both parties to lobby for modification of the Volstead Act. Given Smith's prominent role in working against Prohibition, one newspaper went so far as to dub Smith "the logical candidate for the wets in the [1924] Democratic convention."[25]

Yet Smith's presidential hopes also illustrated how hard it would be to stir American voters to take on the dry crusade. When the Democratic National Convention assembled in New York City in 1924, wet Democrats hoped Smith would win the party's nomination with strong local backing. Democrats saw the Republican Party in 1924 as especially vulnerable, with the bland Calvin Coolidge having inherited the presidency following the unexpected death of President Warren Harding in 1923. The outspoken

Smith seemed a natural antidote to the president popularly known as "Silent Cal," but the Democrats failed to come together in 1924 to exploit Republican vulnerabilities. The party sidestepped the volatile issue of Prohibition entirely, revealing a wide split between Smith's supporters, composed of the growing ranks of wet working-class Democrats from the urban Northeast, and the old guard of dry Democrats from the South and West. Rather than rallying behind the issue of Prohibition, as Smith supporters had hoped would happen, the Democratic factions instead argued ferociously about the Ku Klux Klan and nearly came to blows when urban Democrats' bid to censure the Klan was voted down. The battle over a nominee proved equally contentious. Supporters of Governor Smith and William G. McAdoo of California remained deadlocked through 103 ballots, until the party finally settled on a compromise candidate, John W. Davis, a conservative lawyer from West Virginia who had served in Congress and as Solicitor General of the United States under Woodrow Wilson. Predictably, President Coolidge resoundingly defeated Davis in the fall of 1924.[26]

The 1924 election showed that national public opinion against Prohibition had not reached the point that it had in New York, and that neither party was willing yet to make Prohibition a major issue in a presidential election. Regardless, political opposition to Prohibition was growing, and Smith remained the leading wet on the national scene. As he entered his third term as governor, Smith knew that the majority of voters in his state had no desire to see Prohibition continued. In 1926 he sponsored a statewide referendum on Prohibition in which voters urged modification of the Volstead Act by a margin of nearly three to one statewide, and by a six-to-one margin in New York City. With referenda in Wisconsin, Illinois, Montana, and Nevada producing similar results, Smith remained confident that it was only a matter of time before Prohibition became a dominant issue in national politics. He also used the results of the referenda in New York and other states to dispel the notion that rural and urban voters were hopelessly split on the issue of Prohibition. While urban voters were voting wet by greater margins than their rural counterparts, wet majorities were also clearly emerging in rural areas, and by 1926 few states in the nation could legitimately claim dry majorities any longer.[27]

With wet sentiments growing nationally, it seemed by 1928 that Al Smith's time had come. He had served four successful terms as governor of New York, and he enjoyed a well-deserved reputation as a reformer. He was respected as a champion of personal liberty and viewed as generally friendly to business interests. His stellar legislative record and widespread popularity in his home state made him the most visible Democratic politician in the nation, while his storybook rise from a childhood of poverty on New York's Lower East Side to the highest office in New York made him a hero to urban immigrants and their children across the United States. With more of the nation now sharing New Yorkers' anger over Prohibition, Smith seemed to be the natural choice for voters who wished to see the noble experiment ended. In 1928, it seemed nothing could stand in the way of Al Smith's efforts to win the Democratic nomination. His popularity and the endorsements he received from a wide range of intellectuals and reformers propelled him into the 1928 presidential campaign with the best chances of any Democrat to win the White House since the dry era had begun.[28]

Unlike 1924, when the Democratic National Convention had been marred by ugly disputes over the Ku Klux Klan and a deadlocked nomination, the 1928 convention in Houston was all Smith's. The delegates nominated the New York governor without incident on the first ballot, and Smith personally set out to identify the party with the wet agenda. Though the party sought some measure of balance by nominating the dry Arkansas senator Joseph T. Robinson as Smith's running mate and holding off on the passage of an explicitly wet platform, there was little doubt that with Smith's candidacy the Democratic Party stood for repeal. As one of his first orders of business, Smith set a wet tone for the campaign by appointing his friend and fellow wet, financier John J. Raskob, to serve as chairman of the party and to direct the campaign. More dramatically, Smith sent a widely publicized telegram to the convention as it closed, personally pledging to make modification of the Volstead Act one of his highest priorities, and arguing that "there should be fundamental changes in the present provisions for national prohibition."[29]

Wet Democrats and leading figures in the party were delighted with Smith's openly wet stance. Senator David Walsh of Massachusetts called Smith's telegram to the convention "a frank, honest and courageous statement of his political principles," while others in the party praised it as a candid expression of Smith's position on Prohibition, perfectly consistent with his character. Drys in the party, however, were incensed that Smith declared his wetness so openly. And Smith's choice of Raskob as party chairman vexed even some of his closest advisors, who wondered whether Raskob, a lifelong Republican who had only recently joined the Democratic Party, was an appropriate choice to lead the Smith campaign. Some worried that Smith's alliance with Raskob, a wealthy businessman, would alienate his working-class supporters. Other Democrats feared that Raskob, a Catholic son of working-class immigrants like Smith, would make the Democratic ticket appear too Catholic and unnerve Protestant voters. But Smith was adamant that Raskob lead the party, for he believed that Raskob's business ties and Republican Party connections would help broaden the Democratic coalition and appeal to disenchanted Republicans. As a wet, Raskob also bolstered Smith's belief in the need to make repeal a focal point of the Democratic campaign.[30]

To a degree, Raskob's appointment worked as Smith had intended. After the convention, Raskob received numerous letters of congratulation from business associates who assured him that his presence in the Smith camp and Smith's opposition to the Eighteenth Amendment would swing business leaders and other disillusioned Republicans to the Democratic camp. One supporter wrote, "I have heard quite a number of [associates] who lean toward the Republican Party express themselves favorably toward Mr. Smith . . . and they were not Catholics either." He added, "They are not afraid of his religion nor his wet attitude."[31]

The Prohibition issue in particular helped galvanize Smith supporters. A colleague who wrote to Raskob in the summer of 1928 pledged his support for Smith, exclaiming that a Smith presidency would mean that "we may yet be able to think as we please and drink without being hypocrites." He added, "If there are two men in the United States that can bring this about they are you and Al." The enthusiasm for Smith (and Raskob) in these circles led to an unprecedented number of donations, and Democratic Party fundraising for the year surpassed donations to the Republican Party for the first time since 1912. Raskob himself gave $530,000 to the Smith campaign and persuaded many of his business colleagues to donate similarly large sums.[32]

At the same time, Smith's popularity and his ability to tap into growing wet sentiment were shifting the balance of power in the party away from traditional Southern Democrats to the urban working class and the children of immigrants, marking a turning point in the history of the Democratic Party. Through issues like Prohibition, worker's compensation, housing reform, labor laws, and utility regulation, Smith broadened the voting base of the Democratic Party and remade the party around a coalition of voters that would endure for the remainder of the twentieth century.

Many of the urban ethnic voters who rallied behind Smith felt a natural affinity for him as one of their own. The *Irish World,* for example, called Governor Smith "a living example of the fact that anyone born in the United States of America has a chance of rising to the topmost rung of the ladder." Among Irish Americans, support for Smith was solid. He worked quietly to swing African-American voters to the Democratic camp, benefiting from important newspaper endorsements and from the work of advisors who had close ties to civil rights organizations. He won support from second-generation Jewish voters, whom he wooed away from both the Socialist and Republican parties. He appealed to Italian, Polish, and Czech voters as well, and drew them into the Democratic fold in increasing numbers. Smith's appeal to these voters might have been based on his reform record, his Catholicism, his stand on immigration, or the belief that he offered an antidote to the nativist impulses that had swept the country in the 1920s, but in almost all cases, his stance on Prohibition was part of the equation.[33]

Smith's ability to reach these varied constituencies, his skills as a coalition builder, and his identification with the Prohibition issue all boded well for the governor as he embarked on the path toward the White House in 1928. Early in the year, Smith's chances for winning the presidency had seemed excellent, especially when President Calvin Coolidge announced his intention not to run for reelection, a decision that essentially leveled the playing field by removing the incumbent's advantage from the race as Secretary of Commerce Herbert Hoover took Coolidge's place. After winning the nomination in Houston, Smith was greeted by huge crowds as he traveled to cities with large ethnic and Catholic populations like St. Louis, Chicago, St. Paul, and Milwaukee. These raucous gatherings in support of Smith allegedly prompted the governor to comment to journalists, "I'm going to beat the pants off Hoover."[34]

Unhappily for Smith, his attempt to reinvent the Democratic Party in 1928 by focusing on its urban core and by tapping into popular resentment over Prohibition was countered by more potent forces—the still lingering power of the dry crusade and the bigotry associated with it. Though diminished in numbers, the dry lobby found a way to counter Smith by exploiting a wave of virulent anti-Catholicism against the Democratic candidate in 1928, especially in Southern and Western states.

Both Smith and Raskob, it seemed, had miscalculated how effectively the defenders of the Eighteenth Amendment would exploit Smith's Catholicism to stop the wet agenda. Dry leaders knew that Smith presented the greatest challenge to Prohibition they had ever faced, and in the summer of 1928 they mobilized against him, stirring up as much suspicion and bigotry against the Catholic New York governor as they could. As his aide Frances Perkins later recalled, "We who campaigned for Smith in 1928, and also the candidate himself, were not prepared to deal with the degree of prejudice we encountered . . . and were surprised and shocked by the way in which our opponents appealed to the basest passions and lowest motives of the people."[35]

When the 1928 campaign began, Smith optimistically believed that he had already addressed the issue of his religion, and he expressed confidence that it would not emerge again during his presidential bid. In 1927, as Smith put the final touches on his preparation for a presidential run, the *Atlantic Monthly* had published an article by Charles Marshall, a New York lawyer who openly questioned whether it would be proper for a Roman Catholic like Smith to serve as president in a nation that was three-quarters Protestant. In particular, Marshall asked whether Smith's obligations as a Catholic would conflict with his official duties as Chief Executive.[36]

In a carefully planned reply, Smith wrote an open letter to the *Atlantic Monthly* asserting that his Catholicism had never prevented him from doing his job in all his years as an elected official, and that it never would. He stated flatly, "I recognize no power in . . . my church to interfere with the operations of the Constitution of the United States for the enforcement of the law of the land." With his trademark candor, Smith expressed hope "that never again will any public servant be challenged because of his faith." Smith's reply won widespread praise in intellectual circles, and political observers believed that his defense of his religion had added a much-needed and rare dose of tolerance to American politics.[37]

Campaigning in the Midwest in 1928, however, Smith found that the religion issue still haunted him. As he traveled by train across the country, he looked out the window of his coach one night to see a long line of crosses burning in the Oklahoma night. As he made his way through the American heartland, the Ku Klux Klan and other nativist groups actively spread hate literature about Smith, accusing him, among other things, of drunk driving. (It did not matter that Smith could not drive.) He was accused of owning brothels in New York, and the literature promised that if Smith were elected president he would open up the White House to bootleggers and prostitutes. (Apparently, it was also lost on the authors of these diatribes that the late President Harding had enjoyed the services of his own personal bootlegger in the White House throughout his presidency.)[38]

Additional stories circulated by drys and other Smith detractors focused on his alcohol consumption. Some claimed that Smith was a drunkard who drank as many as eight cocktails a day, and that he had appeared at campaign rallies so inebriated that he had to be propped up by aides. The animosity stirred up against Smith finally led to physical violence. While stumping for Governor Smith in Independence, Missouri, his aide Frances Perkins was greeted with cries of "he's a damned Catholic" before she was pelted with eggs and tomatoes.[39]

The dry movement did not invent the anti-Catholic sentiments that threatened to derail the Smith campaign, but it delighted in exploiting them. Fusing Smith's Catholicism and his stance against Prohibition into a single issue, drys worked ceaselessly to sway Southern and Western Democrats to support the Republican candidate Herbert Hoover. One of the most active individuals in this effort was Bishop James Cannon, Jr., a prominent figure in the Methodist Board of Temperance and the Anti-Saloon League who openly expressed his anti-Catholic sentiments.

Bishop Cannon had risen to the top of the dry movement after the death of the Anti-Saloon League's Wayne Wheeler in 1927. As a Democrat, Cannon was incensed by Smith's declaration in favor of repeal at the 1928 Democratic National Convention, and he was convinced that Smith and his supporters were turning the Democratic Party over to Tammany Hall and the Catholic Church. To stop Smith, Cannon hastily called a conference of Southern Democrats in Asheville, North Carolina, in July 1928 to organize against the Smith campaign. With $65,000 in funds donated by Republican insurance executive F. C. Jameson, Cannon used the Asheville conference to launch a vicious campaign against Smith in the summer of 1928. He urged dry organizations to do everything in their power to prevent Smith from carrying the traditionally Democratic South in the fall election.[40]

For the duration of the 1928 campaign, the dry crusade returned to top form, using the tactics it had honed so well nearly a decade before, when William Anderson's pressure politics took New York by storm. In numerous speeches, editorials, and public letters, Cannon personally led the charge against Smith, urging Southerners to reject "the cocktail President." In an editorial in *The Nation*, Cannon complained that "Governor Smith is personally, ecclesiastically, aggressively, irreconcilably wet." Nor did Cannon miss an opportunity to remind readers of Smith's Catholicism. He insisted that "it is a fact that the attacks in Congress upon the prohibition law are made chiefly by men who are themselves Roman Catholics, or who represent constituencies with large Roman Catholic populations." Building from this point, Cannon deduced that "certainly it is likely that the Governor Alfred E. Smith is influenced by the views of the Pope and the cardinals on the subject of prohibition."[41]

Bishop Cannon also used the issues of race and ethnicity expertly, knowing how effective they would be with Southern audiences. Citing Smith's links to Tammany Hall, Cannon explained that Ferdinand Q. Morton, a black Democratic leader in Harlem, had two white secretaries, and he hinted that Southerners could expect to see more such arrangements under a Smith administration. In a Maryland speech, Cannon also warned that Smith would turn the country over to "the Italians, the Sicilians, the Poles, and Russian Jew. That kind has given us a stomach-ache." He concluded: "He wants the kind of people that you find today on the sidewalks of New York."[42]

With Cannon urging them on, the dry movement rallied against Smith as it had not done since the ratification of the Eighteenth Amendment. Drys attacked Smith, his religious beliefs, his ethnic supporters, and his stand on Prohibition. The Woman's Christian Temperance Union joined the fight, campaigning heavily for Herbert Hoover in the South. It distributed ten million pamphlets, put up highway billboards, and employed nine thousand women to persuade Southerners to vote against the wet New Yorker. The newly created National Women's Democratic Law Enforcement League urged women in the South to vote for Hoover rather than for the wet Smith. New York's temperance leaders, who had fought Smith unsuccessfully for years, also contributed to the anti-Smith campaign. To aid the dry effort, Dr. John Roach Straton of the Calvary Baptist Church in Manhattan traveled throughout the South delivering a stump speech entitled "Al Smith and the Forces of Hell." In it, Straton denounced Smith as the "deadliest foe in America today of the forces of moral progress."[43]

Herbert Hoover, Smith's Republican rival for the presidency, welcomed this dry resurgence and benefited immeasurably from the attacks on Smith. While Hoover ostensibly issued orders to his own campaign to keep things clean, the Republican nominee still profited from the efforts of a member of the outgoing Coolidge administration, Mabel Walker Willebrandt, the Assistant Attorney General of the United States in charge of Prohibition enforcement. A seasoned campaigner and one of the most prominent women officials in American government, Willebrandt campaigned behind the scenes on behalf of Hoover at the Republican National Convention in Kansas City, leading to jokes that the nomination had been decided "up in Mabel's room." After the convention, Willebrandt continued to campaign actively for Hoover in 1928, reporting on state campaign efforts, building valuable contacts, and most important, shoring up support for Hoover among drys who had doubts about the Republican nominee's own commitment to Prohibition.

Dubbed "the Joan of Arc of Prohibition" by drys, Willebrandt had no qualms about using her official position to undermine the Smith campaign. In the summer of 1928, she increased the number of Prohibition agents policing New York City, and personally planned a new round of highly publicized raids in the city to underscore the lack of Prohibition enforcement in Smith's hometown. On the eve of Smith's nomination in Houston,

Willebrandt had 160 agents raid eleven of New York's most famous night-clubs, which resulted in the arrests of 102 people, including Texas Guinan and Helen Morgan. (Upon making her court appearance, Guinan called the whole affair a "lot of bologna.") Willebrandt then caused a mini-scandal when she issued subpoenas to 125 prominent New Yorkers known to be nightclub patrons so that she could personally question them in front of a grand jury for evidence in padlocking cases. Finally, she ordered more raids on the eve of the election in November, a move that Governor Smith and Mayor Walker condemned as the lowest form of politics.[44]

As other drys marshaled Smith opponents in the South and West, Wille-brandt went to the key state of Ohio, where she emphasized Smith's wet record and his Tammany Hall roots for the benefit of the Hoover campaign. In a speech to 2,000 Methodist ministers in Ohio in September 1928, Willebrandt urged her audience to rally dry Protestant congregations against the Catholic Smith in order to preserve the Eighteenth Amendment. She reminded the ministers that there were 600,000 Methodist voters in Ohio alone, meaning that the ballots cast by their congregations would be "enough to swing the election."[45]

Willebrandt never specifically mentioned Smith's religion in her speech, but by going directly to Methodist ministers and urging them to save Pro-hibition by mobilizing their congregations to defeat Smith, she had dealt Smith a severe blow. The press cast a critical eye on Willebrandt's speeches, and Smith himself angrily asked what the consequences would have been for him had he gone to a Catholic conference and urged Catholic priests to rally voters to oppose Hoover. As the controversy raged over Willebrandt's speech and many critics argued that Willebrandt should be removed from office, the Republican National Committee denied any responsibility for her actions. To Willebrandt's chagrin, the official party response was that Willebrandt was acting as a "freelancer" and not speaking officially for the Hoover campaign, though the Republican National Committee had signed off on her efforts in advance. For his part, Hoover simply distanced himself from the controversy while letting the issues of Prohibition and Smith's re-ligion fester.[46]

In the end, the efforts of Bishop Cannon, Reverend Straton, and Assistant Attorney General Willebrandt to fuse Smith's opposition to Prohibition with his religion proved enormously destructive to the Democratic campaign. While dry Democrats had been relatively easy to sway to the Hoover camp, drys had even succeeded in winning over wets who had misgivings about a Catholic president. As the election neared, one New York woman, Mrs. George King, wrote a letter to AAPA board member Pierre DuPont in which she expressed her apprehension about a Catholic's riding the wet tide all the way to the White House. "We agree with you that there should be modification of the Volstead Act," she wrote to DuPont, before sharing her concerns about Smith's religion. "It is a well known fact," she wrote, "that the chairman of his national campaign [Raskob] has but recently returned from Rome where he was decorated by the Pope." She added that "in view of the many assurances of Governor Smith and his backers that religion has no bearing on this manner, it gives one reason to question their good faith when their first act is to choose a prominent Catholic for this position." King concluded: "I feel sure that you, Mr. DuPont, as well as the rest of us who are working on [repeal] would be sorry if we had a Dictator in Rome."[47]

The AAPA's response was pathetic. Rather than defending Smith and Raskob from religious attack and embracing the Smith campaign as the best hope for repeal, the AAPA instead refused to endorse Smith in 1928. Though many of the leading figures in the AAPA announced that they were personally abandoning the Republican Party to vote for Smith, the organization officially remained neutral in the election, arguing disingenuously that the Democratic platform was not definitively in favor of repeal.[48]

The anti-Catholicism that came to dominate the 1928 campaign took a heavy toll on Smith. He had entered the race confident of his ability to win the presidency on the issues, including Prohibition, only to find that the issue he could do nothing about, his religion, was being exploited to defeat him. For one of the few times in Smith's political career, "the great commoner" felt out of touch with the voters. Before addressing a crowd in Oklahoma, he confided to a reporter, "I don't know those people out there. I don't speak their language." He tried to speak candidly about his Catholicism in the hope that more frank talk would put the issue to rest, but the anti-Catholic rhetoric continued unabated. After winning the adulation of his core constituents in American cities and thinking that he had finally found the path to the presidency, Smith now saw his campaign sinking, undermined by an organized campaign of bigotry orchestrated by the dry crusade.[49]

When American voters went to the polls on November 6, 1928, they handed the New York governor a crushing defeat. Herbert Hoover defeated Smith 21,391,993 to 15,061,169 votes, and in the Electoral College, Hoover captured 444 votes to Smith's 87 votes. Smith carried only eight states, losing even his home state of New York by a slim margin. Yet the margin of Hoover's victory was in some regards misleading. Despite the common historical interpretation of Smith's defeat as a debacle, his showing indicated that the Democratic Party had indeed been reinvented by Al Smith's attempt to bring urban, working-class wet voters into the party. While Smith's percentage of the popular vote, only 41 percent, was well below Hoover's, Smith managed to draw more than 15 million votes, more than any Democratic candidate before him. His vote tally was almost double what the two previous Democratic candidates, James Cox and John W. Davis, had garnered in 1920 and 1924 respectively. The dry movement's widespread mobilization against Smith had clearly hurt him, especially in the South, where seven solidly Democratic states swung to the GOP. But in a new development, Smith carried the nation's twelve largest cities and fifty of the nation's largest counties, all of which had gone Republican in 1920. He had also given the Democrats rare wins in the Northeast, and had foreshadowed a trend toward a Democratic resurgence in an increasingly urban nation.[50]

The 1928 election also marked a large upturn in voter participation, a sign of both the support for Smith and the mobilization against him. Nationally, voter turnout in 1928 increased to 67.5 percent of eligible voters, almost 11 percent higher than in the previous presidential election. In New England and the Middle Atlantic states, voter participation increased from 54 percent in 1920 to 72 percent in 1928, and in New York City, the Board of Elections had to scramble to accommodate the nearly 500,000 newly registered voters expected to turn out for Smith. The increase in the registration of first-time voters, many of them urban ethnics and Catholics drawn to the voting booth by Smith, revealed a new Democratic Party.

Though he lost the ultimate prize, the 1928 election indicated that Smith had undoubtedly established the Democratic Party as the party of repeal. He had built a new loyal following of wet voters whose allegiance to the party would long outlast the Eighteenth Amendment.[51]

Reflecting on his defeat, Smith was gracious and upbeat. In the week following the election, he argued that "the verdict of the American people last Tuesday was not the crushing defeat of the Democratic Party that some of the headlines in the public press would have us believe. On the contrary, let us see what the facts are: Take the popular vote—a change of 10 per cent of the total number of votes cast would have changed the popular result."[52]

Publicly, Smith attributed his defeat at the polls to what he called the Republican Party's reliance on "the false and misleading issue of prosperity." In his memoirs, Smith wrote that the economic abundance of the 1920s had been responsible for Hoover's election, as the Hoover camp had "once more brought down from the garret the old full dinner pail, polished it up and pressed it into service." Yet privately Smith believed that the issue of his religion, raised by those who wanted to defend Prohibition, had cost him the presidency. On the eve of the election, he commented that "the time hasn't come yet when a man can say his beads in the White House."[53]

Certainly the Democrats' 1928 campaign was flawed, and Smith and Raskob may have relied too heavily on the Prohibition issue to carry the election. There were other issues for voters to consider in 1928, namely tariff policy, agricultural relief, foreign policy, and utility regulation, but as contemporary analysts of the election noted, "the only real issues were prosperity, prohibition and religion." How much the anti-Catholic rhetoric of the campaign influenced the vote is impossible to quantify, but the *New York Times* confirmed that "the Republicans have profited by the appeals to bigotry and fanaticism in the South." It added that the votes against Smith, especially in Southern dry strongholds, were cast for one of two reasons. Some "were cast against the Democratic candidate because he is a Catholic; the rest because he is an anti-Prohibitionist." The Catholic weekly *Commonweal* also saw the influence of anti-Catholicism in the 1928 race, and added that "this prejudice, and this only, swayed hundreds of thousands." While political scientists for decades after argued that the prosperity of the country kept the presidency in Republican hands, more recent studies have shown what many political observers saw plainly at the time: that Smith was defeated because he was a Catholic, a point that the dry lobby pushed ceaselessly.[54]

Dry leaders heralded Herbert Hoover's victory at the polls in 1928 as one of their greatest hours. The Republican win had not only extinguished the greatest political threat to Prohibition by keeping Al Smith out of the White House but also swayed the balance of power in Congress back in favor of the drys, giving the dry movement more allies in Congress than it had ever had before. Ella Boole of the Woman's Christian Temperance Union rejoiced at the dry gains in Congress in 1928, arguing that Hoover's win had vanquished the wet forces once and for all. Bishop Cannon wrote to Mabel Walker Willebrandt, "Yours is the outstanding victory of the entire election." Yet in many regards, Hoover's victory in 1928 was as misleading as Smith's loss. Hoover owed a significant part of his victory margin to the anti-Catholicism stirred up by drys like Cannon, Straton, and Willebrandt. Though this tactic had worked in the short term, it caused a backlash as well, for millions of voters now identified the Republican Party with intolerance and bigotry. As Smith noted several years later, "the 1928 national campaign and the use by the drys of their power over the President, disgusted decent people all over the country." Hoover's victory had forged the lasting impression in wet voters' minds that Republicans and drys were one in the same—an impression that wet Republicans like Fiorello LaGuardia and Nicholas Murray Butler had desperately sought to avoid. While Republicans could also credit the nation's prosperity with helping them carry the election, within a year's time that prosperity would disappear with the stock market crash of 1929. The taint of bigotry, by contrast, would remain.[55]

For all the joy the drys had found in Herbert Hoover's election, they failed to see the costs of their tactics. For the duration of Hoover's presidency, wets, urban immigrants, and Catholic voters seethed, waiting to exact their revenge. Alienated by the Republicans, they had found refuge in Al Smith's Democratic coalition, and they would remain loyal to that coalition no matter who led it. In the meantime, wets from both parties saw clearly from the alliance brokered between Herbert Hoover and the dry lobby that there would be no room for repeal within the Republican agenda any time soon.

Though the results of the 1928 election were plainly visible, the lasting effects of the election were not immediately clear. Although Al Smith may have failed in his bid for the presidency, he had actually succeeded in one important regard by gathering together a nascent coalition for repeal that would grow in the coming years. The 1928 election had shown that New York's resistance to the Eighteenth Amendment was not an aberration but a starting point from which all wets could begin to join forces. And the dry crusade, believing it had vanquished the wets in 1928, instead had managed only to draw a starker line between wets and drys. The dry lobby had stopped Governor Smith from reaching the White House by engineering one last campaign to defend the noble experiment, but it had won only by using fear and hatred to shore up a declining base of support. It would be the last time the dry crusade would be able to muster such a victory. After 1929, no amount of pressure politics would conceal the failure of Prohibition nor change the growing sense that the dry lobby had held sway in American politics for far too long.

10

The End of the Party

After the presidential election of 1928, the nation's dry leaders confidently claimed that Herbert Hoover's election had validated their cause. They argued that Hoover's victory over Al Smith proved that the nation still supported Prohibition, and they promised that the New York governor's defeat would mark the end of opposition to the Eighteenth Amendment. With Al Smith forced into political retirement, the drys expected resistance to Prohibition finally to subside, and the nation to ease into a long-overdue acceptance of the dry agenda. Commenting on the election outcome, Ella Boole of the Woman's Christian Temperance Union argued that "it was proof enough that . . . politically the Dry side was the winning side and it should have been enough to convince the Wet politicians—who seemed to die hard."[1]

But the final years of the Prohibition experiment would be marked by anything but a true acceptance of the Eighteenth Amendment. Within months of Herbert Hoover's taking office, a stark contrast could be seen between the further degeneration of the dry experiment in cities like New York, and the optimistic picture presented by the dry crusade. In particular, the effects of organized crime, drunkenness, violence, and corruption, all of which had thrived under Prohibition, were mounting faster than ever in the late 1920s, giving many Americans a sense that the noble experiment had gone terribly wrong. The problems became even more pronounced after the stock market crash of 1929, which replaced the exuberant, buoyant attitude that had accompanied prosperity with a sense of economic and cultural desperation.

As the Roaring Twenties came to a close, the speakeasies and nightclubs that had characterized the "smart," carefree atmosphere of the era were now becoming backdrops to unspeakable acts of violence. A few incidents stood out as evidence that the conditions engendered by Prohibition were spiraling out of control. Late one evening in July 1929, an ex-convict named Simon Walker and two brothers with reputations as waterfront street fighters, William "Red" Cassidy and Peter Cassidy, stopped in for drinks at the Hotsy-Totsy Club at Broadway and Fifty-fourth Street, a speakeasy owned by the gangster Jack "Legs" Diamond. The three men, according to news reports, had already consumed a good deal of alcohol earlier in the evening, and they grew rowdy when their bartender was not quick enough with their beers. An argument followed, and soon the Cassidy brothers were brawling with Diamond and his partner, Charles Entratta, also known as Charles Green. Diamond and Entratta reached for their pistols, and "Legs" Diamond shot and killed "Red" Cassidy. Red's brother Peter was shot and seriously wounded, and Simon Walker, who had been watching the altercation but had not taken part in the original argument, was killed. All the while, another partner in the Hotsy-Totsy Club, Hymie Cohen, ordered the orchestra to play on to drown out the sounds of gunfire.

The double murder in the Hotsy-Totsy Club was a sign to New Yorkers that Prohibition culture had gone awry. Twenty-five patrons had witnessed the shooting, but fearing for their lives, none would admit to having witnessed any of the events that had unfolded in the club that evening. Charles Entratta, who fled to Chicago after the incident, was later brought back to New York and tried for the murders of Walker and Cassidy, but was acquitted for lack of evidence. A few months later, he was found dead. Two other waiters who had witnessed the shooting in the Hotsy-Totsy Club were also later found dead, and Hymie Cohen, the partner who had ordered the band to play on during the shooting, disappeared. When "Legs" Diamond emerged from hiding eight months later to answer questions about the murders in his club, police were forced to release him for lack of evidence. As the journalist Stanley Walker noted, "No one was alive to give evidence against him."[2]

The murders in the Hotsy-Totsy Club indicated that Prohibition culture in New York was entering a darker period, more vicious than what the city had known previously. Prohibition-related violence erupted with fearful regularity in the city in the late 1920s and early 1930s, and every morning, the press carried new stories about the ugly side of the "anything goes" atmosphere that had been fostered by Prohibition.

Murder was the most common indicator of the darker mood. Saturday night drunkenness in the city's speakeasies was responsible for much of it, as patrons got into deadly fights and bartenders were killed or injured at the hands of robbers and drunks. In one instance in 1931, the *Amsterdam News* described how "his bacchanal majesty, gin, mounted a gory throne in Harlem . . . when three men died violently, a fourth was mortally wounded, and several persons slashed and seriously injured in the aftermaths of drinking bouts and brawls in the community within twelve hours."[3]

The extremes of this violence could be gruesome. In February 1933, the press reported that a deliveryman entered Porky Murray's speakeasy on West Fifty-second Street at 2:30 in the morning for a late drink, only to find it eerily deserted. Looking behind the bar, he saw the body of the bartender, Patsy Griffin, lying dead of a gunshot wound. Nearby lay the bodies of two patrons, a man and a woman. As far as police detectives could gather from the subsequent investigation, a drunken patron had murdered Griffin for asking him to keep his voice down, and then shot the two other victims because they had witnessed the incident.[4]

As grisly murders like these became more common in New York in the unregulated world of the Prohibition era, the city's murder rate more than doubled. In 1921, the Magistrate's Court had recorded 712 arraignments for homicide in the city, but by 1931, the number had crept to nearly 1,500.[5]

According to Judge Alfred J. Talley of the New York State Court of General Sessions, murder was only one part of the problem. Crime of all sorts soared as law and order eroded under the effects of Prohibition. Testifying before Congress in 1926, Talley observed that not only in New York but throughout the nation, "crime has increased in such amazing proportion that it has become the dominant consideration of most of the state and municipal governments of the nation." Calling Prohibition the "breeder of crime," Talley argued that it was responsible for an escalation not only of homicide rates but also of juvenile crime, assault, and crimes committed by women. "The increase of crimes of violence or passion," he explained, "the increase of intoxication, [and] the breakdown of the administration of the law, can be traced primarily to the disrespect for the law which has been engendered . . . by the operation of this prohibition law."[6]

Statistics supported Talley's argument. In 1929 the NYPD reported a "big increase" in murder, theft, and robbery rates, and a 9 percent rise in arrests. District Attorney Joab Banton complained that Prohibition was responsible for the proliferation of crime, for "night clubs are hangouts of criminals who watch for women with jewelry and men with money, follow them when they leave and rob them or blackmail them." The crime statistics should have been even higher, Banton argued, given that many nightclub patrons who were victimized by criminals failed to file complaints with the police.[7]

The high crime rate in the city was exacerbated by long-standing problems regarding the allocation of police resources to Prohibition enforcement. Since Richard Enright's tenure as police commissioner in the early 1920s, New Yorkers had complained that pressure to enforce the dry laws had continually distracted the Police Department from more serious crimes. As one 1926 editorial in the *Daily News* put it, "The police commissioner ought to let [U.S. Attorney Emory] Buckner do his own snooping, and the city police ought to be sicked on such real, dangerous, and plentiful criminals as murderers, second-story men, stick-up men, rapists, and fences."[8]

Illegal stills posed another major problem. During the Prohibition era, one-gallon stills were widely available for purchase in New York City hardware stores for six or seven dollars, and instructions on how to use them could easily be obtained from dated Department of Agriculture publications available at the public library. While most "urban moonshiners" who operated these stills made alcohol only for their own personal consumption, more ambitious amateurs found that much larger stills could be set up for $500 and could pay for themselves in as little as four days.[9]

Home stills were most common in the poorer neighborhoods of the city, where the noxious odors they produced annoyed neighbors and sometimes betrayed their presence to police and Prohibition agents. While the homemade liquor produced in these stills could kill those who consumed it, the stills themselves posed even greater dangers when they exploded or started tenement fires. On a regular basis in the late 1920s, the New York papers documented numerous deaths or injuries resulting from still fires and explosions, such as the explosion in a West Eleventh Street apartment kitchen that killed the infant son of a grocery importer and injured his parents, daughter, and seven firemen in the resultant fire. In a similar case in 1930, a large still exploded in a building across the street from P.S. 83 in Brooklyn, injuring fifteen school children. The widespread distribution of stills, however, made them impossible to police. Testifying before Congress in 1926, U.S. Attorney Emory Buckner confessed that federal enforcers seized on average only five stills a week in New York, while Senator James Reed of Missouri suspected that there were as many as 50,000 active stills in the city.[10]

Even more dangerous was the questionable quality of the city's liquor supply under the Volstead Act. In the 1920s, the federal government added poison to industrial alcohol to "denature" it and prevent it from being diverted for human consumption. Yet bootlegging operations routinely used denatured alcohol anyway, redistilling it in an attempt to remove the poisons. The process usually left trace amounts of poison in the reprocessed liquor to be consumed by unwitting drinkers. Additionally, homemade alcohol sold by bootleggers was often tainted with fusel oil, a poisonous byproduct of the distilling process. The quality of liquor available in the city was so inferior that in 1926 the Social Science Research Council reported that 99 out of 100 liquor samples tested by New York City laboratories contained traces of poison or fusel oil, which were almost certain to cause long-term medical harm. In the words of the report, "a tremendously high death rate is sure to result." U.S. Attorney Buckner agreed, and reported to Congress that 98 percent of the liquor samples his office tested over a two-year period were impure. A 1929 investigation conducted by the *New York Telegram* reached the same conclusion. After sampling liquor from 400 sources around the city, the paper reported that poisonous liquor abounded and was as likely to show up in the city's most exclusive clubs as it was in waterfront dives. As a result of Prohibition, New Yorkers were now drinking bootleg alcohol containing antifreeze or sterno, consuming "needle" beer mixed with ether, and being poisoned by Jamaica ginger extract, which produced the paralytic condition commonly known as "jake leg."[11]

Even when the alcohol itself was not poisonous, the continuous and excessive consumption of liquor in the city during the late years of Prohibition had devastating effects. New York's speakeasy culture and the identification of alcohol with urban sophistication had encouraged the widespread abuse of alcohol, and as a result, alcoholism rates in the city skyrocketed. According to a 1926 report by the Social Science Research Council, alcoholism wards in city hospitals were filled to capacity during Prohibition, both in public hospitals and in the private hospitals that catered to the "better class of people." Judge Talley's testimony to Congress confirmed the tendency toward excess. In 1926, he noted a 100 percent increase in the number of alcoholism cases treated at Bellevue Hospital. According to Talley, arrests for intoxication in the city had also risen steadily in the 1920s, as had revocations of chauffeurs' licenses for drunk driving and instances of children drinking. A New York City probation officer shared Talley's dismay over drinking among children. "As a result of my own experience and observation," he noted, "I cannot come to any conclusion other than this— that more young girls are drinking than ever." He added, "Boys ranging from ten to fifteen years are brought in dead drunk and when questioned it is found that they bought the 'white mule' themselves at a quarter a pint."[12]

The writer and photographer Carl Van Vechten aptly characterized the overindulgence of the period, admitting that for many of his colleagues, life in New York in the 1920s had become an endless cycle of drunken binges. "We'll get drunker and drunker, and drift about nightclubs so drunk we won't know where we are," he wrote. "We'll . . . go to bed late tomorrow morning and wake up and begin it all over again."[13]

Whether tainted or simply consumed in large quantities, Prohibition-era liquor was wreaking havoc in the city, claiming the lives of hundreds of New Yorkers every year and blinding or hospitalizing many more. In 1930 alone, the city medical examiner reported 625 deaths directly attributable to the ingestion of poisoned alcohol, while another 1,295 New Yorkers suffered other alcohol-related deaths. Often fatalities resulting from poisoned alcohol were reported in groupings of 10 or 20 at a time, the result of a single shipment of tainted liquor hitting the streets and claiming its victims in a matter of hours. The actual death tolls from poisoned liquor and alcoholism were thought to be even higher, however, as the illegality of drinking and the stigma attached to alcoholism resulted in alcohol-related deaths being regularly disguised on death certificates.[14]

The problems of alcoholism and random violence in Prohibition-era New York were compounded by the equally daunting problem of competition among organized criminals who battled for control of the city's profitable liquor and beer markets during the late 1920s. While organized crime in New York was hardly born in the Prohibition era, the Eighteenth Amendment gave Jewish, Italian, and Irish gangs more lucrative opportunities in the illegal liquor and beer trade than they had ever seen before. Though these organized crime gangs often avoided violence out of fear that it would only bring more law enforcement pressure upon them, when the competition for the alcohol trade in New York intensified, deadly altercations quickly flared, resulting in more than one thousand gangland murders during the Prohibition era.[15]

Organized crime's control over the city's liquor trade, the largest market for alcohol in the nation, was rooted in an impressive infrastructure engineered by the famed racketeer Arnold Rothstein. With Rothstein's initial investment, liquor traffickers set up centralized purchasing rings in Canada, England, and the West Indies. Rothstein also purchased the speedboats used to smuggle the liquor into the United States, as well as warehouses in which to store it. Before long, 80 percent of the liquor distilled in Canada was making its way into the United States, while the Bahamas, which had imported 944 gallons of whiskey in 1918, were importing close to 400,000 gallons a year, with most of it destined for the American market.[16]

The daily operations of this large-scale system were handled by Rothstein's ethnically diverse group of protégés, among them Irving Wexler (a.k.a. "Waxey Gordon"), Big Maxie Greenberg, Charles "Lucky" Luciano, and Owney Madden. Under Rothstein's tutelage, these figures learned that fixing prices and parceling out the business through negotiated deals with one another was far more profitable than intense and potentially deadly competition. (Not all gangland figures shared this cooperative spirit, however. Arthur "Dutch Schultz" Flegenheimer came to control the Bronx beer trade by stubbornly and violently fighting off his rivals.) Under Rothstein's guidance, his protégés built empires, branching out from bootlegging and beer running to protection schemes, numbers rackets, and other criminal enterprises. Some used their liquor profits to invest in nightclubs or theater productions, and a few even dabbled in smuggling Chinese immigrants into the United States from Cuba, reasoning that it was a simple effort to include them on boats already carrying contraband rum.[17]

With the bootleg liquor trade grossing millions of dollars a year, its leading figures had plenty of funds available to buy police protection and cultivate political connections, thus extending the negative effects of the noble experiment. Tammany Hall boss Charles Murphy, for one, made peace with the city's major bootleggers, while the leader of the Assembly District, James Hines, arranged protection for several notorious gangsters. Through these political arrangements, most well-connected gangsters found that they could operate with relative impunity. As a result, even when authorities intercepted large shipments of bootleg liquor, prosecutors found it nearly impossible to convict the ringleaders of Prohibition violations.

Organized crime's control of the liquor trade was so efficient that New Yorkers came to treat alcohol as just another commodity despite its illegality. Though New Yorkers knew of the corruption and violence endemic to the alcohol trade, they had come to accept purchasing liquor on a daily basis as a routine practice, hardly discernible from buying flowers or groceries. Having no direct interaction with the criminal gangs themselves, New Yorkers instead patronized barely disguised storefront "cordial shops" that dotted residential neighborhoods all over the city, or local bootleggers who specialized in the neighborhood trade by mailing out weekly price lists to area residents. Though these vendors carried only small stocks of liquor in case of raids, often provided liquor of poor quality, and tended to disappear after a few weeks to stay ahead of the law, they offered all the convenience and variety of the modern liquor store and made the purchase of illegal liquor as mundane as any other retail transaction.[18]

These neighborhood cordial shops and local bootleggers, set up in offices with "importer" or "broker" euphemistically painted on their doors, made the liquor trade seem innocent and commonplace. They plied their wares by leaving flyers on car windshields or slipping order forms under apartment doors, while the more savvy dealers offered free samples and home delivery, took telephone orders, and gave out gifts like Bakelite tumblers to regular customers. One bootlegger's menu, which already offered dozens of familiar whiskeys, beers, and wines, promised, "Ask for anything you may not find on this list."[19]

Though in their dealings with local bootleggers New Yorkers were spared the most unsavory aspects of the liquor business for most of the decade, by the late Prohibition era it was harder to ignore the negative side of the trade. Every few weeks, if not every few days, New Yorkers were given fresh evidence of the underworld's violent involvement in the liquor trade. Early one summer evening in 1931, for instance, a twenty-three-year-old renegade from Dutch Schultz's gang named Vincent "Mad Dog" Coll and several of his associates attempted to kill rival gangster Joey Rao as part of a war between beer-running operations. As Rao sat in front of the Helmar Social Club on East 107th Street, a crowded street filled with playing children, Coll and his gang opened fire with submachine guns and shotguns. The blasts from Coll's shotgun missed Rao and instead killed five-year-old Michael Vengalli and wounded four other children, earning Coll the moniker "baby killer."

The carnage on 107th Street horrified the city. Governor Franklin D. Roosevelt called the incident a "damnable outrage," while Mayor Walker responded by launching an all-out war on organized crime in New York, giving the police orders to "shoot to kill" should they encounter Coll. Eventually Coll was arrested and tried for the fatal shooting, but a jury acquitted him after his defense lawyers questioned the credibility of a key witness in the case. Once free, Coll returned to his luxurious apartment in the Cornish Arms Hotel in Chelsea, and immediately resumed his battles with Dutch Schultz's gang for the city's beer-running operations. The violent feud between Schultz and Coll ultimately resulted in more than twenty murders in the city in 1931 and 1932, and ended only when an enforcer from Dutch Schultz's gang, Abraham "Bo" Weinberg, caught Coll in a phone booth in the London Chemists drugstore across the street from his apartment on West Twenty-third Street. While drugstore employees watched in silence, Weinberg fired fifty rounds from a submachine gun into the phone booth, killing Coll instantly. Weinberg then sped away in a black sedan, disappearing in city traffic.[20]

Coll's demise in a drugstore phone booth hardly comforted the city. His acquittal in the Vengalli murder, his brazen defiance of the law, and his spectacular death at the hands of his rivals simply illustrated how far the criminal gangs involved in the beer and liquor trades had moved beyond the reach of the law. The Police Department's occasional battles with organized crime proved incapable of stemming the violence. Only a month after Coll's execution, the city reeled again when three gangsters, one of them a former associate of Coll's, fired at one another in the middle of the late night crowds leaving Connie's Inn and the Lafayette Theater in Harlem. Harlem society matron Lulu Willis was killed in the crossfire, and two other men were wounded. These random shootings cast a pall over the previously festive Harlem nightclub scene and prompted an outraged public to complain that the city was being taken over by criminals.[21]

While New Yorkers spoke out against the increasing regularity of gangland violence in the city, they also expressed resentment at a new, more aggressive push for Prohibition enforcement coming from the federal government. In 1927 Congress passed the Bureau of Prohibition Act, a sweeping new law designed to reinvigorate Prohibition enforcement efforts throughout the nation. The act reorganized the Prohibition Unit of the Internal Revenue Service, making it an independent Bureau within the Treasury Department. It imposed new civil service regulations on its employees, gave agents substantial raises, and effectively replaced 59 percent of the bureau's enforcement staff. To prove the effectiveness of this reorganization, the bureau renewed its efforts to enforce the Eighteenth Amendment in the city in 1928. Under the direction of Major Maurice Campbell, the new Prohibition administrator for the Southern and Eastern Districts of New York, Prohibition agents launched a new effort to police alcohol sales in the city. With 270 agents at his call, Campbell targeted many of the city's most notable clubs during his three-year tenure, raising eyebrows with his aggressive, showy tactics. He embarrassed the Police Department with a midday raid on the Flanagan Brothers restaurant on Grand Street, which was full of whiskey, beer, and police officers eating lunch. His spectacular New Year's Eve raids, his controversial destruction of Helen Morgan's nightclub, and his office's attempts to padlock several notable hotels for alleged Volstead Act violations, guest rooms and all, made him the bane of wet New York.[22]

Campbell's aggressive attempts to shore up Prohibition enforcement pushed New Yorkers to the limit. Many wondered to what extremes the federal government would resort in its efforts to force the city to comply with the dry mandate. In April 1930, Campbell made front-page news when he raided the glamorous Hollywood Restaurant and arrested eleven patrons in evening attire for carrying hip flasks. This rare instance of arresting people for possessing flasks incensed the six hundred patrons in the nightclub. Once the word of the arrests got out, a crowd of thousands gathered outside the Times Square establishment, blocking traffic and jeering as the prisoners were brought out. Even bolder was Campbell's June 1930 raid of the city-owned Central Park Casino, a favorite haunt of Mayor Walker's, where Campbell's agents arrested nine patrons for drinking.[23]

Campbell's uncompromising approach to Prohibition enforcement in New York raised public animosity toward the Bureau of Prohibition to an unprecedented level. Under Campbell's leadership, journalist Stanley Walker argued, "day by day the repudiation of the [Prohibition] agents became worse." The Casino raid in particular, he argued, brought "the agents into lower esteem than ever." The *Daily News,* which had earlier complained that Major Campbell was "hectoring New York City under the Volstead Act" and exacting "honest to God revenge on New Yorkers for being city people," fired off a savage attack on Campbell's latest raids. "We do not want the dry laws enforced in New York City," it declared. "We think they represent an attempt by small town and country people, who cannot know metropolitan conditions, to tell us how we shall conduct our private and personal lives. We don't propose to take such dictation."[24]

As if Campbell's raids were not enough, animosity toward the Bureau of Prohibition increased with the enactment of the Jones Law, passed in 1929 by a compliant Congress at the insistence of the dry lobby. The statute, referred to sarcastically as the "Five and Ten Law," drastically increased federal penalties for Volstead Act violations, calling for first-time Prohibition violators to be sentenced to a maximum of five years in prison and a $10,000 fine, whereas previous guidelines had set a maximum of six months in prison and a $1,000 fine for first-time offenders. The new law also provided for the deportation of aliens convicted of Volstead Act violations, made liquor buyers subject to felony prosecution if they refused to divulge their sources of liquor, and required those convicted under the new law to work off their fines in prison at the rate of one dollar a day if they were unable to pay them outright, a provision that would confine first-time violators to federal prison for up to thirty-two years to satisfy a $10,000 fine.[25]

To New Yorkers, the severity of the Jones Law only highlighted the enduring inequities of Prohibition enforcement. With the federal government imposing ever-stricter punishments on small-time offenders like waiters and bartenders, U.S. Attorney Emory Buckner complained that Prohibition was turning the Manhattan federal court into "a seething mass of bartenders, peddlers, waiters, bond runners [and] fixers." The *Irish World* opined that the new law was simply a reminder that "up to the present, the Prohibition law has been a law for the poor and a joke for the rich." It continued, "let it be a law for all, and then we can all laugh."[26]

Not surprisingly, the Jones Law proved no more effective in deterring Prohibition violators than the measures that had been put in place ten years earlier. What the Jones Law did accomplish, however, was to push New York's state and city prisons (as well as federal prisons) well past their already overflowing capacities. In 1926, the city prison on Welfare Island already held 1,800 prisoners, its largest population in ten years, while the state prison population exceeded 7,200, the highest level it had seen in fourteen years. With the passage of the Jones Law in 1929, arrests for liquor sales in the city jumped sharply from their 1928 levels, further overwhelming the overcrowded prisons with both convicted Prohibition offenders and defendants awaiting trial.[27]

In December 1928, New Yorkers' frustrations with the Jones Law and Major Campbell's aggressive enforcement of the Volstead Act were compounded by another factor, the appointment of Mayor Walker's third police commissioner, the independent-minded department store executive Grover Whalen. Walker appointed Whalen out of desperation, eager to combat a crime wave that had pushed the number of homicides, burglaries, robberies, and assaults in the city sharply upward. Amid criticism of the Police Department's handling of gangland cases, especially the unsolved 1928 murder of Arnold Rothstein, Mayor Walker dismissed Commissioner Joseph Warren and turned to Whalen to reverse the NYPD's declining fortunes. Upon his appointment, Commissioner Whalen insisted that Mayor Walker give him free reign with the Police Department. Given the political demands of an election year in which crime was a major issue, the mayor complied, leaving the Police Department in the hands of a man who shared none of Walker's laissez-faire attitude toward drinking in the city. Once he took office, Whalen immediately distinguished himself from his two predecessors, George McLaughlin and Joseph Warren, with a forceful and showy approach to drying up the city that exceeded anything the two men had attempted.[28]

Commissioner Whalen began his tenure by announcing an all-out war on the underworld in New York. Convinced that there was an organic link between the liquor trade and crime in the city, Whalen declared that "breeding places of crime such as speakeasies and gambling resorts must be closed." Not one for constitutional subtleties, Whalen explained to the press that his goal was to "teach these tough guys, these ruthless gangsters who respect no law, that there is still a lot of law at the end of a nightstick." At another gathering, Commissioner Whalen told his audience that the Police Department would make life hard for gangsters in the city through the use of "plenty of lead." True to his promise, Whalen launched a spectacular wave of raids across the city, hitting between forty and one hundred establishments a night, and ordering police officers equipped with hatchets to smash up any businesses that had re-opened after previous violations. On one such expedition, officers destroyed Julius' on Charles Street, a cigar shop on Christopher Street, and nine other establishments in Brooklyn, leaving them, as the *New York World* recounted, "bashed into splinters . . . counters, tables, chairs—all were chopped to bits."[29]

For all the tough talk and the theatrical use of sledgehammers, nightsticks, and axes, Whalen's campaign had little effect on the underworld or the liquor trade in New York. His aggressive tactics briefly shielded Mayor Walker from critics who accused him of not doing enough to address crime in the city, but Whalen's policies did not make the city noticeably drier or safer. They only fueled the argument that the dry crusade had set the nation on an impossible law enforcement mission.

Whalen's desire to become the first police commissioner to successfully enforce Prohibition in New York City was undermined by a predictable set of problems, beginning with the continuing squabbles between the Police Department and the Bureau of Prohibition. Commissioner Whalen and

Major Campbell feuded intensely over who should take charge of Prohibition enforcement in the city, and their mutual love of the limelight fostered acrimonious public clashes between the two men, making cooperation between the Bureau of Prohibition and the Police Department impossible.

Major Campbell, always highly critical of Whalen, blamed the high levels of crime in the city on the Police Department's decade-long neglect of the city's speakeasies. Campbell wanted the New York City Police Department to submit to federal authority and allow the Bureau of Prohibition to direct its enforcement efforts. Whalen in turn rejected Campbell's suggestions outright. In news conferences, he criticized Campbell's strategies for Prohibition enforcement—which included stationing police officers around the clock in alleged speakeasies—as expensive and overblown, arguing that Campbell's plans for Prohibition enforcement would boost Police Department expenditures by $45 million annually. When Campbell instituted his policy of arresting nightclub patrons for carrying hip flasks, Whalen flatly refused to endorse the effort and said that the NYPD would not follow suit.[30]

The feuding between the two men quickly turned into a political soap opera. While the city newspapers agreed with Whalen that Major Campbell's proposals for Prohibition enforcement in New York were impractical, if not outrageous, Whalen's public repudiation of Campbell outraged Governor Franklin D. Roosevelt. Afraid that his political opponents would use the public row between the two men against him, Roosevelt went over Mayor Walker's head and summoned Whalen to Albany, where he threatened to use executive authority to remove the police commissioner from office if he did not cooperate with Campbell. Rather than bow to Roosevelt's pressure, Whalen resigned on May 20, 1930, becoming the latest in a long line of law enforcement officials undone by the challenge of Prohibition enforcement. (Whalen's relationship with Mayor Walker had soured by this time, anyway. Having won reelection in 1929, Walker no longer had much use for Whalen's aggressive style of policing, and there was not enough room in the administration for both men to share the limelight.) Ironically, Campbell was also ousted from his office shortly thereafter, in large part owing to the political fallout from his audacious raid on the Central Park Casino. Upon leaving office, he complained bitterly that political meddling in the bureau's affairs had hindered his work.[31]

The feuding between the Bureau of Prohibition and the Police Department, the proliferation of poison liquor, alcoholism, and gangland violence in the city, and the increasingly draconian application of the Jones Law had finally produced a pattern of law enforcement in New York whose extremes defied common sense. On a daily basis, New Yorkers read examples of Prohibition enforcement that left them aghast. A Brooklyn man, arrested on the Rockaway Beach Boardwalk for selling twenty-five-cent shots of liquor, was held in jail for twenty days in his bathing suit until a judge released him after imposing a one-dollar fine. The Coast Guard fired on and sank pleasure boats involved in rum running off the coast of New York, occasionally with loss of life. Bureau of Prohibition agents set up random roadblocks and searched as many as four hundred automobiles for contraband liquor in a single afternoon. In one case, a Catholic priest stopped by dry agents was arrested for possessing one bottle of liquor in his car. New Yorkers were even more outraged when the federal government announced in 1928 that it was doubling the amount of poison it added to industrial alcohol in order to further discourage its use in illegal liquor production. In each case, New Yorkers were left wondering to what lengths the government would go next in its efforts to enforce a decade-long failed experiment.[32]

To no one's surprise, the new extremes of Prohibition enforcement provoked more emotional outbursts against the Eighteenth Amendment's enforcers. Even in higher-class nightclubs, police and Prohibition agents who were once serenaded with song and treated as part of the entertainment now encountered irate patrons who attacked them physically and verbally. In one Broadway nightclub, a woman patron became so enraged when a Prohibition agent pointed a gun at her that she leapt up and scratched the offending agent in the face. In another nightclub, a male patron punched an agent in the face and broke his nose. According to *Variety,* which regularly tracked these incidents as barometers of public opinion, "vicious battles" were breaking out regularly between agents and patrons in nightclubs and speakeasies by the early 1930s. It added that even young women were joining the fray, further heightening the sense that the crusade to rid the city of alcohol was causing all respect for law and order to evaporate.[33]

In its attempt to regulate the private lives of its citizens, the federal government had gone to extremes no one had thought possible in a democracy. At the same time, the unintended effects of crime and corruption had undermined every rational argument that the Eighteenth Amendment offered benefits to the United States. Neither drunkenness nor alcoholism had gone away over the course of the ten-year dry experiment, and when the stock market crashed in 1929, the stubborn refusal of drys to reconsider any element of Prohibition fostered the sense that the nation's priorities had veered far off course. To New Yorkers at the turn of the 1930s, the fact that Prohibitionists wished to continue their efforts to rid the nation of the alcohol problem while failing to see the other problems stemming from their experiment made it exceedingly clear that repeal was finally in order, if not long overdue.

11

A Surging Wet Tide

If the dry crusade retained any hope that Prohibition could ever be enforced in New York City, that dream vanished when the stock market crashed in October 1929. The national economic crisis that followed the crash brought a sudden end to the gay atmosphere of the Roaring Twenties, and in the context of the ensuing Depression, New Yorkers could only look upon continued efforts to enforce Prohibition as a cruel joke.

The Depression struck New York City harder than any place in America, leaving close to two million people out of work. Given the dire economic situation, many New Yorkers were outraged that the federal government was dedicating nearly $16 million a year to Prohibition enforcement in the early 1930s, and spending $75,000 on each of Major Campbell's detested raids. They questioned why the dry lobby would continue to worry about whether people were drinking while so many in the city went without food. They asked whether the nation would benefit more by continuing a clearly failed experiment or by reopening American breweries and distilleries and creating tens of thousands of jobs for unemployed Americans. Noting that the federal government had collected more than $483 million in liquor taxes in 1919, the last year before Prohibition, some critics argued that the return of legal alcohol, or at the very least legal beer, would yield no less than $495 million in much needed federal revenue, and millions more in additional state taxes. If social conditions had already given New Yorkers sufficient reasons to call for repeal, economic conditions now made the case for repeal even more compelling.[1]

The post-crash arguments for an end to Prohibition were neither celebratory nor characteristic of the festive air of rebellion that had defined city culture in the 1920s. The Depression had cast a pall over New York, and many of the city's nightclubs and cabarets, which had been filled to capacity every night before the crash, were suddenly empty. The most expensive establishments saw their business drop as much as 75 percent. As one club owner complained, "our business . . . is a luxury business, and luxury businesses are not so profitable nowadays . . . [people] don't buy champagne as they used to." Bartenders, waiters, busboys, and hostesses were unceremoniously laid off. Alcohol prices in the city dropped to a ten-year low, and bootleggers found demand for their goods dropping as fewer New Yorkers had the disposable income to spend on liquor. The Depression, *Variety* noted, seemed to be doing what ten years of Prohibition enforcement had not—it was drying up Broadway.[2]

For all its severity, however, the market crash did not eliminate the speakeasy or the desire to drink. Though business certainly fell off because of the economic crisis, the city's drinking establishments adapted as always. Many New York speakeasies switched from serving hard liquor to serving beer instead, which at twenty-five cents a glass was cheaper for patrons and more profitable for bar owners now that organized crime syndicates had succeeded in making it readily available at seven dollars a barrel. Though speakeasies had never been known for their food, the free lunches of saloon days now returned, often proving a bigger draw than the booze. While costly, these giveaways kept the patrons coming, even if they were drinking less. Given the hard times, New Yorkers turned to alcohol for solace more than celebration, but as long as they kept coming, the trickle of customers allowed bars to stay afloat.[3]

In the new economic climate of the Depression, speakeasy jobs became a treasured commodity to New Yorkers. Fearing that they would be unable to find any other work if they lost their jobs, bartenders worked longer hours and paid their own fines if arrested, an arrangement they would have scoffed at before the crash. One man explained, "I'm the only bartender in our place, and if I want to keep my job I've got to take the rap. The boss says he won't pay the fine."[4]

Though most New Yorkers were preoccupied with economic survival, their thoughts still turned to repeal. Already opposed to President Hoover as the nation's leading dry, New Yorkers grew even angrier with him as the Depression set in. He had come to embody two ills in one—the economic crisis gripping the nation and the stubborn persistence of the dry experiment. With public anger mounting, the Depression and Prohibition were becoming inextricably linked as political issues, and the blame for both was falling squarely on President Hoover and the Republican Party.[5]

In essence, Prohibition and the Depression had become a two-headed hydra for President Hoover. The two issues were very different, but in the minds of New Yorkers Hoover's response to them seemed the same. After defeating Al Smith in 1928, he had vowed to "stay the course" with Prohibition. When the economy collapsed in 1929, he adopted a similarly optimistic position. In May 1930 he argued, "I am convinced we have passed the worst and with continued effort we shall recover rapidly." Despite pleas for his administration to do something to alleviate the national crisis, Hoover resisted issuing direct relief to Depression-struck Americans, assuring them that the market would correct the nation's economic downturn in due time. When it came to Prohibition, he seemed equally obstinate in his unwillingness to reconsider the wisdom of the noble experiment.[6]

Hoover's stubborn refusal to yield to calls for the modification or repeal of the Eighteenth Amendment stood out more than ever in January 1931, with the release of the long-awaited report of the National Commission on Law Observation and Enforcement. In 1929 Hoover had appointed former U.S. Attorney General George Wickersham to head a special panel to study Prohibition and issue recommendations to improve its effectiveness. When the Wickersham Commission released its five-volume report, however, its findings were confusing and contradictory. The commission concluded that Prohibition had failed on several major counts. Since the passage of the Volstead Act, the panel determined, drinking in the United States had increased, bootlegging and corruption had become more serious national problems, and public trust in law enforcement had eroded significantly. In separate statements submitted by the eleven panel members, nine expressed the belief that the Eighteenth Amendment lacked public support. Six went so far as to declare Prohibition unenforceable; two suggested that the Eighteenth Amendment be repealed immediately; and four favored modification of the Volstead Act to allow beer and wine. Only five of the eleven commissioners recommended that the Prohibition experiment be continued without significant changes.

The summary statement of the panel, however, completely contradicted the statements of the individual panel members. It recommended that the Eighteenth Amendment be subjected to "further trial" and not revised unless enforcement continued to fail after a longer period of time. It was to this summary statement that President Hoover turned for guidance, using it to reaffirm his desire to see Prohibition continued. Ignoring the critiques offered by the individual commissioners, Hoover interpreted the report as he wanted, stating that "the Commission . . . does not favor the repeal of the Eighteenth Amendment."[7]

The Wickersham Commission's work was greeted with dismay by wets and drys alike, as the report contained little to satisfy either group. In New York, wets had a field day mocking the Wickersham Report as nonsensical. The humorist Franklin P. Adams captured the wet response in a poem for the *New York World* that poked fun at the contradictory conclusions of the committee:

> Prohibition is an awful flop.
> > We like it.
> It can't stop what it's meant to stop.
> > We like it.
> It's left a trail of graft and slime
> It don't prohibit worth a dime
> It's filled our land with vice and crime,
> > Nevertheless, we're for it.[8]

The *Irish World* expressed similar amazement at the conclusions of the report, stating, "We fail to understand why Mr. Hoover . . . should have gone to the trouble of appointing a commission of finding out something that everybody knows . . . The prohibition law is unenforceable." The paper argued that only bootleggers and corrupt officials could possibly want to see Prohibition continued. Nicholas Murray Butler was equally angered by the commission's final report, which he called "new and pathetic evidence that Washington, like the Emperor Nero, fiddles while Rome is burning."[9]

In the context of the Depression, President Hoover's response to the Wickersham Report only strengthened the perception that the president was out of touch with the American people and unresponsive to the nation's problems. Had Hoover paid more attention to the resentment stirred by Prohibition, he might have had a better chance of convincing Americans that he intended to aid them in their time of economic crisis. But Hoover remained committed to Prohibition enforcement, both because of the support the drys had shown him in the 1928 election, and because he believed that as president he had a responsibility to stand by a constitutional amendment. Whatever his reasoning, Hoover's disregard for public opposition to Prohibition fueled an angry backlash against him and inspired an even stronger final push for repeal from Americans weary of the federal government's decade-long attempt to regulate their personal lives at the behest of the dry lobby.[10]

The combination of resentment over Prohibition and despair over the Depression finally created the political conditions that made the repeal of the Eighteenth Amendment possible. The Depression essentially tipped the scales of the Prohibition debate against the dry lobby once and for all, making the choice between the continuation of the dry experiment and repeal a starker choice than it had ever been before. By 1930, drys' insistence on continuing the noble experiment made the movement seem like an anachronism, and even their most loyal supporters found it difficult to take Prohibition seriously in the context of the larger economic problems facing the nation. The only thing that seemed to he holding up repeal, other than the stubbornness of President Hoover, was the need for an effective leader to carry the repeal campaign forward.

With Al Smith essentially retired from politics, Pauline Sabin, the New York socialite who had left the Republican National Committee in 1929 to form the Women's Organization for National Prohibition Reform, emerged as the only repeal leader capable of harnessing the national discontent with Prohibition. Under Sabin's leadership, WONPR had expanded rapidly in 1929 and 1930, reaching far beyond New York to form a national base of support. Through grassroots organizing, its membership quickly eclipsed that of the Association against the Prohibition Amendment and other national repeal organizations. As it grew, WONPR stirred a long-awaited mass movement for repeal.

Sabin's remarkable success leading the campaign for repeal demonstrated her political savvy and her ability to learn from the mistakes of her predecessors, both wet and dry. Though Sabin belonged to the same privileged social class as the leaders of the Association against the Prohibition Amendment, she shunned that group's elitist approach. Whereas the AAPA had operated on the assumption that the opinions and interests of the wealthy should set the standard for the repeal movement, Sabin's WONPR took great pains to reach out to middle-class and working-class women in the belief that a broad coalition of women would pose the greatest challenge to the dry lobby. In recognition of the unfair application of the Prohibition laws in working-class communities, Sabin denounced Prohibition as "the greatest piece of class legislation ever enacted in this country." At the same time, she avoided the partisan approach taken by Al Smith, who had tried to present repeal as an issue of the Democratic Party. While building on Smith's success in making Prohibition a national political issue, Sabin vowed that her organization would support any and all political candidates who favored repeal, regardless of party. She said that Democratic and Republican candidates alike would be responsible for winning the support of the wet voters WONPR was organizing.[11]

The effectiveness of Sabin's strategy was immediately clear. Her bold leadership quickly attracted more than a million American women to WONPR, disproving the dry movement's assertion that the repeal issue had died with Al Smith's 1928 presidential bid. Moreover, the growth of WONPR showed that women struggling to make ends meet and to manage their households in the Depression had come to repudiate their association with the dry cause. Put simply, they were no longer convinced that the noble experiment held any promise for the American people.

National polls confirmed Sabin's insistence that repeal was desired not just by New Yorkers but by more Americans than ever. According to the *Literary Digest,* which polled the public on the issue of Prohibition throughout the 1920s, by 1930 nearly 70 percent of the nation favored the repeal or modification of the Volstead Act, with the majority of respondents favoring outright repeal. Even as the Depression worsened, Prohibition continued to dominate the American political agenda, suggesting that the context of the Depression had made conditions under Prohibition intolerable. Whatever the reason, national sentiments in the early 1930s were clear. When the National Economic League conducted its own poll in January 1930, it listed the top problems facing the nation as

1. Administration of Justice
2. Prohibition
3. Lawlessness / Disrespect for the Law
4. Crime
5. Law Enforcement.

While all top-five issues clearly related to Prohibition, unemployment ranked a distant eighteenth in the poll. The following year, unemployment and economic stabilization had climbed to fourth place in the poll, but "Prohibition," "Administration of Justice," and "Lawlessness" remained in the top three.[12]

Faced with such clear indications that the clamor for repeal was mounting nationally, the dry movement sought to discredit Sabin and WONPR the same way it had attacked Al Smith in 1928. But the most effective issue that drys had been able to use against Smith, his Catholicism, proved irrelevant in Sabin's case, so the dry movement was forced to find another basis for its attacks. In the context of the Depression, drys expected unemployed and struggling Americans to resent the wealthy women who led WONPR, who yachted in their spare time and owned estates in Southampton. Attacking WONPR's leaders and their fellow wets as "damned millionaires," Mamie Colvin of the Woman's Christian Temperance Union insisted that there was no popular support for the movement against Prohibition, and that "the money for the wet organizations comes from a few wealthy persons." Hoping to foster feelings of class animosity, drys depicted WONPR's leaders as an elite cabal scheming to use urban immigrant votes to enact repeal so the rich could once again drink cocktails in their mansions and pay lower income taxes.[13]

In their efforts to stop WONPR, drys attempted to paint Sabin and her colleagues as decadent and greedy, using the same approach that had served the dry lobby so well in the campaign for the ratification of the Eighteenth Amendment in the 1910s. The *American Independent,* a dry newspaper based in Kentucky, took the lead, denouncing Sabin and her fellow WONPR leaders as a "drunken and immoral bunch of women." In a radio address, Mamie Colvin added to this barrage of insults, calling the women repeal leaders "Bacchantian maidens parching for wine, wet women who, like the drunkards their program will produce, would take pennies off the eyes of the dead for the sake of legalizing booze."[14]

Even more telling was the way drys sought to besmirch WONPR and its supporters by identifying them with New York City, insinuating that if the WONPR campaign succeeded, it would contaminate the rest of the nation with the permissive, uninhibited culture of the nation's wettest and least regulated city. For several years, leading wets had anticipated these attacks and worried that the repeal movement could easily be perceived as "too New York." Even before Smith's 1928 campaign, some wet activists had wondered if they were making a grave mistake by letting New Yorkers take such prominent positions in the movement for repeal. For example, the AAPA's Irénée DuPont, concerned about the effect of anti–New York sentiment on the repeal campaign, kept a 1926 press clipping in his collection of anti-Prohibition materials in which a dry columnist argued that "the 'Wets' have made a serious political blunder in opening their guns with a lot of New Yorkers. As a matter of pure politics, 'dry' candidates will get a good response when they ask their constituents if they are going to let New York run the country."[15]

The Woman's Christian Temperance Union and other dry groups repeatedly called attention to the fact that Sabin and many of the leading women in WONPR were New Yorkers and, as such, shared little in common with the way the rest of the nation felt about Prohibition. (They conveniently chose not to emphasize that their own president, Ella Boole, resided in Brooklyn.) In Dubuque, a woman speaking at an Anti-Saloon

League dinner blasted the wet propaganda coming out of New York as treasonous and un-American. Noting the surge of wet activity in New York, she mockingly asked, "Will New York secede from the Union? . . . I wouldn't care, would you?"[16]

This anti–New York sentiment was a serious issue for wets to contend with in the 1920s, when much of the nation enjoyed a love/hate relationship with the city. From the heartland, New York could be seen at once to be re-inventing America with its trendsetting contribution to modern culture and threatening the nation with its refusal to abide by traditional and old-fashioned values. It was by no means certain that the rest of the United States would sign on to a repeal movement rooted so firmly in New York. Even Will Rogers, the quintessentially American humorist who had consistently mocked Prohibition during the 1920s, expressed doubts about a repeal movement led by New Yorkers. Referring to the wealth and urban refinement of the leaders of WONPR, Rogers quipped, "There is but one reason that Prohibition won't be repealed . . . It's because the wrong people want it repealed."[17]

In the face of these criticisms, Pauline Sabin proved to be an exceptionally resilient and skillful repeal leader. Unlike Al Smith, who was devastated by the dry attacks against him, Sabin remained unflappable. She and her colleagues in WONPR skillfully addressed questions about their class standing, morality, and identification as New Yorkers. Responding to Will Rogers's comments, Dr. Mather Abbot, a speaker at a WONPR luncheon, quipped, "Of course Mr. Rogers is a very clever and a very witty man . . . but I have never found a witty man who was a deep thinker." As to the constant onslaught of the drys against WONPR, Abbot added that "the drys are all angry, and when you get angry defeat is in sight."[18]

On the issue of class, Pauline Sabin successfully rebuffed the accusations leveled against her that she was only representing the interests of the economic elite. She knew that a victorious repeal movement had to be based on mass participation, and so she refused to let WONPR be pigeonholed as a group of self-important society women. In 1930, when the Philadelphia socialite Mrs. George Strawbridge publicly called on wealthy women to ban cocktails at their gatherings to set an example for society at large, Sabin seized the opportunity to demonstrate that WONPR women did not see themselves as an enlightened elite. In a press statement, Sabin commented, "I am amazed that Mrs. Strawbridge's grasp of the fundamentals of Prohibition is so slight that she believes this problem, which touches every household in America, can be solved by the agreement of a comparatively few people of social prominence to discontinue serving cocktails at social functions." Sabin concluded, "I am afraid Mrs. Strawbridge overestimates the influence of so-called society upon the great masses of American people."[19]

WONPR's recruitment activities did even more to combat the assertions that the organization was an elitist group for wealthy women. In July 1929, shortly after the group was founded, WONPR embarked on a national effort to measure anti-Prohibition sentiment among working-class women and to enroll as many of them as possible in the organization. By the time the repeal movement reached its peak in 1932, WONPR membership figures revealed that 37 percent of members were housewives, 15 percent were industrial workers, 19 percent were office workers, and 15 percent were business or professional women. This mixture of women from all lines of work, from all over the nation, silenced critics who accused WONPR of being composed only of wealthy society women.[20]

As it turned out, the dry assertions that WONPR members were a "drunken and immoral bunch of women" hardly needed to be addressed at all, as these were undermined by moral failings of the dry leaders themselves, especially of one dry in particular, Bishop James Cannon, Jr. Since his prominent role in the anti-Smith campaign of 1928, when he had emerged as one of the nation's leading dry spokesmen, Bishop Cannon had himself been caught in a widely publicized adultery scandal in 1930 and hit with accusations of financial misdeeds that landed the dry leader in federal court. Though Cannon was eventually cleared of any wrongdoing, in light of his troubles, the strict moralism of the dry crusade looked hypocritical. Sabin and her colleagues seemed relatively upstanding by comparison.[21]

Sensing that the dry movement had reached its weakest moment, the women of WONPR claimed the moral high ground in the Prohibition debate, arguing that they themselves were the genuine advocates of "true temperance." Taking great care never to present WONPR as a champion of drinking, Sabin positioned her organization as a reform group more genuine than any dry organization, as WONPR saw the need to protect American families and children from the most dangerous consequences of the failed Prohibition experiment, namely excessive drinking, violence, organized crime, declining respect for the law, and hypocrisy. By focusing the repeal movement on the negative effects of Prohibition as opposed to the right to drink, WONPR reclaimed the ideal of temperance from the dry movement, arguing that a legal but well-regulated liquor supply would foster more temperance than Prohibition ever had.

With drys increasingly on the defensive, WONPR found the criticisms the group was too "New York" even easier to handle. In one regard, the public identification of Pauline Sabin with the sophisticated urban culture of New York City was not as damaging as the dry crusade had expected it would be. After a decade of Prohibition-inspired cosmopolitan culture being transmitted to the rest of the United States through advertising, music, film, and women's magazines, the "New York" quality of the WONPR movement attracted far more women than it repelled. Despite the attempts by dry women's groups to denigrate WONPR's leaders, magazines like *Vogue, Smart Set,* and *McCall's* profiled them in a flattering light, praising their dedication to their cause, as well as their style and sophistication. With so much positive press, many American women found affiliation with WONPR much more appealing than membership in the "plainer" women's temperance groups. While the WCTU had been in touch with the women of the 1910s, WONPR seemed far more attuned to the cultural and political tastes of women in the late 1920s and early 1930s.[22]

In the end, the dry attacks on WONPR proved entirely ineffective. The organization continued to grow, extending far from urban centers like New York to areas that had once been considered dry strongholds. By early 1930, WONPR was enrolling large numbers of women at county and state fairs throughout the rural areas of the Midwest and West. During the organization's Repeal Week membership drive in May 1932, WONPR made more headway in states like North Carolina, Missouri, and Montana. According to WONPR secretary Grace Root, WONPR organizing drives successfully enrolled up to 60 percent of the women in some rural areas, essentially stealing them away from the temperance movement with a more persuasive argument and a more engaging political style. The phenomenal growth of WONPR outside of urban centers like New York helped undermine the idea that Prohibition was rooted in a split between urban and rural social mores, and demonstrated that by the early 1930s opposition to Prohibition was as strong in some parts of the countryside as it was in the city. By pushing further into rural areas, WONPR made it abundantly clear that women from all over the country were uniting against Prohibition.[23]

As it grew in strength, WONPR devastated the remnants of the American dry lobby. Echoing the famous "do everything" strategy of the WCTU's Frances Willard, the women of WONPR continually demonstrated distinct tactical and organizational advantages over the fading Prohibitionists. Though WONPR preferred to emphasize its grassroots approach to repeal, in the end its financial resources played a central role in its ability to stay ahead of the drys. At the very moment when the Depression wiped out the donations coming in to most temperance groups, WONPR's leaders still had extensive financial resources of their own to contribute to the organization and could appeal to wealthy supporters for cash.

WONPR also successfully countered the dry lobby in the press, reversing two generations of dominant dry propaganda. For decades, the dry movement had maintained the upper hand in American politics through its effective use of the press and its own media outlets. WONPR was the first wet group to confront the dry movement with effective and more modern tactics. For one, WONPR made extensive use of the radio as an inexpensive and efficient way to promote the repeal message to large audiences, airing four-minute radio spots twice a day, targeting women in the morning with female speakers and men in the evening with male speakers. Even when circumstances threatened to prevent WONPR from using the radio to promote its cause, Sabin's political savvy turned the situation to the wet advantage. When the manager of a Rochester radio station barred Sabin and former Senator James Wadsworth from speaking on the subject of repeal for fear of losing his broadcasting license, Sabin's vehement protest against censorship drew even more press coverage for the repeal cause and forced the station manager to reverse his decision.[24]

WONPR's understanding of publicity was impressive. In addition to radio appeals, the organization staged political rallies, town hall meetings, and demonstrations in New York City and throughout the country. While rallies in New York in Times Square, Union Square, Columbus Circle, and at the Brooklyn Academy of Music may have been preaching primarily to the converted, the newsreel and press coverage of the events carried the message of the repeal movement far beyond the city. WONPR also used motorcades to draw attention to the repeal cause, capitalizing on America's love affair with the automobile. These parades ranged from local tours through the Bronx to fifteen-day campaign motorcades for wet congressional candidates. In another instance, WONPR capped off its repeal week events by having a young aviatrix land a sky-blue Curtis-Wright biplane at an outdoor rally in Delaware to deliver a congratulatory message to the group. The event received front-page coverage in the local papers as indicative of the youthful energy of the repeal campaign.[25]

The use of radio, automobiles, and airplanes imbued WONPR's campaign with a modern sensibility that encouraged more and grander expressions of support for the repeal of the Eighteenth Amendment. A final sign of WONPR's forward-looking approach to campaigning for repeal was its unabashed appeal toward American consumer interests. To promote and raise funds for the wet cause, WONPR opened a "repeal shop" on Madison Avenue in October 1932, as well as a separate concession offering repeal novelties in the Bergdorf-Goodman department store. The two stores offered a choice of neckties and chiffon scarves bearing the slogan "Ratify for Repeal," as well as anti-Prohibition buttons, books, and playing cards that, borrowing from presidential candidate Franklin D. Roosevelt's campaign slogan, heralded repeal as a "New Deal for the American People."[26]

Though WONPR had clearly mastered the art of waging a modern political campaign, it also did very well with old-fashioned, grassroots efforts. The group fearlessly canvassed dry strongholds looking for converts to the wet cause, often using door-to-door appeals and home visits to reach would-be members. WONPR also lobbied politicians and elected officials extensively to pressure them into coming out for repeal. Meanwhile, WCTU organizers complained that WONPR organizers were brazenly barnstorming their meetings to confront them and steal away their members.[27]

WONPR emerged as the leading repeal organization in the United States because it successfully mobilized a core of wet supporters, rallied them behind the message that repeal would right all that had gone wrong under Prohibition, and learned how to counter the dry crusade's most aggressive tactics. The combination of tactics used by WONPR to promote repeal presented the dry movement with a formidable challenge, and for the first time in a generation, the dry crusade that had once left its opponents quaking seemed helpless. With their numbers declining, funds disappearing, and inspiration lacking, dry groups were left with traditional church meetings and bake sales. Faced with the spectacles staged by WONPR, the temperance forces, as *Vanity Fair* noted, "had nothing to offer as a counterattraction."[28]

The rise of WONPR was the critical development in the campaign for the repeal of the Eighteenth Amendment. By challenging the dominance of the drys, WONPR gave more wets the courage to speak freely against the Eighteenth Amendment, secure in the feeling that they were part of a growing national movement. With the repeal campaign expanding, prominent defectors from the dry movement came forward in increasing numbers to concede that the Prohibition experiment had not accomplished what drys had promised, and that the continuation of the dry crusade was futile.

The words of onetime drys who had changed their minds about Prohibition now provided some of the most insightful observations of what had gone wrong with the Eighteenth Amendment. Many of those who spoke out most eloquently were government officials and social workers who had initially hoped for great benefits from Prohibition but had been shocked by its results. As early as 1926, New York City's chief probation officer, Edwin Cosley, was quoted in a repeal publication saying, "I started out by believing in Prohibition. For a good many years I had seen homes broken up by the saloon." But because of the increase in drinking he encountered, especially among children, Cosley reversed his thinking, arguing that he had seen more, not fewer, disturbing sights since the introduction of the noble experiment.[29]

A later convert was Franklin Chase Hoyt, a New York City Children's Court justice who communicated his dismay over the effects of Prohibition to WONPR in the early 1930s. From his perspective on the bench, Hoyt believed that Prohibition had only increased delinquency and child neglect in the city. Another Brooklyn Family Court magistrate, Jeannette Brill, expressed a similar view. She explained that the time had come for her to support the modification of the Volstead Act because she had seen plenty of its

negative side effects in her courtroom but no benefits to justify its continuation.[30]

Arguing that repeal would herald a return to more sober times, WONPR
official Mrs. John S. Sheppard told a reporter that "the directors of the social
service departments of two of the largest hospitals in New York were for
Prohibition, but are now against it because of the deplorable conditions
which it has brought about." Sheppard added that the director of nursing
services for the New York City Department of Health had also changed her
mind and turned against Prohibition on the basis of reports she had received from hundreds of home visits all over the city. The executive director
of the Children's Welfare Federation and the director of the New York Tuberculosis and Health Association also abandoned the dry cause, as did the
director of the New York State Reformatory for Women, whom Sheppard
described as "a Prohibitionist for three generations [who] had given up on
it, saying it 'has not worked and never can work.'"[31]

Ministers and church groups in the city, on whom the dry movement
had always relied for undying support, were also defecting to the wet cause.
In 1928, the Church Temperance Society released a poll of its members
showing that only 28 percent of them believed that Prohibition was a success in their church districts. According to the report, many religious leaders
who had been vehement supporters of the Eighteenth Amendment earlier
in the decade returned letters to the effect that they had "nothing to say" in
favor of Prohibition, while others took the bold step of denouncing Prohibition outright. Of the more than 2,000 religious leaders who responded to
the Church Temperance Society's poll, nearly 1,400 said they favored modification of the Volstead Act.[32]

Even leading Bureau of Prohibition administrators were coming out
against the Eighteenth Amendment, criticizing it from their own first-hand
experiences attempting to enforce it. General Lincoln C. Andrews, the assistant secretary of the Treasury in charge of supervising Prohibition enforcement, testified to Congress as early as 1926 that he favored the legalization
of beer because Prohibition was unenforceable in its current form. Major
Maurice Campbell, the Prohibition administrator who had angered all of
New York City with his aggressive campaign of raids and his public feuds
with Police Commissioner Grover Whalen, also threw in the towel. After
leaving the bureau in 1931, he blasted his superiors and derided the Anti-

Saloon League as "a thing contaminated" that had traitorously taken advantage of the crisis of World War I to further its own agenda. In a complete about-face, Campbell spent the next two years devoting his energies to *Repeal,* a new magazine dedicated to the wet cause.[33]

Even more notable was the career shift taken by Mabel Walker Willebrandt, the Assistant U.S. Attorney General for Prohibition Enforcement who had campaigned so fiercely against Al Smith in 1928. After leaving the Department of Justice in 1930 to return to the private practice of law, Willebrandt shocked drys and elicited snickers from wets when she took on as one of her first clients a conglomeration of California grape growers who marketed Vine-Glo homemade wine kits. Willebrandt insisted that she still believed in Prohibition and that she was only acting to aid an ailing legal industry in her home state of California, but her choice to represent the manufacturers of winemaking kits was widely interpreted as a sign that the dry coalition was imploding.[34]

Finally, the most crushing defection from the dry movement came in 1932, when John D. Rockefeller, Jr., an ardent dry who with his father had contributed nearly $350,000 to the Anti-Saloon League since 1920, announced in a public letter to Nicholas Murray Butler that he was abandoning his support for the Eighteenth Amendment. Arguing that the negative effects of Prohibition had come to outweigh any possible benefits, Rockefeller observed that "drinking has generally increased . . . the speakeasy has generally replaced the saloon, not only unit for unit, but probably two-fold if not three-fold . . . [and] a vast array of lawbreakers has been recruited and financed on a colossal scale."[35]

WONPR naturally benefited from these defections from the dry cause, as each further fueled the groundswell of support for repeal. As wet support surged, WONPR's ranks grew to 1.5 million members in 1933, making it three times larger than its chief rival, the WCTU. With WONPR exposing weakness in the dry movement at every turn, the national momentum, having moved beyond urban centers like New York, now clearly favored repeal.

Pauline Sabin's accomplishment in mobilizing a broad political movement for repeal was remarkable. Since 1919, no one had been able to bring together enough different constituencies behind the repeal cause to challenge the strength of the Anti-Saloon League, the Woman's Christian Temperance Union, and the other forces of the dry crusade. In New York City, resisting Prohibition had always been easy owing to the city's culture and politics, but never had New Yorkers been able to make their opposition to Prohibition matter outside of the five boroughs or beyond their influence in Albany. Governor Al Smith had tried, but only through Sabin's leadership did the repeal campaign finally develop true political power and allow New Yorkers to join in a political coalition with opponents of the Eighteenth Amendment across the nation.

WONPR's national strength was immediately visible in the midterm congressional elections of 1930, when the organization campaigned actively for wet candidates regardless of party. When the votes were counted, drys, especially dry Republicans tainted by President Hoover's disastrous management of the Depression, suffered losses in both the House and the Senate, causing the *Philadelphia Record* to proclaim that "the Election day of 1930 marked the turn of the tide." To be certain, the Depression factored largely in voters' anger, but Prohibition remained a central issue in the election. The two main issues in 1930, the *New York Telegraph* argued, were "hunger and thirst . . . hunger for food and jobs and security . . . thirst, if not for decent liquor, then for the right to it." Backed by WONPR, repeal candidates gained widely everywhere, with wet Democrats defeating incumbent dry Republicans in Ohio and Kansas, both considered dry strongholds. In the midterm elections, Democrats gained fifty-three seats in the House of Representatives and eight in the Senate, while voters considering referenda in several states expressed a preference for repeal by a three-to-one margin. When asked about the election results, Sabin modestly responded, "I do think our little organization did something to perfect this wet landslide."[36]

After the 1930 elections, the repeal movement took on a jubilant tone, as if Pauline Sabin and WONPR had found the solution to a puzzle that had stymied wets for a decade. Declarations for repeal became bolder, and inspired wets now believed that repeal had gone from being an impossibility to an inevitability. Bolstered by WONPR's success, repeal organizations like the Crusaders, the Volunteer Committee of Lawyers, and various repeal committees within labor and trade associations increased their activity and transformed the movement into a juggernaut.

Two New Yorkers, Al Smith and Pauline Sabin, had brought the repeal issue to this point. Together, their efforts had shaped a mass movement against the Eighteenth Amendment by taking the campaign for repeal from New York to the rest of the nation. Though Smith had suffered political defeat in his attempt to ride the repeal issue to the White House, he had galvanized the repeal movement in two important ways. He had exposed the bigotry entrenched in the dry crusade, and he had helped identify the Republican Party with Prohibition and the Democratic Party with repeal, helping determine which party would capture the mass of voters yearning to see the noble experiment come to an end.

Sabin, Smith's unlikely successor, had pushed the issue one step further. She had forced American politicians to assert their wet or dry leanings clearly, and she had brought new tactics and energy to the repeal movement, building upon what Al Smith had begun. Together, Smith and Sabin showed New Yorkers, and all Americans, that opposition to Prohibition had to go beyond merely disobeying the Volstead Act. They had opened up a long-overdue political front against the dry crusade and shown that political activity, not just cultural rebellion, was the key to ridding the nation of its failed Prohibition experiment. With the repeal coalition in place and its strength now evident, the only task remaining for the wets was to find a standard bearer who would carry the repeal issue into the presidential election of 1932.

12

The Wet Convention
and the New Deal

In the summer of 1932, the Great Depression, now nearing its third year, loomed large over the American political landscape. More than 10 million people were out of work. While the national unemployment rate hovered near 20 percent, in large cities the number of people without jobs ran closer to 50 percent, with many workers reduced to part-time employment at best. Nationally, 12 million Americans had been displaced from their homes. The value of the stock market had fallen from $87 billion to $19 billion, and more than 2,000 U.S. banks had failed. In New York City, where the Depression hit harder than perhaps anywhere in the nation, 20,000 schoolchildren were reported to be malnourished, and bread lines and soup kitchens were overwhelmed. New Yorkers angry at President Hoover over the nation's economic troubles talked of "Hoovervilles," referring to the shantytowns that had popped up in Central Park; empty pockets, which when turned out were called "Hoover flags"; and most significantly, the "Hoover Depression."[1]

With a presidential campaign taking shape that year, it became clear that the fall election would serve as a referendum on the presidency of Herbert Hoover. In particular, Americans would question whether President Hoover's politics, rooted in the prosperity of the past decade, were now the hallmark of a stubborn man reluctant to adapt to the hard realities of the 1930s. Despite the misery caused by the Depression, Prohibition still played a large role in Hoover's plummeting standing with the American people. While no rational observer could argue that the issue of Prohibition took precedence over the national crisis caused by the Depression, in many regards the Eighteenth Amendment and its effects were easier for Americans to understand. They had lived with Prohibition for a longer time; they were more certain of where it came from; and they knew how it intruded into their daily lives. The Depression, in contrast, conjured fear and uncertainty as Americans struggled to make sense of how the nation's economy had collapsed and wondered what could be done to reverse their fallen fortunes. The twin issues of Prohibition and the Depression came to be seen as inseparable parts of Herbert Hoover's record as president, and the 1932 election would become Americans' opportunity to pass judgment on his handling of both.

Though the two issues were very different, together they revealed the president's inflexibility and unwillingness to listen to the American people in a time of great crisis. Popular resentment of Prohibition in particular contributed greatly to the public perception of Hoover as an unresponsive political leader. The president's unwillingness to consider repeal made it difficult to convince the public of his determination to address the nation's economic crisis in the early 1930s, no matter how effective his policies might have been.

By 1932, the majority of Americans had tired of Prohibition, the myriad adverse effects it had engendered, and the bullying and browbeating of the dry lobby. As the enormity of the Depression's woes dwarfed the moral imperative of the dry experiment, Americans were shocked to see Hoover stand steadfastly by his dry allies. Many wondered why the president was willing to intrude into the personal lives of Americans when it came to keeping them from drinking, but unwilling to send the federal government into their homes to provide food or economic relief.

With the Depression and Prohibition taking hold as the key political issues of the day, the 1932 election had the makings of a watershed moment in American political history. The nation would have to decide either to stick with a brand of political leadership that had consistently bowed to the dry lobby's insistence on a single moral standard for the country, or to embrace a new type of leadership, marked by a responsiveness to popular calls for government action to end both the Depression and the noble experiment. Despite the grave economic situation that preoccupied the nation, the Democratic National Convention assembled in Chicago made clear that the opposition to Prohibition pioneered in New York and other cities had given rise to a national consensus that the Eighteenth Amendment had outlived its usefulness and that decisive action on the federal level to end it was in order.

On the night of June 27, 1932, Senator Alben Barkley of Kentucky delivered the keynote address to the Democratic National Convention. In a raucous display of solidarity, the 24,000 delegates gathered in Chicago Stadium cheered and waved banners as Barkley outlined a vision for the Democratic Party and its ambition to retake the White House for the first time in twelve years. In a two-hour speech, Barkley called for lower tariffs, agricultural aid to farmers, and government relief for the millions of unemployed Americans. When the senator came to the topic of Prohibition, the crowd responded wildly. Barkley, a former dry and co-author of the now-hated Eighteenth Amendment, declared that he and the Democratic Party stood unequivocally for the end of national Prohibition. The convention roared its approval, interrupting the senator's speech with a twelve-minute outburst. "The shouting and uproar grew to a terrific din," reported the *New York Herald Tribune,* as the crowd cheered for repeal and spontaneously began singing verses of the wet anthem "How Dry I Am."[2]

Two nights after Alben Barkley's speech, the Democrats met to vote on a party platform. Once again, the issue of Prohibition brought the assembly to life. A repeal plank, personally engineered by New York's Al Smith, was submitted to the delegates for their approval. The plank, which flatly declared, "We favor the repeal of the Eighteenth Amendment," called on Congress to submit to state conventions as soon as possible a new amendment for the repeal of Prohibition, and demanded the immediate legalization of beer through the modification of the Volstead Act. When Nebraska Senator Gilbert Hitchcock read the plank to the delegates, he incited the biggest demonstration of the convention. For twenty-five minutes, the Democratic delegates stomped, cheered, and waved signs calling for an end to Prohibition, while women wets milled about the convention floor, leading the Democrats in song. When order was restored, the convention approved the plank over a more moderate alternative by a four-to-one margin. Only two states, Georgia and Mississippi, voted against it, showing how significantly Southern support for Prohibition had eroded since the 1928 election.[3]

With the 1932 election shaping up as a referendum on Prohibition, the Depression, and the need for more responsive national leadership, the contrast between the optimistic Democrats, already at a great advantage owing to Hoover's unpopularity, and the Republicans was startling. Meeting two weeks before the Democrats, the Republican convention revealed a party embarrassingly divided over the issue of Prohibition. The wet wing of the party, led by Columbia University President Nicholas Murray Butler, had tried to include a repeal plank in the Republican platform out of fear that if the Republicans failed to change their position on Prohibition, they would certainly lose the White House to the Democrats. "If the convention stops short of Repeal and the Democrats advocate it," Butler warned his colleagues, "our nomination won't be worth the paper it is written on."[4]

While Butler and other wet Republicans rallied an impressive show of force, they could overcome neither President Hoover's determination to stand by Prohibition nor the lingering presence of the dry lobby. The party rejected Butler's wet proposal and instead arrived at a "moist" compromise recommending a national referendum on Prohibition. If passed by a two-thirds majority in national elections, it would allow the states to regulate or ban alcohol as they saw fit. In contrast to the Democrats' unequivocal position, the Republicans' compromise failed on the most basic level to say whether the party supported Prohibition. It angered wet Republicans and was ridiculed by political observers, who called it a masterpiece of vague and ambiguous politicking. Worst of all for the Republicans, the compromise meant the party had missed a valuable chance to seize upon repeal as the one issue that would cheer voters otherwise dismayed by the miserable state of the nation's economy. The *American Monthly* commented that "the Republicans missed a great opportunity to lift the cloud of the depression that rests on everybody's mind when they failed to come out for repeal." By attempting to straddle the issue, the Republicans emerged from their convention as the de facto party of Prohibition, and President Hoover as its dry candidate.[5]

The Republicans' attempt to sidestep the Prohibition controversy only fueled the Democrats' resolve to be identified as the party of repeal. While the more complex economic elements of their platform were crafted behind closed doors, Democrats consistently promoted Prohibition as the most easily understood issue of the election, and the one that most clearly distinguished the two parties. Aptly, when the Democrats approved their wet plank at the convention, the *Washington Post* commented, "The Democratic Party . . . stakes its existence upon this plank," while the *New York Times* noted that the Democrats' position on repeal provided "a new aspect to the whole Presidential campaign."[6]

Although the Democrats were optimistic that they could win the White House by capitalizing on resentment over both the economy and Prohibition, presenting a clear alternative to Hoover's unresponsive leadership proved a more difficult task. They hoped to make Hoover's insensitivity to popular concerns a central theme of the 1932 campaign, but as the Democratic convention wound down, the party still did not have a presidential candidate to offer as a more palatable option than Hoover.

Franklin Delano Roosevelt, Al Smith's successor as the governor of New York, had entered the convention with a majority of the Democratic delegates pledged to him. Despite enjoying broad support within the party, however, he did not have the two-thirds majority necessary to secure the party's nomination, and there were enough Democrats with reservations about Roosevelt to cast doubts on his viability as a candidate. It was by no means certain that Roosevelt was the best choice for the party to present as an alternative to Hoover.

The test for Governor Roosevelt was to prove, to his party and to the nation, that he offered a more responsive style of leadership than President Hoover did, and that his policies would be more in touch with the nation's concerns than Hoover's were. Initially, Roosevelt had a difficult time accomplishing this task. Though he had made a national name for himself with pioneering relief programs to combat the effects of the Depression in New York State, conservative Democrats throughout the United States considered his economic policies too extreme. In addition, a large number of New York's Democrats, beholden to Al Smith, were angered by Roosevelt's apparent lack of party loyalty. Roosevelt's animosity toward New York City's Tammany Hall machine, his strained relationship with his predecessor Al Smith, and his leading role in the anticorruption investigation that had finally ousted the popular Mayor James J. Walker from office all undermined Roosevelt's standing with rank-and-file New York Democrats. Smith in particular felt slighted by Roosevelt. In 1932 he told a colleague, "Do you know, by God, that [Roosevelt] has never consulted me once about a damn thing since he has been governor? . . . He has ignored me!" To many in his own party, Roosevelt came across as elitist, untrustworthy, and unwilling to work with his fellow Democrats.[7]

Roosevelt's biggest problems emerged when it came to the assessment of his character. Critics described Roosevelt as an indecisive leader who lacked conviction. In the pages of *The Nation,* editor Oswald Garrison Villard wrote of Roosevelt, "We still do not know where he stands on the vital issues of the day." Another editorial in *Harper's* took Roosevelt to task for the indeterminate and "shifting" political positions he had taken over the course of his career. *The Crisis* mocked his vacillation on numerous issues. An editorial in the journal characterized the governor as two-faced: "Liquor? He is and he ain't? The League [of Nations]? He was and he isn't. Power control? Yes and no. Tariff? No and yes. And so on, far into the night." Contrasted with the unresponsive Hoover, the unreliable Roosevelt hardly seemed like a better choice.[8]

With many Democrats viewing repeal as a central element of the 1932 campaign, one of the most pressing concerns about Roosevelt's tendency to waver on key issues was his long-standing refusal to take a stand on Prohibition. In the months before the Democratic convention, opinion polls indicated that more than 73 percent of the country, including majorities in forty-six states, now favored modification or repeal of the Eighteenth Amendment. Two weeks before the convention, *Time* reported that the wet sentiment was dominant in every state but Kansas and North Carolina. Even in the middle of the Depression, polls published in the *Literary Digest* continued to show that most Americans saw Prohibition as the paramount problem facing the United States, still ranking far above unemployment. Yet of the five leading Democratic contenders for the nomination in 1932, including Governor Smith, Texas Representative John Nance Garner, former Secretary of War Newton Baker, and Governor Albert C. Ritchie, only Governor Roosevelt refused to commit himself openly to repeal.[9]

Roosevelt's noncommittal position on repeal was nothing new. Despite his own fabled fondness for martinis, FDR had dodged the issue of Prohibition throughout his entire political career out of fear of offending voters on either side of the liquor issue. In 1920, as the vice presidential running mate of Governor James M. Cox, Roosevelt had presented himself as a moderate dry to balance Cox's wet stance. In 1923, when Roosevelt served in the New York State Assembly, he urged Governor Smith not to repeal the Mullan-Gage Act, New York's state law for Prohibition enforcement, suggesting that Smith instead take a more convoluted position by allowing limited state involvement in Prohibition enforcement. At other times during his tenure in the State Assembly, Roosevelt sought to appease New York wets by proposing limits to Prohibition enforcement. In 1928, when Roosevelt first ran for governor of New York, he avoided the issue of Prohibition altogether so as not to alienate dry voters upstate or wets in New York City. Once in the governor's office, he wavered between supporting the dry law and opposing it, depending on what was most politically expedient at any given time. In 1930, when he ran for a second two-year term as governor, Roosevelt danced around the issue again. Though his campaign slogan of "Bread, Not Booze" appealed directly to drys, Roosevelt quietly supported the Democratic repeal position, yet he still preferred to position himself as a moderate alternative to his more outspokenly wet Republican opponent, United States Attorney Charles H. Tuttle. In short, Roosevelt's stance on Prohibition depended on who was asking.[10]

While Roosevelt's wavering on the noble experiment served his political career in the short term, it infuriated Al Smith, the patriarch of New York Democrats. In 1932, Smith was adamant that his fellow Democrats, especially New York Democrats, stand for repeal. Smith, who had staked his own political future on repeal and lost, was livid to see Roosevelt, now sitting in Smith's old Albany office as governor, cultivating the image that he was drier than most of his party. Smith, John Raskob, and other prominent wet Democrats were determined to force Roosevelt to get in line with the rest of the party on the Prohibition issue, but Roosevelt refused to echo their calls for outright repeal. Instead, he supported the more moderate proposal that called for resubmitting the Prohibition amendment to the states. Breaking ranks with the majority of his party, Roosevelt seemed to be risking his nomination on his reluctance to embrace repeal.[11]

Indignant at Roosevelt's refusal to cooperate on the Prohibition issue, a bitter Al Smith launched a last-minute "Stop Roosevelt" campaign at the convention to prevent the governor from winning the nomination. With ninety-two of New York's ninety-four delegates personally pledged to him, Smith planned to sink Roosevelt's candidacy on the convention floor by blocking him from winning the two-thirds vote necessary for the Democratic nomination. (Remarkably, Roosevelt entered the convention with only two of New York's delegates in his camp.) Whether for personal vindication or out of single-minded devotion to the Prohibition issue, Smith threatened to upend the convention.[12]

Sensing trouble from the Smith camp, Roosevelt supporters led by Louisiana's Huey Long responded with an abortive attempt to suspend the traditional convention rule requiring a two-thirds majority to approve the nomination, arguing that a simple majority should be sufficient. Though many Democrats agreed in principle that the two-thirds rule was an antiquated practice left over from the days of Andrew Jackson, the timing of the Roosevelt camp could not have been worse. A floor fight over the two-thirds rule would have injected unnecessary controversy into the convention; moreover, the move suggested to many Democrats that Roosevelt was improperly trying to swindle his way to a nomination that he could not win through the regular procedure. Anti-Roosevelt Democrats cried foul, and Roosevelt's supporters were forced to make an embarrassing retreat. After his last misstep, the *New York Times* predicted that Roosevelt's candidacy would be "soon done for."[13]

With little room to maneuver, Roosevelt finally did what he had steadfastly avoided doing for twelve years. Just fifteen minutes before Al Smith was scheduled to address the convention on the issue of Prohibition, potentially embarrassing FDR, Roosevelt released a brief statement pledging his full support for the party's wet plank for repeal. A showdown with Smith had been averted, but the episode highlighted the willingness of the Democratic Party to stake much of its fate on the Prohibition issue.[14]

Even with this major concession on the wet plank, Roosevelt still faced difficulty at the convention. The New York governor failed to win the nomination in the first round of balloting on June 30. A second round of balloting later that night also failed to secure his place as the Democratic nominee. When the third round of balloting ended at 9:00 A.M. the following morning, the delegates left behind five thousand empty liquor bottles and a stadium in shambles, but they still had not agreed on a candidate. To some observers, FDR now seemed in serious danger of losing the nomination to a compromise candidate. Only after another day of backroom politicking, which saw Al Smith's old nemesis William Randolph Hearst brokering a deal with the Roosevelt camp via telephone from California, did Representative John Nance Garner withdraw his candidacy and release his delegates to Roosevelt. In exchange, Hearst had arranged for Garner to win the vice presidential nomination. When the roll was called that night, Garner's concession gave Roosevelt more than the two-thirds majority he needed for the nomination. Though Al Smith still won sixty-three of New York's ninety-four delegates in the final round of balloting, his plan to block FDR's nomination and his political career were over.[15]

Having secured the nomination, Roosevelt still failed to appease many of his critics. Summarizing the events at the convention in *The Nation,* Oswald Garrison Villard called Roosevelt an "unsatisfactory" candidate. "We can see in him no leader," he added, "and no evidence anywhere that he can rise up to the needs of this extraordinary hour." A pro-Smith newspaper lamented that "in Franklin Roosevelt, we have another Hoover." *Harper's* similarly compared the two men, noting that "neither Mr. Hoover nor Governor Roosevelt stirs much emotion." H. L. Mencken, who had watched the proceedings of the convention closely, observed, "No one really likes Roosevelt, not even his own ostensible friends, and no one quite trusts him." He added that "a majority of the Roosevelt men are really not for Roosevelt at all, but simply against Al Smith." Though a Democratic nominee had been found, the final choice of Roosevelt seemed to sap the spirit of what had begun as a jubilant convention. Noting the lukewarm response for Roosevelt, Villard commented, "Never have I seen a Presidential ticket named at a national convention with so little enthusiasm."[16]

Entering the most important campaign since World War I, many Democrats in 1932 initially appeared more excited about their platform than they were about their candidate. For example, the *Irish World,* which had always staunchly supported Al Smith, told voters in the fall of 1932 that "it is the duty of every American citizen, no matter what his or her political affiliation may be, to vote against Hoover, against Prohibition, against starvation." In another plea, the paper argued that "every vote for a Democrat is a vote for repeal." But it made almost no mention of Franklin Roosevelt; it simply proclaimed that "Prohibition and Hooverism must be defeated on election day." To the *World,* the election would serve as a national referendum on Hoover, Prohibition, and the Depression, in which voters were expected to cast their ballots against Hoover but not *for* anyone in particular.[17]

The damage done by Prohibition, and the deep-seated resentment it had fostered over thirteen years, had prompted a backlash so strong that it distracted Americans from the larger issue of the Depression at a time when the economic crisis required the most consideration. The lukewarm reception Roosevelt initially received from many Democrats in 1932 was a signal that he had not done enough to convince them that he shared their concerns over Prohibition. Ironically, Roosevelt, the political leader who would later be credited with guiding the nation through the enormous challenges of the Great Depression, nearly lost the opportunity to do so because of his reluctance to embrace repeal. Only by agreeing to take up the repeal cause was he able to win over his many skeptics.

As critical as the Prohibition issue was to the 1932 election, the Democratic Party's preoccupation with repeal in 1932 did not sit well with everyone. Many American intellectuals and political writers could not understand the wets' insistence that Prohibition play such a central role in the campaign, and they bemoaned the lack of attention paid to the Depression by either party. At the Republican convention, according to one historian, "the general attitude was 'What Depression?'" A reporter for the *New York Times* who covered the Democratic convention wrote that "an eavesdropper would seldom guess that the country was passing through a serious economic crisis. Unemployment and the depression are seldom mentioned, except by the serious minded elder statesmen." The philosopher and educational reformer John Dewey was shocked by this case of political myopia.

"Here we are in the midst of the greatest crisis since the Civil War," he complained, "and the only thing the two national parties seem to want to debate is booze."[18]

To Dewey, Prohibition warranted far less concern than the Depression, and political thinkers like him desperately hoped that as the 1932 campaign progressed the emotional issue of Prohibition would fade into the background, thus allowing the economy to move to the forefront. Roosevelt stalwarts also felt that the emphasis on repeal within the Democratic Party was shortsighted, and they resurrected FDR's 1930 slogan "Bread, Not Booze" as an unofficial rallying cry to help refocus the campaign. One Roosevelt supporter, Ray Tucker, scoffed at the agenda incessantly pushed by Al Smith, John Raskob, and other wets. He commented that "to the millions who ask for food, Raskob would give drink."[19]

FDR never shared the belief held by many of his fellow New Yorkers that Prohibition was the paramount issue of the day. His political reputation as governor had been built on his economic policies, and he clearly hoped to keep the campaign focused on the Depression and the economy. But Roosevelt had to acknowledge that popular sentiment remained fixed on Prohibition. However misguided, H. L. Mencken expressed the views of many Democrats when he wrote in the *American Mercury,* "The truth is, of course, that Prohibition is immensely more important than any imaginable economic issue. No sensible man believes that either Hoover or Roosevelt can do anything substantial to end the Depression: it must run its course, and soon or late it will end."[20]

Mencken may have had a poor sense of national priorities, but his comments demonstrated that Americans in 1932 grasped Prohibition more easily than the Depression and its causes. Moreover, having already lost so much to the Depression, most people were unwilling to sacrifice even an ounce of their personal liberty to an anachronistic reform cause that may have made sense at one time but now seemed petty. What Americans wanted more than anything was a quick exit from what had become a drawn-out dry experiment, and an end to the moral demands of a dry movement that seemed hopelessly stuck in the past.

The election thus became a perfect litmus test for the two candidates. Even if, as Mencken argued, voters did not believe that there was a political solution to the Depression, in 1932 they could plainly ask the two candidates what they were willing to do about Prohibition. Would they work to repeal the Eighteenth Amendment or stand by it?

In this scenario, President Hoover was suddenly at a great disadvantage. Not only did voters believe that Hoover had taken few steps to ease the suffering caused by the Depression, but he was adamant that the nation not give up on Prohibition. The latter position may have hurt him as badly as did the nation's economic woes, as evidenced by the *American Monthly*'s comment that "of all the Hoover hair-shirts, the hairiest is Prohibition."[21]

By comparison, Roosevelt came out of the convention in a position to gain. Though FDR's plans for the economic recovery of the nation were still vague, unfocused, and contradictory, and would remain so until after he took office, by finally embracing his party's stance on Prohibition, he had distinguished himself from Hoover's "stay the course" mindset. His willingness to do something about Prohibition, even if only at the behest of his party, signaled to voters that Roosevelt was more in touch with them than Hoover was, and that he would respond to their concerns. It was a sign that FDR would not stand steadfastly by economic or social policies that did not work, and that he represented a change from the political leadership of the 1920s, which had always bowed to the dry lobby. FDR's position was by no means a wholesale abandonment of reform; indeed, FDR would leave his mark as one of the greatest reformers in American history. But here, in the 1932 election, he represented a repudiation of the type of paternalistic moral reform that had driven the dry crusade. In its place, Roosevelt offered a more sensible, responsive approach to government reform. The government would still reach into the daily lives of Americans, but in a very different way.[22]

As the reluctant wet candidate of 1932, FDR put aside his past wavering and took up the repeal campaign where Al Smith had left off in 1928, drawing upon the political support of the wet coalition that had been nurtured since then by New Yorkers like Fiorello LaGuardia and Pauline Sabin. When FDR took the unprecedented step of flying to Chicago in 1932 to accept his party's nomination in person, he delivered the speech that brought all the issues together, and began the process of unifying the party, and ultimately the American people, behind him.

In his famous address to the convention, FDR pledged to "restore America to its own people," and for the first time he offered his economic plan for a "New Deal for the American People." Understanding that a large number of Democrats at the convention had not clamored for him so much as for repeal, he also took up the wet standard. He told the delegates, "This convention wants Repeal. Your candidate wants Repeal. And I am confident the United States wants Repeal . . . From this day on, the Eighteenth Amendment is doomed!" Commenting on the outcome of the convention, *Harper's* announced, "There is a wet wave running. It looks like a tidal wave."[23]

The election of 1932 did in fact resemble a tidal wave, and true to Roosevelt's convention promise, the Eighteenth Amendment was doomed when the votes for FDR were counted. Roosevelt won the presidential election of 1932 by a landslide, capturing nearly twenty-three million votes to Hoover's sixteen million. The Depression alone had in all likelihood destroyed President Hoover's chances for reelection in 1932, but by seizing upon the issue of repeal, Roosevelt had reassured many Americans that they would have a president who not only cared about their economic well-being but also listened to and understood their demand to be liberated from the constraints of Prohibition and the intrusion of the state into their private lives.

The results of the vote in New York City gave FDR an even more lopsided victory, undoubtedly demonstrating a repudiation of President Hoover for his inability to address the Depression and for his insistence on continuing the noble experiment in the center of wet resistance. After FDR carried the city with 66 percent of the vote, the editors of the *Amsterdam News* argued that Roosevelt's victory signaled two things: "the people of the country are desirous of a change in administration and . . . they want legalized beer." Similarly, a Lower East Side resident explained that he voted for Roosevelt because, "from what we read in the papers, and from what the leaders in our neighborhood were saying [Roosevelt] was going to bring us through the hard times, and then to the good times." "He was going to repeal Prohibition," he continued. "That was his platform. That's what all the voting was for, as far as I was concerned."[24]

In the national political arena, FDR's election ended all talk of continuing the failed Prohibition experiment and marked the final defeat for a dry lobby that had wielded considerable power for nearly three decades. The *New York Herald Tribune* argued that "whatever else the Democratic sweep may mean . . . it is obviously a mandate to Congress to modify the Volstead law and pass a resolution for the straight repeal of the Eighteenth Amendment." *Variety* echoed this view, summing up the election results with the words: "Beer, Booze and Speaks." The *American Monthly* declared with equal economy, "The people voted for repeal." In spite of his past wavering, voters had identified the president-elect with repeal, and numerous political observers viewed Roosevelt's triumph and the prospect of legal beer as emblematic of the nation's hopes for better times ahead.[25]

Upon taking office on March 4, 1933, President Roosevelt responded quickly to the public clamor for a new style of leadership. His fifteen-minute inaugural address made no specific mention of the Eighteenth Amendment but focused instead on economic issues and the morale of the country. Still, Roosevelt set the tone for his administration, and hinted what would become of Prohibition, when he proclaimed that "this nation asks for action, and action now."[26]

Though Roosevelt had not mentioned Prohibition by name, it was clear what Americans expected of him, and many New Yorkers wrote to the president after the inauguration to urge him to action. The Jamaica Saengerbund, a German-American group in Queens, telegrammed Roosevelt to ask him to modify the Volstead Act quickly, adding, "We promise to stand by you in the future." Another New Yorker, Nathaniel Frankel, wrote, "As you won the confidence of the people in the last election, so will you repeal the Eighteenth Amendment." A letter from John Robert exemplified the way many New Yorkers were linking repeal with the rest of FDR's New Deal agenda. "Your activities since the fourth of March have brought forth the deepest admiration from the people of this nation," Robert wrote, "and your ability to make Congress see, as you see, has been a source of wonderment." He urged the president to move the repeal process forward for the sake of the economy, to put an end to corruption and crime, and to restore personal liberty.[27]

Roosevelt kept his promise by taking swift action on both the Depression and Prohibition. On March 13, 1933, after nine days in office, he asked a special session of Congress to modify the Volstead Act to immediately legalize beer and wine. To cheers from the gallery of "vote—vote—we want beer," Congress hastily complied by passing the Beer and Wine Revenue Act. On March 22, FDR signed it into law. It would be the third major piece of legislation of Roosevelt's first 100 days, coming only after the Emergency Banking Act and the sweeping Economy Act. The complete repeal of Prohibition could be realized only after a new constitutional amendment had been ratified, but Congress had already taken the lead by submitting a proposed Twenty-first Amendment to the states in February, the key phrase of which simply stated, "The eighteenth article of amendment to the Constitution of the United States is hereby repealed." Once thought impossible, repeal now seemed inevitable, in large part owing to the efforts of New Yorkers.[28]

On the afternoon of April 6, 1933, in a nationally broadcast radio address on the topic of repeal, Nicholas Murray Butler reminded Americans that "there can be no more happy sight in the world than a German beer-garden on a summer afternoon or evening." That night at midnight, New York saw the return of legal beer for the first time in nearly fourteen years. At the Savoy Ballroom, the *Amsterdam News* reported that free beer was given away to patrons at the stroke of twelve, and though it was of poor quality and in short supply, it was heartily welcomed. The paper's headline declared, "Hail Beer with Glee in Harlem." A few midtown hotels and nightclubs also supplied midnight parties with beer of questionable provenance, sheepishly refusing to comment on its origins aside from assuring patrons that it was "the real stuff."[29]

For the rest of the city, the celebrations would have to wait until morning for the first deliveries of legal beer. In Manhattan's Yorkville, cheering crowds saluted the departure of the first trucks as they left Jacob Ruppert's Brewery at Ninety-first Street and Third Avenue at 6:00 A.M. Ruppert directed that the first two cases be sent to Al Smith at his office in the Empire State Building. (It would prove a bountiful day for Smith, who also received two cases of Budweiser, sent by airplane from Saint Louis and delivered by a Clydesdale-drawn wagon to his office.) All morning, local breweries dispatched hundreds of trucks laden with beer across the city, only to see the entire supply exhausted by lunchtime as crowds gathered in restaurants, dining rooms, and bars to consume every available drop.

At Lüchow's, the famed German restaurant on Fourteenth Street, the horde of thirsty patrons that included Police Commissioner Edward Mulrooney and Tammany Hall President John F. Curry overflowed into the street. When the beer ran out, the restaurant turned one thousand disappointed customers away. The restaurant manager at the Biltmore Hotel witnessed a similar scene. He told a reporter, "I looked around the dining room at 1 o'clock and I saw nobody who wasn't drinking beer." Despite the jubilation, the celebrants remained remarkably well behaved. The police reported not a single arrest for drunkenness or driving while intoxicated, and the alcoholism wards at the city's hospitals recorded only six new admissions, the lowest number in months. Two months later, police reports would acknowledge that arrests for intoxication in the city had decreased 14 percent since the return of legal beer, supporting the argument that the end of Prohibition would encourage more temperate behavior.[30]

The return of legal beer to the Depression-struck city gave New York more reason to celebrate in the form of jobs. Inundated with patrons, Lüchows hired back thirty-five former waiters and twenty kitchen workers to help it cope with beer-thirsty crowds. Ruppert's Brewery, which had shipped 250,000 cases of bottled beer and 18,000 kegs on April 7, hired 200 permanent and 100 temporary brewery workers to keep up with demand. In Brooklyn, neighborhood residents lingered expectantly outside the borough's several breweries, hoping to be hired by plants operating around the clock to label bottles and fill wooden crates. Some breweries reported that they had doubled their number of employees, while others scrambled to find truckmen to deliver their goods. Bartenders also saw their fortunes rise. Eagerly awaiting the call back to work, Emanuel Koveleski of the New York Bartenders' Union promised that his members were ready for work. "We're all set," he said. "The bartenders will be all fine, clean upstanding young men."[31]

The return of legal beer so early into Roosevelt's presidency ensured that FDR would remain forever identified with repeal. With the Twenty-first Amendment already speeding through state legislatures and the final end of

Prohibition only months away, letters from New Yorkers continued to pour in to Roosevelt's office, offering advice on liquor regulation and praising his leadership in dealing with Prohibition and the Depression.

As the reluctant wet became the hero of repeal, Roosevelt's constituents marveled at the rapidity with which FDR was taking decisive action against both Prohibition and the Depression. One New Yorker, commenting on Roosevelt's handling of the economy, the nation's banking crisis, and repeal, wrote, "[You] have demonstrated behind the shadow of the most critical doubters that you are the leader needed at this time of dire emergency." Another admirer assured the president that "in New York, as everywhere . . . the acts of the President are thought ideally human and right."[32]

Most of all, these observers were quick to note the change in style and temperament that FDR had brought to government. In the magazine *Liberty*, columnist Bernarr MacFadden exclaimed, "Much of our sanctimonious fanatical prohibition law was wiped out in a few days." With Roosevelt in office, he concluded, "our government became human overnight." These comments highlighted how differently Americans viewed their relationship with the government now that the New Deal had begun and the dry crusade was over. (Only occasionally was a discordant note heard. Though supportive of the New Deal, *The Crisis* correctly cautioned that repeal would not end the Depression. It commented that "those morons who see salvation in beer are in for disillusion.")[33]

The nation's drys naturally made last-ditch efforts to preserve national Prohibition. They, too, wrote numerous letters to Roosevelt, pleading with him to recognize that repeal was a "false panacea," and arguing that legalizing alcohol would only encourage more drinking and harm the welfare of families. In a personal plea to Roosevelt, Ella Boole of the Woman's Christian Temperance Union declared, "We do not believe the government should derive revenue from the vices of the people." While the petitions from Boole and the other drys received cordial responses from the White House, their arguments, which had once proved so persuasive, no longer held any weight.[34]

The inevitable and final end of Prohibition came at 5:32 P.M. on December 5, 1933, when Utah became the thirty-sixth state to ratify the Twenty-first Amendment. In New York's bars, the news of Utah's vote was eagerly awaited over the radio, as was the proclamation from Acting Secretary of State William Phillips that the Twenty-first Amendment had become law. Upon hearing the news, Justice Learned Hand wrote, "God! How good it is to speak freely about it! Free, free, free!!!! Curst be its name, its memory, its parent, its fosterers, its designers, its sycophants, its proposers, its backers, its executors." *The Nation,* reflecting the relief felt by millions of Americans now that Prohibition was over, commented, "It is probably not an exaggeration to say it was the worst legislative mistake this country ever made."[35]

The city greeted repeal, according to headlines, with "quiet restraint." Though New York's entire police force had been called out in case celebrations got out of hand, no more arrests were reported than usual, and Greenwich Village, the center of so much riotous behavior during the Prohibition era, was described in newspaper reports as "dull." Part of the subdued atmosphere was due to the dearth of legal liquor in the city. Though more than a thousand establishments had received licenses to serve liquor from the newly created state Alcohol Control Board, only fifty truckloads of legal liquor were available in the entire city. Those most likely to be serving alcohol that evening were New York's hotels, which simply dusted off their wine cellars, uncached what they insisted were legal supplies of pre-Prohibition liquor, rehired old bartenders, and reopened their bars.

Contrary to dry fears that repeal would unleash a bacchanalia, the return of legal liquor was characterized by an abundance of caution. New York saloons and bars that had brazenly sold illegal liquor throughout the Prohibition era now adopted a more careful attitude, taking care to stick to the letter of the law. They had stopped selling liquor with the return of legal beer in the spring, wary of jeopardizing their chances to obtain a legal liquor license once new state regulations were in place. The hundreds of cordial shops, which had slyly supplied New Yorkers with liquor for the past decade, vanished, replaced by legal liquor stores.

In the place of criminal bootlegging syndicates, New York's major department stores now became reliable purveyors of wine and spirits. In fact, Bloomingdale's recorded the first legal liquor sale in the city after repeal, selling a bottle of port and a bottle of rye to its first customer. Most of the city's speakeasies quietly disappeared, though famous midtown establishments like the "21" Club and the Stork Club went legitimate, and ended up giving away their stocks of illegal liquor as they waited for legal supplies of alcohol to arrive. Given this abundance of caution, the lack of drunkenness on the first night of repeal makes sense, but there was certainly revelry. Effigies representing Prohibition were hung, drowned, and in one case electrocuted in an electric chair. In a brief respite from the misery of the Depression, bands played drinking songs and clubs hosted repeal balls, dinners, and dances. At the Club Richman, a new cocktail was named in honor of Al Smith, while other bars concocted "New Deal" cocktails in tribute to Roosevelt.[36]

The end of Prohibition revealed how much New York City had changed during the thirteen years, ten months, and eighteen days of national Prohibition. Hotel stewards were alarmed to find their wine cellars rattled by vibrations from subway lines that had not existed a decade earlier. Denizens of the old-time saloon fumed that drinks were, according to a new state regulation, not allowed to be consumed standing, while women who had found their way into the world of the speakeasy planned to stay there, ensuring that there would never be a return to the all-male saloon, McSorley's on East Seventh Street excepted. (It would remain an all-male enclave until 1970.) Drinking styles had also changed significantly during the dry era, and the city stuck with its taste for more elaborate cocktails rather than the beer and whiskey of pre-Prohibition days. Nightlife, which had raged so boundlessly during the 1920s, also evolved with repeal, taking a more sedate turn on account of the Depression and the return of enforceable regulations.[37]

The end of the Prohibition era marked the demise of a moral crusade meant to impose a uniform standard of social behavior in the United States. Unrealistic and unforgiving, Prohibition had allowed a vocal minority to regulate the personal habits of all Americans, especially those who lived and worked in cities like New York. While the desire of the dry crusade to uplift and improve the United States by banning alcohol and the saloon had in some ways been understandable in the Progressive era that spawned the Prohibition movement, the shortcomings of the dry crusade manifested themselves as soon as the dry experiment had begun. Anachronistic and unworkable, the Prohibition experiment was ill suited to the diversity and dynamic of the modern United States, which by the 1920s had grown too large and too varied a nation to be governed by an impulse as intrusive as the dry crusade. Despite the force of federal law, the use of authoritarian tactics to enforce it, and the expenditure of millions of dollars a year, in fourteen years Prohibition succeeded neither in changing Americans' behavior nor in eliminating the problems caused by alcohol abuse. When Prohibition failed, and it did so spectacularly, it revealed the limits of moral reform movements, and specifically the paternalistic, prejudiced, and undemocratic ideals behind the dry crusade.[38]

New Yorkers' resistance to the Eighteenth Amendment, and their cultural rebellion against Prohibition, were the inevitable results of such an ill-advised and overly ambitious reform agenda. In breaking the law, New Yorkers who opposed Prohibition rejected the idea that the state had a right to dictate the private conduct of its citizens. They rebelled against the dry crusade because it was an affront to their values and their identities as Americans. Knowing well that the dry crusade had specifically targeted New York and had intended to make an example of the city, New Yorkers defied the Volstead Act as a way of saying that the diverse culture and cosmopolitanism of the modern city was their American ideal. As their rebellion moved from simple everyday acts like making their own wine or drinking and dancing in speakeasies to more focused wet activism in the realm of politics, New Yorkers helped steer the nation away from the moral absolutism of the drys and toward both a more tolerant view of American society and a more practical understanding of the relationship between the government and its citizens.

It is unlikely that William Anderson of the Anti-Saloon League fully anticipated the long-term effects of the noble experiment, or the cultural and political ramifications of the rebellion against it, when he arrived at the Hotel McAlpin on New Year's Day, 1914, on his ill-fated mission to dry up New York. But in the two decades between the launch of Anderson's dry crusade in New York and FDR's decisive push for the repeal of the Eighteenth Amendment as part of the New Deal, New Yorkers found themselves at the center of something much larger than a debate over alcohol. Prohibition, and the rebellion against it, had been a struggle over the direction American society would take for the rest of the century.

Abbreviations

CU	Columbia University Archives
CUOHC	Columbia University Oral History Collection, Columbia University
FDR	Franklin D. Roosevelt Library
HML	Hagley Museum and Library
LOC	Library of Congress
MANY	Municipal Archives of the City of New York
MNHS	Minnesota Historical Society
NARA	National Archives and Records Administration, Northeast Branch
NYHS	New-York Historical Society
NYPL	New York Public Library
UCL	University of Chicago Library, Special Collections Research Center

Notes

Introduction

1. *New York Times,* September 24, 1929, p. 8; September 25, 1929, p. 64; September 26, 1929, p. 18; September 24, 1929, p. 8; September 28, 1929, p. 12; September 29, 1929, Section XX, p. 9; *The Crisis,* November 1929, p. 365.

2. Roy V. Peel and Thomas C. Donnelly, *The 1928 Campaign: An Analysis* (New York: Richard R. Smith, 1931; repr. New York: Arno Press, 1974), p. 57; Charles Merz, *The Dry Decade* (New York: Doubleday, Doran and Company, 1930; repr. Seattle: University of Washington Press, 1969), pp. 221–224, 329–331.

3. Not all historians regard Prohibition as a failure. Since the late 1960s, a revisionist school has argued that Prohibition, despite popular sentiment to the contrary, was a modestly successful reform that curbed the corrupt influence of the liquor trade in the United States and reduced drinking rates nationally. The pioneering study in this school of thought was John C. Burnham's 1968 article "New Perspectives on the Prohibition 'Experiment' of the 1920s," *Journal of Social History* 1 (Fall 1968): 51. K. Austin Kerr's book *Organized for Prohibition: A New History of the Anti-Saloon League* (New Haven: Yale University Press, 1985) builds on this premise by arguing that the Prohibition movement, despite being depicted popularly as the work of fanatics, was in fact rooted in the larger social reform movements of the late nineteenth and early twentieth centuries, and must be understood in the context of those reforms. For an overview of the arguments that Prohibition was a success, see Norman H. Clark, *Deliver Us from Evil: An Interpretation of American Prohibition* (New York: W. W. Norton and Company, 1976), pp. 145–150.

4. F. Scott Fitzgerald, "Echoes of the Jazz Age," *The Crack-Up* (New York: New Directions, 1956), p. 14.

5. Ann Douglas, *Terrible Honesty: Mongrel Manhattan in the 1920s* (New York: Farrar, Straus and Giroux, 1995), p. 24.

6. Paula Fass, *The Damned and the Beautiful: American Youth in the 1920s* (New York: Oxford University Press, 1977), p. 4.

1. The Dry Crusade

1. *Baltimore Sun,* January 2, 1914, cited in Peter H. Odegard, *Pressure Politics: The Story of the Anti-Saloon League* (New York: Columbia University Press, 1928; repr. New York: Octagon Books, 1966), p. 231.

2. K. Austin Kerr, *Organized for Prohibition: A New History of the Anti-Saloon League* (New Haven: Yale University Press, 1985), p. 2.

3. *New York Times,* January 2, 1914, p. 8; Odegard, *Pressure Politics,* pp. 228–232.

4. Kerr, *Organized for Prohibition,* pp. 137–138.

5. *New York Times,* January 1, 1914, p. 1; *New York World,* January 2, 1914, p. 7.

6. *New York Sun,* January 2, 1914, p. 8; *New York Tribune,* January 2, 1914, p. 12; *New York World,* January 2, 1914, p. 7; *New York Times,* January 2, 1914, p. 8; CUOHC, *Reminiscences of William H. Anderson* (1950), p. 7.

7. *New York World,* January 2, 1914, p. 7; *New York Times,* January 2, 1914, p. 8.

8. Ibid.

9. *New York World,* January 2, 1914, p. 7; Catherine Gilbert Murdock, *Domesticating Drink: Women, Men, and Alcohol in America, 1870–1940* (Baltimore: Johns Hopkins University Press, 1998), pp. 22–23; Kerr, *Organized for Prohibition,* p. 142.

10. *New York World,* January 2, 1914, p. 7; *Reminiscences of William H. Anderson,* p. 7.

11. Richard F. Hamm, *Shaping the Eighteenth Amendment: Temperance Reform, Legal Culture, and the Polity, 1880–1920* (Chapel Hill: University of North Carolina Press, 1995), p. 247; Odegard, *Pressure Politics,* p. 174.

12. Odegard, *Pressure Politics,* p. 174.

13. *New York Times,* March 22, 1918, p. 12.

14. *New York Times,* January 28, 1919, p. 1.

15. *New York Times,* January 31, 1919, p. 1; Gene Fowler, *Beau James: The Life and Times of Jimmy Walker* (New York: Viking, 1949), p. 92; Odegard, *Pressure Politics,* pp. 177–178.

16. Hamm, *Shaping the Eighteenth Amendment,* p. 255; Odegard, *Pressure Politics,* p. 177.

17. Odegard, *Pressure Politics,* p. 177.

18. Andrew Barr, *Drink: A Social History of America* (New York: Carroll and Graf, 1999); Frederick Binder and David Reimers, *All the Nations under Heaven: An Ethnic and Racial History of New York City* (New York: Columbia University Press, 1995), pp. 83–84; William Grimes, *Straight up or on the Rocks: The Story of the American Cocktail* (New York: North Point Press, 2001), pp. 18–19.

19. Ernest H. Cherrington, ed., *Anti-Saloon League Yearbook, 1913* (Westerville, Ohio: American Issue Press, 1913), pp. 173–174.

20. *Anti-Saloon League Yearbook, 1913,* p. 174; Kerr, *Organized for Prohibition,* p. 147; *New York Times,* December 29, 1913, p. 2.

21. Edward Marshall, "Is National Prohibition Actually Close at Hand?," *New York Times,* April 19, 1914, Section VI, p. 10.

22. Norman H. Clark, *Deliver Us from Evil: An Interpretation of American Prohibition* (New York: W. W. Norton and Co., 1976), Ch. 6; Kerr, *Organized for Prohibition,* p. 96.

23. Ruth Bordin, *Woman and Temperance: The Quest for Power and Liberty, 1873–1900* (New Brunswick: Rutgers University Press, 1990), p. 4; Kerr, *Organized for Prohibition,* p. 81.

24. Odegard, *Pressure Politics,* pp. 104–126.

25. Marshall, "Is National Prohibition Actually Close at Hand?," p. 10.

26. Kerr, *Organized for Prohibition,* p. 147; *New York Times,* June 3, 1914, p. 3; Odegard, *Pressure Politics,* p. 177.

27. Odegard, *Pressure Politics,* pp. 104–105.

28. Ibid., pp. 96–97.

29. *New York Times,* April 4, 1914, p. 9; Marshall, "Is National Prohibition Actually Close at Hand?," p. 10.

30. Odegard, *Pressure Politics,* p. 232; *New York Times,* November 22, 1915, p. 6; *Reminiscences of William H. Anderson,* pp. 28–29.

31. *New York Times,* January 26, 1915, p. 1.

32. *New York Times,* November 9, 1915, p. 22; December 19, 1916, p. 10; November 4, 1917, p. 6; Ernest H. Cherrington, ed., *Anti-Saloon League Yearbook, 1914* (Westerville, Ohio: American Issue Press, 1914), p. 174; *Reminiscences of William H. Anderson,* p. 88; Odegard, *Pressure Politics,* p. 95, 238.

33. *Anti-Saloon League Yearbook, 1913,* pp. 171–172.

34. *New York Times,* January 14, 1915, p. 6; *New York World,* January 2, 1914, p. 7.

35. *New York Times,* March 8, 1917, p. 8; May 4, 1917, p. 10; May 23, 1917, p. 11.

36. *New York Times,* December 29, 1913, p. 2; January 2, 1914, p. 8; November 10, 1916, p. 4; Steven J. Diner, *A Very Different Age: Americans of the Progressive Era* (New York: Hill and Wang, 1998), pp. 1–13.

37. George Kibbe Turner, "Beer and the City Liquor Problem," *McClure's,* September 1909, pp. 528–543; "The Story of an Alcohol Slave," *McClure's,* August 1909, pp. 426–430.

38. Charles Stelzle, *A Son of the Bowery: The Life Story of an East Side American* (New York: George H. Doran, 1926), p. 192.

39. *Literary Digest,* February 1, 1919, p. 11; James H. Timberlake, *Prohibition and the Progressive Movement, 1900–1920* (Cambridge: Harvard University Press, 1963), pp. 52, 102–107, 125–148; Blocker, *Retreat from Reform,* pp. 8–10; Kerr, *Organized for Prohibition,* pp. 4–9, 19, 33–35; Hamm, *Shaping the Eighteenth Amendment,* pp. 45–47.

40. Odegard, *Pressure Politics,* p. 248; William L. Riordon, *Plunkitt of Tammany Hall* (1905, repr., New York: E. P. Dutton, 1963), pp. 48, 77–80, 84–87; George Kibbe Turner, "Tammany's Control of New York by Professional Criminals," *McClure's,* June 1909, pp. 117–119; Edward M. Levine, *The Irish and Irish Politicians* (Notre Dame: University of Notre Dame Press, 1966), pp. 117–119; Caroline Ware, *Greenwich Village, 1920–1930: A Comment on American Civilization in the Post-War Years* (1935, repr., New York: Octagon Books, 1977), pp. 55; *The Messenger,* February 1920, p. 11.

41. Turner, "Tammany's Control of New York by Professional Criminals," pp. 119–134.

42. Odegard, *Pressure Politics,* p. 44; Paula Eldot, *Governor Alfred E. Smith: The Politician as Reformer* (New York: Garland Publishing, 1983), p. 345.

43. Timberlake, *Prohibition and the Progressive Movement,* pp. 151, 168–169; Roy Rosenzweig, *Eight Hours for What We Will: Workers and Leisure in an Industrial City, 1870–1920* (Cambridge: Cambridge University Press, 1983), pp. 93–126.

44. Lewis A. Erenberg, *Steppin' Out: New York Nightlife and the Transformation of American Culture, 1890–1930* (Chicago: University of Chicago Press, 1981), pp. 63–65, 77, 130, 134; Timothy J. Gilfoyle, *City of Eros: New York City, Prostitution, and the Commercialization of Sex, 1790–1920* (New York: W. W. Norton and Co., 1992), pp. 304–305.

45. Gilfoyle, *City of Eros,* pp. 243–248; Edwin G. Burrows and Mike Wallace, *Gotham: A History of New York City to 1898* (New York: Oxford University Press, 1999), p. 1203.

46. Timberlake, *Prohibition and the Progressive Movement,* pp. 111, 153; *Anti-Saloon League Yearbook, 1913,* p. 173.

47. *New York Times,* February 6, 1915, p. 8; March 16, 1916, p. 14; March 17, 1916, p. 12; March 21, 1916, p. 7; March 29, 1916, p. 15.

48. Marshall, "Is National Prohibition Actually Close at Hand?," p. 10; David J. Goldberg, *Discontented America: The United States in the 1920s* (Baltimore: Johns Hopkins University Press, 1999), p. 55.

49. Marshall, "Is National Prohibition Actually Close at Hand?," p. 10; *New York Times,* February 2, 1916, p. 5; *The Reminiscences of William H. Anderson,* pp. 12, 17, 88; Odegard, *Pressure Politics,* p. 232.
50. *New York Times,* March 13, 1917, p. 5; March 14, 1917, p. 6; March 15, 1917, p. 7.
51. *New York Times,* March 15, 1918, pp. 1, 7.
52. *New York Times,* January 29, 1918, p. 12.
53. Nuala McGann Drescher, "The Opposition to Prohibition, 1900–1919: A Social and Institutional Study" (Ph.D. diss., University of Delaware, 1964), pp. 330–331; Odegard, *Pressure Politics,* p. 167; *New York Times,* December 29, 1917, p. 10; January 29, 1918, p. 12.
54. Frederick Lewis Allen, *Only Yesterday: An Informal History of the Nineteen Twenties* (New York: Harper and Brothers, 1931), p. 12; *The Outlook,* November 6, 1918, p. 334; Timberlake, *Prohibition and the Progressive Movement,* pp. 149–180; Odegard, *Pressure Politics,* pp. 67–69, 166–171; Kerr, *Organized for Prohibition,* pp. 200–207; *New York Times,* May 1, 1917, p. 10.
55. Robert A. Hohner, *Prohibition and Politics: The Life of Bishop James Cannon, Jr.* (Columbia, SC: University of South Carolina Press, 1999), pp. 109–112.
56. *New York Times,* April 19, 1917, p. 14; May 8, 1917, p. 6; January 8, 1918, p. 4; January 29, 1918, p. 13.
57. Odegard, *Pressure Politics,* p. 71.
58. Ibid., p. 70; Timberlake, *Prohibition and the Progressive Movement,* p. 179; "The National German-American Alliance and Its Allies—Pro German Brewers and Liquor Dealers: A Disloyal Combination" (Westerville, OH: American Issue Publishing, 1918), p. 18.
59. Drescher, "Opposition to Prohibition," p. 172; Odegard, *Pressure Politics,* pp. 71–72.
60. Odegard, *Pressure Politics,* pp. 71–72; Timberlake, *Prohibition and the Progressive Movement,* p. 165; Binder and Reimers, *All the Nations under Heaven,* pp. 150–151.
61. Drescher, "Opposition to Prohibition," pp. 35–48, 207.
62. Chris McNickle, "When New York Was Irish, and After," in Ronald H. Bayor and Timothy J. Meagher, eds., *The New York Irish* (Baltimore: Johns Hopkins University Press, 1996), p. 350; Binder and Reimers, *All the Nations under Heaven,* pp. 151–152.
63. *New York Times,* January 16, 1919, p. 12.
64. Andrew Nilsen Rygg, *Norwegians in New York, 1825–1925* (Brooklyn: Norwegian News Company, 1941), pp. 173–176.
65. *The Messenger,* February 1920, p. 11.
66. *The Crisis,* April 1920, pp. 327–328.
67. *Variety,* December 26, 1919, p. 9; April 30, 1919, p. 4.
68. *New York Times,* February 2, 1919, Section II, p. 7; "Prohibition's Effect on Meals and Movies," January 19, 1919, Section IV, p. 1; April 11, 1920, Section VI, p. 10.
69. *New York Evening Post,* January 17, 1919, p. 8; *New York Sun,* January 17, 1919, p. 6; *New York Times,* January 17, 1919, p. 12.
70. *New York Times,* January 26, 1919, p. 5; *New York Sun,* January 14, 1919, p. 5.
71. "The Prohibition Amendment," *The Outlook,* February 5, 1919, pp. 212–213; *New York Sun,* January 14, 1919, p. 5.

2. A New Era?

1. *New York Herald,* January 15, 1920, p. 1.
2. *Current Opinion,* May 1920, p. 613.

3. *New York Times,* January 17, 1919, p. 4.

4. MANY, District Attorney Scrapbooks, April 11, 1921.

5. Lewis A. Erenberg, *Steppin' Out: New York Nightlife and the Transformation of American Culture, 1890–1930* (Chicago: University of Chicago Press, 1981), pp. 234–235; *New York Times,* April 18, 1917, p. 4; February 21, 1919, p. 1.

6. *New York Times,* November 20, 1918, p. 14; November 22, 1918, p. 1; K. Austin Kerr, *Organized For Prohibition: A New History of the Anti-Saloon League* (New Haven: Yale University Press, 1985), pp. 206–207.

7. *New York Evening Post,* June 30, 1919, p. 1.

8. *New York Times,* June 6, 1919, p. 11; June 30, 1919, pp. 1, 7; July 3, 1919, p. 9; *New York Evening Post,* June 30, 1919, p. 1; July 2, 1919, p. 2; July 3, 1919, p. 2.

9. *New York Times,* August 3, 1919, Section II, p. 1.

10. *New York Evening Post,* June 30, 1919, p. 1; *New York Times,* July 3, 1919, p. 4; July 5, 1919, p. 22.

11. Kerr, *Organized for Prohibition,* pp. 225–226.

12. Nuala McGann Drescher, "Labor and Prohibition: The Unappreciated Impact of the Eighteenth Amendment," in David E. Kyvig, ed., *Law, Alcohol, and Order: Perspectives on National Prohibition* (Westport, CT: Greenwood Press, 1985), pp. 41–42; David J. Goldberg, *Discontented America: The United States in the 1920s* (Baltimore: Johns Hopkins University Press, 1999), p. 55.

13. Goldberg, *Discontented America,* p. 56; Jenna Weissman Joselet, *Our Gang: Jewish Crime and the New York Jewish Community, 1900–1945* (Bloomington: Indiana University Press, 1983), p. 89.

14. Kerr, *Organized for Prohibition,* pp. 222–226; Charles Merz, *The Dry Decade* (Seattle: University of Washington Press, 1969), pp. 105–106.

15. *New York Times,* October 28, 1919, pp. 1, 3; Kerr, *Organized for Prohibition,* p. 225; Merz, *The Dry Decade,* pp. 49–50.

16. *New York Herald,* January 17, 1920, p. 10.

17. *New York Clipper,* July 9, 1919, p. 6.

18. *New York Clipper,* November 5, 1919, p. 4; *Variety,* December 30, 1921, p. 126; NYPL, Committee of Fourteen Papers, Box 34, Folder "1920," report signed H. K., November 11, 1920; William Grimes, *Straight up or on the Rocks: The Story of the American Cocktail* (New York: North Point Press, 2001), p. 86.

19. District Attorney Scrapbooks, April 23, 1921; *Variety,* December 26, 1919, p. 18; May 21, 1920, p. 1; October 25, 1923, p. 3; June 10, 1925, p. 1; *Gaelic American,* December 20, 1919, p. 7.

20. *New York Herald,* January 2, 1920, p. 8.

21. *New York Evening Post,* March 6, 1920, p. 10; *The Crisis,* April 1920, pp. 327–328; *Variety,* April 16, 1920, p. 10; August 18, 1922, p. 5; August 25, 1922, p. 1.

22. *New York Times,* April 28, 1919, p. 8; May 22, 1919, p. 22; "Plans for Dry New York," June 8, 1919, Section VII, p. 1.

23. *New York Evening Post,* July 2, 1919, p. 2; James H. Timberlake, *Prohibition and the Progressive Movement, 1900–1920* (Cambridge: Harvard University Press, 1963), p. 77; Raymond Calkins, *Substitutes for the Saloon* (Boston: Houghton Mifflin Co., 1919), p. xxii.

24. *New York Times,* January 17, 1919, p. 4; January 25, 1920, p. 19; *Variety,* December 31, 1920, p. 11; Robert E. Corradini, *Broadway, the Greatest Street in America, under Prohibition: A Survey of This Great Thoroughfare, Comparing Present Conditions with Those of Pre-*

Prohibition Days (Washington, D.C.: World League against Alcoholism, [1924]), pp. 11, 20–21; Grimes, *Straight Up*, p. 6.

25. *New York Times,* January 24, 1919, p. 4; February 2, 1919, Section II, p. 1; August 11, 1919, p. 5; Kyvig, *Repealing National Prohibition*, p. 39; *Variety*, May 13, 1921, p. 21; *Literary Digest*, July 12, 1919, pp. 32–33; August 16, 1919, p. 60; Calkins, *Substitutes for the Saloon*, pp. x–xi; Corradini, *Broadway*, pp. 20–21.

26. Corradini, *Broadway*, pp. 11, 20–21, 24; *New York Times*, August 13, 1919, p. 2.

27. Corradini, *Broadway*, p. 11.

28. *New York Clipper*, July 9, 1919, pp. 3, 6; Erenberg, *Steppin' Out*, p. 207.

29. *Variety*, November 11, 1921, p. 1; December 9, 1921, p. 20; *New York Evening Post*, July 1, 1919, p. 1; Corradini, *Broadway*, p. 11; Erenberg, *Steppin' Out*, pp. 36, 238; Michael and Ariane Batterberry, *On the Town in New York* (New York: Routledge, 1999), p. 203.

30. Committee of Fourteen Papers, Box 34, Folder "1920," report by "HK," dated April 11, 1920; unsigned report dated December 5, 1919; *Variety*, April 30, 1920, p. 5.

31. Robert E. Corradini, *Saloon Survey—New York City: Changes in Saloon Property after the First Three Years and after Five Years of Prohibition* (Westerville, OH: World League against Alcoholism, [1925]), pp. 11–12, 24; *New York Times*, February 22, 1920, p. 1; Arnold Shaw, *The Street That Never Slept: New York's Fabled 52nd Street* (New York: Coward, McGann and Geoghegan, 1971), p. 13.

32. Corradini, *Saloon Survey*, p. 12.

33. Corradini, *Broadway*, pp. 11, 24; Stanley Walker, *The Night Club Era* (New York: Frederick A. Stokes, 1933), p. 57.

34. *What Became of Distilleries, Breweries and Saloons in the United States of America?* (Washington, D.C.: World League against Alcoholism, n.d.), pp. 11–13.

35. Corradini, *Saloon Survey*, pp. 12, 19.

36. *New York Clipper*, August 13, 1919, p. 5; September 17, 1919, p. 7; *Variety*, April 22, 1921, p. 13; June 3, 1921, p. 11.

37. *New York City under Prohibition* (Washington, D.C.: World League against Alcoholism, [1923]), pp. 1–2; *The Outlook*, April 28, 1920, pp. 741–742.

38. "Bowery Is Rolling in Wealth, Day of Down-and-Outer Gone," *The Sun and New York Herald*, March 14, 1920, Section VII, p. 1.

39. "Making a Joke of Prohibition in New York City," *New York Times*, May 2, 1920, Section VII, p. 1.

40. *Amsterdam News*, February 21, 1923, p. 12; December 29, 1926, p. 14; *The Minute Man*, December 22, 1925, p. 126; District Attorney Scrapbooks, January 22, 1921; *Variety*, March 3, 1922, pp. 1, 2; *New York Times*, September 18, 1922, p. 7; Isidore Einstein, *Prohibition Agent #1* (New York: Frederick A. Stokes, 1932), p. 120.

41. *Address of Police Commissioner Richard E. Enright, New York City, by Radio on Police Problems,* "Prohibition," October 23, 1923; New York City Magistrate's Court, *Annual Report*, 1920, p. 52; Annual Report, 1927, p. 61.

42. *New York Times*, May 9, 1920, Section VIII, p. 9; *New York Evening Post*, January 7, 1921, p. 5; NYPL, Social Science Research Council Papers, Box 5, Folder 2.

43. Peter H. Odegard, *Pressure Politics: The Story of the Anti-Saloon League* (New York: Columbia University Press, 1928, repr., New York: Octagon Books, 1966), p. 234; Merz, *The Dry Decade*, pp. 216–220.

3. A Hopeless and Thankless Task

1. *New York Evening Post,* December 27, 1920, p. 2; December 28, 1920, p. 2; January 3, 1921, p. 1; *New York World,* December 27, 1920, pp. 1, 3; December 28, 1920, p. 6; December 29, 1920, p. 4; January 4, 1921, p. 7; MANY, District Attorney Scrapbooks, January 1–4, 1921.

2. District Attorney Scrapbooks, January 1–4, 1921.

3. Ibid.

4. *New York Times,* January 6, 1921, p. 3.

5. Richard F. Hamm, *Shaping the Eighteenth Amendment: Temperance Reform, Legal Culture, and the Polity, 1880–1920* (Chapel Hill: University of North Carolina Press, 1995), pp. 250–255.

6. Rayman L. Solomon, "Regulating the Regulators: Prohibition Enforcement in the Seventh Circuit," in David E. Kyvig, ed., *Law, Alcohol, and Order: Perspectives on National Prohibition* (Westport, CT: Greenwood Press, 1985), p. 93; Hamm, *Shaping the Eighteenth Amendment,* pp. 250–255; Norman H. Clark, *Deliver Us from Evil: An Interpretation of American Prohibition* (New York: W. W. Norton and Co., 1976), pp. 160–162; David E. Kyvig, *Repealing National Prohibition* (Chicago: University of Chicago Press, 1979), p. 23.

7. Clark, *Deliver Us from Evil,* pp. 161–165; Charles Merz, *The Dry Decade* (Seattle: University of Washington Press, 1969), pp. 81–84.

8. *New York Times,* December 18, 1921, Section II, p. 1.

9. Merz, *The Dry Decade,* p. 56.

10. K. Austin Kerr, *Organized for Prohibition: A New History of the Anti-Saloon League* (New Haven: Yale University Press, 1985), pp. 222–228; Kyvig, *Repealing National Prohibition,* p. 31.

11. *New York Evening Post,* March 12, 1920, p. 7; March 15, 1920, p. 1; *New York Times,* October 12, 1920, p. 17; October 15, 1920, p. 10; October 16, 1920, p. 23; October 20, 1920, p. 32; District Attorney Scrapbooks, March 13, 1920; October 12, 14, 21, 1920.

12. *New York Times,* April 22, 1920, p. 17; April 26, 1920, p. 8.

13. NARA, Record Group 21, Southern District of New York, Box 171, Docket Number C26–351; *New York Times,* December 30, 1920, p. 9; *New York Sun,* December 29, 1920, p. 2; *New York Evening Post,* December 29, 1920, p. 1.

14. *New York Evening Post,* January 6, 1921, p. 1; *New York Times,* January 14, 1921, p. 2; October 16, 1919, p. 16.

15. *New York Times,* December 2, 1920, p. 8.

16. Southern District of New York, Box 168, Docket Number C26–71; Box 163, September 8, 1920.

17. District Attorney Scrapbooks, March 13, 1920; *Variety,* June 3, 1921, p. 37; October 20, 1922, p. 9; May 19, 1922, p. 38; November 2, 1922, p. 21.

18. *New York Times,* August 11, 1920, p. 15; *Variety,* May 19, 1922, p. 38.

19. *New York Times,* October 9, 1921, p. 2; October 10, 1921, p. 15.

20. *New York Times,* January 14, 1921, p. 2; April 2, 1921, p. 9; December 3, 1921, p. 12; *Variety,* July 14, 1922, p. 11; Laurence F. Schmeckebier, *The Bureau of Prohibition: Its History, Activities and Organization* (Washington, D.C.: Brookings Institution, Institute for Government Research, 1929, reprint, New York: AMS Press, 1974), pp. 45, 47.

21. *New York Sun,* November 30, 1920, p. 11; December 28, 1920, p. 3; *New York Times,*

December 1, 1921, p. 15; Schmeckebier, *Bureau of Prohibition*, pp. 51–52; Thomas Repetto, *American Mafia: A History of Its Rise to Power* (New York: Henry Holt and Co., 2004), p. 108.

22. Hamm, *Shaping the Eighteenth Amendment*, p. 254.

23. William F. Swindler, "A Dubious Constitutional Experiment," in Kyvig, ed., *Law, Alcohol, and Order*, pp. 57–58.

24. *New York Times*, February 3, 1920, p. 4.

25. MNHS, Andrew J. Volstead Papers, Folder "Correspondence and Other Papers, September 22 to November 28, 1921," Letter from "Democritus," October 20, 1921.

26. Stephen Graham, *New York Nights* (New York: George H. Doran, 1927), pp. 71, 73; *New York Times*, June 9, 1920, p. 17; February 24, 1921, pp. 1–2.

27. CUOHC, *The Reminiscences of August W. Flath* (1958), p. 18; NYPL, Committee of Fourteen Papers, Box 35, Folder "1926," report on Pete's Place, 2064 Eighth Avenue, n.d.

28. *New York Times*, June 23, 1921, p. 7; July 4, 1921, p. 14; September 14, 1922, p. 23.

29. NYPD, *Annual Report*, 1921, p. 10.

30. *New York Times*, April 12, 1920, p. 14; May 9, 1920, Section VIII, p. 9; January 14, 1921, p. 2; *New York Sun*, November 19, 1920, pp. 1, 3.

31. District Attorney Scrapbooks, April 5–16, 1921; *New York Times*, April 5, 1921, p. 21; April 13, 1921, p. 14.

32. District Attorney Scrapbooks, April 5, 1921; *New York Times*, January 21, 1921, p. 1; April 5, 1921, p. 21; April 13, 1921, p. 14.

33. CUOHC, *Reminiscences of William H. Anderson* (1950), pp. 32–33; *New York Evening Post*, January 13, 1921, p. 6; *New York Times*, January 21, 1921, p. 1; April 8, 1921, p. 12.

34. *New York Times*, April 11, 1921, p. 1; District Attorney Scrapbooks, April 7, 1921, April 12, 1921; *Variety*, May 6, 1921, p. 33; NYPD, *Annual Report*, 1921, p. 387.

35. *The Minute Man*, December 22, 1925, p. 134.

36. *New York World*, July 23, 1921; District Attorney Scrapbooks, September 1, 1921.

37. District Attorney Scrapbooks, April 30, 1921; *New York Times*, May 26, 1921, p. 17; *Variety*, January 19, 1923, p. 25.

38. Merz, *The Dry Decade*, pp. 205–206.

39. NYPD, *Annual Report*, 1921, pp. 8–9.

40. *New York Herald*, May 22, 1921, p. 1; District Attorney Scrapbooks, August 21, 1921; *New York Times*, January 6, 1923, p. 15; December 10, 1920, p. 4.

41. *Between Wars: An Oral History* (New York: Community Documentation Workshop at St. Mark's Church-in-the-Bowery, 1980), p. 22; *New York Times*, December 18, 1921, Section II, p. 1.

42. Humbert S. Nelli, *The Business of Crime: Italians and Syndicate Crime in the United States* (New York: Oxford University Press, 1976), pp. 160–161; Caroline Ware, *Greenwich Village, 1920–1930: A Comment on American Civilization in the Post-War Years* (1935, repr., New York: Octagon Books, 1977), pp. 57, 60, 72–73.

43. *New York Times*, September 5, 1920, Section VII, p. 20; *Between Wars*, p. 16.

44. District Attorney Scrapbooks, *New York World*, February 10, 1921.

45. District Attorney Scrapbooks, February 10, 1921, April 16, 1923; Ware, *Greenwich Village*, pp. 61–62; Graham, *New York Nights*, p. 75; James Lardner and Thomas Repetto, *NYPD: A City and Its Police* (New York: Henry Holt and Co., 2000), p. 200.

46. Graham, *New York Nights,* p. 187; Mary Kingsbury Simkhovitch, *Neighborhood: My Story of Greenwich House* (New York: W. W. Norton and Co., 1938), p. 205; Peter Kriendler's comments were made at a panel discussion on Prohibition at the New-York Historical Society, April 12, 1997.

47. *New York Times,* June 9, 1920, p. 17; District Attorney Scrapbooks, April 11, 1921, November 24, 1921.

48. CUOHC, *The Reminiscences of William O'Dwyer* (1962), p. 99.

49. Committee of Fourteen Papers, Box 36, Folder "First Street—," report on Mingo's speakeasy, 167 E. Fourth St., n.d.; *Reminiscences of William O'Dwyer,* p. 99; *New York Times,* May 2, 1920, Section VII, p. 1.

50. District Attorney Scrapbooks, July 30, 1921, August 2, 1921, October 15, 1921.

51. Gerald Gunther, *Learned Hand: The Man and the Judge* (New York: Alfred A. Knopf, 1994), pp. 271, 305–306; *New York Times,* January 26, 1920, p. 2.

52. William E. Nelson, "The Changing Meaning of Equality in Twentieth-Century Constitutional Law," *Washington and Lee Law Review,* vol. 52, no. 1 (1995), pp. 10–19; Lardner and Repetto, *NYPD,* pp. 207–208; *New York Times,* August 12, 1920, p. 15; October 19, 1920, p. 32; District Attorney Scrapbooks, July 23, 1921.

53. New York City Magistrate's Court, *Annual Report,* 1920, p. 5.

54. Southern District of New York, Box 161, various cases; District Attorney Scrapbooks, March 10, 1921.

55. District Attorney Scrapbooks, March 19, 1921.

56. NYPD, *Annual Report,* 1921, pp. 11, 88–89.

57. District Attorney Scrapbooks, April 5–16, 1921, July 23, 1921; *New York Journal,* April 28, 1921, p. 1; *New York Times,* April 5, 1921, p. 21.

58. District Attorney Scrapbooks, July 24, 1921.

59. District Attorney Scrapbooks, April 17, 1921, July 23, 1921.

60. *New York Herald,* May 20, 1921, p. 18; *New York Times,* September 10, 1921, p. 4; September 17, 1921, p. 15; October 15, 1921, p. 1; District Attorney Scrapbooks, April 29, 1921.

61. Albert W. Altschuler, "Plea Bargaining and Its History," *Law and Society Review,* Winter 1979, p. 230; Lawrence M. Friedman, "Plea Bargaining in a Historical Perspective," *Law and Society Review,* Winter 1979, p. 255.

62. *New York Times,* June 22, 1920, p. 5.

63. Southern District of New York, Box 145, Docket Nos. C21–84 (Landraf); C21–83 (Berger); C21–85 (Rose); C21–91 (Gorman); C21–96 (Schiff); C21–88 (Cohen); Box 151, Docket No. C22–246 (Fitzgerald); MANY, Department of Probation Records, 1923, Loc. No. 127577, cases 12004, 12005, 12006, 12007, and 12024.

64. Southern District of New York, Box 145, Docket No. C21–25 *(U.S. v. James J. Murphy);* Box 147, C21–278 *(U.S. v. Anthony Solitore).*

65. District Attorney Scrapbooks, April 11, 1921.

66. District Attorney Scrapbooks, January 17, 1921, April 10, 1921; NYPD, *Annual Report,* 1924, p. 111; *Address of Police Commissioner Richard E. Enright, New York City, by Radio on Police Problems,* "Prohibition," October 23, 1923; New York City Magistrate's Court, *Annual Report,* "Ten Year Comparison of Arraignments," 1931, p. 39.

67. Robert A. Slayton, *Empire Statesman: The Rise and Redemption of Al Smith* (New York: The Free Press, 2001), pp. 154–155.

68. Richard O'Connor, *The Last Hurrah: A Biography of Alfred E. Smith* (New York: G. P.

Putnam's Sons, 1970), p. 143; Paula Eldot, *Governor Alfred E. Smith: The Politician as Reformer* (New York: Garland Publishing, 1983), p. 361; Slayton, *Al Smith,* pp. 196–200.

69. O'Connor, *The Last Hurrah,* p. 143.

70. Alfred E. Smith, "Memorandum Accompanying Approval of the Bill to Repeal the Mullan-Gage Law," *Progressive Democracy: Addresses and State Papers of Alfred E. Smith* (New York: Harcourt, Brace and Co., 1928), p. 284; Slayton, *Al Smith,* pp. 197–199.

71. *New York Times,* June 2, 1923, p. 2; June 26, 1923, p. 12; Slayton, *Al Smith,* pp. 196–201.

72. *Amsterdam News,* June 6, 1923, p. 3.

73. Enright, "Prohibition," October 23, 1923.

4. The Brewers of Bigotry

1. MANY, District Attorney Scrapbooks, May 13, 1921.

2. Kenneth D. Rose, *American Women and the Repeal of Prohibition* (New York: New York University Press, 1996), p. 165; Robert A. Hohner, *Prohibition and Politics: The Life of Bishop James Cannon, Jr.* (Columbia: University of South Carolina Press, 1999), pp. 149, 232–233; David M. Fahey, *Temperance and Racism: John Bull, Johnny Reb, and the Good Templars* (Lexington: University Press of Kentucky, 1996); Ruth Bordin, *Woman and Temperance: The Quest for Power and Liberty, 1873–1900* (New Brunswick: Rutgers University Press, 1990), pp. 82–85.

3. Maxine S. Seller, "Protestant Evangelism and the Italian Immigrant Woman," in Betty Boyd Caroli, Robert F. Harney, and Lydio F. Tomasi, eds., *The Italian Immigrant Woman in North America* (Toronto: Multicultural History Society of Ontario, 1978), pp. 124–125; Edward A. Ross, "Italians in America," *Century,* May-October 1914, p. 443; Robert Alston Stevenson, "Saloons," *Scribner's,* May 1901, p. 573; George E. Pozzetta, "The Mulberry District in New York City: The Years before World War I," in Robert F. Harney and J. Vincent Scarpaci, eds., *Little Italies of North America* (Toronto: Multicultural History Society of Ontario, 1981), p. 36.

4. Paul S. Boyer, *Urban Masses and Moral Order in America, 1820–1920* (Cambridge: Harvard University Press, 1978), p. 205; Peter H. Odegard, *Pressure Politics: The Story of the Anti-Saloon League* (New York: Columbia University Press, 1928), p. 29.

5. *New York Times,* January 17, 1919, p. 4.

6. *New York Times,* August 5, 1923, Section VII, p. 4; Ira Rosenwaike, *Population History of New York City* (Syracuse: Syracuse University Press, 1972), Ch. 5; *New York City under Prohibition* (Washington, D.C.: World League against Alcoholism, [1923]), p. 1; Odegard, *Pressure Politics,* p. 233; Deborah Dash Moore, *At Home in America: Second Generation New York Jews* (New York: Columbia University Press, 1981), p. 21; George E. Pozzetta, "The Italians of New York City, 1890–1914" (Ph.D. diss., University of North Carolina, Chapel Hill, 1971), p. 78; Pozzetta, "The Mulberry District," p. 7; Marion R. Casey, "'From the East Side to the Seaside': Irish Americans on the Move in New York City," in Ronald H. Bayor and Timothy J. Meagher, eds., *The New York Irish* (Baltimore: Johns Hopkins University Press, 1996), p. 396; Gilbert Osofsky, *Harlem: The Making of a Ghetto* (New York: Harper and Row, 1968), pp. 128–130.

7. Robert E. Corradini, *Saloon Survey—New York City: Changes in Saloon Property after the First Three Years and after Five Years of Prohibition* (Westerville, OH: World League against Alcoholism, [1925]), pp. 6–7.

8. NYPL, Committee of Fourteen Papers, Box 34, Folder "1920," various reports.

9. Ibid.; Travis Hoke, "Corner Saloon," *American Mercury*, March 1931, p. 314; Clyde V. Kiser, *Sea Island to City: A Study of St. Helena Islanders in Harlem and Other Urban Centers* (1932, repr. New York: Atheneum, 1969), p. 46.

10. Corradini, *Saloon Survey*, p. 10; Frederick Binder and David Reimers, *All the Nations under Heaven: An Ethnic and Racial History of New York City* (New York: Columbia University Press, 1995), pp. 61, 64; *New York City under Prohibition*, p. 1.

11. Charles Stelzle, *A Son of the Bowery: The Life Story of an East Side American* (New York: George H. Doran, 1926), pp. 47–48.

12. Perry Duis, *The Saloon: Public Drinking in Chicago and Boston, 1880–1920* (Urbana: University of Illinois Press, 1983), pp. 95–97, 105–106, 191–192.

13. Raymond Calkins, *Substitutes for the Saloon* (Boston: Houghton Mifflin, 1919), pp. 9, 22; Hasia Diner, *Hungering for America: Italian, Irish, and Jewish Foodways in the Age of Migration* (Cambridge: Harvard University Press, 2001), pp. 134–140; Stevenson, "Saloons," p. 573; Stephen Graham, *New York Nights* (New York: George H. Doran, 1927), p. 72; Kathy Peiss, *Cheap Amusements: Working Women and Leisure in Turn-of-the-Century New York* (Philadelphia: Temple University Press, 1986), p. 18; Madelon Powers, "The 'Poor Man's Friend': Workers and the Code of Reciprocity in U.S. Barrooms, 1870–1920," *International Labor and Working-Class History*, Spring 1994, p. 2.

14. Jon D. Cruz, "Booze and Blues: Alcohol and Black Popular Music, 1920–1930," *Contemporary Drug Problems*, Summer 1988, pp. 149–186; Richard Stivers, *Hair of the Dog: Irish Drinking and American Stereotype* (University Park, PA: Pennsylvania State University Press, 1976), pp. 127–129; Committee of Fourteen Papers, Box 35, Folder "1926," report dated October 29, 1926; Folder "1930," various reports; Michael Gold, "East Side Memories," *American Mercury*, September 1929, p. 97.

15. Jon M. Kingsdale, "The 'Poor Man's Club': Social Functions of the Working-Class Saloon," *American Quarterly*, October 1973, p. 487.

16. Calkins, *Substitutes for the Saloon*, p. 62.

17. Stelzle, *Son of the Bowery*, p. 48.

18. Duis, *The Saloon*, pp. 54, 121–127, 182; Powers, "The 'Poor Man's Friend,'" p. 8; Calkins, *Substitutes for the Saloon*, p. xxii.

19. Stelzle, *Son of the Bowery*, pp. 24, 48–49; Caroline Ware, *Greenwich Village, 1920–1930: A Comment on American Civilization in the Post-War Years* (1935, repr., New York: Octagon Books, 1977), pp. 55–56; Hutchins Hapgood, "McSorley's Saloon," *Harper's Weekly*, October 25, 1913, p. 15.

20. *Literary Digest*, January 25, 1919, p. 9; *Il Progreso*, January 17, 1919, advertisement of A. J. Musco, 178 Mott Street.

21. Rollin Lynde Hart, "Made in Italy," *The Independent*, July 23, 1921, p. 19; Binder and Reimers, *All the Nations under Heaven*, p. 166; Mary Kingsbury Simkhovitch, *Neighborhood: My Story of Greenwich House* (New York: W. W. Norton and Co., 1938), p. 204; Ware, *Greenwich Village*, pp. 56–58; Martha Bensley Bruère, *Does Prohibition Work?: A Study of the Operation of the Eighteenth Amendment Made by the National Federation of Settlements* (New York: Harper and Brothers, 1927), p. 257.

22. *American Monthly*, January 1919, p. 143; February 1919, p. 174; *Literary Digest*, January 25, 1919, p. 9; *Irish World*, February 15, 1919, p. 5.

23. *New York Times*, March 13, 1920, p. 4.

24. *New York Times,* February 21, 1920, p. 1; *The Sun and New York Herald,* "Rush of Aliens Home Puzzling Labor Men," March 14, 1920, Section VII, p. 2.

25. *New York Times,* July 3, 1919, p. 12.

26. *Daily News,* January 23, 1920, p. 3.

27. *New York Sun,* November 19, 1920, p. 3.

28. NARA, Record Group 21, Southern District of New York, Box 165, Docket Number C25–172.

29. Southern District of New York, Box 147, Docket Number C21–253.

30. District Attorney Scrapbooks, August 10–29, 1920; *New York Times,* August 11, 1920, pp. 1, 4.

31. District Attorney Scrapbooks, August 10–29, 1920; *New York Times,* August 19, 1920, p. 7; August 23, 1920, p. 6; August 28, 1920, p. 18; August 29, 1920, p. 5; *New York Herald,* May 3, 1921, p. 24.

32. District Attorney Scrapbooks, September 1, 1920.

33. *Between Wars: An Oral History* (New York: Community Documentation Workshop at St. Mark's Church-in-the-Bowery, 1980), p. 24.

34. Southern District of New York, Box 169, Docket Number C26–123; Albert W. Altschuler, "Plea Bargaining and Its History," *Law and Society Review,* Winter 1979, p. 233.

35. NYPL, Social Science Research Council Papers, Box 1, Folder 1, letters to American Management Association, n.d.; letter from Eda A. Effeld, Research Secretary, Charity Organization Society, March 27, 1926; Matthew Josephson, *Union House, Union Bar: The History of the Hotel and Restaurant Employees and Bartenders International Union* (New York: Random House, 1956), p. 131fn.

36. Lillian D. Wald, *Windows on Henry Street* (New York: Little, Brown and Co., 1933), pp. 211, 221; Bruère, *Does Prohibition Work?* p. 272.

37. Committee of Fourteen Papers, Box 35, Folder "1926," Letter from Cranston Brenton, November 4, 1926; Isidore Einstein, *Prohibition Agent #1* (New York: Frederick A. Stokes, 1932), pp. 37–38.

38. Einstein, *Prohibition Agent #1,* pp. 4, 15, 30–31.

39. Timothy J. Gilfoyle, *City of Eros: New York City, Prostitution, and the Commercialization of Sex, 1790–1920* (New York: W. W. Norton and Co., 1992), pp. 303–306; Kevin J. Mumford, *Interzones: Black/White Sex Districts in Chicago and New York in the Early Twentieth Century* (New York: Columbia University Press, 1997), p. 21.

40. Committee of Fourteen Papers, Box 34, Folder "1920," reports signed "H. K." [Harry Kahan], dated June 16, 1920; June 19, 1920; December 11, 1920; Folder "1921," unsigned report dated September 9, 1921.

41. Committee of Fourteen Papers, Box 35, Folder "1924—Democratic Nat'l Convention," Letter from District Attorney's office to Harry Kahan, n.d.; *New York Times,* November 12, 1922, p. 21; August 3, 1922, p. 17; May 8, 1922, p. 5; February 27, 1921, pp. 1, 6.

42. Southern District of New York, Boxes 145, 146, Docket Numbers C21–29, C21–35, C21–134.

43. *New York Times,* December 19, 1923, p. 8.

44. *New York Sun,* November 16, 1920, p. 3.

45. Odegard, *Pressure Politics,* p. 233; *New York Times,* November 5, 1919, p. 15; June 12, 1923, p. 3; July 11, 1923, p. 3.

46. *America,* March 15, 1919, p. 587.

47. *New York Evening Post,* March 6, 1920, p. 3; "Mr. Anderson's Quarrel with Roman Catholics over the Liquor Question," *Current Opinion,* May 1920, p. 674.

48. *New York Daily Tribune,* March 9, 1920, pp. 1, 6; *New York Evening Post,* March 9, 1920, p. 16; *Irish World,* March 20, 1920, p. 2; "Mr. Anderson's Quarrel," p. 675.

49. *New York Evening Post,* March 9, 1920, p. 16; "False Witness," *The Outlook,* March 24, 1920, pp. 504–505.

50. Odegard, *Pressure Politics,* p. 27.

51. *The Sun and New York Herald,* March 12, 1920, p. 2.

52. *New York Herald,* May 27, 1921, p. 22; *Irish World,* November 17, 1923, p. 7.

53. Jenna Weissman Joselet, *Our Gang: Jewish Crime and the New York Jewish Community, 1900–1945* (Bloomington: Indiana University Press, 1983), p. 86.

54. Ibid., p. 88; Hannah Sprecher, "'Let Them Drink and Forget Our Poverty': Orthodox Rabbis React to Prohibition," *American Jewish Archives,* Fall/Winter 1991, p. 141.

55. Sprecher, "Let Them Drink," pp. 136–140.

56. Ibid., pp. 153–154, 163.

57. *New York Times,* November 12, 1922, p. 21; December 23, 1921, pp. 1, 6; December 25, 1921, p. 5; February 1, 1922, p. 21; Sprecher, "Let Them Drink," pp. 143–149, 163; LOC, Lincoln C. Andrews Scrapbooks; District Attorney Scrapbooks, May 18, 1921.

58. Lincoln C. Andrews Scrapbooks; Laurence F. Schmeckebier, *The Bureau of Prohibition: Its History, Activities and Organization* (Washington, D.C.: Brookings Institution, Institute for Government Research, 1929, reprint, New York: AMS Press, 1974), p. 98; Sprecher, "Let Them Drink," p. 154.

59. District Attorney Scrapbooks, April 22, 1921.

60. Sprecher, "Let Them Drink," p. 165.

61. Ibid., pp. 163–164.

62. *New York Times,* September 15, 1922, p. 21; January 25, 1923, p. 10; January 26, 1923, p. 11; January 27, 1923, p. 4; January 28, 1923, p. 5.

63. MNHS, Andrew J. Volstead Papers, Folder "Correspondence and Other Papers— June 15 to July 14, 1921," Letter from "Jas. Intolerance," June 22, 1921; unsigned letter c. June 28, 1921; *Daily News,* March 11, 1920, p. 9.

64. *New York Times,* June 19, 1921, Section VII, p. 1; *New York Herald,* July 5, 1921, pp. 1, 6.

65. *New York Herald,* May 23, 1921, p. 20.

5. The Itch to Try New Things

1. Billy Altman, *Laughter's Gentle Soul: The Life of Robert Benchley* (New York: W. W. Norton and Co., 1997), pp. 222–223; Babette Rosmond, *Robert Benchley: His Life and Good Times* (New York: Doubleday and Co., 1970), pp. 112–113; Marion Meade, *Dorothy Parker: What Fresh Hell Is This?* (New York: Villard Books, 1988), p. xviii; Harrison Kinney, *James Thurber: His Life and Times* (New York: Henry Holt and Co., 1995), pp. 378–380.

2. Altman, *Laughter's Gentle Soul,* pp. 222–223.

3. Meade, *Dorothy Parker,* pp. 93–94; Rosmond, *Robert Benchley,* p. 100.

4. Altman, *Laughter's Gentle Soul,* pp. 30, 36–38, 98, 221–222; Meade, *Dorothy Parker,* pp. 93–94.

5. Meade, *Dorothy Parker,* pp. 93–94; Rosmond, *Robert Benchley,* pp. 100, 111, 119.

6. Rosmond, *Robert Benchley*, p. 111; Altman, *Laughter's Gentle Soul*, pp. 357–360.

7. Meade, *Dorothy Parker*, pp. xvi–xviii.

8. Ibid., p. xvi; Kinney, *James Thurber*, p. 378.

9. Lewis Erenberg, *Steppin' Out: New York Nightlife and the Transformation of American Culture, 1890–1930* (Chicago: University of Chicago Press, 1981), pp. xi–xv, 33–59.

10. *Irish World,* April 30, 1921, p. 5; *Amsterdam News,* August 24, 1927, p. 20; Martha Bensley Bruère, *Does Prohibition Work? A Study of the Operation of the Eighteenth Amendment Made by the National Federation of Settlements* (New York: Harper and Brothers, 1927), p. 275.

11. *Literary Digest,* August 16, 1919, p. 59.

12. William Grimes, *Straight up or on the Rocks: The Story of the American Cocktail* (New York: North Point Press, 2001), pp. 88–89.

13. H. I. Brock, "New York's Cocktail Hour," *New Republic,* January 11, 1922, pp. 180–181.

14. Ibid.

15. *New York Times,* April 5, 1921, p. 21.

16. Stanley Walker, *The Night Club Era* (New York: Frederick A. Stokes, 1933), pp. 81–82.

17. John Mariani, *America Eats Out* (New York: William Morrow and Co., 1991), p. 96; Walker, *The Night Club Era,* p. 82.

18. Walker, *The Night Club Era,* pp. 77–83.

19. *The New Yorker,* February 28, 1925, p. 3.

20. Thomas Kunkel, *Genius in Disguise: Harold Ross of the "New Yorker"* (New York: Random House, 1995), pp. 101–102; James Thurber, *The Years with Ross* (New York: Perennial Classics, 2001), pp. 19–22.

21. Kunkel, *Genius in Disguise,* pp. 101–102; Thurber, *The Years with Ross,* pp. 19–22.

22. Ellin Mackay, "Why We Go to Cabarets: A Post-Debutante Explains," *The New Yorker,* November 28, 1925, p. 7.

23. Thurber, *The Years with Ross,* p. 28; Mary Ellin Barrett, *Irving Berlin: A Daughter's Memoir* (New York: Limelight Editions, 1996), p. 42.

24. Kunkel, *Genius in Disguise,* p. 107; Kinney, *James Thurber,* pp. 378–380.

25. *The New Yorker,* June 13, 1925, p. 20; Caroline Ware, *Greenwich Village, 1920–1930; A Comment on American Civilization in the Post-War Years* (1935, repr., New York: Octagon Books, 1977), p. 370; Ben Yagoda, *About Town: "The New Yorker" and the World It Made* (New York: Da Capo Press, 2001), pp. 96–97.

26. *Variety,* January 3, 1924, p. 15; Howard McLellan, "The High Cost of Nullification," *Review of Reviews,* April 1930, pp. 56–61; *The New Yorker,* January 16, 1926, p. 13; April 18, 1925, p. 18.

27. Mariani, *America Eats Out,* pp. 96–97; Michael and Ariane Batterberry, *On the Town in New York* (New York: Routledge, 1999), pp. 205, 207; Andrew Sinclair, *The Era of Excess* (Boston: Little, Brown and Company, 1962), pp. 230–232; *Variety,* October 14, 1921, p. 12; March 11, 1925, p. 47; *The New Yorker,* January 16, 1926, p. 13; Walker, *The Night Club Era,* p. 102; Grimes, *Straight up or on the Rocks,* pp. 77–82.

28. *The New Yorker,* January 16, 1926, p. 14.

29. Grimes, *Straight up or on the Rocks,* pp. 90–91.

30. Mariani, *America Eats Out,* p. 97; Batterberry, *On the Town in New York,* p. 205; Sinclair, *The Era of Excess,* pp. 230–232.

31. Kinney, *James Thurber,* p. 348.

32. Walker, *The Night Club Era,* pp. 94–102.
33. Ibid., pp. 83, 88.
34. Helen Bullit Lowry, "New York's After Midnight Clubs," *New York Times,* February 5, 1922, Section III, p. 3.
35. Frederic Arnold Kummer, "When Night Clubs Are Trumps," *Ladies' Home Journal,* October 1929, p. 10.
36. MANY, District Attorney Scrapbooks, March 10, 1927; Benjamin de Casseres, "Joel's," *American Mercury,* July 1932, p. 361.
37. Ware, *Greenwich Village,* p. 118.
38. *Variety,* March 24, 1922, p. 1.
39. *Variety,* September 23, 1921, p. 8; December 1, 1922, p. 9; Benjamin de Casseres, *Mirrors of New York* (New York: Joseph Lawren, 1925), pp. 167–168.
40. District Attorney Scrapbooks, July 24, 1921; Louis Graves, "Relative Values in Prohibition," *Atlantic Monthly,* April 1921, p. 527.
41. Warren I. Susman, *Culture as History: The Transformation of American Society in the Twentieth Century* (New York: Pantheon Books, 1984), p. 111.
42. Carl Van Vechten, "A Note on Breakfasts," *American Mercury,* August 1925, p. 488.
43. *Ladies' Home Journal,* August 1931, p. 22.
44. *Irish World,* January 2, 1926, p. 6; Ernest W. Mandeville, "The Biggest City and Its Booze," *Outlook,* March 4, 1925, p. 341.

6. Vote as You Drink

1. *New York Times,* July 4, 1926, p. 3.
2. *New York Times,* March 28, 1923, p. 5.
3. *New York Times,* June 12, 1921, p. 1; *Address of Police Commissioner Richard E. Enright, New York City, by Radio on Police Problems,* "Prohibition," October 23, 1923.
4. Frederick Lewis Allen, *Only Yesterday: An Informal History of the 1920s* (New York: Harper and Row, 1964, repr. 1931), p. 84.
5. *New York Times,* January 17, 1925, p. 4; October 4, 1925, p. 1.
6. *New York Times,* December 11, 1923, p. 23.
7. *New York Times,* January 7, 1922, pp. 1, 11.
8. *Variety,* January 20, 1926, p. 13; March 10, 1926, p. 44; July 14, 1926, p. 45; Edward Robb Ellis, *The Epic of New York City: A Narrative History* (New York: Old Town Books, 1966), pp. 540–543.
9. *New York Times,* March 9, 1925, pp. 1–2; "To Dry New York with Padlocks," *Literary Digest,* March 21, 1925, p. 8.
10. "To Dry New York with Padlocks," p. 9; "Mr. Buckner and His 'De-Bunking' Padlocks," *Literary Digest,* April 11, 1925, p. 56.
11. *New York Times,* April 21, 1925, p. 1; "To Dry New York with Padlocks," p. 9; "Mr. Buckner and His 'De-Bunking' Padlocks," p. 56.
12. *New York Times,* March 7, 1925, p. 12; "To Dry New York with Padlocks," p. 9.
13. Stanley Walker, *The Night Club Era* (New York: Frederick A. Stokes, 1933), pp. 60–61; *New York Times,* April 17, 1925, p. 1; April 21, 1925, p. 20; July 3, 1925, p. 3.
14. *New York Times,* August 1, 1925, pp. 1, 5.
15. *New York Times,* November 21, 1925, pp. 1–2; *Variety,* October 21, 1925, p. 41; October 28, 1925, p. 1; November 18, 1925, p. 1; July 16, 1924, p. 31.

16. Lewis A. Erenberg, *Steppin' Out: New York Nightlife and the Transformation of American Culture, 1890–1930* (Chicago: University of Chicago Press, 1981), p. 239; *The New Yorker*, April 18, 1925, p. 18; *New York Times*, July 16, 1926, p. 14; *Variety*, January 13, 1926, p. 18.

17. Walker, *The Night Club Era*, pp. 240–245; NYPL, Billy Rose Theatre Collection, John S. Stein [and Grace Hayward], "Hello, Sucker! (The Life of Texas Guinan)" (unpublished MS, 1941).

18. *New York Times*, July 3, 1925, p. 3; October 6, 1925, p. 8; November 13, 1925, p. 40; *The New Yorker*, November 14, 1925, pp. 7–8.

19. *The New Yorker*, November 14, 1925, pp. 7–8; *New York Times*, November 13, 1925, p. 40.

20. *New York Times*, November 19, 1925, p. 4; November 21, 1925, p. 1; Justin Steuart, *Wayne Wheeler: Dry Boss* (New York: Fleming H. Revell, 1928), pp. 254–259.

21. *New York Times*, July 3, 1925, p. 3.

22. Gene Fowler, *Beau James: The Life and Times of Jimmy Walker* (New York: Viking Books, 1949), p. 140; Walker, *The Night Club Era*, p. 154; *The New Yorker*, January 16, 1926, p. 11.

23. *New York Times*, November 4, 1925, p. 1; Robert A. Slayton, *Empire Statesman: The Rise and Redemption of Al Smith* (New York: The Free Press, 2001), pp. 221–225; Fowler, *Beau James*, pp. 152–153.

24. Henry F. Pringle, "Jimmy Walker," *American Mercury*, November 26, 1925, p. 272.

25. *The New Yorker*, August 1, 1925, p. 2.

26. Fowler, *Beau James*, pp. 95–109.

27. Ibid., pp. 92–95.

28. *New York Times*, August 24, 1925, pp. 1–2; November 6, 1925, p. 25.

29. Pringle, "Jimmy Walker," p. 273; MANY, James J. Walker Papers, Box 16, Folder "Office of the Mayor—1926," undated speech to Wall Street Firms Association; Ann Douglas, *Terrible Honesty: Mongrel Manhattan in the 1920s* (New York: Farrar, Straus and Giroux, 1995), pp. 12–13.

30. *Between Wars: An Oral History* (New York: Community Documentation Workshop at St. Mark's Church-in-the-Bowery, 1980), pp. 16, 24; *The New Yorker*, August 29, 1925, p. 10.

31. *Between Wars*, pp. 16, 24; *The New Yorker*, August 29, 1925, p. 10.

32. "Tammany in Modern Clothes," *The New Yorker*, January 16, 1926, pp. 11–12; MANY, District Attorney Scrapbooks, January 6, 1926; NYPD, *Annual Report*, 1926, pp. 3–4.

33. James J. Walker Papers, Box 32, Folder "Department of Licenses—1927," Report of the Department of Licenses, 1927; *Variety*, December 15, 1926, p. 1; NYPL, Committee of Fourteen Papers, Box 82, Folder "Dance Hall Laws—1915–30"; Paul Chevigny, *Gigs: Jazz and the Cabaret Laws in New York* (New York: Routledge, 1991), p. 57.

34. *New York Times*, December 18, 1926, p. 36; James J. Walker Papers, Box 44, Folder "Police Dept.—Sept.–Dec. 1928," Letter from NYPD Secretary James Sinott to JJW, dated October 25, 1928; Box 51, Folder "Department of Licenses—1929," Report of the Department of Licenses, 1929; *Variety*, November 23, 1927, p. 57.

35. Chevigny, *Gigs*, pp. 55–57; *Variety*, August 31, 1927, pp. 1, 36.

36. James J. Walker Papers, Box 43, Folder "Office of the Mayor—1928," undated draft of letter from JJW to Mabel Walker Willebrandt; Box 44, Folder "Police Dept.—May–Aug. 1928," Letter from Joseph Warren to Mabel Walker Willebrandt, dated September 7, 1928.

37. James J. Walker Papers, Box 94, Folder "1926—July–Dec—Letters Rcvd—Anonymous," Letter dated August 12, 1926.

38. Douglas, *Terrible Honesty,* p. 12.

39. Ellis, *Epic of New York City,* pp. 523–527, 540–548; *Vanity Fair,* August 1926, p. 30; Herbert Mitgang, *Once upon a Time in New York: Jimmy Walker, Franklin Roosevelt, and the Last Great Battle of the Jazz Age* (New York: The Free Press, 2000), p. 34.

40. Alyn Brodskey, *The Great Mayor: Fiorello LaGuardia and the Making of the City of New York* (New York: St. Martin's Press, 2003), pp. 214–222; Ellis, *Epic of New York City,* p. 527; *Vanity Fair,* August 1926, p. 30.

41. District Attorney Scrapbooks, January 30, 1924; K. Austin Kerr, *Organized for Prohibition: A New History of the Anti-Saloon League* (New Haven: Yale University Press, 1985), pp. 244–248; Paula Eldot, *Governor Alfred E. Smith: The Politician as Reformer* (New York: Garland Publishing, 1983), pp. 368–369; *New York Times,* August 29, 1925, p. 6.

42. Committee of Fourteen Papers, Box 82, Folder "Attacks on Committee of Fourteen," clipping from *New York Telegram,* November 26, 1930.

7. I Represent the Women of America!

1. *New York Times,* November 14, 1920, p. 19; June 7, 1922, p. 40; March 20, 1923, p. 19; NARA, Record Group 21, Southern District Court of New York, Box 163, Docket Nos. C24–482, 483; Box 317, Docket Nos. C46–39, 349; MANY, District Attorney Scrapbooks, April 5, 1921, May 23, 1921.

2. *New York Times,* April 14, 1925, p. 39.

3. *New York Times,* May 11, 1921, p. 1.

4. William H. Chafe, *The Paradox of Change: American Women in the Twentieth Century* (New York: Oxford University Press, 1991), pp. 46–47; Kenneth A. Yellis, "Prosperity's Child: Some Thoughts on the Flapper," *American Quarterly,* Spring 1969, pp. 44–64; Gerald E. Critoph, "The Flapper and Her Critics," in Carol V. G. George, ed., *"Remember the Ladies": New Perspectives on Women in American History* (Syracuse: Syracuse University Press, 1975), pp. 145–160; Bruce Bliven, "Flapper Jane," *The New Republic,* September 9, 1925, p. 67.

5. Stephen Graham, *New York Nights* (New York: George H. Doran, 1927), p. 74; Margaret Culkin Banning, "Anti-Prohibitionette," *Vogue,* September 1, 1930, p. 55; Stanley Walker, *The Night Club Era* (New York: Frederick A. Stokes, 1933), p. 30.

6. Carroll Smith-Rosenberg, *Disorderly Conduct: Visions of Gender in Victorian America* (New York: Alfred A. Knopf, 1985), pp. 14–15; Catherine Gilbert Murdock, *Domesticating Drink: Women, Men, and Alcohol in America, 1870–1940* (Baltimore: Johns Hopkins University Press, 1998), pp. 20–34.

7. Kenneth D. Rose, *American Women and the Repeal of Prohibition* (New York: New York University Press, 1996), p. 32; James H. Timberlake, *Prohibition and the Progressive Movement, 1900–1920* (Cambridge: Harvard University Press, 1963), p. 123.

8. *New York Times,* July 2, 1919, p. 1.

9. Estelle Freedman, "The New Woman: Changing Views of Women in the 1920s," *Journal of American History,* September 1974, pp. 372–393; Smith-Rosenberg, *Disorderly Conduct,* p. 284.

10. Chafe, *Paradox of Change,* p. 106; Bliven, "Flapper Jane," pp. 65–67.

11. Mary Murphy, "Bootlegging Mothers and Drinking Daughters: Gender and Prohi-

bition in Butte, Montana," *American Quarterly*, June 1994, pp. 175–177; Lewis A. Erenberg, *Steppin' Out: New York Nightlife and the Transformation of American Culture, 1890–1930* (Chicago: University of Chicago Press, 1981), p. 135; Perry Duis, *The Saloon: Public Drinking in Chicago and Boston, 1880–1920* (Urbana: University of Illinois Press, 1983), pp. 102–103; Kathy Peiss, *Cheap Amusements: Working Women and Leisure in Turn-of-the-Century New York* (Philadelphia: Temple University Press, 1986), p. 28; Roy Rosenzweig, *Eight Hours for What We Will: Workers and Leisure in an Industrial City, 1870–1920* (Cambridge: Cambridge University Press, 1983), pp. 42–45, 63; Madelon Powers, *Faces along the Bar: Lore and Order in the Workingman's Saloon, 1870–1920* (Chicago: University of Chicago Press, 1998), pp. 32–35, 210–212; Christine Stansell, *American Moderns: Bohemian New York and the Creation of a New Century* (New York: Henry Holt and Co., 2000), p. 12.

12. John Mariani, *America Eats Out* (New York: William Morrow and Company, 1991), p. 207; Graham, *New York Nights,* pp. 63–64; *Variety,* May 24, 1932, pp. 1, 57.

13. *New York Times,* October 12, 1913, Section VIII, p. 2.

14. Harrison Kinney, *James Thurber: His Life and Times* (New York: Henry Holt and Co., 1995), pp. 378–380.

15. Southern District of New York, Box 165, Docket No. C25–174; NYPL, Committee of Fourteen Papers, Box 34, Folder "1920," report dated September 28, 1920; *New York Times,* April 5, 1920, p. 17; Paula S. Fass, *The Damned and the Beautiful: American Youth in the 1920s* (New York: Oxford University Press, 1977), pp. 310–324.

16. H. I. Brock, "New York's Cocktail Hour," *The New Republic,* January 11, 1922, pp. 180–181.

17. *Variety,* December 20, 1926, p. 25.

18. *Variety,* February 15, 1923, p. 30; February 8, 1923, pp. 9, 32; Committee of Fourteen Papers, Box 34, Folder "1921," report on Garden of Joy, dated July 18, 1921, signed H. K.; Folder "1920," report on Hotel Koenig Ballroom, dated May 29, 1920; Box 35, Folder "1926," report on Jewel Restaurant, dated October 5, 1926; *Variety,* February 8, 1923, pp. 9, 32; February 15, 1923, p. 30; George Chauncey, *Gay New York: Gender, Urban Culture and the Making of the Gay Male World, 1890–1940* (New York: Basic Books, 1994), pp. 304–321.

19. Kinney, *Thurber,* pp. 378–380.

20. *Amsterdam News,* March 17, 1926, p. 3; Committee of Fourteen Papers, Box 34, Folder "1920–22," report dated March 10, 1920, signed H. K.; Box 35, Folder "1931–32," report dated May 26, 1932, signed H. K.

21. Committee of Fourteen Papers, Box 82, Folder "Report re: Transfer of Dance Hall Licenses," Confidential Report [1926?], pp. 3–6; James J. Walker Papers, Box 94, Folder "1926—Letters Received—Whi—Why," Letter from Frederick C. Whitin to JJW, April 26, 1926; "What the Night Clubs Really Are," *The Survey,* August 15, 1928, pp. 506–507.

22. "What the Night Clubs Really Are," pp. 506–507; *Variety,* July 18, 1928, p. 46.

23. "What the Night Clubs Really Are," pp. 506–507; C14, Box 34, Folder "1920," report on Peter's Restaurant, dated February 12, 1920, signed H. K.

24. Committee of Fourteen Papers, Box 34, Folder "1920," report dated July 11, 1920, signed H. K., report dated November 10, 1920, signed H. K.

25. Peiss, *Cheap Amusements,* pp. 110–113; Timothy Gilfoyle, *City of Eros: New York City, Prostitution, and the Commercialization of Sex, 1790–1920* (New York: W. W. Norton and Company, 1992), pp. 309–313.

26. Committee of Fourteen Papers, Box 35, Folder "1930," report on the Rendezvous, dated December 14, 1930.

27. Committee of Fourteen Papers, Box 82, Folder "Dance Hall Law 1915–1930," assorted clippings; *Variety*, July 1, 1925, p. 11; Paul G. Cressey, *The Taxi-Dance Hall* (1932, repr. Montclair, NJ: Paterson Smith, 1969), pp. 35–45; "The Night Club as an Institution," *Vanity Fair*, May 1926, p. 116.

28. Committee of Fourteen Papers, Box 34, Folder "1921," report on Orange Grove, dated November 20, 1921, signed H. K.

29. Helen Bullit Lowry, "New York's after-Midnight Clubs," *New York Times*, February 5, 1922, Section III, pp. 3, 25.

30. Committee of Fourteen Papers, Box 34, Folder "1920," report on Orange Grove, dated April 5, 1920, signed H. K.

31. Lowry, "New York's after-Midnight Clubs," p. 25.

32. Ellin Mackay, "Why We Go to Cabarets—A Post-Debutante Explains," *The New Yorker*, November 28, 1925, p. 7; *The New Yorker*, January 30, 1926, p. 30.

33. Miriam Hopkins, "Make Mine a Speakeasy," *Collier's*, August 27, 1932, pp. 31, 43–44.

34. Belle Livingstone, *Belle out of Order* (New York: Henry Holt and Company, 1959), pp. 311–312, 326; Walker, *The Night Club Era*, pp. 92–93.

35. Walker, *The Night Club Era*, pp. 63–68; Gilbert Maxwell, *Helen Morgan: Her Life and Legend* (New York: Hawthorn Books, 1967), pp. 49–57; District Attorney Scrapbooks, January 1, 1928, February 20, 1928.

36. Graham, *New York Nights*, pp. 87, 92–103.

37. *Variety*, August 13, 1924, p. 37; Graham, *New York Nights*, pp. 88–91; *The New Yorker*, January 23, 1926, p. 34; Southern District of New York, Equity case 46–94, *U.S. v. Salon Royal et. al.*; Equity case 41–54, *U.S. v. Guinan et. al.*, transcript.

38. *Variety*, February 3, 1926, pp. 1, 61; Walker, *The Night Club Era*, p. 241; *New York Times*, July 4, 1926, p. 3; Southern District of New York, Equity case 41–54, *U.S. v. Guinan et. al.*

39. Murdock, *Domesticating Drink*, pp. 116, 149–150; "Impossible Interviews—No. 14: Mrs. Ella Boole vs. Ms. Texas Guinan," *Vanity Fair*, January 1933, p. 36.

40. Freedman, "The New Woman," pp. 372–393.

41. "Ladies at Roslyn," *Time*, July 18, 1932, pp. 8–10.

42. *New York Times*, February 28, 1920, p. 10; June 29, 1924, Section VIII, p. 13.

43. *New York Times*, May 15, 1929, p. 1; Rose, *American Women and the Repeal of Prohibition*, pp. 67–68; David E. Kyvig, "Women against Prohibition," *American Quarterly*, Fall 1976, pp. 446–447.

44. NYPL, M. Louise Gross Papers, Box 1, Folder "Correspondence 1927–29," clippings; "Secretary's Report of Activities, 1927–8."

45. M. Louise Gross Papers, Box 1, Folder "Correspondence 1927–29," clippings.

46. Ibid.; Secretary's Report of Activities, 1927–1928, Form Letter to Congressmen, dated December 6, 1928; Rose, *American Women and the Repeal of Prohibition*, pp. 67–74; HML, Association against the Prohibition Amendment Papers, File 1023–18, Box 3, Folder "Printed Matter—Moderation League, 1925–31," pamphlet "Repeal or Rebellion?"

47. M. Louise Gross Papers, Box 1, Folder "Correspondence 1927–29"; Secretary's Report of Activities, 1927–1928, Form Letter to Congressmen, dated December 6, 1928; Rose, *American Women and the Repeal of Prohibition*, pp. 67–74.

48. M. Louise Gross Papers, Box 1, Folder "Women's Committee for the Repeal of the

18th Amendment, 1929–30," Folder "Women's Committee for the Repeal of the 18th Amendment, 1931–32."

49. Caroline Ware, *Greenwich Village, 1920–1930: A Comment on American Civilization in the Post-War Years* (1935, repr., New York: Octagon Books, 1977), pp. 276–277; Murdock, *Domesticating Drink,* pp. 136–137.

50. Martha Bensley Bruère, "What Will We Do with It?," *Outlook,* October 10, 1928, pp. 923–927, 958; Pauline Morton Sabin, "I Change My Mind on Prohibition," *Outlook,* June 13, 1929, p. 254.

51. Freedman, "The New Woman," pp. 372–393; Kyvig, "Women against Prohibition," pp. 467–468.

52. Kyvig, "Women against Prohibition," p. 468; "Ladies at Roslyn," p. 9.

53. *New York Times,* April 4, 1929, pp. 1, 4.

54. Grace C. Root, *Women and Repeal: The Story of the Women's Organization for National Prohibition Reform* (New York: Harper and Brothers, 1934), pp. 5, 9.

55. Root, *Women and Repeal,* pp. 110, 13.

56. Milton MacKaye, "The New Crusade," *The New Yorker,* October 22, 1932, p. 20; Isabel Leighton, "A Charming Aristocrat," *Smart Set,* March 1930, pp. 37, 82.

57. "Ladies at Roslyn," p. 9; Rose, *American Women and the Repeal of Prohibition,* pp. 76–77, 102.

58. Jefferson Chase, "The Sabines Ravish the Senators," *Vanity Fair,* August 1931, pp. 42, 80.

59. *New York Times,* August 5, 1929, p. 20; October 17, 1929, p. 2; January 27, 1930, pp. 1, 17; May 27, 1930, p. 2; February 17, 1931, p. 12; December 2, 1931, p. 6; Grace Robinson, "Women Wets," *Liberty,* November 1, 1930, p. 30.

60. *New York Times,* February 17, 1931, p. 12.

61. FDR, Eleanor Roosevelt Papers, Box 14, Folder "ER Gen. Corr.—Proh. Letters 1928–32," Letter from Mrs. D. Leigh Colvin to ER, March 4, 1930; Letter from C. Charlotte Wilkinson to ER, April 7, 1930; reply, April 12, 1930; Letter from Elizabeth Lovett to ER, December 6, 1930; Rose, *American Women and the Repeal of Prohibition,* p. 124.

62. *New York Times,* December 2, 1931, p. 6.

63. *New York Times,* February 11, 1931, p. 25; Banning, "Anti-Prohibitionette," p. 55.

64. Robinson, "Women Wets," p. 30.

8. Hootch Joints in Harlem

1. Ira Reid, "Why I Like Harlem," *The Messenger,* January 1927, p. 2; Ernestine Rose, "Books and the New Negro" and "Books and the Color Line," *Library Journal,* November 1, 1927, pp. 75, 1012.

2. *Amsterdam News,* August 15, 1923, p. 12; August 22, 1923, p. 12; August 23, 1923, p. 1; Magistrate's Court, *Annual Reports,* 1920, 1922, 1924.

3. Ann Douglas, *Terrible Honesty: Mongrel Manhattan in the 1920s* (New York: Farrar, Straus and Giroux, 1995), p. 261; *The Crisis,* August 1929, p. 257.

4. *Amsterdam News,* December 29, 1926, p. 15; January 11, 1928, p. 3.

5. *Amsterdam News,* June 6, 1923, p. 12; September 7, 1932, p. 11.

6. *Amsterdam News,* February 7, 1923, p. 12; October 17, 1923, p. 6; December 21, 1927, p. 20.

7. *Amsterdam News,* September 2, 1925, p. 9; December 21, 1927, p. 20; *The Crisis,* October 1928, p. 348.

8. *Amsterdam News,* March 1, 1933, p. 6; Martha Bensley Bruère, *Does Prohibition Work? A Study of the Operation of the Eighteenth Amendment Made by the National Federation of Settlements* (New York: Harper and Brothers, 1927), p. 293.

9. *Amsterdam News,* August 29, 1923, p. 1; August 3, 1928, p. 2; September 7, 1932, p. 2.

10. Jon D. Cruz, "Booze and Blues: Alcohol and Black Popular Music, 1920–1930," *Contemporary Drug Problems,* p. 164; Bruce M. Tyler, "Black Jive and White Repression," *Journal of Ethnic Studies,* Winter 1988, pp. 38–39; Carole Marks, "The Social and Economic Life of Southern Blacks during the Migration," in Alferdte Harrison, ed., *Black Exodus: The Great Migration from the American South* (Jackson: University of Mississippi Press, 1991), p. 46.

11. *Amsterdam News,* June 3, 1925, p. 16; March 7, 1928, p. 1; *The Crisis,* May 1931, pp. 160–161, 176; George S. Schuyler, "New York: Dream Deferred," in Tom Lutz and Susanna Ashton, eds., *These "Colored" United States: African American Essays from the 1920s* (New Brunswick, NJ: Rutgers University Press, 1996), p. 198.

12. Clyde V. Kiser, *Sea Island to City: A Study of St. Helena Islanders in Harlem and Other Urban Centers* (1932, repr. New York: Atheneum, 1969), p. 32; LOC, Manuscript Division, WPA Federal Writers' Project Collection, Frank Byrd, "Harlem Rent Parties," 1938.

13. *Amsterdam News,* June 8, 1927, p. 16.

14. Byrd, "Harlem Rent Parties."

15. Katrina Hazzard-Gordon, *Jookin': The Rise of Social Dance Formations in African American Culture* (Philadelphia: Temple University Press, 1990), pp. 94–119; CUOHC, *The Reminiscences of Benjamin McLaurin* (1960), p. 120; Byrd, "Harlem Rent Parties."

16. *Amsterdam News,* April 6, 1927, p. 16; July 25, 1923, p. 7.

17. Bruère, *Does Prohibition Work?,* p. 294.

18. Hazzard-Gordon, *Jookin',* p. 91; *Amsterdam News,* June 8, 1927, p. 16.

19. *Amsterdam News,* September 2, 1925, p. 9.

20. *Amsterdam News,* June 8, 1927, p. 16; WPA Federal Writers' Project Collection, Dorothy West, "Cocktail Party: Personal Experience," 1939.

21. Schuyler, "New York: Utopia Deferred," pp. 203–204.

22. *Amsterdam News,* April 6, 1927, p. 16; March 1, 1925, p. 16; January 20, 1926, p. 16.

23. *Amsterdam News,* July 25, 1923, p. 7; October 20, 1926, p. 8; August 31, 1932, p. 10.

24. Arnold Rampersad, *The Life of Langston Hughes—Volume 1: I, Too, Sing America* (New York: Oxford University Press, 1986), p. 97; *Amsterdam News,* February 10, 1926, p. 15; October 12, 1927, p. 7; CUOHC, *The Reminiscences of George S. Schuyler* (1962), p. 108.

25. *Amsterdam News,* April 6, 1927, p. 16.

26. *New York Age,* September 3, 1927, p. 2.

27. *Amsterdam News,* August 23, 1927, p. 4.

28. Ibid.

29. *Amsterdam News,* August 25, 1927, pp. 1, 7; August 26, 1927, p. 4; April 6, 1927, p. 16; July 6, 1927, p. 16.

30. Kevin J. Mumford, *Interzones: Black/White Sex Districts in Chicago and New York in the Early Twentieth Century* (New York: Columbia University Press, 1997), pp. 164–165; Earl Lewis and Heidi Ardizzone, *Love on Trial: An American Scandal in Black and White*

(New York: W. W. Norton and Company, 2001), pp. xi, 54; *Amsterdam News,* November 25, 1925, p. 1.

31. Josephine Schuyler, "Does Intermarriage Succeed? II" in Cloyte M. Larson, *Marriage across the Color Line* (Chicago: Johnson Publishing, 1965), pp. 166–172; *Amsterdam News,* August 23, 1927, p. 4; *The Messenger,* August 1922, p. 461.

32. *Amsterdam News,* March 26, 1930, p. 9.

33. Chandler Owen, "The Cabaret—A Useful Social Institution," *The Messenger,* August 1922, p. 461; "The Black and Tan Cabaret—America's Most Democratic Institution," *The Messenger,* February 1925, pp. 97, 100.

34. *Variety,* November 10, 1926, p. 47; December 1, 1926, p. 22; May 16, 1928, p. 1; *Amsterdam News,* August 6, 1923, p. 5.

35. NYPL, Committee of Fourteen Papers, Box 34, Folder "1921," Report on Astoria Restaurant, dated November 3, 1921, signed H. K.; Box 34, Folder "1920," Report on Baron Wilkin's, dated July 30, 1920, signed H. K.

36. Committee of Fourteen Papers, Box 35, Folder "1924—Democratic Nat'l Convention," "Report of Investigation of Vice Conditions in Harlem"; Box 82, Folder "Harlem—Report on Conditions"; Box 34, Folder 1921, report on the Old Lybia, dated November 3, 1921; Box 34, Folder 1920, report on Baron Wilkins, July 30, 1920; *Variety,* March 17, 1922, p. 28; August 13, 1924, p. 37; March 27, 1929, p. 59; *Amsterdam News,* July 11, 1928, p. 1; September 5, 1928, p. 3; January 2, 1929, p. 3.

37. Rudolf Fisher, "The Caucasian Storms Harlem," *American Mercury,* August 1927, p. 398; Bruce Kellner, "'Refined Racism': White Patronage in the Harlem Renaissance," in Victor A. Kramer and Robert A. Ross, eds., *The Harlem Renaissance Re-examined: A Revised and Expanded Edition* (Troy, NY: Whitson Publishing Co., 1997), pp. 121–132.

38. *Amsterdam News,* August 26, 1927, p. 4.

39. Stephen Graham, *New York Nights* (New York: George H. Doran, 1927), pp. 252–254.

40. Ibid., pp. 244–245, 254.

41. *Variety,* March 27, 1929, p. 59; George S. Schuyler, "Our White Folks," *American Mercury,* December 1927, p. 391.

42. Edgar Grey, "Intimate Glimpses of Harlem," *Amsterdam News,* August 26, 1927, p. 4.

43. *Amsterdam News,* October 16, 1929, p. 3; August 17, 1932, p. 1; Kevin Mattson, "The Struggle for an Urban Democratic Public: Harlem in the 1920s," *New York History,* July 1995, p. 313; Committee of Fourteen Papers, Box 82, Folder "Harlem—Report on Conditions."

44. *Amsterdam News,* July 4, 1923, p. 12; February 17, 1926, p. 16; Mattson, "Struggle for an Urban Democratic Public," pp. 313–314.

45. *Amsterdam News,* July 4, 1923, p. 12.

46. *New York Age,* November 6, 1926, p. 2; January 1, 1927, p. 2; Committee of Fourteen Papers, Box 82, Folder "Attacks of Committee of 14."

47. *The New Yorker,* May 9, 1925, p. 18; *Variety,* February 17, 1926, pp. 4, 8.

48. Committee of Fourteen Papers, Box 96, Clippings Folder; "Unique Theatres of America—A Negro Theatre, New York," *Brevities,* April 7, 1932, p. 13; Mumford, *Interzones,* pp. 168–171.

49. *Amsterdam News,* February 3, 1926, p. 12; January 9, 1929, p. 1.

50. *Amsterdam News,* March 27, 1929, p. 1; *Amsterdam News,* November 24, 1926, p. 2.

51. Southern District of New York, *U.S. v. Jesse J. Harvey, et. al,* C46–440; *Amsterdam News,*

January 5, 1927, p. 1; June 22, 1927, pp. 1, 3; June 29, 1927, p. 1; July 6, 1927, p. 1; *New York Times,* June 28, 1927, pp. 1, 11; *New York Age,* January 8, 1927, pp. 1–2.

52. *The Messenger,* April 1927, p. 120.
53. *Amsterdam News,* March 24, 1926, p. 15.
54. Fisher, "The Caucasian Storms Harlem," p. 398.
55. *Reminiscences of George S. Schuyler,* p. 116.

9. Al Smith, the Wet Hope of the Nation

1. MANY, District Attorney Scrapbooks, October 19, 1928; LOC, James J. Wadsworth Papers, Box 19, File "Prohibition Feb. 22, 1923–May 15, 1923," Letter from Wadsworth to James R. Sheffield dated May 9, 1923.
2. *Irish World,* January 8, 1927, p. 4.
3. Charles Merz, *The Dry Decade* (Seattle: University of Washington Press, 1931), p. 329.
4. *New York Times,* April 8, 1926, p. 24; *Irish World,* August 8, 1931, p. 4.
5. David E. Kyvig, *Repealing National Prohibition* (Chicago: University of Chicago Press, 1979), pp. 2, 32–33; NYPL, Committee of Fourteen Papers, Box 83, Folder "Prohibition," Statement by Frederick C. Whitin, c. 1926; Isidore Einstein, *Prohibition Agent #1* (New York: Frederick A. Stokes, 1932), p. x.
6. Kyvig, *Repealing National Prohibition,* p. 2.
7. *New York Times,* November 3, 1926, p. 1.
8. *Irish World,* March 21, 1931, p. 2.
9. Kyvig, *Repealing National Prohibition,* p. 49; Carter Field, "Captain Bill Stayton—Guiding Spirit of the 'Little Group of Millionaires,'" *Life,* July 24, 1931, p. 15.
10. Ernest Gordon, *Brewers and "Billionaires" Conspire against the Working Classes* (New York: Alcohol Information Committee, 1930), pp. 215–220; Kyvig, *Repealing National Prohibition,* pp. 89, 95, 145; *New York Times,* April 24, 1930, p. 1.
11. HML, Irénée DuPont Papers, Box 62, Folder "AAPA October–December 1928," Outline of 1929 Program, p. 4; Box 63, Folder "July—August 1929," Memo from Irénée Dupont, May 16, 1929.
12. Irénée DuPont Papers, Box 61, Folder "AAPA 1928," Letterhead; Box 63, Folder "July–August 1929," Financial Statement; HML, John J. Raskob Papers, File 102, Box 1, Folder "AAPA 1928," Letter from E. Livingston to H. G. Greer, June 31, 1928; Kyvig, *Repealing National Prohibition,* pp. 46–47, 95–96; LOC, AAPA Collection, Box 1, Pamphlet, "Who, How, Why of the Association against the Prohibition Amendment" (1931), p. 4.
13. *Gaelic American,* June 23, 1928, p. 4; CU, Nicholas Murray Butler Papers, CB II-17 Prohibition, Folder "NMB Prohibition," Letter from LaGuardia to NMB, August 18, 1930.
14. *New York Times,* June 7, 1925, p. 26; April 29, 1926, p. 20.
15. Nicholas Murray Butler Papers, CB II—19 Prohibition, Folder "NMB Prohibition," Letter from NMB to "Fritz," September 4, 1928.
16. *Congressional Record,* 66:1, August 20, 1919, p. 4071; Fiorello LaGuardia, *The Making of an Insurgent—An Autobiography: 1882–1919* (Philadelphia: J. B. Lippincott, 1948), pp. 211–212.
17. Lowell M. Limpus and Burr W. Leyson, *This Man LaGuardia* (New York: E. P. Dutton and Co., 1938), pp. 301–302; Alyn Brodsky, *The Great Mayor: Fiorello LaGuardia and the*

Making of the City of New York (New York: St. Martin's Press, 2003), pp. 186–188; John Kobler, *Ardent Spirits: The Rise and Fall of Prohibition* (New York: Da Capo Press, 1973), pp. 283–284; Howard Zinn, *LaGuardia in Congress* (Westport, CT: Greenwood Press, 1958), p. 155.

18. *Variety*, September 1, 1926, p. 31; *New York Times*, June 20, 1926, pp. 1, 5; July 6, 1926, p. 23.

19. *New York Times*, July 18, 1926, p. 8.

20. Ernest Cuneo, *Life with Fiorello* (New York: The Macmillan Company, 1955), p. 26; Zinn, *LaGuardia in Congress*, p. 155; *New York Times*, December 10, 1926, p. 2; February 9, 1927, p. 7.

21. LaGuardia, *The Making of an Insurgent*, pp. 211–212.

22. Duff Gilford, "LaGuardia of Harlem," *American Mercury*, June 1927, p. 153.

23. *Anti-Saloon League Yearbook*, 1931, p. 82.

24. Richard O'Connor, *The First Hurrah: A Biography of Alfred E. Smith* (New York: G. P. Putnam's Sons, 1970), pp. 139, 168–171; *Variety*, September 1, 1922, p. 12; *Outlook*, November 22, 1922, p. 511; Alfred E. Smith, *Up to Now: An Autobiography* (New York: Viking Press, 1929), pp. 220–221, 230–231, 236–239, 245; Paula Eldot, *Governor Alfred E. Smith: The Politician as Reformer* (New York: Garland Publishing, 1983), p. 357.

25. *Literary Digest*, June 16, 1923, pp. 5–7; Eldot, *Governor Alfred E. Smith*, p. 364; Robert A. Slayton, *Empire Statesman: The Rise and Redemption of Al Smith* (New York: The Free Press, 2001), p. 202.

26. Conrad Black, *Franklin Delano Roosevelt: Champion of Freedom* (New York: Public Affairs, 2003), pp. 166–167; Slayton, *Empire Statesman*, pp. 207–215.

27. HML, Pierre S. DuPont Papers, AAPA File 1023–18, Box 3, Folder "Printed Matter— Moderation League," Pamphlet, "Prohibition and the 1928 Campaign"; Smith, *Up to Now*, p. 185; *Anti-Saloon League Yearbook*, 1931, p. 84.

28. Allan J. Lichtman, *Prejudice and Old Politics: The Presidential Election of 1928* (Chapel Hill, NC: University of North Carolina Press, 1979), p. 5; Felix Frankfurter, "Why I Am for Smith," *New Republic*, October 31, 1928, pp. 292–295; John Dewey, "Why I Am for Smith," *New Republic*, November 7, 1928, p. 321; E. C. Lindeman, "The Education of Al Smith," *New Republic*, November 7, 1928, p. 320.

29. Roy V. Peel and Thomas C. Donnelly, *The 1928 Campaign: An Analysis* (New York: Richard R. Smith, 1931, repr. New York: Arno Press, 1974), p. 34; Slayton, *Empire Statesman*, pp. 258–259.

30. *New York Times*, June 30, 1928, pp. 1, 2; Matthew and Hannah Josephson, *Al Smith: Hero of the Cities* (Boston: Houghton Mifflin, 1969), pp. 350–357, 369–372; Slayton, *Empire Statesman*, pp. 260–262.

31. John J. Raskob Papers, File 602, Box 1, Folder "Democratic National Committee— 1928, A-C," Letter from H. P. Cannon to Raskob, dated July 12, 1928.

32. John J. Raskob Papers, File 602, Box 1, Folder "Democratic National Committee— 1928, I-O," Letter from Charles Keck to Raskob, dated July 12, 1928; Kyvig, *Repealing National Prohibition*, pp. 102, 143.

33. *Irish World*, July 7, 1928, p. 4; Deborah Dash Moore, *At Home in America: Second Generation New York Jews* (New York: Columbia University Press, 1981), pp. 206–208, 211– 212; Stephen P. Erie, *Rainbow's End: Irish Americans and the Dilemmas of Urban Machine Politics, 1840–1985* (Berkeley: University of California Press, 1988), p. 108; Eldot, *Gover-*

nor Smith, pp. 122–123; Lichtman, *Prejudice and Old Politics,* pp. 107–121; Slayton, *Empire Statesman,* pp. 14–15, 176–177.

34. Slayton, *Empire Statesman,* pp. 251–259; Christopher M. Finan, *Alfred E. Smith: The Happy Warrior* (New York: Hill and Wang, 2002), pp. 221–223.

35. Josephson, *Al Smith,* p. 394.

36. Charles C. Marshall, "An Open Letter to the Honorable Alfred E. Smith," *Atlantic Monthly,* April 1927, p. 540.

37. Josephson, *Al Smith,* pp. 358–366; Alfred E. Smith, "Catholic and Patriot: Governor Smith Replies," *Atlantic Monthly,* May 1927, pp. 721–728.

38. Josephson, *Al Smith,* pp. 380–381.

39. Ibid., pp. 390–391; Slayton, *Empire Statesman,* p. 313.

40. Robert A. Hohner, *Prohibition and Politics: The Life of Bishop James Cannon, Jr.* (Columbia: University of South Carolina Press, 1999), pp. 220–222.

41. K. Austin Kerr, *Organized for Prohibition: A New History of the Anti-Saloon League* (New Haven: Yale University Press, 1985), pp. 257–258; James Cannon, Jr., "Al Smith—Catholic, Tammany, Wet," *The Nation,* July 4, 1928, pp. 9–10.

42. Hohner, *Prohibition and Politics,* p. 227.

43. Ella Boole, *Give Prohibition Its Chance* (Evanston, IL: National Woman's Christian Temperance Union Publishing House, 1929), pp. 123–125, 130–136; Josephson, *Al Smith,* p. 385; *Irish World,* August 18, 1928, p. 1.

44. *New York Times,* June 29, 1928, p. 27; June 30, 1928, p. 1; August 7, 1928, p. 23; August 18, 1928, pp. 1, 4; August 20, 1928, pp. 1, 9; Dorothy M. Brown, *Mabel Walker Willebrandt: A Study of Power, Loyalty and Law* (Knoxville: University of Tennessee Press, 1984), pp. 157–158.

45. LOC, Mabel Walker Willebrandt Papers, Box 4, File "Speeches and Writings, 1923–9 and undated"; District Attorney Scrapbooks, November 19, 1928; *Variety,* August 22, 1928, p. 1; Stanley Walker, *The Night Club Era* (New York: Frederick A. Stokes, 1933), pp. 65–66; Wayne Gard, "Mabel Pulls the Bung," *Vanity Fair,* August 1931, p. 29; Josephson, *Al Smith,* p. 382; Peel, *The 1928 Campaign,* p. 63; Martin L. Fausold, *The Presidency of Herbert C. Hoover* (Lawrence, KS: University Press of Kansas, 1985), pp. 29–30; Edmund A. Moore, *A Catholic Runs for President: The Campaign of 1928* (New York: Ronald Press, 1956), pp. 190–191; Mabel Walker Willebrandt, "The Inside of Prohibition," *New York Times,* August 5, 1929, p. 23.

46. Slayton, *Empire Statesman,* pp. 307–308; Brown, *Willebrandt,* pp. 160–165.

47. Irénée DuPont Papers, Box 62, Folder "AAPA, August–September 1928," Letter from Mrs. George F. King to Pierre DuPont, dated August 10, 1928.

48. Kyvig, *Repealing National Prohibition,* pp. 102–103.

49. Josephson, *Al Smith,* pp. 388–389; Paul A. Carter, *The Twenties in America* (New York: Crowell, 1968), p. 75.

50. Slayton, *Empire Statesman,* pp. 322–325; Fausold, *The Presidency of Herbert C. Hoover,* p. 31.

51. Slayton, *Empire Statesman,* pp. 318, 322; Peel, *The 1928 Campaign,* p. vii; *Recent Social Trends in the United States* (New York: Whittlesey House, 1930), p. 1507; Charles Willis Thompson, "The Campaign Closes," *Commonweal,* November 7, 1928, p. 9.

52. Peel, *The 1928 Campaign,* p. vii; *Recent Social Trends in the United States,* p. 1507; Thompson, "The Campaign Closes," p. 9; Josephson, *Al Smith,* pp. 397–400; *Campaign Addresses of Governor Alfred E. Smith* (New York: J. B. Lyon, 1929), p. 317.

53. Smith, *Up to Now,* pp. 407–408; Josephson, *Al Smith,* p. 398.

54. Peel, *The 1928 Campaign,* pp. 52, 71; Lichtman, *Prejudice and Old Politics,* p. 89; *New York Times,* November 7, 1928, p. 24; *Commonweal,* November 14, 1928, p. 30; Slayton, *Empire Statesman,* pp. 322–324.

55. Kyvig, *Repealing National Prohibition,* p. 103; Hohner, *Prohibition and Politics,* p. 234; Alfred E. Smith, "On the Way to Repeal," *New Outlook,* August 1933, p. 10.

10. The End of the Party

1. Ella Boole, *Give Prohibition Its Chance* (Evanston, IL: National Woman's Christian Temperance Union Publishing House, 1929), p. 131.

2. *New York Times,* July 14, 1929, p 20; July 16, 1929, p. 22; July 19, 1929, p. 22; July 21, 1929, p. 8; July 22, 1929, p. 21; Stanley Walker, *The Night Club Era* (New York: Frederick A. Stokes, 1933), pp. 236–237; *Variety,* July 31, 1929, p. 45.

3. *Amsterdam News,* December 9, 1931, p. 1.

4. NYPL, Committee of Fourteen Papers, Box 96, unmarked folder, clipping dated January 20, 1932, "Slash Man in 'Ex-Cop's' Speakeasy"; *Amsterdam News,* March 9, 1933, p. 1; Walker, *The Night Club Era,* pp. 216–217.

5. MANY, Magistrate's Court, *Annual Reports,* 1930, 1932.

6. *National Prohibition Law: Hearings before the Subcommittee of the Committee on the Judiciary, United States Senate, Sixty-Ninth Congress, Vol. I* (Washington, D.C.: Government Printing Office, 1926), pp. 142, 154.

7. *New York Times,* October 12, 1928, p. 9; March 15, 1929, p. 27.

8. MANY, District Attorney Scrapbooks, September 15, 1926.

9. Humbert S. Nelli, *The Business of Crime: Italians and Syndicate Crime in the United States* (New York: Oxford University Press, 1976), pp. 159, 162.

10. District Attorney Scrapbooks, November 20, 1921; Nelli, *The Business of Crime,* pp. 158–159; Howard McClellan, "The High Cost of Nullification," *Review of Reviews,* April 1930, pp. 56–61; *National Prohibition Law,* p. 203.

11. NYPL, Social Science Research Council Papers, Box 5, Folder 2; *National Prohibition Law,* pp. 74, 114; *Variety,* July 2, 1924, p. 9.

12. Social Science Research Council Papers, Box 5, Folder 2; Box 2, Folder 4, clipping from *Periscope,* July 1926, pp. 8–9; *National Prohibition Law,* pp. 145–146.

13. Steven Watson, *The Harlem Renaissance: Hub of African American Culture, 1920–1930* (New York: Pantheon Books, 1995), p. 99; Ann Douglas, *Terrible Honesty: Mongrel Manhattan in the 1920s* (New York: Farrar, Straus and Giroux, 1995), pp. 22–24.

14. Social Science Research Council Papers, Box 5, Folder 2, Survey of City Testing Labs, 1926; Committee of Fourteen Papers, Box 63, Folder "Clippings-Raids"; *New York Telegram,* January 2, 1929; *Irish World,* March 7, 1931, p. 6.

15. Nelli, *The Business of Crime,* pp. 168–172.

16. Rich Cohen, "Gun, Gangster and the Business of Crime," *Financial Times,* June 27, 1998, p. 4; Nelli, *The Business of Crime,* p. 155; David E. Kyvig, *Repealing National Prohibition* (Chicago: University of Chicago Press, 1979), p. 21.

17. MANY, William O'Dwyer Papers, Box 9422, "Breweries Operated by the Jewish Syndicate, 1928–1933" (n.d.); James Lardner and Thomas Repetto, *NYPD: A City and Its Police* (New York: Henry Holt and Co., 2000), p. 200; Thomas Repetto, *American Mafia: A History of Its Rise to Power* (New York: Henry Holt and Co., 2004), pp. 103–108; Cohen, "Gun, Gangster and the Business of Crime," p. 4.

18. *Variety,* October 20, 1931, pp. 1, 62.

19. NYHS, Speakeasy Cards and Prohibition Ephemera; Ernest W. Mandeville, "The Biggest City and Its Booze," *Outlook,* March 4, 1925, p. 341.

20. *New York Times,* July 29, 1931, pp. 1, 6; July 30, 1931, pp. 1, 12; July 31, 1931, pp. 1, 12; February 8, 1932, pp. 1, 2; Nelli, *The Business of Crime,* p. 150; Walker, *The Night Club Era,* p. 137.

21. *Amsterdam News,* March 30, 1932, p. 1; *New York Times,* March 26, 1932, p. 16.

22. *New York Times,* March 4, 1927, p. 2; John Kobler, *Ardent Spirits: The Rise and Fall of Prohibition* (New York: Da Capo Press, 1973), pp. 236–237; *The New Yorker,* December 7, 1929, p. 21; Walker, *The Night Club Era,* pp. 63–70.

23. *New York Times,* April 26, 1930, pp. 1, 8; June 25, 1930, pp. 1, 18.

24. District Attorney Scrapbooks, December 31, 1927; *Variety,* June 11, 1930, p. 59; Walker, *The Night Club Era,* pp. 68–69.

25. *New York Times,* March 1, 1929, p. 1; March 3, 1929, p. 3; Kyvig, *Repealing National Prohibition,* pp. 32, 112.

26. *National Prohibition Laws,* p. 97; *Irish World,* April 13, 1929, p. 4.

27. Social Science Research Council Papers, Box 2, Folder 4, Report in *Periscope,* July 1926, p. 12; *Variety,* March 7, 1929, p. 1; March 20, 1929, p. 57; Mark Edward Lender and James Kirby Martin, *Drinking in America* (New York: The Free Press, 1982), pp. 163–164.

28. Herbert Mitgang, *Once upon a Time in New York: Jimmy Walker, Franklin Roosevelt, and the Last Great Battle of the Jazz Age* (New York: The Free Press, 2000), pp. 29–30; Lardner and Repetto, *NYPD,* pp. 205–206.

29. *New York Times,* December 20, 1928, p. 1; April 11, 1929, p. 29; *New York World,* January 5, 1929, p. 1; Magistrate's Court, *Annual Report,* 1930; Committee of Fourteen Papers, Box 63, Folder "Clippings-Raids."

30. *New York Times,* January 15, 1930, p. 18; April 27, 1930, pp. 1, 2.

31. Gene Fowler, *Beau James: The Life and Times of Jimmy Walker* (New York: Viking Press, 1949), pp. 265–268; *New York Times,* May 21, 1930, pp. 1, 20; June 25, 1930, p. 1; July 1, 1930, p. 1.

32. *Amsterdam News,* August 26, 1931, p. 15; *Wall Street Journal,* April 21, 1929, p. 1; Nelli, *The Business of Crime,* p. 157; LOC, James J. Wadsworth Papers, Box 19, File "P Feb 22–May 15, 1923," Letter from James R. Sheffield, May 1, 1923; District Attorney Scrapbooks, October 10, 1928; Committee of Fourteen Papers, Box 96, unmarked folder, anonymous broadsheet, c. 1928; *Irish World,* January 8, 1927, p. 4.

33. *Variety,* January 5, 1932, pp. 9, 35.

11. A Surging Wet Tide

1. Kenneth D. Rose, *American Women and the Repeal of Prohibition* (New York: New York University Press, 1996), pp. 46–47; LOC, AAPA Collection, Box 1, Pamphlet, "Cost of Prohibition and Your Income Tax," pp. 2, 5; HML, John J. Raskob Papers, File 102, Box 2, Folder "AAPA 1933," Flyer from the Beer for Prosperity Campaign; William Preston Beazell, "The Facts of Prohibition's Life," *World Week,* June 1932, p. 25.

2. F. P. Dunne, "Dark Days for Bootleggers," *Outlook and Independent,* December 25, 1929, pp. 652–653, 679; *Variety,* November 6, 1929, pp. 1, 16; January 1, 1930, p. 44; May 14, 1930, p. 1; September 24, 1930; August 11, 1931, pp. 1, 43.

3. *Amsterdam News,* December 28, 1932, p. 2.

4. *New York Times,* June 28, 1932, p. 18.

5. MANY, James J. Walker Papers, Box 185, Folder "1930—July–Dec Letters Received, Anonymous," Letter dated September 14, 1930, signed "A Friend."

6. David M. Kennedy, *Freedom from Fear: The American People in Depression and War, 1929–1945* (New York: Oxford University Press, 1999), p. 58.

7. *Official Records of the National Commission on Law Observance and Enforcement* (Washington, D.C.: United States Government Printing Office, 1931); David E. Kyvig, *Repealing National Prohibition* (Chicago: University of Chicago Press, 1979), pp. 111–113; Martin L. Fausold, *The Presidency of Herbert C. Hoover* (Lawrence: University Press of Kansas, 1985), p. 127.

8. David E. Kyvig, ed., *Law, Alcohol, and Order: Perspectives on National Prohibition* (Westport, CT: Greenwood Press, 1985), p. 11.

9. *Irish World,* January 16, 1930, p. 4; *New York Times,* January 15, 1930, p. 18.

10. Fausold, *Herbert Hoover,* pp. 127–129.

11. Rose, *American Women and the Repeal of Prohibition,* pp. 91–92.

12. Frederick Lewis Allen, *Since Yesterday: The Nineteen-Thirties in America* (New York: Harper and Brothers, 1940), p. 31.

13. *New York Times,* April 22, 1930, p. 4; *Time,* "Ladies at Roslyn," July 18, 1932, p. 10.

14. Grace C. Root, *Women and Repeal: The Story of the Women's Organization for National Prohibition Reform* (New York: Harper and Brothers, 1934), p. 110; *Vogue,* "Workers for Repeal," August 1, 1932, p. 34.

15. HML, Irénée DuPont Papers, Box 61, Folder "AAPA April–Dec. 1926," news clippings enclosed in letter from George Alberger to Irénée DuPont.

16. *American Mercury,* "Fanning the Home Fires," October 1930, p. 149.

17. *New York Times,* May 20, 1932, p. 21.

18. *New York Times,* May 21, 1932, p. 32.

19. *New York Times,* June 10, 1930, p. 29.

20. *New York Times,* July 2, 1929, p. 12; May 29, 1932, p. 2.

21. Robert A. Hohner, *Prohibition and Politics: The Life of Bishop James Cannon, Jr.* (Columbia: University of South Carolina Press, 1999), Ch. 14–15; Root, *Women and Repeal,* p. 13.

22. Rose, *American Women and the Repeal of Prohibition,* pp. 109–113; Margaret Culkin Banning, "Anti-Prohibitionette," *Vogue,* September 1, 1930, pp. 55, 82, 84; Isabel Leighton, "A Charming Aristocrat," *Smart Set,* March 1930, pp. 36–37, 82; Dorothy Ducas, "In Miniature: Mrs. Charles H. Sabin," *McCall's,* September 1929, p. 4.

23. Rose, *American Women and the Repeal of Prohibition,* pp. 95–101; *New York Times,* May 10, 1929, p. 56; December 2, 1931, p. 6; Root, *Women and Repeal,* pp. 107–108.

24. Rose, *American Women and the Repeal of Prohibition,* pp. 80–81; Nancy F. Cott, *The Grounding of Modern Feminism* (New Haven: Yale University Press, 1987), pp. 261–266; WONPR papers, Box 3, Folder "Correspondence, Sept–Dec. 1930–1," Letter from Brooks Darlington to WONPR, dated September 23, 1931; *New York Times,* September 12, 1930, p. 3; October 31, 1931, p. 23; *New York Evening Post,* May 12, 1932, p. 3.

25. *New York Times,* May 19, 1932, p. 14; *New York Evening Post,* May 12, 1932, p. 3; Root, *Women and Repeal,* pp. 59, 114; WONPR Papers, Box 9, Folder "Repeal Week 1932."

26. *New York Times,* October 29, 1932, p. 5.

27. Rose, *American Women and the Repeal of Prohibition,* pp. 96–97, 101.

28. WONPR Papers, Box 9, Folder "Radio Data—1933"; Jefferson Chase, "The Sabines Ravish the Senators," *Vanity Fair,* p. 80.

29. NYPL, Social Science Research Council Papers, Box 2, Folder 4, *The Periscope,* July 1926, pp. 8–9.

30. Committee of Fourteen Papers, Box 83, Folder "Prohibition."

31. Grace Robinson, "Women Wets: A New Voice Is Heard in American Politics," *Liberty,* November 1, 1930, p. 34.

32. *Prohibition as We See It* (New York: Church Temperance Society, 1928), pp. 14, 20, 40; *Irish World,* September 1, 1928, p. 7.

33. *New York Times,* November 2, 1931, p. 24.

34. Wayne Gard, "Mabel Pulls the Bung," *Vanity Fair,* August 1931, p. 29; Dorothy M. Brown, *Mabel Walker Willebrandt: A Study of Power, Loyalty and Law* (Knoxville: University of Tennessee Press, 1984), pp. 177, 179–189; Rose, *American Women and the Repeal of Prohibition,* pp. 124–127.

35. *New York Times,* June 7, 1932, pp. 1, 12; Kyvig, *Repealing National Prohibition,* p. 152; Rose, *American Women and the Repeal of Prohibition,* pp. 123–124; Hohner, *Prohibition and Politics,* p. 284.

36. Kyvig, *Repealing National Prohibition,* p. 145; *Irish World,* November 15, 1930, p. 1; *Literary Digest,* "The Democratic Landslide," November 15, 1930, p. 9; "How the 'Digest' Poll Stood the Election Test," p. 10; Kennedy, *Freedom from Fear,* p. 60.

12. The Wet Convention and the New Deal

1. David M. Kennedy, *Freedom from Fear: The American People in Depression and War, 1929–1945* (New York: Oxford University Press, 1999), pp. 77, 85–88; Nathan Miller, *New World Coming: The 1920s and the Making of Modern America* (New York: Scribner, 2003), pp. 375–376.

2. Richard Oulahan, *The Man Who . . . : The Story of the 1932 Democratic Convention* (New York: Dial Press, 1971), pp. 93–94; *Literary Digest,* July 9, 1932, pp. 4–5; *New York Times,* June 28, 1932, pp. 1, 12.

3. Oulahan, *The Man Who . . . ,* pp. 100–101; David E. Kyvig, *Repealing National Prohibition* (Chicago: University of Chicago Press, 1979), pp. 157–158; *Literary Digest,* July 9, 1932, pp. 4–5; *Irish World,* July 8, 1932, p. 3.

4. Oulahan, *The Man Who . . . ,* p. 62.

5. *American Monthly,* August 1932, p. 10; Oulahan, *The Man Who . . . ,* p. 62; Kyvig, *Repealing National Prohibition,* pp. 154–156; Martin L. Fausold, *The Presidency of Herbert C. Hoover* (Lawrence: University Press of Kansas, 1985), p. 195.

6. *Literary Digest,* July 9, 1932, pp. 4–5; *New York Times,* June 30, 1932, p. 22.

7. Robert A. Slayton, *Empire Statesman: The Rise and Redemption of Al Smith* (New York: The Free Press, 2001), pp. 370–371.

8. *The Nation,* June 1, 1932, p. 612; *Harper's,* November 1932, p. 719; *The Crisis,* March 1932, p. 80; Slayton, *Empire Statesman,* pp. 370–371.

9. Kyvig, *Repealing National Prohibition,* pp. 151–152, 157; *Literary Digest,* April 30, 1932, pp. 6–7; *Time,* June 13, 1932, p. 11; Frederick Lewis Allen, *Since Yesterday: The Nineteen-Thirties in America* (New York: Harper and Brothers, 1940), p. 31.

10. Sean Dennis Cashman, *Prohibition: The Lie of the Land* (New York: The Free Press, 1981), pp. 231–232; Kyvig, *Repealing National Prohibition,* pp. 147–148; *Literary Digest,*

"The Democratic Landslide," November 15, 1930, p. 7; Slayton, *Empire Statesman,* p. 197; Conrad Black, *Franklin Delano Roosevelt: Champion of Freedom* (New York: Public Affairs, 2003), p. 233.

11. *New York Times,* June 23, 1932, p. 10; *Literary Digest,* July 9, 1932, pp. 4–5; Slayton, *Empire Statesman,* p. 371.

12. *New York Times,* June 22, 1932, p. 1; William E. Leuchtenburg, *Franklin D. Roosevelt and the New Deal* (New York: Harper and Row, 1963), pp. 4–7; Kyvig, *Repealing National Prohibition,* pp. 146–147.

13. Oulahan, *The Man Who . . . ,* pp. 83–86; *New York Times,* June 28, 1932, p. 29.

14. *Literary Digest,* July 9, 1932, pp. 4–5.

15. Black, *Franklin Delano Roosevelt,* pp. 233–237; Slayton, *Empire Statesman,* pp. 371–373.

16. Oulahan, *The Man Who . . . ,* pp. 112–113; *New York Times,* July 2, 1932, pp. 1, 4; *The Nation,* July 13, 1932, pp. 22, 27; *Harper's,* October 1932, p. 637; H. L. Mencken, *Making a President* (New York: Alfred A. Knopf, 1932), p. 106; Richard O'Connor, *The First Hurrah: A Biography of Alfred E. Smith* (New York: G. P. Putnam's Sons, 1970), pp. 248, 254, 256.

17. *Irish World,* July 9, 1932, p. 4; September 24, 1932, p. 1.

18. Oulahan, *The Man Who . . . ,* p. 57; William E. Leuchtenburg, *Perils of Prosperity* (New York: Harper and Row, 1963), p. 266.

19. Matthew Josephson and and Hannah Josephson, *Al Smith: Hero of the Cities* (Boston: Houghton Mifflin, 1969), p. 439; *Literary Digest,* July 9, 1932, pp. 4–5.

20. *American Mercury,* November 1932, p. 383.

21. *American Monthly,* April 1930, p. 7.

22. Black, *Franklin Delano Roosevelt,* pp. 244–249.

23. *New York Times,* July 3, 1932, p. 1; *Harper's,* August 1932, pp. 383–384; Oulahan, *The Man Who . . . ,* p. 136.

24. *Amsterdam News,* November 9, 1932, p. 1; *Between Wars: An Oral History* (New York: Community Documentation Workshop at St. Mark's Church-in-the-Bowery, 1980), p. 24; Black, *Franklin Delano Roosevelt,* p. 250.

25. Grace C. Root, *Women and Repeal: The Story of the Women's Organization for National Prohibition Reform* (New York: Harper and Brothers, 1934), pp. 114–115; *Time,* November 7, 1932, p. 16; *New York Herald Tribune,* November 19, 1932, p. 8; *Variety,* November 15, 1932, p. 1; *American Monthly,* December 1932, p. 18.

26. Black, *Franklin Delano Roosevelt,* p. 292.

27. FDR, Franklin Delano Roosevelt Papers, Record Group OF 75, Folder "Prohibition: Against 1933–38," Telegram from Carl Kruening to Roosevelt, March 16, 1933; Letter from Nathaniel Frankel to Roosevelt, May 24, 1933; Folder "Prohibition: Against 1933–37, N–Z," Letter from John M. Robert to Roosevelt, April 10, 1933.

28. Leuchtenburg, *Roosevelt and the New Deal,* p. 46; Kennedy, *Freedom from Fear,* pp. 138–139.

29. CU, Nicholas Murray Butler Papers, CB I–16, "Prohibition," Speech, April 6, 1933; *Amsterdam News,* April 12, 1933, p. 1.

30. *New York Times,* April 7, 1933, pp. 1, 2; April 8, 1933, pp. 1, 2; May 9, 1933, p. 4; *Amsterdam News,* April 12, 1933, p. 16; *New York Evening Post,* April 7, 1933, pp. 1–3.

31. *New York Times,* December 20, 1932, p. 1; April 7, 1933, pp. 1, 2; April 8, 1933, pp. 1, 2; *New York Evening Post,* April 7, 1933, pp. 1–3; Leuchtenburg, *Roosevelt and the New Deal,* pp. 46–47.

32. Franklin Delano Roosevelt Papers, Record Group OF 75, Folder "Prohibition: Against 1933–38," Letter from Frank G. Mattern to Roosevelt, March 21, 1933; Folder "Prohibition: Against 1933–37, N-Z," Letter from M. A. Seligmann to Col. Louis Howe, March 17, 1933.

33. Bernarr MacFadden, "The New Deal Is Here—God Be Praised!," *Liberty,* April 22, 1933; *The Crisis,* May 1933, p. 101.

34. Franklin Delano Roosevelt Papers, Record Group OF 75, Folders "Prohibition: In Favor of, 1933–7, A–I," "Prohibition: In Favor of, 1933–7, J-R"; *Congressional Record,* Seventy-third Congress, First Session, p. 290.

35. Gerald Gunther, *Learned Hand: The Man and the Judge* (New York: Alfred A. Knopf, 1994), p. 306; *The Nation,* December 12, 1932, p. 663.

36. *New York Times,* December 5, 1933, pp. 1, 2, 16; December 6, 1933, pp. 1–3.

37. *The Nation,* March 29, 1933, p. 331.

38. *The Nation,* December 12, 1932, p. 663.

Acknowledgments

It would be an exaggeration to say that it took me as long to write this book as it took for the United States to repeal Prohibition, but only a slight one. At times while working on *Dry Manhattan,* I felt as though I were watching the history of the fourteen-year "noble experiment" unfold in real time. Given the lengthy nature of this project, I have accumulated more than my fair share of debts, and I am happy finally to have the opportunity to acknowledge them.

At New York University, Carl Prince's enthusiasm for the topic of Prohibition convinced me that this was a subject worth pursuing. Lizabeth Cohen, who expertly guided me during my graduate studies at NYU, did everything that could be asked of a mentor and more. Her unwavering commitment to her students, and the high standards of scholarship on which she insisted, profoundly influenced me. I feel very fortunate to have benefited from her training, and I am grateful for all the advice she has continued to offer. Thomas Bender, Daniel Walkowitz, and William Nelson also offered valuable insights as I worked on this project in its early stages. I owe special thanks as well to the late Paul Avrich, who selflessly encouraged me to pursue the study of history in my undergraduate years. I never took a class with him, yet he taught me more about how to look at history and how to listen to historical voices than many of my own professors. I regret that I did not finish this book in time to share it with him.

In the course of writing this book, I was aided immeasurably by the librarians, archivists, and staff members of the many institutions and libraries where I conducted my research. I especially wish to thank the archivists and staff at the New York Public Library, the Municipal Archives of the City of New York, the Hagley Museum and Library, the New-York Historical Society, the Library of Congress, the Museum of the City of New York, the Franklin D. Roosevelt Presidential Library, the Minnesota Historical Society, the University of Chicago Library Special Collections Research Center, and the Northeast Branch of the National Archives in New York City.

Writing can be a lonely endeavor, so having supportive family, friends, and colleagues matters enormously. I offer my sincere thanks to all those who encouraged me, read parts of this manuscript, offered research tips, helped track down rare books, songs, and cocktail recipes, offered me a place to stay, or simply bought me a drink when I needed one. I am indebted especially to Joan Saab, Louise Maxwell, Neil Maher, Louis Anthes, Duane Corpus, Andrew Darien, Mark Elliot, Scott Messinger, David Quigley, Morris Adjmi, John Jesurun, the late Frank Maya, David Coughlin, Mary Stricker, Andrew Webster, Julie Stepanek, Jenny Weisberg, Mark Landsman, Mahinder Kingra, Melissa Halley, Lydia Ely, Marianna Cherry, Laura Cantrell, Tim Merello, Liz Eckstein, John Logie, Carol Logie, Camille Gage, David Greenberg, Nina Morrison, Peter Dizikes, Kristi Powell, Willy Lee, David Power, and Suzanne Power.

At the Bard High School Early College, where I am the Associate Dean of Studies, I have been fortunate to have had the support of many wonderful colleagues, including Ray Peterson, Patricia Sharpe, U Ba Win, Stuart Levine, Martha Olson, Camille Sawick, Sara Yaffee, and especially my past and present colleagues in the Social Sciences Department, Bronwen Exter, David Serlin, Steven Mazie, Ed Vernoff, Mary Ellen Lennon, Rene Marion, and Bruce Matthews. I am especially grateful for release time and financial support granted from the Bard High School Early College Faculty Development Fund, which assisted me in the final stages of editing this book. I would be remiss if I didn't also thank all of my students at Bard. They are a big part of why this book was so long in coming, but they also reminded me daily of the importance of history in our lives and the joy that can be found in teaching something you love.

When I began working with Harvard University Press, I was fortunate to have had in David Lobenstine a supportive and enthusiastic editor. His guidance in the early stages of developing this book went above and beyond the call of duty. Joyce Seltzer saw me through the completion of this book, and I could not have asked for more from an editor. She patiently accommodated the demands of my teaching schedule, offered valuable feedback, and did me (and my readers) an enormous service by pressing me to develop and bring to light the key questions at the heart of this book. Christine Thorsteinsson made the process of manuscript editing not only painless but fun. For that I owe her a world of thanks. I also wish to thank my readers for their comments, and in particular Robert Slayton for his generous and insightful readings of this manuscript.

My parents, Marie and Michael Lerner, will be happy that they can now stop asking me, "How is the book coming along?" They have been an abundant source of support. I also wish to thank my brother John for offering me a quiet place to which to escape, complete with access to trout fishing, when I was consumed with revising this book. Most of all, I owe my gratitude and love to "Two-Sip" Susie Walter, my partner in drinking and in life, who lived with me and this book from the beginning to the end. She was gracious and understanding when this book came with us to dinner, joined us on vacation, followed us through two cross-country moves, and literally took over our small Manhattan apartment. I don't think either of us can quite believe it is finished. Now that it is, Susie, I promise to buy every round for the rest of our lives.

Index